Nine Days Of
WAR

Nine Days Of
WAR

Peter Stiff

LEMUR
BOOKS

*For General Hans Dreyer, SWA Police, and his men,
who saved the day and the peace with their courage
and their blood*
and
*For Prime Minister Margaret Thatcher, whose strength of
purpose ensured reluctant action on the part of the
Security Council*
and
*For Foreign Minister Pik Botha, who quite rightly, didn't
give an inch or a damn*
and
*For UN Special Representative Martti Ahtisaari,
on whose shoulders much of the immediate future of
Namibia now rests*
also
*In memory of my late father, Robert James ... Bob, one of
nature's true gentlemen*

© Peter Stiff 1989
All Rights Reserved
ISBN 0 620 14260 X

First published by Lemur Books (Pty) Ltd
P O Box 1645 Alberton 1450. Rep. South Africa

Type computer set by S A Book Society
Interfaced to 10/11 Times Roman by Gutenberg Book Printers, Pretoria
Colour and half tones by Gutenberg
Printed and bound by Printpak Books

Book and dust jacket design by Francis Lategan

Acknowledgements

Many people were interviewed when researching this book, some were seen individually and some in groups, some interviews were in depth and others only fleeting. When speaking to people in groups and in passing, names were not always recorded, but this in no way diminishes their contributions.

Special thanks are due to Gen Jannie Geldenhuys, Chief of the SADF, who set aside valuable time to guide me through many labyrinths, Derek Auret, Director Foreign Affairs who detailed the peace process and events on the diplomatic front, Administrator General of SWA/Namibia, Advocate Louis Pienaar, who took me behind the scenes of international political events and his dealings with British Premier, Mrs Margaret Thatcher, on that fateful 1st April, Gen Hans Dreyer, SWA Police, who played such an important role before, during and after the April incursion, General Niel Knoebel, Surgeon General the SADF who sketched an important overview of the duties and responsibilities of SAMS and Lt Gen Dewan Prem Chand, who explained his responsibilities as UNTAG Force commander and events as seen from that viewpoint.

Thanks are also due to Maj Gen Willie Meyer, SWATF commander, Brig Johan Louw, Chief of Staff Operations SWATF, Brig Bischeff, Col Jan Bierman, Col de Jager, Col Japie Dreyer, Commdt du Toit, Commdt Fanie Krige, Commdt Sophia du Preez, Sergeant Henk Rheeder and Mr Gerhard Roux of the Administrator General's office.

In the SWA Police invaluable help was extended by Lt Gen Dolf Gouws, Commissioner, Maj Gen Piet Fouche, Deputy Commissioner, Brig Nel, C/Inspector Derek Bruno, C/Insp Kierie du Rand, Insp Willem Botha, Insp Jumbo de Villiers, Insp Lucas Koen, Insp Nick Peens and Insp Chris Ronne.

Policemen from the fighting groups who detailed their many remarkable stories, in alphabetical order, were: Const Ray Archer, Const Wynand Bezhuidenhout, Sgt Johan Bosch, Const Chips Bosman, Const Jimmy Botha, Sgt Nick Coetzee, Sgt Piet Cronje, Sgt Thys de Jager, Const Duppie du Plessis, W/O Fanna du Rand, Sgt Herman Grobler, W/O Jackie Grobler, Const Freddie Harding, W/O Herman Havenga, Const Willie Hough, Const Sakkie Jooste, Const Theunis Kruger, Const Mike Maree, Const Willie Meyer, Const Peet Nel, Sgt Dewald Pretorius, W/O Corrie Prinsloo, Sgt Wayne Prinsloo, Sgt Rassie Ras, L/Cpl Jose Saayman, (medic attached), Const W Scholtz, Const Stony Steenkamp, Const Koos Swart, Const Kobus Theron, Const Assie van As, Const Fires van Vuuren, Sgt Fires van Vuuren, Sgt Fanie van der Westhuizen, Sgt Dolf van Tonder (attached), Sgt Fires van Vuuren and Sgt Wessie Wessels.

The air war was related by Col Koos Botha, Maj Alan McCarthy, Maj Wimpie Kruger, Capt Pierre Steyn, Capt Jamie Burger and Capt Keith Fryer. 101 Battalion's role was detailed by Col Kotze, Commdt Jaco Kruger and Capt Sys Prinsloo and 102's by its commander and officers at a conference laid on for me at Ehomba forward base.

Thanked also are the Dakota, Bosbok, Kudu and chopper pilots, who at various times flew me to remote destinations in the operational area at the mandatory altitude of 50 feet, to avoid the lurking danger of SWAPO SAM-7s.

Of UNTAG, although no fullscale interviews, were given, assistance was extended by Fred Eckhard, Cedric Thornberry and Police Commissioner, Maj Gen Stephen Fanning.

Also thanked are Albert Nakawa and James Sikalungu, for their honest and frank accounts of the fighting from SWAPO's side.

Particular thanks are due to Commdt Paul Balko-Mertz and Maj Connie du Toit, my constant companions on the border, who uncomplainingly and even cheerfully, at my behest, clambered from their sleeping bags before dawns and worked with me late into the nights.

A particular debt of gratitude is due to Col Johan Beyers of the SADF's Directorate of Public Relations, who immediately grasped the importance of this book when the concept was first broached, and who spent a weekend on the phone explaining it to many people of influence, thereby obtaining for me a previously unheard of *carte blanche*.

Consequently, nothing in this book has been subjected to any form of censorship.

The facts in the book speak for themselves, the opinions and conclusions are mine, except where they have been specifically attributed.

Picture Credits

Johan Bosch, Attie Dippenaar, Herman Havenga, L Lombard, Paul Balko-Mertz, Nick Peens, W Scholtz and Peter Stiff.
  Cover picture Peter Stiff.
  Maps by Francis Lategan.

Contents

Bibliography

The following newspapers have been an invaluable source of information regarding the passing scene in Namibia: The *Citizen*, *The Namibian*, *New Nation*, *Die Republikein*, *The Star*, *The Sunday Star*, *Sunday Times*, *Times of Namibia*, *Weekly Mail*, *The Windhoek Adveriser* and *The Windhoek Observer*.

Various official documents like the SWATF battle log were also made available to me, but as always with those kind of documents, the detailed reports from fighting men on the ground have proved more accurate.

Also used were press releases of the Administrator General and UNTAG, various tape recordings of press conferences made available to me to me by the kindness of Attie Dippenaar and records of the Supreme Court of SWA/Namibia.

Willem Steenkamp's *Borderstrike* (Butterworths, Durban, 1983), Helmoed-Romer Heitman's *South African War Machine* (Galago, London 1985), both friends and respected fellow writers, *Namibian Independence and Cuban Troop Withdrawal* (SA Ministry of Foreign Affairs, Pretoria 1989), *The Choice* (NPP 435 and Contact Group, Windhoek), *Human Rights Violations In SWAPO Camps In Angola and Zambia* (International Society for Human Rights, London, 1988) and my own *Taming The Landmine* (Galago, Alberton, 1986), are indispensable works of reference on the border war and related political, human rights and diplomatic matters.

Foreword

The 1st April 1989 marked the first day of peace in Namibia.

After seemingly endless years of dispute between South Africa and the United Nations, after 23 years of bush warfare between the Marxist orientated South West Africa People's Organisation – SWAPO, and South African forces, which had spread from Namibia into Angola and, at times, into Zambia, and after eight months of American brokered talks between South Africa, Cuba and Angola, Namibia was finally on course for UN supervised 'free and fair elections' in November 1989, which would lead to independence in 1990.

The South Africans had stuck strictly to the letter of the agreements and even more. By the 1st April they had demobilised the powerful SWA Territory Force, drastically reduced the strength of the SADF and confined the residue still remaining in Namibia to bases.

When the sun rose on that fateful day, it would catch the shadows of only five SAAF Alouette helicopter gunships, emasculated of their deadly cannons, and dispersed along 400 kilometres of Namibian border with Angola.

SWAPO's leader, Sam Nujoma, knew it, for the knowledge was international property via the UN.

Nujoma had transmitted his written agreement to a ceasefire to the UN Secretary General in late March.

But while smilingly professing he was for peace, he was treacherously behind the scenes preparing for war.

More than 1 600 of his PLAN fighters, who should have long been removed to camps north of the 16th parallel by the Angolan and Cubans, under UN supervision, were massing in Angola along the Namibian border, heavily armed with everything from anti tank to sophisticated anti aircraft weapons.

On the night of the 31st March-1st April, they surged over in what they obviously believed was an unstoppable wave. A wave which once it broke into pools, they believed, would be allowed by a weak UN to remain in Namibia and subvert the elections by means of a brutal intimidation campaign.

But they overlooked a wild card. It was a thin blue line of some 1 200 SWA Policemen of the northern border command, many of them former members of the counterinsurgency unit, Koevoet, whose heavy weapons had been removed from their Casspirs in terms of the peace plan.

But what those policemen, mostly black with a sprinkling of white commanders, lacked in weaponry, they more than made up with sheer guts, fighting skills and undying courage.

For nine bitter days until the Mount Etjo Agreement was signed, they fought the SWAPO infiltrators to a grim standstill, in the closing stages with air force and military help, beating them hands down.

Peter Stiff was there while the fighting was on.

He spoke to Administrator General Louis Pienaar and people in his administration, Gen Prem Chand and men of his UN command, South African diplomat Derek Auret, SADF Chief Gen Geldenhuys, SWA Police Commissioner Gen Dolf Gouws, Regional Commissioner for the northern border, Gen Hans Dreyer and many other senior military, police and civilians as well.

But above all he spoke to the policemen, airmen, soldiers, medics and even captured SWAPO fighters in the field, often when they were fresh from battle, from whose stories he has written this unmatched almost blow by blow account of the fighting.

It is all here.

It is Peter Stiff's story, without any form of censorship or restriction, of Namibia before it happened, while it was happening and what has happened since.

It is a thought provoking account, impossible to ignore, impossible to put down.

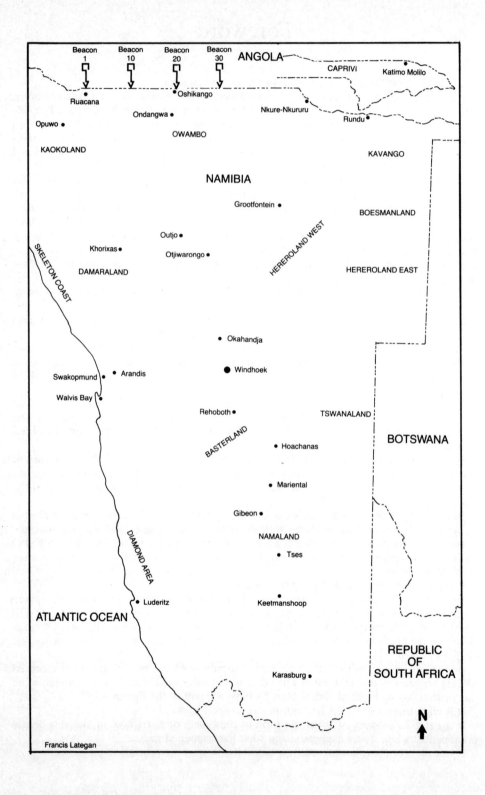

1

The Namibian War

As Africa moved towards the 1960s, African nationalism began to stir as a political force, a force which would one day sweep the continent, but in South Africa and South West Africa the winds of change were scarcely a breeze.

The Owambo People's Congress – OPC, was formed by Owambos working in Cape Town, who became politically aware by learning of the heady and seemingly impossible dreams and aspirations of the politics of black rule, by rubbing shoulders with members of organisations like the African National Congress, the South African Communist Party and the Liberal Party.

One of the founders was Andimba Herman Ja Toivo, who had risen to corporal in the Native Military Corps of the Union Defence Force during World War-2.

Their original aims were politically unambitious, they merely wished to see an end to the contract labour system – the hated odalate, a product of apartheid that had been imposed in South West Africa, and which prevented Owambos from freely leaving Owamboland to seek work, unless it was as a contracted labourer.

Within South West Africa one of its early members was Sam Nujoma, then working for the railways in Windhoek.

Early in 1959 the organisation's name was changed to the Owambo People's Organisation – OPO, and Sam Nujoma became its leader.

Seizing on social grievances as vehicles for agitation, as was happening in other white ruled African countries to the north, the OPO under Sam Nujoma learned fast and became increasingly militant.

In December 1959 OPO-inspired civil unrest broke out in Windhoek and this soon escalated into violence, culminating in police opening fire on rioters in the Old Location.

Sam Nujoma fled the country and sought support from President Julius Nyerere of Tanzania, a black leader of Marxist persuasion who had turned his country into a one party state.

Tanzania had become the cockpit from which many African nationalist movements launched subversion back into their own countries.

From there the South West Africa Peoples' Organisation – SWAPO, which the OPO was renamed in April 1960, never looked back.

SWAPO's purely nationalistic character, thanks to extensive financial backing and the provision of weapons by the Soviets, soon changed so that it became a Marxist revolutionary organisation. SWAPO cadres were sent to various communist countries for guerrilla training.

9

This led to the formation of SWAPO's military wing in 1962 – the Peoples' Liberation Army of Namibia – PLAN.

By the mid I960s, like the ANC and liberation movements from such places as Rhodesia [now Zimbabwe], Mozambique Angola and elsewhere, SWAPO had established offices in Moscow, London, New York, Stockholm, as well as in various newly independent black states, the most important being Dar es Salaam in Tanzania and Lusaka in Zambia.

By early I966 SWAPO insurgents were ensconced in rear bases in Zambia, while some were cooperating with Jonas Savimbi's UNITA movement, with which the Owambos have tribal affiliations, who were fighting Portuguese colonialism in southern Angola.

The armed struggle, SWAPO style, was poised and ready to begin.

Their first flexing of muscles occurred in February I966, when a gang attacked two Portuguese trading stores in southern Angola, killing two Portuguese citizens and three of their Owambo employees.

In August I966 the South African Police, supported by SAAF helicopters, attacked a large group of armed SWAPO guerrillas they had tracked to Ongulumbashe in Owamboland. There was a brief contact in which two SWAPO dissidents were killed and nine captured. More were arrested afterwards when Owambo locals, who were unsympathetic to SWAPO, passed on information regarding their hideouts to the police.

Those fortunate enough to escape with their lives, adopted the name Do Momfitu – Soldiers of the Bush. After some impromptu planning, they decided to attack and lay waste to the little settlement of Oshikango, just south of the Angolan border, in the early hours of 27th September 1966.

By a stroke of good fortune, although they managed to burn some buildings and fire off much ammunition, the only casualty was a wounded Owambo night watchman.

Another SWAPO group mounted an attack in December 1966 against a white owned farm at Maroelaboom in northern Owamboland. Their straightforward terrorist plan was to murder a white farmer – any white farmer would have done – but they failed.

In the police follow-up operation afterwards, three armed guerrillas were captured.

Although occasional incidents of SWAPO terrorism continued occurring in Owamboland, they switched their main operational thrust after this to the Caprivi Strip, which because of their rear bases in Zambia, was easier to mount attacks against.

In March 1967 they opened their Caprivi campaign with the ambush of a police patrol, but this went so dramatically awry and all ambushers were captured, without the police suffering a casualty.

The PLAN supreme commander, Tobias Hanyeko, became a statistic himself in May 1967 when he was killed in an exchange of fire after being recognised by police aboard a Zambesi ferry.

Sporadic incidents of armed terrorism continued to occur both in Owamboland and in the Caprivi.

SWAPO then began to use the landmine, a weapon of indiscriminate destruction, which had proved successful against the Portuguese in Angola and Mozambique.

On the 22nd May 1971, a South African Police vehicle on general patrol near Katima Mulilo in the Caprivi Strip, detonated a SWAPO planted landmine. Two policemen, Constables J J Henning and W P Dobbin, were killed while another nine, two of them in the following vehicle, were injured.

Police trackers picked up the spoor of seven insurgents, which they tracked until they crossed the border into Zambia.

During the evening of the 4th October 1971, another SWAPO landmine was detonated by a police vehicle near Katima Mulilo, seriously injuring four constables.

The next day Captain van Eeden, investigating the incident, stepped on an anti personnel mine at the scene and was killed.

A follow-up team with trackers found and made safe three more landmines, one each on the following three days, but again they had to abandon the trail when it led into Zambia.

According to press speculation, South African Premier, John Vorster, was supposed to have authorised a hot pursuit operation into Zambia to catch the culprits and this made banner headlines around the world. That one was planned is doubtful, but the possibility remains that some free thinking spirits in the SAP and SADF out there in the bush, might well have been tempted to do just that. But in the event, the SWAPO guerrillas responsible got away scot free.

SWAPO headquarters in Lusaka, Zambia, issued a press statement on the 7th October saying its fighters had been operating from bases within South West Africa, not from Zambian territory.

President Kenneth Kaunda had the gall to ask for an emergency meeting of the UN Security Council on the 8th October, when his representatives complained of '... a series of incidents and violations of Zambia's sovereignty, air space and territorial integrity by the forces of the fascist government of South Africa ...'

The Security Council, as was par for the course when African ruled states complained about white ruled ones, made no comment on South Africa's own complaint that '... armed bands infiltrating across the border from Zambia into Caprivi in order to cause death and destruction ...' and preferred to adopt a resolution calling on South Africa ' to respect Zambia's sovereignty.'

This low key insurgency, with SWAPO occasionally infiltrating into the Caprivi and then into Owambo and planting landmines, continued unabated for some years.

Then the whole balance of power in the southern African sub continent changed overnight, when in far away Lisbon, a left wing *coup d'etat* toppled the regime of Portuguese dictator, President Caetano.

Since I96I the Portuguese had been fighting an insurgency war against three organisations of black nationalist guerrillas in Angola.

To the north, led by Holden Roberto, was the National Front For The Liberation of Angola – FNLA. His grass roots support came from the Bakongo tribe of which Roberto is the hereditary king, while his logistical support in the main came from Zaire – where his brother-in-law of the time, Mobuto Sese Seko – is State President – as well as from the Red Chinese and various Arab states.

To the south was the National Union For the Total Independence of Angola – Unita, led by Dr Jonas Savimbi and drawing its tribal support from the Ovimbundu. This movement was the weakest of them all, for Savimbi, although an ardent nationalist, was and still is a dedicated anti-communist.

His logistical support came only in thin trickles from various sympathisers, but mainly at that time from Zambia, into which there is a tribal spillage. Zambian assistance ceased after the MPLA had grabbed power in Angola, after which South

African and later American support commenced. The communists supplied nothing, for the last thing they looked forward to was UNITA emerging as the victor in the bush war against the Portuguese.

In central Angola was the Popular Movement For The Liberation of Angola – MPLA, led by the late Dr Agostinho Neto. This movement, although having some tribal support, drew its recruits from a wider cross section of society, appealing in the classical communist fashion to the urban poor and the intellectual classes.

It was heavily backed with money and arms by the Soviets and the Warsaw Pact countries and it was no secret that they were being groomed as the Soviet's tool to transform Angola into a communist state by revolutionary means.

Gradually over the years since the war had started in 1961, the Portuguese, who had got off to a disastrous start, had regained the ascendancy until by early 1974 the fortunes of all three rebel organisations had reached a low ebb. In fact it is doubtful, working as they were, if any of them could ever have succeeded in overthrowing Portuguese rule in Angola.

The Lisbon coup changed all that.

After several contradictory alterations of stance, the Portuguese Government declared that Angola would become independent on the 11th November 1975.

The Angolan scene was chaotic.

The Portuguese troops stayed sullenly in barracks, not even protecting their own nationals.

The three rebel movements, with no one to control them, bloodily jockeyed to grab control of the country when independence day came.

In spite of this, many people, both in southern Africa and elsewhere, sublimely believed all the black movements were committed to working together in a transitional government, which would be replaced later by the people's choice, established by the means of free and fair elections.

The Soviets – who by no stretch of the imagination, can be regarded as potential guardians of democratic options – cared nothing for the people's choice, and they certainly had no intention of losing Angola to their cause by default.

By April 1975 the first of Fidel Castro's Cuban soldiers, whom the Russians had begun to use widely in Africa as surrogates for the Red Army, which had that been used would have invited intervention by the Americans, arrived to act as 'advisers' to the MPLA.

Shipments of communist arms for the movement began to flood in.

To make matters worse for the FNLA and UNITA movements, which by agreement with the Portuguese were supposed to be treated on an equal footing with the MPLA, found that the Portuguese military and civil leadership handling the transition to black rule, who were heavily infiltrated by communists at all levels, were actively working to ensure the MPLA took over the reins of power. By August 1975, it was clear to all thinking people that a Soviet takeover of Angola, through their surrogates, was all but complete.

It was apparent to the South Africans, who stood to lose the most by having a communist state bordering South West Africa, that something had to be done.

Many western countries, including the USA, Great Britain and France, agreed with this position, but were prepared to offer little more than covert support and diplomatic tea and sympathy.

Black states, though, like Zambia and Zaire, normally sworn enemies of white ruled Africa, made approaches to the South African government and pointed out its responsibilities as the only regional power, asking them to intervene.

The South Africans were placed in a quandry.

Since March 1975 they had been rejecting entreaties by both Holden Roberto and Jonas Savimbi for arms and supplies, to help them stand up to the MPLA.

Eventually they relented, but only to a limited degree, and they set up training camps, one at Calembo to train UNITA troops, and the other at Mapupa to train the Daniel Chipembe breakaway faction of MPLA, who had joined FNLA in the south.

This essentially half hearted program of military assistance, proved woefully inadequate and by September 1975 the Cuban supported MPLA, awash with Soviet supplied weapons of war, had grabbed every important town between Luanda and the South West Africa border.

The South African advisers began taking a more active part in FNLA and UNITA operations in an effort to halt the MPLA advance. A few scrappy actions were fought with limited successes, but this only made it clearer that unless a more effective military intervention was embarked on, Angola would be lost to the communists.

With the secret encouragement of the USA, who had commenced covert CIA support for the FNLA, South Africa decided the time had come to act.

On the 14th October 1975, Task Force Zulu, commanded by Colonel Koos van Heerden, moved into Angola.

Zulu was made up of two columns of fighting troops, one consisting of Caprivi Bushmen, commanded by Commandant Delville Linford, and the other Daniel Chipembe's FNLA troops, numbering about one thousand, commanded by Commandant Jan Breytenbach. Both columns were strengthened by the addition of SADF officers and NCOs as well as supporting elements.

Its successes were outstanding and the MPLA and their Cuban backers, despite vastly superior equipment, crumpled before their onslaught.

In thirty three days, the South African columns rampaged an incredible 3 159 kilometres, fighting and winning numerous engagements, both major and minor, and capturing many important towns and villages.

Total casualties were five killed and forty one wounded.

Meanwhile other South African task forces, notably Foxbat and Orange, consisting of mixed elements of UNITA and South African troops, were also committed to action.

They would later be supplemented by a training mission sent to assist Holden Roberto's FNLA in November and by Task Force X-Ray, which would be committed in December 1975.

In January 1976, once it became clear that covert support by the West for their operations in Angola had evaporated, and after the USA had reneged on various promises, South Africa decided to pull her forces back to South West Africa.

Even South Africa's covert supporters in black Africa had been dithering and were in two minds over the Angolan question.

An OAU vote to decide on the recognition of an MPLA government in Angola, had resulted in a split vote.

The Cubans by then had a troop level of 15 000 in Angola and their numbers were rapidly increasing.

At one stage the South Africans were almost within artillery range of Luanda, and there is little doubt that with a determined push they could have taken it. Many people were then of the opinion they should have, including the author, but latterly more information has been revealed which indicates that such a move would have proved disastrous.

It was all very well assisting anti Marxist forces in their efforts to take over the government of the country, but even had the country been 'captured' by the South Africans, there was no one they could hand it to who was capable of holding on to it.

So Luanda would have become South Africa's Saigon, with the Angolan hinterland her Vietnam, and the real war would have then begun. The situation for South Africa after the MPLA's final takeover was bad enough anyway, without that.

After the intervention, UNITA took to the bush, where with South African and American succour, the organisation has continued a brave and successful fight against the MPLA and its Cuban allies to this very day, although at the time of writing peace negotiations between the UNITA and the MPLA are in the offing.

The FNLA remained halfheartedly on the Angolan stage for a while, then slipped away with the might have been into history.

The MPLA victory was a big win for SWAPO as well, because the new Angolan rulers were sympathetic and immediately granted them guerrilla base facilities, while the Cubans took over responsibility for their military training.

The prospect faced by South Africa, the establishment of SWAPO bases along the Angolan border, facing directly into Owamboland and Kaokoland, was dismal – and so it turned out to be.

For a time after the MPLA takeover in Angola, SWAPO concentrated almost entirely on building up its PLAN organisation in southern Angola, which gave a respite to Caprivi, allowing time for the authorities to develop a 'hearts and minds' programme, which did much to turn the populace against SWAPO.

Until September 1977, the South African Police were responsible for countering SWAPO insurgency, with the SADF acting in support of the civil power when required, but with the escalation of the bush war the SADF took over the responsibility.

In October 1977 the SADF announced that contacts between the Security Forces and SWAPO gangs infiltrating Owamboland, were running at more than a hundred per month. According to estimates about 300 insurgents had recently infiltrated Owamboland, while another 2 000 stood ready in Angolan rear bases to come in. In addition another 1 400 SWAPO were waiting in Zambia, ready to recommence armed infiltrations into the Caprivi Strip.

A major infiltration of some eighty SWAPO guerrillas into Owamboland followed a few days later.

After a series of running battles, lasting almost a week, sixty one insurgents had been killed for the loss of six South Africans.

The South African military commanders knew something had to be done to curb SWAPO's build-up in southern Angola.

The problem from the military 'hawks' point of view, was that Premier John Vorster, although tough and craggy in appearance, was a dove who couldn't make up his mind. He was totally opposed to cross border raids. It was his threat to cut back on the movement of their strategic supplies, which had stopped the Rhodesians from mounting cross border raids in the middle years of the war there.

Prime Minister Vorster's major political problem, of which he undoubtedly had more than just a few, was that South Africa had just accepted the Western Five's proposals. These provided for a withdrawal of South African forces from SWA/

Namibia and other matters leading to the adoption of UN resolution 435 – so there couldn't have been a worse time for a cross border foray.

Yet SWAPO inspired incidents of terrorism, with the black civilian population being the prime target, had escalated alarmingly.

A minister in the Owambo tribal government, Toivo Shiyagaya, had been assassinated, a South African soldier, Sapper van der Mescht, had been captured by SWAPO and their landmines continually devastated civilian and Security Force vehicles alike.

If SWAPO were allowed to continue unchecked, the situation in Owamboland would soon get completely out of control.

The South Africans had no illusions about Sam Nujoma. They knew he believed his future power in Namibia would probably have to come, in the classical communist fashion, from the barrel of a gun.

On the 28th February 1978 he had admitted as much during a television interview in New York, saying that on assuming power in Namibia 'SWAPO would do away with a variety of traitors, including Namibians in the armed forces and puppets belonging to the internal political parties'.

When asked what he would do after UN supervised elections if SWAPO was 'left out in the cold' and another party gained political power in Namibia instead, Nujoma immediately set the record straight.

'The question of black majority rule is out,' he said. 'We are not fighting even for majority rule. We are fighting to seize power in Namibia, for the benefit of the Namibian people. We are revolutionaries. We are not counter-revolutionaries . . .

When the storm burst around his head, Nujoma vehemently denied the statements, alleging the original tape had been tampered with. Experts who viewed it, though, pronounced it genuine, saying tampering would have been impossible.

Politically the South African government had lots to lose by raiding SWAPO bases in Angola. What the likely effects on the current UN initiatives would be, was a matter for conjecture, but obviously it wouldn't be good. It would probably result in a UN armaments boycott, but this was all but a fait accompli anyway. At least an economic boycott seemed unlikely.

Another problem was the electorate's mood. If a military adventure north was necessary, they would support it, except for protests by the highly vocal left. But if the SADF paid the blood price of an undisguised defeat, with heavy casualties, it would probably prove disastrous for the government.

Eventually, after much prevarication, Premier Vorster gave the word for the SADF to go ahead with Operation Reindeer.

Three main target areas had been identified by Intelligence.

The first and by far the most difficult was Cassinga, a small Angolan town 250 kilometres north of the SWA/Namibian border, which had been developed as SWAPO's main base in Angola.

The second was Chetequera, 25 kilometres north of the Angolan border, scattered around which were several bases containing upwards of 570 PLAN fighters. Two had been code named Moscow and Vietnam by SWAPO, which are hardly names chosen by an organisation with an inclination towards democracy.

The third target area was another cluster of bases, some 25 kilometres east of Chetequera.

It was a major operation and 500 paratroopers of the 2nd and 3rd Parabats, commanded by Colonel Jan Breytenbach, would be dropped in for the Cassinga strike, while a column of sixty three armoured vehicles, including nine infantry fighting vehicles, would strike north across the border and handle the second. 32 'Buffalo' Battalion, which had been formed from former FNLA troops who had fought under South African officers during Operation Savannah, were tackling the final target.

The para strike against Cassinga went in on the 4th May 1978, and although it turned out to be a tougher nut to crack than anticipated, it was a complete success.

SWAPO lost over a 1 000 guerrillas dead or captured, against South African casualties of four dead and eleven wounded.

The Cubans tried to intervene and attempted to smash their way through with a fighting column of Soviet supplied T-34 tanks and BTR-152 armoured personnel carriers, but they suffered a major reverse. They lost at least fourteen armoured vehicles, but probably more, to RPG rocket launchers, South African laid landmines and air strikes by Buccaneers and Mirages.

The South African attack with light armour on Chetequera was also eminently successful. 248 SWAPO were killed and another 200 captured.

The Buffalo Battalion's task was also well and successfully performed.

Operation Reindeer had the immediate effect of curbing SWAPO's armed incursions into Owamboland.

To reestablish their neglected image in Caprivi, SWAPO mounted an attack with 122mm rockets on the South African base at Katima Mulilo on the 23rd August 1978, and ten South African soldiers asleep in their barrack room, died from a direct hit.

The South Africans mounted an immediate follow-up, achieving minor successes, then shortly afterwards embarked on a major raid, Operation Saffron, against SWAPO's PLAN bases in south western Zambia, from where the attackers had originated.

SWAPO abandoned their bases and took to the bush, unwilling to face the South Africans in open combat. The Zambian National Defence Force which was supposed to be protecting SWAPO, adopted a similar stance, sensibly keeping well out of the way.

It was a salutary lesson for President Kaunda of Zambia, who suddenly realised that if he continued allowing SWAPO to use his country as a springboard to mount attacks against the Caprivi, then the South Africans would probably give Zambia the same devastating treatment they had begun to mete out in southern Angola.

He had already had more than just a taste of that from the Rhodesians – and he didn't like it.

So he banned SWAPO from mounting cross-border raids from Zambia into the Caprivi, and no infiltrations worth speaking about have taken place since.

SWAPO were to suffer a final blow to their Caprivi aspirations, when the Caprivi African National Union – CANU, which had once amalgamated with SWAPO, split once again because of discrimination against non Owambo cadres. The CANU faction constituted the majority of SWAPO in Zambia, but at Sam Nujoma's request, President Kaunda rounded them all up and detained them.

Then a new factor entered the bush war to assist the Security Forces.

In late 1978 Colonel Hans Dreyer, a South African Police officer who had served his guerrilla war apprenticeship in Rhodesia in the early 1970s, and who was then commanding the SAP Security Branch in Natal, was sent for by the Commissioner of Police.

In Pretoria he found himself in conference with the Commissioner of Police, the

Chief of the SADF, General Magnus Malan, and the founding Commander of the Recce Commandos, Major General Fritz Loots.

Something had to be done about the situation in Owamboland where SWAPO were poised to make deep inroads.

The suggestion was that the Recces and the Security Branch should get together and form a unit similar to the Selous Scouts of Rhodesia, whose prime task was to operate as pseudo terrorists in a counterinsurgency role.

Colonel Dreyer was sent to Rhodesia where he spent some time working with BSA Police Chief Superintendent Mac McGuinness, a highly experienced police officer who commanded the Special Branch team supplying the knowhow and intelligence responsible for the spectacular successes achieved by the Selous Scouts' during operations.

On his return to Pretoria there were more conferences, more discussions.

'The army had fixed ideas,' recalled Hans Dreyer, 'I had my own.'

Eventually he was ordered to select five police officers of his own choice, who would accompany him to SWA/Namibia. The police, in most countries, unlike the military, are invariably parsimonious when it comes to providing staff.

'How do you think I can fight a bloody war with only five men?' Hans Dreyer asked the Commissioner.

'It will have to do for a start,' the Commissioner told him tartly.

The SWA/Namibian exercise was coded Operation Koevoet – Koevoet being Afrikaans for crowbar.

On the 11th January 1979 Colonel Dreyer, together with five Security Branch policemen, equipped with two vanettes and two sedan cars, arrived by road at Ondangwa in the heart of the Owamboland bush, feeling like poor relations compared to the well equipped SADF, and attached themselves to the Recce Commando's base.

In the event the concept of a joint police/army unit, as originally envisaged, didn't work out. The policemen had expected the Recces would be bringing in prisoners for them to interrogate, but it was a cart and horse situation, because without police information, the soldiers were unable to produce prisoners.

Eventually, the policemen got down to gathering information themselves, using normal police methods, which quickly resulted in the arrest of some SWAPO insurgents who had been hiding out amongst the tribal population.

This quickly snowballed.

In this way the unit developed and military assistance as originally envisaged became superfluous.

Nothing, of course, succeeds like success, and it was not long before the code name of the operation became accepted as the unofficial name of the unit, then when it stuck, it became the official one.

It stayed as Koevoet until mid 1985, when SAP personnel serving in SWA/Namibia were seconded to the SWA Police. Then officially it became the SWA Police Counter Insurgency Unit – SWAPOL COIN.

Unofficially, though, to those who served in it and to its SWAPO foes, it remained Koevoet. The names of highly successful units defy alteration no matter what is said and done, they become part of tradition, and those who serve in them develop an overweening pride which cannot be disposed of by the stroke of a pen.

And so it was with Koevoet, a name that refused to die.

The unit expanded and became many times the size originally intended, the black policemen, mainly recruited from the Owambo tribe, eventually constituted more than 90% of its personnel.

Major General Hans Dreyer, 'Sterk Hans' [Strong] to his men both black and white, was the type of fighting officer men will cheerfully follow to hell and back, when he gives the nod.

He introduced simple fighting tactics that weren't in the military text books, but in the flat grasslands of Owamboland they worked.

Most successes were gained by using the ubiquitous Casspir and its derivative the Wolf, infantry fighting vehicles supreme, the design and manufacture of which had been sponsored by the police, in support of police trackers from local tribes, who nowadays must number amongst the finest in the world.

Then, when operations became necessary in the mountains and desert of Kaokoland to the west, they adapted their tactics and operated just as successfully on foot as they did in their Casspirs.

Many soldiers from high rank to low, regarded these tough and experienced fighters with respect, amazement, and no little puzzlement. They seemed by army standards, undisciplined. They had their own individualistic rules by which the group leader finding the enemy spoor, became the ground commander for an operation. This meant that sometimes everything was according to military protocol, with sergeants and constables following the officers, but at other times it meant officers ended up following a sergeant or maybe even a constable – which seems highly irregular to the average soldier, even in time of war.

It was finally disbanded in December 1988 as a sop to the United Nations, where there was and still is much sympathy towards SWAPO propaganda and where it had been outrageously labelled it as a unit responsible for atrocities against the black populace, instead of one where the men had merely performed their duties, and performed them well.

Certainly there had been scattered allegations of assault and suchlike against members of Koevoet and its successor, this happens in every police force, but they had mostly come to public light in the courtroom – where police investigations had put them.

Most allegations, though, were patently false and formed part of a determined campaign, orchestrated by the far left, to discredit Koevoet and its successor SWA Police COIN, because they were so successful in operations against SWAPO.

Yet in spite of the lies, no one could deny their successes. During their almost ten years of existence, in 1 615 contacts, they killed 2 812 insurgents and captured 463, for the loss of 151 policemen killed in action, with another 940 men of all ranks wounded.

Amongst the armaments captured were 2 349 AK-47 and other carbines, 203 light machineguns, 145 mortar tubes ranging from 50–82mms, 334 RPG rocket launchers, 11 SAM-7 ground to air launchers complete with missiles, B-10 cannons, grenades of many varieties, sniper rifles, pistols and countless tons of ammunition – conservatively valued at more than US$6 000,000.

For the guerrilla it has often been said that time is on his side, but this was not the case for SWAPO.

SWAPO's intention was to work towards escalating the guerrilla war into a classical one, but the closest they got to it was in 1978, when South Africa's new policy of striking at their bases deep within Angola put paid to that.

In 1978 it was estimated that PLAN had a strength of 16 000 fighters, but as the war against them toughened up recruiting became difficult. There were fewer volunteers filtering across the border into Angola to join their ranks, expeditions into Owamboland to kidnap school children in the time honoured fashion of the press gang, became suicide missions and casualties rose.

While successes had brought recruits, stalemate – even failure, brought desertions, and many cadres decided they'd had enough and once back in Namibia volunteered to fight their erstwhile comrades in the ranks of units of the SWA Territory Force, particular 101 Battalion.

By 1987 it was estimated PLAN's fighting strength had been reduced to about 8 700 men, of whom only about 1 200 were directly available for operations against Namibia.

Of the rest, some 2 280 were involved in administrative, logistic, command and control or base protection work – including the protection of bases in Zambia and Botswana, as well as in Angola, and recruits in training.

Another 5 200 paid the rent due for FAPLA and Cuban assistance, by fighting against UNITA, or being deployed in defensive roles to combat UNITA or SADF raids.

SWAPO quickly discovered that cross border incursions into Namibia by large numbers of men, were invariably costly in men and war material, so they reduced the numbers in the infiltrating gangs, most of whom were still hunted down and brought to combat by the Security Forces.

In an effort towards effectiveness, SWAPO formed so called special force teams, codenamed Typhoon and Volcano, whose task was to get through Owamboland to the white farming areas in the south, where they were to concentrate on terrorist attacks on farms, sabotaging the railway line, electricity installations and other key points.

SWAPO incursions into Namibia gradually developed into a pattern, with the peak of incursions taking place during the rainy season, when the bush is thick and there is plenty of surface water about to replenish water bottles.

The Security Force's response, too, developed into a predictable pattern, as regular raids in force into Angola were mounted to devastate SWAPO build-ups. The South Africans mounted numerous hot pursuit operations into Angola, mostly of a minor nature, against exfiltrating SWAPO bands, staging posts or minor bases, and a number of major ones as well.

The next major operation launched by the South Africans after Operation Reindeer, was Operation Sceptic, which went in on the 10th June 1980. It was directed against PLAN's command headquarters in the Kunene Province, 150 kilometres north of the Namibian border.

The attack was a marked success, with SWAPO losing 360 men killed and captured. As a direct result, SWAPO were forced to move their PLAN headquarters back nearly 300 kilometres, well away from the Namibian border, for safety's sake.

Gradually the situation was reached where the South Africans controlled large areas of southern Angola, forcing SWAPO infiltrators to run a long gauntlet before they could even set foot in Namibia.

Operation Protea, mounted in August 1981, resulted in two FAPLA brigades being defeated in open battle, and the destruction of several PLAN bases.

It was estimated that 1 000 SWAPO insurgents were killed, while 3 000- 4 000 tons of Soviet supplied war material was captured. Amongst the booty was eleven tanks, three scout cars, fifty five artillery pieces – including a Stalin's Organ multiple rocket launcher, and a haul of about two hundred trucks and lorries.

For the first time Soviet advisers were counted amongst the casualties. Two colonels and their ladies, attempting to flee the combat area, were killed, while a tough but bewildered Russian warrant officer was taken prisoner.

On the 6th December 1983 the SADF and SWA Territory Force launched Operation Askari across the border into Angola, with the objective of knocking out PLAN elements that had been building up in preparation for a new offensive.

During the raid there were a number of clashes with FAPLA, who extended their protection to SWAPO units. This culminated in FAPLA's 11th Brigade, especially stiffened up for the occasion by two Cuban battalions, engaging a South African mechanised combat group near Cuvelai.

The FAPLA/Cuban force came second, losing eleven T-54 tanks and abandoning 324 of their dead on the field of battle.

Much fascinating intelligence was gained, including their battle orders, written in Russian and then translated into Portuguese, showing how much the Angolans relied on their advisers.

Just prior to Operation Askari, the South Africans had invited the Angolans to talk about the border war, but they responded only after the operation.

Talks were held in Lusaka during February 1984, where it was eventually agreed the South Africans would withdraw from southern Angola, which the MPLA would keep free of SWAPO.

The Joint Monitoring Commission – JMC, consisting of South African and Angolan elements was formed, to police the agreement, but it soon became clear that Angola was still actively assisting SWAPO to make infiltrations into Namibia.

After a year of really trying to make the agreement work, despite hundreds of violations by PLAN, South Africa finally withdrew from the JMC.

Officially South Africa had withdrawn all military elements from southern Angola after the agreement had lapsed, but it was not long before units were once again operating against SWAPO inside southern Angola.

In 1986 the 10 000th PLAN fighter was killed by South African Security Forces.

In the same year the Soviets began to adopt a more high profile position, and it is reasonable to assume they took charge and ordered a long overdue review of strategy, arising from which they must have taken a hand in formulating a new one.

They had seen vast quantities of their military hardware, countless millions of dollars worth, junked during South Africa's offensive raids into Angola – so it was not only Angola and Cuba who had suffered humiliating losses of prestige from the failure to administer a defeat on South Africa.

By intelligent conjecture, one must believe they redecided their short term objectives as:

  (i) By military means, breaking the South Africans and getting SWAPO installed as the government of Namibia; or alternatively
 (ii) By political means, primarily by exerting pressures through the United Nations, get resolution 435 implemented and use this as a vehicle by which a SWAPO government could be installed in Windhoek; and
(iii) Breaking and disposing of UNITA by military means, because if the MPLA were eventually forced to negotiate at a conference table, it would likely result in the communist aims already achieved in Angolabeing dramatically watered down, or even dispensed with.

There must have been many things military the Soviets discussed with the Angolans and Cubans.

For instance, everyone understood the principles of insurgency communist style, because apart from a few hiccups like Malaya, it had been brought down to a fine art.

The point was an insurgency had to start as a low key terrorist affair. Then when the time was right, it had to be escalated into a full scale conventional war.

The problem was that while it had escalated into a full scale conventional one, it had happened in the wrong place, in Angola and not in the Namibia, where it still grumbled on only as a low key insurgency.

Clearly something had to be done about rectifying that.

It didn't require much expertise either, to understand why the war had remained a Mexican standoff.

The more the Soviets aided the MPLA to aid SWAPO in their efforts to overthrow South African rule in Namibia, the more did the South Africans and the Americans aid UNITA, who from their positioning inside Angola, had become the proverbial thorn in the side.

The revised strategy demanded they should first destroy UNITA, after which they would tackle the South Africans in Namibia, having taken effective steps to restrict their abilities to range freely and without restriction in southern Angola, like in the past.

To effect this, the Soviets first went all out to improve the Angolan air defences, by providing military aircraft of a greater sophistication than the SAAF possessed and making radical upgrading of radar detection facilities. It was intended this would provide the twin effects of keeping the SAAF out, and giving the combined Angolan/Cuban air forces a better chance of shooting them from the sky when they did come in.

At the same time moves were commenced which they hoped would eventually culminate in the destruction of UNITA.

This would be achieved by advancing in massive force and overrunning Jamba, Jonas Savimbi's stronghold in south eastern Angola.

The military movement would be made, one step at a time, with the forces stopping and consolidating, establishing forward airfields and radar cover, as they progressed.

The logistics of such an attack, made it imperative the troop movements south were made in the dry season, as during the rains all transport bogged down in the roadless, muddy bush.

The obviously ponderous overtones to this Soviet planning, reminds one of troop movements conducted in the 19th century, like by the British in their campaigns against Afghanistan and during the Zulu War of 1879.

But movements in those days were carried out using oxen, wagons and horses.

The first attempt was made by combined FAPLA/Cuban forces during the dry season of 1986, but their armoured columns were bloodily repulsed, it was said by UNITA, but there can be little doubt that South Africa played a vital hand in the game as well.

There were no official admissions, but stories in the press spoke of logjams of enemy transport being attacked and decimated by South African jets.

From this time on stories, which until then had been little more than rumours, that the Angolans and Cubans were using Soviet supplied chemical weapons – in blunt terms, poison gas – against UNITA, began to firm.

The Soviets, who have long been preparing to use chemical and biological weapons in the event of World War-3 breaking out against NATO in the West, had always suffered an obvious disadvantage in testing them.

Conventional weapons can be tested and their effectiveness judged in conventional conditions. Nuclear weapons can and have been tested in controlled conditions, by small undergrounds detonations and so forth. Chemical and biological weapons are different, because other than by tests on animals to adjudge their likely effects on humans, not much else can be done. There is no way one can judge the effects of wind and weather on such weapons in a laboratory.

Yet to upgrade them from test tube into a nation's armoury, such things must be established. So testing in battle conditions, against human targets, is essential. But because of natural repugnance towards their use by civilised peoples, it would have to be done in secret.

This would pose difficulties even for a totalitarian state like Soviet Russia, unless, as would probably have happened in Stalin's day, there was a remote area in a place like Siberia, and a few thousand unwanted political dissidents available for experimentation.

The other alternative was to use them secretly during a low key war in a highly remote area not normally frequented by journalists ... like in south eastern Angola.

And this, it seems, is what the Soviets through their surrogates so callously did.

So much for Perestroyka and what have you, when the state remains totalitarian. Evidence proving chemical weapons were used in Angola by the Cuban and Angolans, and were still being used there as recently as April 1989, is available.

Professor Aubin Hendrickx, the eminent head of the Department of Toxicology at the University of Ghent in Belgium, carried out prolonged and thorough investigations within Angola, establishing that the Cubans/Angolans had used Soviet supplied bombs containing a cheaply manufactured and deadly compound of calcium and cyanide $Ca(CN)2$, mixed with gas and dust.

There are sites in Angola where traces of the calcium cyanide dust still remains. UNITA provided conclusive proof by producing an unexploded Soviet chemical bomb, which has since been broken down and tested.

Profess Hendrickx's findings have been supported by academics in other European capitals, but as can be expected, there are still apologists who dismiss it and suggest the victims were suffering from tropical diseases, or had contacted viruses.

He has challenged doubters to visit UNITA controlled Angolan bush areas and satisfy themselves by taking their own samples.

They should also, like he did, carry out medical examinations and tests on the 400–500 black Angolan civilians who have suffered irreversible damage to their sensory organs as a result of the use of Soviet chemical weapons by the Angolans and Cubans.

Most Western countries have closed their eyes to the atrocity of chemical warfare in Angola. Responsible for this is their new anxiety to improve relations with the Soviets, and probably, as well, because of UNITA's close association with South Africa, on the unjust basis that any friend of South Africa must be a supporter of apartheid.

So, who cares if they are gassed!

In July 1987, after a further beefing up of their air capability, the replacement of losses and a huge increase in their armoured strength, the Angolans and Cubans again ventured forth in two columns in what seemed irresistible force, intent again on the eventual capture of Jamba and the destruction of UNITA.

This time the combined forces were estimated to be 25 000 men strong, with masses of armour and heavy weapons and to show that this time the Russians wanted things done correctly, a Soviet officer, General Konstantin Shagnovitch, was placed in command.

He divided his forces into two armoured columns, one of which struck out from Luiana and the other from the by then massively strengthened air base at Cuito Cuanavale.

Both were aimed at Mavinga, which was targeted for capture in September, when the Angolan President, Eduardo dos Santos, was scheduled to make an official visit to Portugal.

It seems the communist columns, with no delegation of authority by the top Russian commander, were able to exercise the flexibility and easy manoeuvrebility of a concrete block.

For the communists the operation turned out a total disaster.

The South Africans responded to UNITA's call for assistance with Operation Modular, which according to reports issued at the time, consisted of G-5 and G-6 long range and pin pointedly accurate artillery support, which together with UNITA infantry, bloodily repulsed the Luiana column at the Lomba River.

The communists suffered heavy casualties in both men and war material.

Whether other South African units took part in the Lomba River battle, to lend armoured, infantry and air support to UNITA, must at the moment remain a matter for conjecture, but in spite of official silence, it seems improbable that air support was denied to UNITA, particularly when South Africa's prime artillery weapons had already been committed and would likely have been vulnerable without it.

But whatever happened there, the South Africans certainly assisted UNITA in breaking the other column, which after taking a grievous mauling, the remnants crawled bleeding and bruised back to Cuito Cuanavale.

It has been estimated the combined communist forces lost over seven thousand dead during this campaign, to say nothing of wounded. Their losses in Soviet supplied war material was staggering, with an estimated value of well over a billion US dollars. Amongst their material losses were ninety four main battle tanks, captured or destroyed.

The South Africans lost thirty one soldiers dead. Three of their tanks fell prey to landmines, but none to artillery fire or to other tanks.

By November 1987, South African and UNITA forces had reached Cuito Cuanavale, which was their objective, and put it under siege.

That Cuito Cuanavale was their objective cannot be emphasised too strongly, because it was the main start point from which the joint Cuban- Angolan army had set out on their campaign to crush UNITA.

The Cuban propaganda ploy during the latter stages of the campaign, that the South Africans were unable to cross from the eastern to the western side of the Cuito River because they were cut off and surrounded, was false. The facts were that the combined South African/UNITA forces halted their advance as intended on the eastern bank.

They had no intention of going farther.

If they had crossed the river purely as a movement of prestige, they would have been in the bad tactical position of defending themselves with their backs to the river, rather than facing across it.

The South Africans were back in the same old situation they had faced during Operation Savannah in late 1975, when they could have captured Luanda. But like Luanda in 1975, what would they have done with the spoil of a captured Cuito Cuanavale in 1987 – remembering that on their own UNITA were incapable of holding it.

And what is more important, where would they have gone from there? The reality was that once again the South Africans had stepped aside to avoid the 'Vietnam' trap.

The communists well knew they had taken a hammering, even if they so often tried to claim victory or stalemate at Cuito Cuanavale, but the truth was they had been beaten back to their campaign's start point, which does not indicate any sort of victory at all for them – even a hollow one.

What must obviously be true, is that the longer they stayed in their static position, the greater was there a build of enemy forces facing them. Which meant in the unlikely event of South African changing its mind and deciding to adventure on to Luanda, they would probably have had a hard time doing it

On the other hand what the South Africans achieved there, proved to be highly useful negotiating cards at the peace talks then about to begin.

Much of the truth was revealed by President Fidel Castro of Cuba when he made damaging admissions during a major two hour speech at a full Council of State meeting in Havana on 9th July 1989, which was afterwards broadcast on the State radio and television services.

The prime purpose of the speech was to denounce and lay the blame for the Cuban/Angolan reverses at the feet of the Cuban commander, General Arnaldo Ochoa Sanchez, who had been executed by firing squad after being found guilty by a military tribunal of theft, corruption and racketeering.

He explained that when General Sanchez should have been devoting himself to working for his country in its hour of need, he was engaged in enriching himself on the black market.

While Castro's obvious purpose was to stress a Cuban-Angolan victory over South Africa, the opposite became apparent.

After all, why should one speak of hours of need and Dunkirk, when you have just won a war.

Castro emphasised the seriousness of events in Angola at the time by saying: 'We were in charge of the [Angolan] government from mid November [1987] until the end of that year. We devoted all our time to that struggle, to the war. It could not have been otherwise. We had to take responsibility for whatever happened there.'

He conceded that at one stage the SADF came close to destroying three FAPLA brigades at Cuito Cuanavale. He said the situation became so serious that he dropped all official duties to personally take over tactical control of the war from Havana. He ordered troop movements, directed contingency planning on the southern front and so on, bypassing his own commanding general in Angola, the doomed General Sanchez, and presumably the much abashed Soviet General Konstantin Shagnovitch as well.

There was a real danger of defeat by South Africa and Castro feared that not only would Cuba's honour be lost, but the whole revolution would have been lost as well.

The South Africans stayed in position at Cuito Cuanavale, using it as a painful hook in the mouth of the communists, until a ceasefire between Angola/Cuba and herself had been finally negotiated.

The Soviets must have realised the idea of breaking South Africa and UNITA by military means, and installing a communist SWAPO government in Namibia as a result of their defeat, was too expensive an option to pursue.

Which is why, one must believe, they changed to using their good offices to assist in the quest for a peace agreement, which would inevitably lead to the implementation of resolution 435.

This, as they undoubtedly once feared, is now leading to the probability of another peace agreement being concluded between the MPLA and UNITA, which could result in communist influences diminishing in south western Africa, as was speculated earlier in this chapter.

But then on the other hand, perhaps not if Sam Nujoma and SWAPO gain power in Namibia. This would more than regain the balance for the Soviets.

So no matter how much one might wish to view Perestroyka through rose tinted spectacles, it would be foolish indeed to believe the Soviets would easily abandon all the political gains and influence they have achieved from military adventures during the chilly years of the cold war.

After all, why hasn't the Berlin Wall yet been reduced to rubble?

Which indicates, no matter the protests to the contrary, that it would be naive indeed to believe they had no prior knowledge and absolutely nothing to do with stacking the deck when the time would come for Sam Nujoma to play his April fool's joker.

The final withdrawal of South African troops from the Cuito Cuanavale area, was completed by the 30th August 1988.

The war was all but over.

2

Namibia and the United Nations

World War-1, which began in 1914 and ended in 1918, started with military pomp, the squeaking leather of cavalry saddles, the romantic notion of dying for one's country and the blare of bugles. It ended as the most extravagant bloodbath that the world has ever seen.

In terms of article 119 of the Peace Treaty of Versailles, signed on the 28th June 1919, a defeated Germany ceded all rights and titles to its former colonies, including South West Africa, to the victors.

The Union of South Africa, who had captured the territory from the Germans in 1915, first asked for it to be incorporated in the Union as a fifth province, but this was refused. She was then given a mandate to govern the territory in terms of article 22 of the Covenant of the League of Nations.

South Africa, in effect, was given a guardianship of the territory. Or as was said in treaty language in the mandate:

> To those colonies and territories ... inhabited by peoples not yet able to stand by themselves under the strenuous conditions of the modern world, there should be applied the principle that the well being and development of such people form a sacred trust of civilisation, and that securities for the performance of this trust should be embodied in this Covenant.

High flown language indeed, but it was only words, for times were different then and the atlas was marked in colours depicting European empires, the greatest and the most widespread of which was the red of the British Empire. Few in those days believed or even remotely considered that the patchwork of colonies throughout Africa and Asia would within a few decades become self governing states.

The government of the Union of South Africa, a British Dominion, was undoubtedly of the same mind as the rest when she duly got down to brushing the map of South West Africa red as well.

By 1946 much had changed, there had been another world war and the League of Nations had ceased to exist. Replacing it, in the high hopes that a brave new world and peace had come to stay, the United Nations Organisation had been created.

The government of Prime Minister General Jannie Smuts asked the United Nations for consent to incorporate South West Africa into the Union of South Africa as a fifth province, but this request was once again refused.

Nothing further happened until 1950, after the Nationalist Party had been governing South Africa for two years, when they pronounced that the mandate for South West Africa had ceased to exist with the demise of the League of Nations, so consequently the territory was of no concern to the United Nations.

The UN strongly opposed this move, but because South Africa was in *de facto* control, there was little that could be done about it.

The question was taken to the International Court of Justice, which in 1966 ruled by a majority of one vote that it had no jurisdiction to give a binding and enforceable decision.

In 1969 the General Assembly of the UN voted to revoke South Africa's League of Nations mandate. This was confirmed by the Security Council, which recognised 'the legitimacy of the struggle of the people of Namibia against the illegal presence of South African authorities in the territory.'

Then in 1971, the International Court of Justice ruled that the revocation of the mandate was valid, that South Africa's presence in the territory was illegal and its acts on behalf of or concerning Namibia were illegal.

The South African government rejected the judgement, but this didn't stop it from becoming the legitimate foundation for the past as well as the future actions of the United Nations.

In spite of this rejection South African Premier, John Vorster, commenced negotiations with the Secretary General to try to reach a compromise. In pursuit of a solution the political parties and groupings in South West Africa were independently consulted by South Africa and by the United Nations to seek their views.

The majority of political parties and groupings, with the notable exception of the exclusively white National Party – affiliated to the ruling party of the Republic of South Africa, welcomed a United Nations role in SWA/Namibia.

The negotiations between South Africa and the Secretary General made some progress during 1972 and 1973, but they then broke down, probably because South Africa thought the Secretary General wanted to go too fast, while the Secretary General believed South Africa was dragging its heels.

The United National South West Party, which later became the United Party, and was then the official opposition, had been unsuccessfully campaigning for the independence of SWA/Namibia for a number of years. In 1974 they began to opt for a policy of power sharing as well as the abolition of apartheid in the territory.

The National Party in SWA/Namibia, under the leadership of Mr A du Plessis, rejected this concept out of hand and at that time he undoubtedly had the support of the country's exclusively white electorate.

In early 1974, the General Assembly of the United Nations adopted a resolution, resulting from 'South Africa's continued refusal to withdraw from Namibia and to allow Namibians their right to self determination and independence', recognising SWAPO as the 'sole and authentic representative of the people of Namibia.'

This move, which was a shock one for South Africa, had been easily orchestrated in the General Assembly, where the vast majority of its members, particularly the Afro-Asian and Communist Blocs, were supportive of SWAPO. The recognition was based on the 'reality' that SWAPO had become the most 'effective' Namibian movement and there was the need for a united stand to oppose South Africa.

In the same year 'Namibia' was adopted by the United Nations as the official name for the territory.

In 1975 the South African government responded to pressures, both local and international, by unilaterally establishing the Turnhalle Constitutional Conference, to which they invited the various leaders of ethnic groupings within Namibia. The official white opposition were snubbed.

With the fall of Portuguese colonialism in Africa, international pressure against South Africa, much of it due to the Namibian question, began to build up.

Security Council resolution 385 of 1976 called for the holding of 'free elections' in Namibia under 'United Nations supervision and control.'

South Africa's main allies and trading partners, the United Kingdom, the United States of America and France, who are all permanent members of the Security Council, had long shielded South Africa from attempts within the world body to impose mandatory sanctions against her, by their use of the veto. In the process, though, they had been embarrassed because none wished to appear as supportive of the apartheid system in force within South Africa, as well as in Namibia.

In 1977 in an effort to overcome the impasse, a grouping consisting of the United States of America, Great Britain, France, West Germany and Canada, came together, becoming known as the 'Western Five'.

They launched a joint initiative involving intensive negotiations and discussions with the government of South Africa, the so called Frontline States, SWAPO and political parties within Namibia.

The Western Five's final proposals were finalised the same year, and to everyone's astonishment, considering the situation prevailing at the time, they had been approved by South Africa, the Frontline States, SWAPO and by several of the internal parties.

South Africa also agreed to jettison the blueprint for a go it alone plan for an interim government, which had recently been completed by the Turnhalle Constitutional Conference.

The full proposals of the Western Five can be seen in Appendix 1, but in general terms they allowed for free elections for Namibia as one political entity with the UN playing an appropriate role, for the appointment of a UN Special Representative for Namibia who would work with the South African appointed Administrator General to oversee the process, the repeal of restrictive or discriminatory laws, the release of political prisoners, the return to Namibia of refugees, the cessation of hostilities and a ceasefire, the return to South Africa of all but 1 500 members of the SADF, the demobilisation of citizen, commando and ethnic forces, the return to Namibia of SWAPO personnel and the formation of UNTAG.

Primary responsibility for maintaining law and order in Namibia during the transition period would remain with the police [then the SA Police and not the SWA Police as it is now], who would be limited to the carrying of smallarms only for the purposes of self defence during the normal performance of their duties.

Arising directly from this, Security Council resolution 431 of the 27th July 1978 recorded:

The Security Council,
Recalling its resolution 385/1976 of 30th January 1976,
Taking note of the proposal for a settlement of the Namibian situation contained in document S/12636 of 10th April 1978,
1 Requests the Secretary General to appoint a Special Representative for Namibia in order to ensure the early independence of Namibia through fair elections under the supervision and control of the United Nations;
2 Further requests the Secretary General to submit at the earliest possible date a report containing his recommendations for the implementation of the proposal in accordance with Security Council resolution 385/1976.

3 Urges all concerned to exert their best efforts towards the achievement of independence by Namibia at the earliest possible date.

The resolution was adopted by 13 votes to none, with two abstentions - Czechoslovakia and the USSR.

Mr Martti Ahtisaari of Finland, was subsequently appointed Special Representative by the Secretary General. He immediately undertook a fact finding survey mission to Namibia and submitted a report of his findings to the Secretary General. (For full text of the Secretary General's resulting report in minute I2827, see Appendix 2).

Resulting from this, the Security Council in their resolution 435 of the 29th September 1978 resolved:

The Security Council,

Recalling its resolutions 385/1976 of 30th January 1976 and 431/1978 of 27th July 1978,

Having considered the report submitted by the Secretary General pursuant to para 2 of resolution 431/78 and his explanatory statement made in the Security Council on 29th September 1978,

Taking note of the relevant communications from the Government of South Africa addressed to the Secretary General,

Taking note also of the letter dated 8th September 1978 from the President of the South West Africa People's Organization (SWAPO) addressed to the Secretary General (minute S/12841),

Reaffirming the legal responsibility of the United Nations over Namibia,

1 Approves the report of the Secretary General (minute S12827) for the implementation of the proposal for a settlement of the Namibian situation (minute S12636) and his explanatory statement (minute S12869);

2 Reiterates that its objective is the withdrawal of South Africa's illegal administration of Namibia and the transfer of power to the people of Namibia with the assistance of the United Nations in accordance with resolution 385/1976,

3 Decides to establish under its authority a United Nations Transition Assistance Group – UNTAG, in accordance with the above mentioned report of the Secretary General for a period of up to twelve months in order to assist his Special Representative to carry out the mandate conferred upon him by para 1 of Security Council resolution 431/1978, namely, to ensure the early independence of Namibia through free and fair elections under the supervision and control of the United Nations;

4 Welcomes SWAPO's preparedness to cooperate in the implementation of the Secretary General's report, including its express readiness to sign and observe the ceasefire provisions as manifested in the letter from the President of SWAPO dated 8th September 1978 (minute S12841);

5 Calls on South Africa forthwith to cooperate with the Secretary General in the implementation of this resolution;

6 Declares that all unilateral measures taken by the illegal administration in Namibia in relation to the electoral process, including unilateral registration of voters, or transfer of power, in contravention of Security Council resolutions 385/1976, 431/1978 and this resolution, are null and void;

7 Requests the Secretary General to report to the Security Council no later than 23rd October 1978 on the implementation of this resolution.

The resolution was adopted by twelve votes to none, with two abstentions – Czechoslovakia and the USSR.

At first it appeared the independence process would proceed without a major hitch, but then South Africa and several internal parties found serious objections to the Secretary General's interpretation of the settlement plan, particularly with reference to the provision of SWAPO bases within Namibia – where SWAPO had not 'liberated' ground the size of a matchbox.

This came about because Nujoma fictitiously, while Secretary General Waldheim happily agreed to enhance, the claim that SWAPO already had bases within Namibia. Waldheim was also prepared to support SWAPO's claim for 'additional' bases within Namibia.

To bring this about Waldheim issued a report which provided 'that any SWAPO armed forces in Namibia at the time of the ceasefire would be restricted to base at designated locations inside Namibia to be specified by the Special Representative after necessary consultations. The monitored move of these armed forces to base could not be considered as a tactical move in terms of the ceasefire'.

There were also South African objections to the Secretary General failing or refusing to make provision for the proper monitoring of SWAPO bases within the Frontline States.

The external bases were covered in Waldheim's report by a paragraph which read: 'All SWAPO armed forces in neighbouring countries would, on the commencement of the ceasefire, be restricted to base in these countries'.

There was no mention of them being monitored by UNTAG.

These objections, particularly now one has the benefit of hindsight, were not unreasonable demands by South Africa. SWAPO's main guerrilla bases were within Angola and Zambia and leaving them unmonitored would have enabled them to deal their military cards as they chose.

The April 1989 armed incursion by SWAPO clearly shows this was not a remote possibility either.

When it became clear the Secretary General had no intention of reacting to these objections, the negotiations broke down.

South Africa decided that matters could not remain in abeyance indefinitely and in December 1978 unilaterally went ahead with internal elections in which the internal wing of SWAPO (which has never been a banned organisation in Namibia) and the Namibia National Front refused to participate.

The election was won by the multi racial Democratic Turnhalle Alliance.

The DTA were installed in 1979 as an interim government by South Africa, ignoring objections by the Western Five.

They also ignored Security Council resolution 439/78, the text of which was:

The Security Council,

Recalling its resolutions 385/1976 of 30th January 1976, 431/1978 and 432/1978 of 27th July and 435/1978 of 29th September 1978,

Having considered the report of the Secretary General submitted pursuant to paragraph 7 of resolution 435/1978,

Taking note of the relevant communications addressed to the Secretary General and the President of the Security Council, [text5]Having heard and considered the statement of the President of the United Nations Council for Namibia,

Taking note also of the communication dated 23rd October 1978 from the President of the South West Africa People's Organisation to the Secretary General,

Assuming the legal responsibility of the United Nations over Namibia and its continued commitment to the implementation of resolution 435/1976, in particular the holding of free elections in Namibia under United Nations supervision and control,

Reiterating the view that any unilateral measure taken by the illegal administration in Namibia in relation to the electoral process, including unilateral registration of voters, or transfer of power, in contravention of the above mentioned resolutions and the present resolution, is null and void.

Gravely concerned at the decision of the government of South Africa to proceed with unilateral elections in Namibia in clear contraventions of resolutions 385/1976 and 435/1978,

1 Condemns the decision of the South African government to proceed unilaterally with the holding of elections in the territory from 4th – 8th December 1978 in contravention of Security Council resolutions 385/1976 and 435/1978;

2 Considers that this decision constitutes a clear defiance of the United Nations and, in particular, the authority of the Security Council;

3 Declares those elections and their results null and void and states that no recognition will be accorded either by the United Nations or any member to any representative or organ established by that process;

4 Calls upon South Africa immediately to cancel the elections it has planned in Namibia in December 1978;

5 Demands once again that South Africa cooperate with the Security Council and the Secretary General in the implementation of resolutions 385/1976, 431/1978 and 435/1978;

6 Warns South Africa that its failure to do so would compel the Security Council to meet forthwith to initiate appropriate actions under the Charter of the United Nations, including Chapter V11 thereof, so as to ensure South Africa's compliance with the aforementioned resolutions;

7 Calls upon the Secretary General to report on the progress of the implementation of the present resolution by 25th November 1978.

The resolution was adopted by ten votes to none, with five abstentions – Canada, France, West Germany, United Kingdom, and the United States.

Yet in spite of the lack of agreement, negotiations continued. Many were the all party conferences held, some in New York and some in Geneva, but resolution 435 remained unimplemented.

From time to time representatives of the Western Five paid visits to the African continent, sometimes to consult with South Africa, on occasions to hold discussions with the Frontline States, or to speak to SWAPO or the internal Namibian parties.

Then the interim government, installed by South Africa in early 1979, was summarily dismissed and the territory entered into a period of direct rule by the then Administrator General, Mr van Niekerk.

On the 20th June 1980, Secretary General Kurt Waldheim, resolved South Africa's problem relating to the monitoring of external bases in Angola and Zambia. The demand for SWAPO bases within Namibia was also dropped. The relevant portion of his letter of that date to South Africa's Minister of Foreign Affairs, read as follows:

Your letter also refers to that part of the settlement proposal dealing with the closure of SWAPO bases in Angola and Zambia one week after the certification of the result of the election. The governments of Angola and Zambia have reassured me that no infiltration of armed SWAPO personnel will take place from their territory into Namibia after the ceasefire. By their acceptance of the settlement proposal they had undertaken to ensure that the provisions of the transitional arrangements, and the outcome of the election for a constituent assembly, would be respected. In the interest of establishing a climate of confidence, the Frontline States informed me of a desire for a reciprocal undertaking by the Government of South Africa that it would also accept and abide by the outcome of free and fair elections held under UN supervision and control. As sovereign states they would diligently exercise their responsibilities in compliance with the letter and spirit of the proposal. It follows, therefore, that the closure of the bases and the disposition of the arms and equipment would be the responsibility of the host government. Their final disposition would be undertaken by them in consultation with the government of the independent state of Namibia. The personnel previously resident in such bases would, of course, have the opportunity of peaceful repatriation to Namibia.

As regards the question of SWAPO bases in Namibia, I would recall that, as your government has been informed, the Frontline States and SWAPO decided, in August 1979, that upon South Africa's acceptance of the demilitarised zone, and upon implementation of resolution 435/1978, this question would no longer arise.

On 12th July 1982, the Western Five, on the initiative of the United States, in letter S/15287 to the Secretary General, submitted additional proposals which had been agreed to by all parties to the negotiations, which provided for decisions of the Constituent Assembly to be taken by a two thirds majority and for important constitutional guidelines and principles, including a declaration of fundamental rights and other matters.

Immediately after the acceptance of this agreement by the Security Council, South Africa and the United States acting together, put forward a new precondition before resolution 435 could be implemented. This was that a firm agreement had first to be reached on the withdrawal of Cuban troops from Angola, the so called linkage condition.

It was considered by South Africa, with the firm support of the United States, that allowing the Cubans to remain in Angola, would, in effect, create instability and a danger to peace on the sub continent.

The United States, through Assistant Secretary of State Dr Chester Crocker, gave the assurance that 'South Africa has accepted resolution 435 of 1978 and has made it about as unambiguously clear as it can be made' that provided there is a commitment on the Cuban question, she would go ahead with the implementation of resolution 435.

Dr Crocker continued by saying that the United States were not proposing any alternatives to resolution 435 pointing out '. . . we are the ones who, in a sense, gave birth to this whole plan. We are not suggesting changes in it and it will only be if everybody else in the world were to agree to have consensus for some other approach, that you would see a shift in our position.'

There was widespread disagreement with the linkage principle – in the Security Council, by the Frontline States, by SWAPO, by Angola and by Cuba, so progress on the implementation of resolution 435 once more ground to a halt.

On the 31st May 1983, the Security Council passed resolution 532/1983, in which it called on South Africa to make a firm commitment as to its readiness to comply with resolution 435 and to 'cooperate forthwith and fully with the Secretary General in order to expedite its early implementation.

This was followed by Security Council resolution 539/1983 of the 28th October 1983, which resolved:

The Security Council,
Having considered the report of the Secretary General (S/15943) of 29th August 1983,

Recalling General Assembly resolution 1514 of 14th December 1960 and 2145 of 27th October 1966,

Recalling and reaffirming its resolution 301/1971, 385/1976, 431/1978, 432/1978, 435/1978, 439/1978 and 532/1983,

Gravely concerned at South Africa's continued illegal occupation of Namibia,

Gravely concerned also at the tension and instability prevailing in southern Africa and the mounting threat to the security of the region and its wider implications for international peace and security resulting from continued utilisation of Namibia as a springboard for attacks against and destabilisation of African states in the region,

Reaffirming the legal responsibility of the United Nations over Namibia and the primary responsibility of the Security Council for ensuring the implementation of its resolutions, in particular, resolutions 385/1976 and 435/1978, which call for the holding of free and fair elections in the territory under the supervision and control of the United Nations,

Indignant that South Africa's insistence on an irrelevant and extraneous issue of 'linkage' has obstructed the implementation of Security Council resolution 435/1978,

1 Condemns South Africa for its continued illegal occupation of Namibia in flagrant defiance of resolutions of the General Assembly and decisions of the Security Council of the United Nations,

2 Further condemns South Africa for its obstruction of the implementation of Security Council resolution 435/1978 by insisting on conditions contrary to the provisions of the United Nations' plan for the independence of Namibia;

3 Rejects South Africa's insistence on linking the independence of Namibia to irrelevant and extraneous issues as incompatible with resolution 435/1978, other decisions of the Security Council and the resolutions of the General Assembly on Namibia, including General Assembly resolution 1514 (XV) of 14th December 1960;

4 Declares that the independence of Namibia cannot be held hostage to the resolution of issues that are alien to Security Council resolution 435/1978;

5 Reiterates that Security Council resolution 435/1978, embodying the United Nations plan for the independence of Namibia, is the only basis for a peaceful settlement of the Namibian problem;

6 Takes note that the consultations undertaken by the Secretary General pursuant to paragraph 5 of resolution 532/1983 have confirmed that all the outstanding issues relevant to Security Council resolution 435/1978 have been resolved;

7 Affirms that the electoral system to be used for the elections of the Constituent Assembly should be determined prior to the adoption by the Security Council of the enabling resolution for the implementation of the United Nations' plan;

8 Calls upon South Africa to cooperate with the Secretary General forthwith and to communicate to him its choice of the electoral system in order to facilitate the immediate and unconditional implementation of the United Nations' plan embodied in Security Council resolution 435/1978;

9 Requests the Secretary General to report to the Security Council on the implementation of this resolution as soon as possible and not later than 31st December 1983;

10 Decides to remain in active contact with this matter and to meet as soon as possible following the Secretary General's report for the purpose of reviewing progress in the implementation of resolution 435/1978 and, in the event of continued obstruction by South Africa, to consider the adoption of appropriate measures under the Charter of the United Nations.

The resolution was adopted by fifteen votes to none – the United States of America, clearly because it was as one with South Africa on the question of linkage, abstained.

In 1984 South Africa had secret talks with SWAPO on the Cape Verde Islands, where it was suggested, according to SWAPO sources only, that they should participate in the existing constitutional process then proceeding in Namibia under South African auspices. SWAPO refused, according to them, saying they adhered to resolution 435.

Then, in June 1985, with no agreement with the UN on the withdrawal of Cuban military forces from Angola on the horizon, South Africa went ahead and installed an interim government in Namibia for the second time, because it was felt if progress couldn't be made through the UN, then South Africa had to proceed alone until such time as agreement could be reached. This time representatives were drawn from the ranks of the Multi Party Conference – MPC. All the internal political parties were given the opportunity to participate in this interim measure, but SWAPO, the CDA, the Damara Council, the NCDP and several other parties declined.

Before the interim government was installed, the Secretary General reported to the Security Council in document S/17242 on the 6th June 1985, summarising 'significant new developments' in the Namibian situation, concluding that it was only South Africa's insistence on the Cuban troop withdrawal which was barring the implementation of resolution 435.

The report opposed the South African plan to establish an interim government in Namibia, and urged them to 'reconsider carefully the implications' of the decision to do so.

The South African government ignored this report and went ahead with implementation.

The almost inevitable happened and in Security Council resolution 566 of the 19th June 1985, the Security Council condemned South Africa for its installation of an interim government in Windhoek and declared it to be illegal, null and void.

The Council mandated the Secretary General to resume immediate contact with South Africa, with a view to obtaining its choice of the electoral system to be used for the elections, in terms of resolution 435, and demanded that South Africa cooperate fully with the Security Council and the Secretary General in the implementation of the resolution.

The resolution strongly warned South Africa that failure to do so would compel the Security Council to consider the adoption 'of appropriate measures' under the United Nations Charter, including under Chapter 11V, to ensure South Africa's compliance.

It also urged UN member states that had not done so to consider in the meantime taking appropriate voluntary measures against South Africa, which could include:

(a) The stopping of new investments and the application of disincentives to this end;
(b) The reexamination of maritime and aerial relations with South Africa;
(c) The prohibition of the sale of krugerrands and all other coins minted in South Africa; and
(d) Restrictions in the field of sports and cultural relations.

On the 6th September 1985 the Secretary General in minute S/17442 reported to the Security Council as required in terms of resolution 566 that there had been no progress in the latest discussions concerning the implementation of resolution 435.

Negotiations continued, but little was achieved. In one of his periodical reports to the Security Council, in minute S/18767 of the 31st March 1987, the Secretary General noted that South Africa's Foreign Minister, Mr Pik Botha, had indicated there was no objection by South Africa to a system of proportional representation as a framework for elections leading to the independence of Namibia, providing agreement was reached on how the system would be implemented in practise.

The final obstacle of the Cuban troop withdrawal, the Secretary General reported, still remained.

In October 1987, the Secretary General again reported to the Security Council in minute S/19234 of the 27th October 1987, that attempts to finalise arrangements for UNTAG and the implementation of resolution 435 had once more been blocked by South Africa's demand of the Cuban troop withdrawal as a precondition.

Following this, on the 30th October 1987 in Security Council resolution 601 the Security Council, again ignoring the Cuban linkage issue, affirmed that all outstanding issues relevant to the implementation of resolution 435 had been resolved. It then authorised the Secretary General to proceed to arrange a ceasefire between South Africa and SWAPO in order to undertake the administrative and other practical steps necessary for the emplacement of UNTAG.

In spite of this display of wishful thinking by the Security Council, the Cuban linkage problem had not just gone away, but there were other stirrings behind the scenes which would eventually resolve the impasse. problem had not just gone away, but there were other stirrings behind the scenes which would eventually resolve the impasse.

3

The Winding Road To Peace

To those involved in wars politically, and certainly to the fighting man, they always seem interminable. Perhaps they are more so nowadays because in a historical sense, the old way of settling a conflict – by bringing an opponent to his knees and then occupying his territory – has become almost impossible since the end of World War-2 and the formation of the United Nations, which by its very presence has achieved much more than is generally accepted.

The ancient law of 'by right of conquest' has become abrogated by disuse, for it is no longer acceptable by the people of the world for any nation to conquer and hold a territory alien to them. It is for this reason that the UN forces in Korea, even as early as the fifties, were unable to advance beyond the 38th parallel and occupy North Korea. The man who so nearly did it on his own initiative, US General Douglas McArthur, was sacked by President Truman and saw the end of his truly distinguished military career as a result.

It is for the same reason that US forces in Vietnam made no attempt to end the war there by invading and occupying North Vietnam and why Israel is still facing an almost impossible struggle to retain captured territories, like the west bank of the Jordan River, and why she reluctantly handed back the Sinai to Egypt.

Another pertinent example is the slaughterous war between Iraq and Iran, where at the end of so much blood letting and unspeakable atrocities by both sides, to say nothing of gas attacks, both sides withdrew to their own territories without retaining an inch of ground.

This, too, has a relevance for South Africa where twice in the past two decades there has been enormous public and political pressure brought on by emotion, for the SADF to forge on during major anti SWAPO operations within Angola. The popular idea was that they should capture the country for friendly surrogates, like, as it was in 1975, Holden Roberto's FNLA and Jonas Savimbi's UNITA, and as it was in 1988, Jonas Savimbi's UNITA, by which means the SWAPO/Angolan/Cuban/Soviet threats would have been solved once and for all.

But this is the real world and it would never have worked, because not only would the Soviets and their allies have seen that it didn't, but so would the Western allies and the full weight of the United Nations as well.

There are always fewer people wishing to make peace than there are wishing to make war. Perhaps this is why in the scriptures the 'peacemakers' are blessed.

War in SWA/Namibia certainly seemed a never ending story, with a negotiated peace appearing to be a near impossibility. From South Africa's viewpoint, a straight handover to the Marxist leaning SWAPO, with all its implications for the future of the sub continent – which was clearly what the main body weight of the UN were opting for, whether there were 'free and fair' elections or not – was an unthinkable option.

The Angolans were faced with different difficulties, because even if it hadn't been their original intention, they had become an unhappy part of the East-West conflict. Without the help of the communists, particularly the Cubans, the Marxist MPLA would never have been able to grab control and thwart the democratic process when the Portuguese gave up the struggle and relinquished their African colonial empire in 1974.

This meant they couldn't just stop the war, unless the Cubans and most particularly the Soviets, agreed. The Soviets had been using the Angolan-SWA/Namibian situation as a vehicle from which they eventually hoped to dominate, then finally control, the rich plum of South Africa, with all its wealth of gold and strategic minerals, and its control of the strategic sea route around the Cape of Good Hope.

Of equal importance, though, from the Angolan point of view, was the fact they had willingly suffered, and suffered mightily, for the cause of seeing SWAPO established as the government of Namibia.

For thirteen all but unendurable years their country had been a battlefield, with UNITA fighting for their downfall in a never ending guerrilla war – which without South African support might have petered out long ago, and with South Africa regularly mounting major armed incursions against SWAPO military bases.

To crown the indignity, they had watched impotently while the southern part of their country had been occupied by South African forces, and the infrastructure in the way of towns and villages, bridges and roads, had been devastated.

Having gone through all that, it was not an easy decision to unilaterally abandon their allies.

For these reasons this holding and certainly no win war could easily have dragged on for another decade.

The reason it didn't was because the East-West armed standoff, the cold war took an unexpected turn when Mikhail Gorbachev, a wild card in the pack, took over as leader of the Soviet Union and introduced his new policies of openness and reconstruction.

While suspicion alternated wildly with optimism in the West, the Soviets began making moves indicating their new policy was a genuine one and not just another power play as had so often happened in the past.

While little seemed to be happening in SWA/Namibia, things had definitely started to move in Afghanistan.

Reagan-Gorbachev Summit in Reykjavik

The seeds of peace for south western Africa, however, were not even planted in Africa, but in the unlikely permafrost ground of Reykjavik, the capital city of Iceland, which was selected as a neutral venue for an October 1986 summit meeting between the Soviet leader, Mikhail Gorbachev, and US President, Ronald Reagan.

One item on the agenda, apparently, was the suggestion of a new cooperation to solve regional conflicts. This openly included Afghanistan, but less obviously also included the war in Angola and the vexed question of the implementation of UN resolution 435 in Namibia.

The general conclusion of the press afterwards, was that the summit had not been one of the most successful in history. What, if anything, it had achieved, became obscured by speculation about whether or not Reagan and Gorbachev had hit it off, and whether or not Mrs Gorbachev had put Nancy Reagan's nose out of joint by her fashionable clothes.

Dr Chester Crocker and Mr Anatoly Adamishin Meet

Things, though, had begun to happen behind the scenes. By July 1987 enough progress had been made to bring about a meeting in London between the US Assistant Secretary of State for African Affairs, Dr Chester Crocker, and Soviet Minister Anatoly Adamishin. At this meeting they exchanged mutual assurances.

Both South Africa and Angola were ready for peace negotiations.

After this Dr Chester Crocker had talks in Luanda with the Angolan government, and probably with the Cubans as well. Little if anything appeared to have been achieved, because at a press conference given on his return to Washington, he described his mission as a 'waste of time'.

Reagan-Gorbachev Summit in Washington

December 1987 saw another Reagan-Gorbachev summit, this time in Washington. The Angolan conflict and the implementation of resolution 435 was mentioned briefly, but it didn't feature in the formal statements. In spite of this, Dr Chester Crocker was again in Luanda shortly afterwards. This time it was breakthrough, for he returned with the clear message that the Angolans were ready to talk.

Dr Crocker discussed this with Foreign Minister Pik Botha and other top South African officials at a meeting in Geneva, during February 1988.

Were the South Africans ready to talk as well?

It was a question the South African Cabinet would have to decide.

After protracted discussion at various levels in South Africa, the Cabinet gave the Department of Foreign Affairs the go ahead to join initiatives with Angola and Cuba, in an attempt to find peaceful solutions to the Angolan and the SWA/Namibia problems.

The Director General of Foreign Affairs, Mr Neil van Heerden, and Director, Mr Derek Auret, both urbane diplomats experienced in Namibian negotiations, flew to Washington for discussions with Dr Chester Crocker.

A few days later a letter from Dr Chester Crocker was personally delivered by the US Ambassador, Mr Ed Perkins, to the South African Foreign Affairs Ministry. It proposed 'exploratory' talks in London at which the US would play a 'facilitating' role during direct negotiations between the South Africans and the Angolans and Cubans.

The South Africans agreed and so did the Angolans and Cubans.

The ball game was on.

Just prior to the opening of the London talks, Dr Crocker and Mr Anatoly Adamishin met. Afterwards Dr Crocker told the South African delegation the Soviets would be watching unobtrusively from the wings, assisting where they could.

The two most powerful nations in the world had come to some sort of secret agreement on the future of south western Africa.

When their delegation arrived at Heathrow, the British – who quite understandable frown on the Cuban revolutionaries' easy attitudes towards guns being practised in London – unexpectedly searched their aircraft and grabbed a bonanza of Soviet made Tokarev and Makarov pistols, an assortment of grenades and a goodly supply of ammunition.

'We never asked them, obviously, what their intentions were, but there was a lot of amused speculation,' commented Derek Auret.

One can assume that the British, who were not amused, did.

But whatever happened the Cubans didn't appear with guns slung and grenades clipped to chest webbing when the meetings took place.

The South Africans, used to a sunny clime and more spaciousness in their surroundings, were bemused when they first saw the dismal and small basement conference room at the hotel they were staying in.

There was much speculation as to why such a funny little cramped Victorian premises had been selected. It could have been either because being old it was particularly easy to bug – for the shared benefit of the Americans and Soviets, and undoubtedly for the British as well, or because by snuggling the delegations up together, it helped encourage a social intercourse impossible in larger and more formal surrounds.

While the rain, in good old London fashion, drizzled down outside, sixty negotiators drawn from the two warring sides, edged their ways into chairs wedged against a 'U' shaped conference table. The joint Angolan/Cuban delegation sat along one leg of the 'U', while the South Africans faced them along the other. The Americans sat at the top, in the bride's position as it were.

The South African delegation was led by Foreign Affairs Director General, Neil van Heerden, Chief of the SADF, General Jannie Geldenhuys, and the Director General of the National Intelligence Service, Dr Niel Barnard.

Facing them were Cuban Politburo member for foreign affairs, Jorge Risquet – a respectable former revolutionary, who had gained his credentials by fighting in the Sierra Madres with Fidel Castro in the good old bad old days, the Cuban Chief of Staff, General Ulises Rosales del Toro, the Angolan Foreign Minister, Mr Alfonso van Dunem, the Angolan Minister of Justice, Mr Fernandes van Dunem and the Angolan Chief of Staff, General Antonio dos Santos Franco.

Mr Neil van Heerden, is his opening statement, stressed that in South Africa's view the negotiations should be conducted on the basis that in the end, there should be no losers.

This sensible standpoint became the main foundation stone for eventual success.

Because of the intimate atmosphere of the conference room, the talks sometimes spilled over into informal meetings during coffee breaks, cocktail parties and meals.

The proceeding alternated between spells of friendliness and periods of suspicion, but the atmosphere was often a curtain of unconcealed dislike. Although this was discouraging to the Americans, they stuck gamely to their self appointed task of creating harmony and goodwill.

Each side knew the other had good reasons for wanting to see the war ended, but no one was prepared to admit it.

Both the Cubans and Angolans had accepted that, militarily, after their costly and painful bloodletting during the Lomba River and Cuito Cuanavale battles, any form of victory over the South Africans had become a pipe dream.

The South African military, despite having always won the battles, also knew they couldn't win the war.

There were sound economic reasons for settling, as well.

For Cuba the halcyon days of generous Russian handouts were gone. Without those the country's economy has been left almost entirely dependent on sugar, and this has long been a depressed commodity. For health reasons, primarily, sugar has become almost as unfavoured as nicotine in recent years.

It was the same with Angola, which possessed a ruined economy that had proved itself incapable of raising itself above ground level since independence, because of the ravages of war.

South Africa, too, was economically beleaguered, beset by a plunging rand, raging inflation, international sanctions caused by a repugnance of apartheid, and political discontent. It couldn't afford to continue paying the bills for SWA/Namibia, and for the increasingly costly war in Angola.

The Americans had prepared a detailed paper setting out the Angolan-Cuban position, which they handed to the South Africans before the conference began.

The South Africans prepared detailed answers, which seemed pretty good and sensible at the time, but they lacked tact for they amounted to what was almost a complete out of hand rejection of the opposition's position.

The Angolans and Cubans weren't impressed.

After considerable argument, it was finally agreed that as the South Africans didn't like the Angolan-Cuban proposals, they should lay out their own. This was noted for the agenda for the next meeting. This spelt out the only agreement achieved. That although their differences appeared irreconcilable, they would meet again and attempt to resolve them.

Meeting privately outside of the conference, the South Africans and Angolans had agreed to meet soon somewhere in Africa, to discuss bilateral matters affecting the peace process.

The most important were the future positions of UNITA, SWAPO and the ANC. Another was the rising tide of war in Angola. The Cubans and Angolans were engaged in large scale troop movements south, which the South Africans believed were needling the situation. This, it was apparent, would ultimately result in the cutting of the water flow from the Calueque Dam to draught stricken Owambo. This South Africa couldn't and wouldn't tolerate, which meant a danger was looming of the SADF being forced to make a military response.

Eventually the Angolans came up with Brazzaville, capital of the Congo Republic, as the place for the meeting.

Brazzaville

The Congo Republic, a former French colony, was unfamiliar, even hostile territory, to the South Africans. It had hosted the MPLA during the guerrilla warfare years, when they had fought the Portuguese – then South Africa's allies. It was also away from the normal sphere of South African influence.

The South African's main problem, however, was not the dusting off of old or imagined grudges, but how to get there. There were no air routes leading there from the south. Another complication was that many of the black state inbetween, refused landing and overflying rights to South African aircraft. The only practical way was to go the long way around non stop, avoiding the air space of hostile black countries, but the only available aircraft capable of this, were the passenger Boeings of SAA, but they were considered too expensive.

Eventually business magnate, Dr Anton Rupert, and the Anglo Vaal Corporation, agreed to assist by lending their executive jets, a Falcon 900 and a Hawker-Siddely 125.

The route chosen was west across Namibia and out over the South Atlantic for 120 nautical miles, then north, staying parallel with the west coast of Africa until reaching the latitude of the mouth of the Congo River, then turning east and flying up its course to Brazzaville.

It took two flights to Brazzaville using both aircraft. The first took the advance party of administrative officials, communications staff and security men.

The Minister of Foreign Affairs, Mr Pik Botha, and the Minister of Defence, General Magnus Malan, accompanied the delegation. This pleased the Angolans because no South Africans of ministerial rank had attended the London meeting, which, in diplomatic terms, indicated they looked on it as a low key affair. Both ministers had met the Angolans before, at prior unsuccessful meetings held on the Cape Verde Islands. The South Africans were courteously received by the government of the Congo Republic, who took great pains to make them feel at home.

The meetings, which began on the 13th May, were held in premises within the presidential palace's grounds.

After these meetings, it was announced that 'substantial agreement' had been achieved.

Negotiations Continue

In South Africa work, immediately commenced on an extensive exercise to determine precisely which options were open, what had been agreed to, what hadn't been agreed to and where to go from there.

South African envoys were secretly despatched abroad to many different countries on many occasions, to sort out matters of detail. Mr Derek Auret alone went on 38 missions abroad, while the gruelling negotiations continued at low key.

While all parties at the London talks, including the Cubans, had agreed the next round of talks would take place in an African state, the Cubans suddenly became obdurate. It seems they believed the Brazzaville talks, between the Angolans and the South Africans and to which they were not a party, had been an attempt to squeeze them out of the picture. So, diplomatically, they set out to make the other parties suffer, and suffer they did.

The Cubans rejected venue after venue, until the issue of where the talks should be held, assumed an importance almost as great as the talks themselves. Eventually the Angolans, working behind the scenes, were able to persuade them to accept Cairo – as much an extremity of Africa as the Cape is.

Meanwhile, as had been agreed in London, the South Africans had painstakingly drawn up their own set of proposals, concentrating on the vexed question of linkage – where the South Africans backed by the Americans but violently disagreed to by the Angolans and Cubans, most African states and the United Nations, demanded that the independence of Namibia be linked to the withdrawal of Cuban troops from Angola.

Having listened intently to what their adversaries had to say and having examined the question in detail, the South Africans had accepted that it was unreasonable to expect the Cubans to pull out of Angola in one fell swoop, like the Americans had in Vietnam.

While the Cubans' primary task there was one of military support, they had also became part of the country's fragile infrastructure. They provided medical staff for hospitals and clinics, engineers for road and bridge construction and maintenance, teachers for schools and so on.

The South Africans understood this, because to a lesser but still vital extent, the SADF had been assisting with much the same sort of services in the remote areas of Namibia. They knew, too, that when those services were withdrawn, it would be a hard blow to that Namibia's infrastructure.

Consequently, the South Africans accepted that the Cuban withdrawal should be phased.

Cape to Cairo

For the first time in three decades, a South African aircraft, a SAA Boeing 747, took off from Jan Smuts airport on the 23rd June 1988 and flew by the most direct route north to Cairo, having obtained special clearance to overfly the independent black states on route.

This time the whole party was accommodated in the same aircraft.

Heading the delegation were Ministers Pik Botha and Magnus Malan, while the non ministerial members were led by Mr Neil van Heerden with General Jannie Geldenhuys, Dr Niel Barnard, Mr Derek Auret, Mr Andre Jaquet of the Department of Foreign Affairs, Major General Neels van Tonder of Military Intelligence and Mr Joe Boshoff of the National Intelligence Service.

The South Africans were again treated with the utmost courtesy by the Egyptians. All delegations, with the exception of the Cubans, stayed in the Hyatt el Salaam Hotel.

For the first time there was a Soviet presence in the form of Mr Vladilen Vasev, head of the Directorate for Africa in the Soviet Foreign Ministry.

At the first formal session, the joint Angolan-Cuban delegation delivered a bombshell by rejecting half of South Africa's key proposals.

They then launched into an irrelevant ideological tirade.

This provoked an equally irrelevant response by Foreign Minister Pik Botha, on which Dr Crocker decided it was a time to suggest an adjournment.

Mr Derek Auret said afterwards that he believed 'it was just a case of tit for tat . . . because we had rejected most of their proposals in London they felt they should do the same to ours, which meant that we didn't get anywhere.'

For a time the Americans believed the Angolan-Cuban delegation might stage a walk out and if they didn't, the South Africans might do it instead.

Fortunately, common sense prevailed.

'We [the South Africans] realised,' said Mr Auret later, 'that the technique of putting a substantive proposal on the table and have the other side add or subtract from it, was not going to work. We had not found it acceptable in London and they did not find it acceptable in Cairo.'

That evening the hotel laid on a buffet meal in the gardens. The South Africans hoped this would provide an opportunity to pick up the pieces by resuming informal contacts with the other delegations, but it didn't work, and the Cubans and Angolans kept their distances.

Later both delegations retired to separate quiet corners of the grounds, where huddling around tables, they discussed their strategies for the morrow. The fact the gardens were chosen in preference to hotel rooms, indicates that both sides believed they were being monitored by bugs.

The South Africans made a fresh start by identifying principles likely to be acceptable to both sides, which could become a basis for further discussion. It was no longer possible to even think of forging ahead with discussions – it had become a question now of building an agreement, using one brick at a time.

When talks resumed the next morning, they submitted 18 principles for discussion, discovering shortly afterwards to their surprise, that the Angolans/ Cubans had spent the night carrying out a similar exercise.

It was a pleasant surprise, because they had begun to wonder if, in reality, the Angolans and Cubans weren't stringing them along and didn't want to settle anyway.

Afterwards, a rumour filtered back via the Americans that Mr Vladilen Vasev had reemphasised Moscow's interest in the peace initiatives to the Angolan-Cubans, which had forced a change of heart.

Again, the talks had accomplished little, only two differing sets of proposals, illustrating the yawning differences between the parties.

Dr Chester Crocker suggested both sets of proposals be accepted as working documents, and before the next meeting took place at another venue, lower level officials from both sides should get together and attempt to marry them up.

For the South Africans it had not been all work, and they managed to get in some sightseeing. They visited the Egyptian Museum and saw the fabulously rich exhibits of the Tutunkhamen collection and visited the Great Pyramids. On a more solemn note, Mr Pik Botha approached the Egyptian government and arranged for his delegation to visit the Commonwealth War Cemetery at Heliopolis, where a wreath was laid in memory of South Africans who fell in battle during the 1941–42 North African campaigns.

Havana, Pretoria and Luanda

Low level discussions began immediately afterwards, with envoys constantly on the move between the three capitals.

Finally the next high level meeting was scheduled for New York on the 11th July

New York in July

The venue laid on by the Americans was the US Coast Guard's club on Governor's Island, a five minute ferry trip from the heart of Manhattan.

Neil van Heerden opened the first session.

He was followed by Mr Carlos Aldana of Cuba, another old revolutionary comrade of President Fidel Castro, who was the new leader of the Cuban delegation.

He spoke frankly, astonishing the South Africans, by saying he recognised the 'fact of linkage' between the implementation of resolution 435, and the withdrawal of Cuban forces from Angola.

Until this new departure, the Angolans/Cubans had consistently and heatedly repudiated this contention.

Their new position was that although the question continued to give them 'political problems' in public, they accepted its reality in private.

To get this recorded in the minutes, though, was another story altogether. Using super efficient centralised secretarial services provided by the Americans, both sides got to work drafting and redrafting, discussing and rediscussing, all the while being nudged on by Dr Chester Crocker, until gradually they got down to the meat of what eventually became known as the New York principles.

The language of diplomacy was argued over and reargued over, the whole process coming to a standstill at one time over the implications of using the word 'and'. This occurred because of a phrase put forward by the South Africans, which directly implied linkage by using the words: '[the] implementation of resolution 435 'and' the Cuban troop withdrawal from Angola'.

The Cubans and Angolans believed this would commit them publicly to the linkage principle, which for political reasons they had already made clear they were not yet prepared to do.

Agreement was finally achieved in a draft which declared: 'the parties accept the following principles, each of which is indispensible to a comprehensive agreement.'

When complete, neither side was really satisfied, but at least everyone believed they were getting somewhere.

That they had got so far, was a fruit of the diplomatic genius of Dr Chester Crocker, ripened by the use of his so called 'synthesis papers.'

His technique, which proved remarkably effective, involved bilateral meetings between the negotiating parties, followed by separate ones between each of the negotiating parties and the Americans. From these Dr Crocker's staff would take the elements common to both sides and draw him up a synthesis paper.

'Synthesis' by definition of the Concise Oxford Dictionary is 'Combination, composition, putting together, building up of separate elements especially of conceptions or propositions or facts, into a connected whole . . . '

Another effective technique of Dr Crocker was to draw up a document dealing with a particular area, adopting a negotiating position uncommon to both sides, and which they could attack. This had the effect of gradually edging the parties towards common ground, and eventually to agreement.

'What we had achieved was in danger of being undone by a single bullet, it was that precariously balanced.'

This was the remark of a South African delegate after the conference.

He would soon know how prophetic his words were.

Calueque Water Works

It was more than a single bullet, it was probably the first really successful air attack by the Cubans against the South Africans and was directed against the Calueque water works, just inside Angola.

It coincided with the southwards advance towards the Namibian border by Cuban, Angolan and suspected SWAPO forces.

Twelve SADF soldiers were killed, the eldest was Lieutenant Noah Tucker (23), from Johannesburg and the youngest, Rifleman Stefanus Johannes Els (19), of Bethel.

South Africa was shocked.

'Is it war or peace?' blazed the newspaper headlines.

A snap debate was held in Parliament where the mood of the opposition Conservative Party was hawkish. Had the government benches adopted the same position, as had often happened in the past, the whole process could have been buried overnight.

Urgency of Peace

The mood on the border was like touchpaper, needing only the slightest spark to ignite.

The Cubans and the Angolans were closer to the Namibian border than they had been for years, and their forces were undoubtedly still smarting for revenge, after the drubbings they had been dealt with at the Lomba River and at Cuito Cuanavale.

So far as the SADF were concerned, it goes without saying, that as the undoubted masters of the quick thrust of mobile warfare and aware of the value of a preemptive strike, they must have been ready to lunge northwards at short notice.

If either side had made a wrong move, both armies would probably have been at each other's throats within hours, which would have ended all chances of peace negotiations, for maybe two or three years to come.

Attempts were made to end to hostilities officially, at a secret meeting of military delegations on the Cape Verde Islands during the period 22nd-23rd July.

The South African delegation submitted a detailed plan, involving gun ranges, time lags and response times, by which the warring forces would distance themselves from each other.

Nothing firm was agreed, so the risk of war continued to hang like a dark cloud over the negotiations.

Geneva Protocol

The threat of war stayed bubbling near the surface, until the full negotiating teams met again at Geneva from the 2nd-8th August.

The South Africans started by eddying the water with a surprise rock. Without giving prior notice, they formally proposed that the 1st November become the implementation date of Resolution 435, leading to Namibian independence. In accordance with this, they undertook to withdraw all South African still remaining in Angola by then.

The Cubans and Angolans, caught on the wrong foot, stalled, saying it was more within the realm of authority of the Secretary General of the UN to decide the implementation date, and not for the parties to decide unilaterally.

The South Africans said the negotiations lacked a benchmark. A firm date for the implementation of resolution 435 would provide that. It would be a target at which all parties could aim. A 1st November deadline didn't seem unrealistic to South Africa.

Although probably against their better judgement, the Angolan-Cuban delegation finally agreed to this date.

After this point had been dealt with, the Cubans indicated that they were bound by a treaty of friendship, obligating them to supply troops to Angola.

It was decided the answer was to conclude a bilateral agreement between the two countries, to release Cuba from its obligation.

To the South African's satisfaction, the Cubans said they wanted their troop movements, first a movement northwards and then a phased withdrawal, monitored by the UN Security Council.

The South Africans suggested that in view of their proposal for a 1st November implementation of resolution 435, the timetable for the Cuban troop redeployments and eventual withdrawal, should be agreed to by the 1st September.

The delegations agreed on the need for a trilateral agreement between the parties, covering all the preceding steps.

It was also agreed, after much argument, that the Cubans wouldn't undertake military action south of latitude 15 degrees 30, or east of 17 degrees longitude – which was an imaginary line drawn from Cuamata in the west, to Ngiva in the east. This was conditional on them not being harassed or attacked.

Another point agreed to, was that the Angolans/Cubans would continue to allow activity associated with the provision of water and power for Owamboland from Ruacana and Calueque.

More importantly, providing all South African troops were moved from Angola, the Angolans agreed to 'use their good offices' to pressure SWAPO into moving its bases to the north of the 16th parallel.

In later months, when fingers of suspicion were being pointed, many asked why the Angolans had not phrased their agreement on the question of SWAPO redeployments north of the 16th parallel more definitely. In diplomatic language, though, the statement was apparently satisfactory because it was a positive commitment. In those terms it meant they agreed to it, but reserved their sovereignty on the matter – because it was a sovereign decision.

The South Africans asked for a stronger phrase during the negotiations, but the Angolans baulked, saying it would cause them 'political problems'.

Nevertheless, there can be absolutely no doubt that they formally committed themselves to ensuring SWAPO redeployment north of the 16th parallel.

Security Council minute 20109 of the 10th August 1988 records:

> By this note verbale addressed to the Secretary General, the Permanent Mission of the United States to the United Nations transmitted the text of a joint statement issued on 8th August 1988 at Geneva by the governments of Angola, Cuba, South Africa and the United States. The delegations of Angola, Cuba and South Africa had agreed, inter alia, on a sequence of steps necessary to prepare the way for the independence of Namibia in accordance with Security Council resolution 435, and to achieve peace in south western Africa. They agreed to recommend to the Secretary General the date of 1st November 1988 for the beginning of the implementation of resolution 435.
>
> The parties approved the text of a tripartite agreement between Angola, Cuba and South Africa. On their side, Angola and Cuba reiterated their decision to subscribe to a bilateral accord, including a timetable acceptable to all parties for the staged and total withdrawal of Cuban troops from Angola.

Security Council minute 20129 of the 12th August 1988 records the receipt of a letter from the President of SWAPO, Mr Sam Nujoma, the full text of which reads:

> Against this background of both setbacks and tremendous progress in the heroic struggle, I wish to inform Your Excellency that, SWAPO has by its own sovereign and unilateral decision, as a national liberation movement, in accordance with the spirit of the Geneva agreement reached by the parties participating in the quadripartite talks,

committed itself to take the necessary steps to help make the peace process in the south west African region irreversible and successful.

In this context, SWAPO has agreed to comply with the commencement of the cessation of all hostile acts which started as of 10th August 1988 in Angola. By the same token, SWAPO will be ready to continue to abide by this agreement until the formal ceasefire, under resolution 435, is signed between SWAPO and South Africa, thereby triggering the implementation process.

Once home, the South Africans got down to deciding their next move. Being faced with a self imposed deadline of the 1st November, they needed to start planning the move of the SADF from Angola by the suggested date of the 1st September.

They also had to decide what would be a reasonable and acceptable timetable for a Cuban troop withdrawal.

Brazzaville Again

The delegations met again at Brazzaville in late August. They soon discovered that on the question of Cuban troop withdrawals, yawning differences between their opening positions remained.

The Angolan/Cuban delegation wanted a forty eight month withdrawal period, while the South Africans proposed it should be completed in no more than seven.

Dr Chester Crocker began mediating between the parties, drawing them together in areas of commonalty in his own inimitable way, ensuring direct and sterile confrontations were avoided.

His task was simpler than before, because of a mood of optimism prevailing amongst all parties, who were eager to progress.

When discussion became deadlocked, Dr Crocker arranged for two of each of the most senior Cuban and Angolans delegates, the top four South Africans and four Americans, including Dr Crocker, to meet informally so they speak their minds off the record.

When the conference was adjourned, so the South Africans could return home for the visit of the UN Secretary General, Dr Crocker made a statement phrased 'in a general way' pointing out 'areas of commonalty'. He also pointed out matters needing attention, particularly the timetable for the Cubans withdrawal.

The Secretary General of the United Nations, Dr Perez de Cuellar, visited South Africa over the period 22nd-24th September, when he had discussions with President Mr P W Botha, the Administrator General of Namibia, Mr Louis Pienaar, and with the leaders of various Namibian political parties.

From there he went on to have talks in Luanda with the Angolan President on the general situation in south western Africa and with Sam Nujoma, on the peace plan.

Brazzaville yet again

The talks resumed in Brazzaville on the 26th and lasted until the 28th September. When the time came for Dr Crocker's closing statement, it was generally recognised that agreement was near – a draft of the Brazzaville Protocol had even been drawn – but the vexed question of the Cuban withdrawal still eluded agreement.

Security Council minute 20208 of the 29th September 1988 recorded in a note that the President of the Security Council, acting on behalf of the council, had indicated its members' support for resolute action led by the Secretary General with a view to the implementation of resolution 435, and encouraged him to continue his efforts to that end. It indicated that the Security Council had noted recent developments in efforts by a number of parties to find a peaceful solution to the conflict in south western Africa as had been reflected in the joint statement of 8th August 1988 by the Governments of Angola, Cuba, South Africa and the United States.

Also noted was SWAPO's expressed readiness to sign and observe a ceasefire agreement with South Africa, as stated in the letter of 12th August 1988.

The President also noted that the Security Council had urged the parties to display the necessary political will to translate the commitments they had made into reality so as to bring about a peaceful settlement of the Namibian question and peace and stability in the region.

New York Again

Early in October the talks resumed at the UN Plaza Hotel, New York, where finally, it was agreed in principle it would be impossible for the Cubans to make a total and rapid withdrawal in the short term. There had to be a timetable prepared which would need to be strictly adhered to.

It became clear the 1st November as the implementation date for resolution 435, was premature. A later date had to be set.

Geneva Once More

The talks resumed in Geneva on the 11th November, with agreement tantalisingly near. A protocol might perhaps have been finalised there, except that President Denis Sassou-Nguesso of the Congo Republic, who had hosted the talks on a number of occasions, had especially asked that the formal document be signed in Brazzaville.

Brazzaville Protocol

After more toing and froing than had been expected, the Brazzaville Protocol, the forerunner of the final agreement to be signed at the United Nations in New York, was ready to be signed on the 13th December 1988.

The final agreement would be in three parts – the Brazzaville Protocol, the trilateral agreement between South Africa, Cuba and Angola and the bilateral agreement between Cuba and Angola, releasing Cuba from its treaty of friendship.

The Brazzaville Protocol stipulated the 22nd December 1988 as the deadline by which the Cubans and Angolans must reach agreement with the UN, regarding the mechanisms of monitoring the Cuban redeployment and withdrawal.

The bilateral agreement between Angola and Cuba would also be monitored by the United Nations.

President Sassou-Nguesso turned the signing ceremony into a gala occasion. In true African fashion, the music was supplied by xylophones accompanied by the deep beat of native drums.

The diplomatic corps as well as the entire Congolese cabinet and representatives of the Organisation of African Unity attended.

Speeches were made and South African Foreign Minister, Mr Pik Botha, was given a standing ovation when he stressed that Africa should stand together.

French champagne flowed freely, as did a supply of *witblitz*, thoughtfully provided by Mr Pik Botha.

The guests, including Soviets Mr Anatoly Adamishin and Mr Vladilen Vasev, mixed freely exhibiting great friendliness.

Security Council minute 20325 of the 14th December 1988 recorded:

> In a note verbale addressed to the Secretary General, the Charge d'affaires of the United States transmitted the text of the Protocol of Brazzaville, which was signed by the representatives of the Governments of Angola, Cuba and South Africa on 13th December 1988, with the mediation of the Government of the United States.
>
> The parties agreed to meet in New York on 22nd December 1988 to sign tripartite and bilateral agreements in the context of which they recommended to the Secretary General that 1st April 1989 be established as the date for implementation of Security Council resolution 435. The parties to the tripartite agreement agreed to exchange prisoners of war upon signature of the agreement. The parties also agreed to the establishment of a Joint Commission to facilitate the resolution of any dispute regarding the interpretation or implementation of the tripartite agreement.

Signing at the UN

South African diplomat, Mr Derek Auret, who had been involved in the negotiations since the outset, flew to New York ahead of the main South African delegation, where the signings would take place on the 22nd December. He was working on papers in his hotel room, when the news came that Pan Am flight 103 had crashed at Lockerbie, Scotland, killing all persons aboard and eleven unfortunates on the ground.

It was later learned the disaster had been engineered and caused by the dastardly terrorist actions of the Popular Front for the Liberation of Palestine – PFLP, who had planted a bomb aboard.

He knew the rest of the South African delegation had been due to board a Pan Am flight in London, bound for New York, at about that time.

He was aghast and immediately contacted his US counterparts, telling them he suspected the South African delegation were on the doomed flight.

It took the US Secret Service ten minutes to come back with the reassurance that his colleagues were safe and sound. They had flown out of London an hour before, on Pan Am flight 101.

'It was the longest ten minutes of my life,' Derek Auret recalled later.

Regretably, the UN Commissioner for Namibia, Mr Bernt Carlsson, was less fortunate, for he had been on flight 103 flying to New York for the signing ceremony, and he perished in the crash.

The signing ceremony was held in the Economic and Social Council chamber at UN headquarters at 10:00 on the 22nd December 1988.

The agreement giving independence to Namibia was signed by Foreign Ministers, Mr Pik Botha for South Africa, and Mr Alfonso van Dunem for Angola. Seated between and witnessing the signing were the UN Secretary General, Dr Javier Perez de Cuellar, and US Secretary of State, Mr George Shultz.

Resolution 435 was scheduled for implementation on the 1st April 1989.

After eight months of wearing negotiations, Namibia was finally assured of peace.

At least, that is what everyone thought.

4

The Three Months Before

SWAPO

On Christmas Eve, 24th December 1988, two days after the signing in New York, SWAPO's Chief Representative in Zimbabwe, Mr Kapuka Nauyala, said SWAPO 'was not excited' about the event.

He accused the South Africans of using stop start tactics, saying they had often raised false hopes in the past and had then gone back on them.

Three black Owambo civilians, two men and a woman, had no reason to be excited about SWAPO either, because on the same day close to Oshakati, their private car detonated a SWAPO laid landmine, killing two of them and grievously wounding the poor man who survived.

In spite of this SWAPO's ceasefire applied in the last half of 1988 had been generally effective.

In March 1989 there were only four SWAPO related incidents reported in Namibia. One was classified as a contact, one was a report of intimidation and two involved the laying of landmines on public roads.

The United Nations and UNTAG

According to the *New York Times* on the 3rd January 1989, Brigadier General Pericles Ferreira Gomez of Brazil established his headquarters in Luanda from where his UN verification mission of 90 soldiers and civilians drawn from Argentina, Algeria, Congo, Brazil, Czechoslovakia, India, Jordan, Norway and Spain, would monitor the Cuban withdrawal from Angola.

He said in an interview he wasn't expecting his job to be difficult as the world body would 'simply trust Cuba' to adhere to their agreement to withdraw 50 000 troops from Angola.

The Angolan news agency *Angop* reported General Gomez as saying the appointment of a Brazilian officer to lead the mission 'demonstrated the international prestige of Brazil.' He expressed admiration for the Angolan people and stressed the cultural links between Brazil and Angola.

On the 10th January Foreign Minister Pik Botha reacted to the remarks of UNTAG's General Gomez in Luanda on the 3rd January.

He said the Secretary General's report had been accepted by Security Council resolution 626/1988. The South African government was satisfied with this report and other assurances given over a period of time concerning the withdrawal of

Cuban troops, including the monitoring of their departure by the UN at sea and air ports.

He warned that should any of the parties involved not fulfill their obligations, the whole process laid out by the interlocking agreements would be endangered.

On the 12th January Brigadier General Gomez again spoke in relation to the Cuban withdrawal, saying 'there will be no difficulties in carrying out this assignment.' He stressed that his twenty seven month mission depended on the 'goodwill of the Angolan and Cuban governments'.

On the 24th February it was revealed the Americans were also unhappy with General Gomez saying he would 'trust' the Cubans so far as their withdrawal from Angola was concerned, and as a consequence would be stationing their own observers in Luanda to monitor the monitors.

An example of UN assistance extended to SWAPO was a talk program on a 'Seminar for SWAPO foreign service personnel' produced by United Nations Radio for Radio Maputo, Mozambique.

In this program Ms Lucia Hamuteyna of the Office of the United Nations Commissioner for Namibia, spoke to Comrade Helmut Angula, SWAPO's permanent observer to the United Nations.

During discussions Helmut Angula mentioned that SWAPO maintains 22 missions abroad, saying: 'Some of them are fully diplomatic. For example in India we have a fully fledged embassy – in Iran it is the same – in the Soviet Union almost the same. We have the same status in the GDR and almost the same in the Republic of Cuba.

'In many other instances, like in the Western world, we have kind of representation – like information bureaus, but again they differ from country to country.

'For example that one we have in Sweden is quite very large. In London it is quite a large mission. This is not supposed to be information, but in actual fact it acts in its way like a diplomatic mission, although with no political or diplomatic mission, although with no political or diplomatic recognition at all.

'And then, of course, you come to the African countries where we have large representation in west Africa and east central Africa whereby actual political relations with those countries are very strong . . .'

According to a report in *Business Day* of the 6th February, the Frontline States had pressed various conditions on SWAPO to ensure the question of UN impartiality, when the UN plan went into effect on the 1st April.

The discussions and agreements relating to this had apparently taken place in 1982, when they had been presented to Secretary General Dr Perez de Cuellar by the Frontline States. He had, however, kept this secret since then for reasons best known to himself and the other parties involved.

The document comprised seventy agreements on various matters. Six prohibited a special relationships between SWAPO and the UN saying:

1 The UN will not provide funds for SWAPO, nor any other party during the transition period;
2 The UN Council for Namibia should refrain from engaging in all public activities, once the Security Council authorized the implementation of the plan;
3 The Commissioner for Namibia should suspend all political activities during the transition period;

4 SWAPO will voluntarily forego all special privileges granted by the General Assembly of the United Nations;

5 Consideration of questions relating to Namibia should be suspended during the transition period; and

6 At the Security Council meeting to authorise the implementation of resolution 435, all speeches should be kept to a minimum. None of the parties to the forthcoming elections or to the ceasefire should speak.

According to the agreement, all provisions were to be covered by, even if not specifically enumerated, in the final Security Council enabling resolution.

Dr Perez de Cuellar was, according to *Business Day*, intending to cover all these points in his report to the Security Council of the 23rd January 1989, dealing with the proposed budget cuts for UNTAG, for his reports are normally adopted as Security Council resolutions.

With the passage of time since 1982, though, it seems the Frontline States had become embarrassed by the number of concessions they had screwed SWAPO into accepting.

Consequently, they persuaded De Cuellar to omit the details from his report.

On the 26th February the *Observer*, London, dealt with the question of SWAPO losing its long standing position of privilege at the United Nations with effect from the 1st April, as the 'sole and authentic representative of the Namibian people'.

UN funding of SWAPO would also cease. The existing funding was US$450 000 to pay for its New York office, and US$150 000 for travelling expenses.

The government of Finland announced it had cut off a grant of 400 000 marks to SWAPO so as to secure a place for Finnish troops in UNTAG. This was to comply with South Africa's demand that countries participating had to display neutrality.

On the 15th March, Soviet officials at a London press conference, said Moscow wouldn't provide funding for SWAPO during the election run up.

On the 17th March it was reported that Secretary General Dr Perez de Cuellar, had personally sent out invitations to UN member states, asking them to donate monies for the UN Fund For Namibia, the UN Trust Fund for the Nationhood Program of Namibia and the Trust Fund for the UN Institute for Namibia.

In the many years since the funds came into existence, all monies donated to them had been spent solely on the advice of SWAPO, and used only for that organisation's benefit. This was common knowledge in UN circles and would have been well known to the Secretary General.

Dr Perez de Cuellar had planned a conference for the 22nd March, the UN's International Day for Elimination of Racial Discrimination, only nine days before the implementation of resolution 435, when it was expected that many millions of dollars would be collected for SWAPO's benefit.

Dr de Cuellar even sent an invitation to Mr Jeremy Shearer, South Africa's permanent representative at the UN, inviting them to contribute to the SWAPO front funds.

53

South Africa's Director General of Foreign Affairs, Mr Neil van Heerden, said it was 'a most serious complication . . . the Secretary General is sponsoring a fund which seriously compromises his impartiality.'

When questioned further he said: 'I nearly had a heart attack. If the parties inside Namibia here about this, there's going to be hell to play'.

Understandably, on the same day, South Africa accused the Secretary General of favouring SWAPO in the UN supervision of Namibia's transition to independence.

On the 23rd March, the OAU Assistant Secretary General, Mr Yilma Tedesse, told a meeting that the organisation would provide SWAPO with R4 8 million to assist them in their election campaign.

This was in addition to R12 million already approved by the OAU's Council ministers in February.

He also announced that another R2 4 million had been set aside, to allow the organisation to participate fully in the implementation of resolution 435.

On the 17th February, only a day after the UN budget for UNTAG had been authorised by the Security Council, after the exercise of stalling tactics and much wrangling by the non aligned members, Major General Stephen Fanning, the UNTAG Police Commissioner, arrived in Windhoek by a scheduled SAA flight on a preliminary fact finding visit.

During his visit he had talks with the Commissioner of SWA Police, Lieutenant General Dolf Gouws.

Commissioner Fanning served as a police officer for forty years, retiring in 1987 as Ireland's most senior police officer. He was the head of National Security in Ireland, and reponsible for the security of the President, the Prime Minister and other government ministers, foreign embassies, national airports, government buildings and VIP visitors.

He first visited Namibia in 1978 and again during 1979, which was in the hot and heady early days of resolution 435, as a UN adviser on police matters.

Although primary responsibility for the maintenance of law and order in Namibia during the transitional period would rest with the SWA Police, Commissioner Fanning, through the authority of Special Representative, Mr Martti Ahtisaari, would be responsible for 'the good conduct of the police force and shall take the necessary action to ensure their suitability for continued employment.' And, where appropriate, 'he shall make arrangements' for his men 'to accompany the police forces in the discharge of their duties.'

The most important of his responsibilities would be 'to take steps to guarantee against the possibility of intimidation or interference with the electoral process from whatever quarter.'

To assist him in carrying out his responsibilities, Commissioner Fanning would command a force of some 500 UN police monitors drawn from fifteen contributing countries, namely Austria, Bangladesh, Barbados, Egypt, Fiji, Ghana, Hungary, Ireland, Jamaica, Netherlands, New Zealand, Nigeria, Philippines, Sweden and Tunisia.

While the experience and integrity of the men of the UN police team, from the Commissioner down, can be undoubted, few of the countries from which police officers were drawn had experienced recent insurgencies of major note, and none which approached the scale of the Namibian insurgency, which had persisted for the best part of three decades.

It would become an important question of attitude.

In Europe if a PLO or IRA terrorist is on the loose with an RPG-7 rocket launcher, and even more so if he has a SAM-7 ground to air missile, it is enough to get every police force in the region, plus Interpol, running in the proverbial small circles.

In Namibia such weapons in the possession of insurgents had become common-place, but this didn't mean their possession by insurgents shouldn't be judged, both police and politicallywise, by the same stern and condemnatory standards as in Europe.

But, of course, they won't be.

On the 24th March Commissioner Fanning arrived in Windhoek to take up his duties, bringing with him nine senior police officers, which constituted the police advance party. Two came from Austria, one from Fiji, one from Ghana, one from Ireland, two from Holland and one from Sweden.

It was announced the remainder were expected to arrive in phases during April.

Nine policemen plus the UNTAG Commissioner would not be many to have around by the 1st April.

General Prem Chand, the commander of the military component of UNTAG, together with about twenty other senior military officers and officials, flew into Windhoek by SAA flight on the 27th February. They were there to finalise preliminary arrangements and be briefed by senior military and police officers on the security situation in Namibia.

He would also meet the Administrator General, Advocate Louis Pienaar.

Huge crowds of SWAPO supporters, there to greet him, thronged the arrivals area at Windhoek Airport. Many wore SWAPO t-shirts or were dressed in the organisation's colours of blue, red and green.

Placards displayed slogans like: 'Namibia will be free', 'Welcome to colonised Namibia, Gen Prem Chand', 'Reduction of UNTAG is UN's partiality towards South Africa', and so on.

There were few police on hand to deal with the demonstration, but the crowd was described in one press report as 'generally well disciplined'.

A German tour group leaving for home, however, were harassed by a barrage of political slogans, banner waving and 'freedom' songs sung right in their faces.

General Prem Chand made a short and noncommittal statement at the airport saying he was looking forward to the cooperation of all parties involved in the peace process.

General Prem Chand (73), an Indian Army general officer, was commissioned in 1937, after which he saw service in the North West Frontier Province and in Malaya during the closing stages of World War-2.

Thereafter he held various appointments, becoming a major general in 1961.

After that he was seconded to the UN for peacekeeping operations. He was involved in the Congo as Commander UN Forces in Katanga (1962–63), in Cyprus (1969–70) and in Rhodesia (now Zimbabwe) as a representative of the Secretary General (1977–78).

By the middle of March General Prem Chand and his senior staff were back in Windhoek and had commenced work.

One of the first tasks undertaken by the General and his military staff, complete except for his Kenyan deputy, Brigadier Daniel Opande, was a comprehensive familiarisation and orientation tour of the northern border area.

They were first given an extensive briefing by senior officers of the SWA Territory Force and then conducted around, going wherever they chose, and seeing whomsoever they liked.

They travelled extensively around Kaokoland, Bushmanland, Owamboland, Kavango and Caprivi.

They visited military bases and spoke to soldiers, both officers and men, and to civilians, from senior headmen to the ordinary men in the street, as well as to primitive tribesmen in the remote bush, who didn't know streets existed.

In Kaokoland, as became usual in the course of their travels, they met a gathering of tribal headmen.

These headmen were particularly anxious to speak to General Prem Chand, wanting his confirmation that UNTAG would protect his people from SWAPO, once the SADF left. They didn't expect SWAPO to honour their word and abide by the restrictions imposed on them.

They believed a real danger to their lives and freedom at the hands of SWAPO would develop, and that they asked for UNTAG protection.

Nowhere during this comprehensive tour did either General Prem Chand or his officers find a scrap of evidence, or even a hint, to suggest that SWAPO had military bases within Namibia.

General Prem Chand confirmed this to many people of prominence, after SWAPO mounted their 1st April border adventure.

Friday the 10th March 1989, perhaps more than the date way back in 1978 when resolution 435 was first adopted by the Security Council, really signified to Windhoekers, the capital of the last remaining colonial territory in Africa, that the winds of change had finally started to blow down Kaiser Street.

For this was the day of the blue berets – the blue berets of the United Nations' troops. Until then there had been newspaper, radio and television reports that South West was soon finally and irrevocably to be Namibia, but this was something which seemed remote, something they had all heard about before, but never expected to see in reality. Sure there had been news stories of the odd UN official arriving before, but they had been virtually unnoticeable.

But now it was different, it had to be different, because seeing a huge three hundred ton Galaxy transport painted in the drab greens and browns of the Military Airlift Command of the US Air Force, landing at Windhoek airport was decidedly different.

The Galaxy had flown from its home base at Travis, california, via Australia where it had picked up thirty six Australian sappers and seventy tons of equipment. While on route to Namibia it had been delayed at Nairobi with technical problems.

The scores of spectators who had braved the tedious journey from town to the Windhoek Airport, had a grandstand view when the huge aircraft made two cumbersomely grand circuits of the airfield before making its landing approach. The pilot explained later that this was standard procedure when landing at a strange airport, because of the size of the aircraft. This certainly seemed wise, particularly when it was pointed out that the Windhoek runway only allowed a margin of a meter on either side of the giant's wheel base.

The Ausies gave the spectators an unexpected treat and the journalists an unexpected tongue in the cheek story, for instead of merely filing off the aircraft with kitbags on shoulders and slouch hats on heads as everyone had expected, they deplaned in full kit at a rush the moment the aircraft landed, M16 rifles at the tactical ready, and doubled to take up defensive positions around the aircraft.

This was a sufficiently unusual sight to cause glasses of Windhoek lager moving in regular arcs from counter to mouths in the airport bar to hesitate momentarily, for this was nothing like the easy going Crocodile Dundees, everyone had been expecting.

Eventually, though, when the officer in command realised that his first day in Windhoek was not going to be at all like the last day in Saigon, but more like a dry and dusty Friday afternoon in Alice Springs, they relaxed, abashed and a trifle sheepish.

The US Air Force crew of the Galaxy had a far greater sense of the historic moment, and produced with considerable aplomb, in an inimitable American way, their own press and public relations unit.

As the days passed advance parties of the Finnish and Danish contingents arrived, then a group of Malaysian admin staff, a few Jugoslavs, some Canadians, Spaniards and a few Italians, some on SAA's scheduled flight from Frankfurt. The British component of seventy signallers and their equipment arrived on the 13th.

There was a sudden acute shortage of both office and living accommodation in Windhoek, a small town by any standards. Since resolution 435 had been put back on the rails, property had begun changing hands at greatly enhanced prices, as countries began buying for future diplomatic and consulate purposes, and international businesses made accommodation provisions for future opportunities.

Overnight the situation worsened when UNTAG took up anything and everything anywhere that was vacant for rent.

Hotel accommodation became impossible and everything available was grabbed by the UN. The Kalahari Sands Hotel, Windhoek's premier hotel, became an almost completely UNTAG hostelry overnight.

On the 25th March, during a rugby match at the country town of Tsumeb, relations between UNTAG and local civilians became somewhat strained when a fight broke out between four Australian and four British soldiers on the one side and white civilians on the other.

One British soldier suffered a broken jaw, while five civilians were detained on assault charges. No charges were laid against the UN troops.

After that, on orders from the Australian Defence Department in Canberra, the Australian troops, who were based at Grootfontein, were confined to barracks during their off duty hours, 'for their own safety.'

According to news reports on the 29th March, UNTAG had advertised widely in South Africa for the supply of various requirements, but they were shipping motor vehicles and four wheeled drive truck direct from Japan, because Japanese prices were more competitive than South African ones.

The West German government had donated a large number of vehicles, but until they and the Japanese ones arrived, UNTAG had hired some 200 locally.

In addition the UNTAG authorities were seeking suppliers of foodstuffs, prefabricated housing units, office chairs, desks, caravans, tents and so on.

Rifleman Johan Papenfus

With the tripartite agreement between Angola, Cuba and South Africa on track and scheduled for signature in New York on the 22nd December 1988, there seemed to be no reason why the release of South African POW, Rifleman Johan Papenfus, should not be imminent, because the agreement made provision for prisoner exchanges to take place immediately afterwards.

Foreign Minister Pik Botha, obviously taking this into consideration, proposed on the 15th December that South Africa should fly Domingo Vinez, the Cuban pilot of the MIG-21 who had recently crash landed near Otjiwarongo, Namibia, to New York for the signing of the agreements and that Cuba should do the same with Rifleman Papenfus.

A formal exchange could take place immediately afterwards.

It seems the Foreign Minister's suggestion was premature, because there was no response from Cuba and Angola, not a public one anyway, and the day of the signing came and went, with Papenfus still a prisoner.

Hopes were raised on the 27th December when a SADF spokesman said in an official statement, that the exchange of South Africa, Cuban and Angolan prisoners of war was 'already underway.'

When nothing seemed to happen, there was speculation in the South African press that Papenfus might become part of a broader prisoner swop involving Heleen Passtoors, the Dutch born white ANC saboteur then undergoing a prison sentence in South Africa and Odile Harrington, the white South African who had been convicted of spying on the ANC and sentenced to a long prison term in Zimbabwe.

On the 7th January 1989, Cuba's Ambassador to Zimbabwe, Mr Alfonso Farga, said at a press conference to mark the 30th anniversary of the Cuban Revolution, that before any repatriation 'we would ask Papenfus if he is in agreement with apartheid, and if he wants to go back to South Africa.'

When asked about the use of chemical weapons against UNITA, for which overwhelming evidence existed, he lost his smugness and ranted away, saying the suggestion was absurd, describing it as typical CIA propaganda.

Intense negotiations were proceeding behind the scenes, but it was only on the 28th February that the media began getting close to what was really happening.

Before releasing Papenfus, the Cubans and Angolans wanted to know how many of their men were held as prisoners of war by UNITA.

This created a problem, for UNITA was not a party to any of the agreements signed between Cuba/Angola and South Africa. Neither were there understandings in the agreements that South Africa would pressure UNITA for any purpose, unlike the situation pertaining between Angola and SWAPO.

Neither Cuba nor Angola could or would negotiate directly with UNITA, because they didn't recognise the organisation, so holding back on Papenfus' release, was their way of pressurising the South Africans to use their 'good offices' to get POWs in UNITA's hands released.

Fair enough, one might say, that Cuba and Angola should wish to look after their POWs in UNITA's hands, but nevertheless by failing to immediately release Rifleman Papenfus, they were clearly in breach of a solemn agreement signed at the United Nations headquarters in New York, but no one outside of South Africa had a word to say in condemnation.

According to media reports there were other complications, some of which were caused by the belief of the Cubans and Angolans that certain of their men were POWs, while the South Africans either knew nothing about them or had good reason to believe they had been killed in action. Those in question were, in the main, soldiers missing during the Cuban-Angolan rout at the Lomba River, and afterwards at the siege of Cuito Cuanavale.

Most such queries were difficult to resolve, particularly as the SADF had withdrawn from the battle areas many months before.

The negotiations were ongoing and protracted and seemed a long way from finalization.

At the JMMC meeting on the 21st March at Havana, Cuba, members of the South African delegation, including the Chief of the SADF, General Jannie Geldenhuys, were allowed to speak to Rifleman Papenfus.

Reports filtering out described him as 'morose and lonely' and that he believed, with some justification, he was being used as a political pawn.

He was also presented to reporters at the Military Police camp where he had been kept in detention for the previous eight months.

Understandably he appeared nervous, probably because he was worried he might say something wrong which could prejudice his release, so perhaps wisely, he rarely extended his replies to questions beyond a simple yes or no.

There was no doubt where his heart lay, though, for when asked what he missed most, he unhesitatingly replied : 'My Fatherland, South Africa.'

This if he heard about it, which is somehow doubtful, would have proved a disappointing answer to Mr Alfonso Farga, Cuban Ambassador to Zimbabwe.

Press reports of the 21st March said negotiations for Papenfus' release 'were ongoing'.

On the 22nd March both South African and Cuban sources said that Papenfus would 'almost certainly' be released soon.

On the 23rd March, after the final session of the JMMC, Foreign Minister Pik Botha made a brief statement saying that South Africa, Cuba, and Angola had agreed to 'exchange a prisoner' on the 1st April.

Although unsaid, it was generally assumed that 'a prisoner' referred to Rifleman Papenfus.

This agreement was seen as a major breakthrough by the JMMC.

On the 25th March media reports suggested the price for Papenfus' exchange had been set at three Cubans and twenty Angolans.

On the 28th March the Cuban Prensa Latina New Agency reported that Papenfus would be released later that day, but this was immediately refuted by South African diplomatic sources.

Finally, on the 29th March, an announcement was made that the prisoner exchange would go ahead at Ruacana on Friday the 31st March.

SWAPO's Deployments in Angola

On the 24th January it was announced in New York that agreement had been reached on the establishment of a Joint Military Monitoring Commission – JMMC, comprising of South African, Angolan and Cuban delegates, with observers supplied by the United States and the Soviet Union.

Its purpose was to provide a forum where any problems relating to the agreements that might arise from time to time could be dealt with. It would automatically fall away when UNTAG assumed its responsibilities on the 1st April.

On the 25th January at a Cape Town press briefing, Foreign Minister Pik Botha expressed concern regarding 'ongoing SWAPO military activity south of the 16th parallel'.

He said he had instructed the South African delegation, still in New York discussing the formation of the joint monitoring commission, to convey his concern to representatives of the US, Soviet, Cuban and Angolan governments.

Although it is doubtful that anyone would suggest otherwise, the fact that discussions between the upper levsl of SWAPO and the Angolan government were ongoing can be seen from a talk program on 'A seminar for SWAPO foreign service personnel' produced by United Nations Radio for Radio Maputo, Mozambique when it was said by Helmut Angula, SWAPO's permanent observer to the UN, that during the plenary session of the seminar a delegation from the Angolan Foreign Affairs Ministry 'cleared up hitherto unclear matters – the position of Angola vis-a-vis the quadripartite talks ... the talks involving Angola, Cuba on the one hand and South Africa and the United States on the other ...' He then continued by saying how they had benefitted from an address by the Ambassador of Brazil to Angola.

On the 20th February SWA Territory Force Headquarters, Windhoek, released a statement saying that Simon Shilongo (22), a SWAPO section leader of the Red Square battalion, had deserted in early February from his unit's base at Peu-Peu, which is about ninety kilometers north of the Namibian border and sixty kilometres south of the 16th parallel, and had escaped to Namibia where he gave himself up.

His reasons for deserting were 'bad conditions in SWAPO camps, a lack of food and clothing and bad treatment from both SWAPO and the Cubans'.

He said he left Namibia to join SWAPO in Angola during 1980 to take up a promise of schooling, but instead they used him as a labourer, gave him infantry training and sent him into action against UNITA.

Shilongo confirmed that SWAPO remains deployed south of the 16th parallel, in direct contravention of the Geneva Protocol.

The SWAPO Operational Commanding HQ – OCHQ and the HQ Central Area were still based at Peu-Peu, as was the Red Square battalion, deployed there on protective duties. To his personal knowledge SWAPO's Ongehete military clinic to the west of Xangongo was still in operation, as was the Katanga logistics unit to the northwest of the same town.

The SWA Territory Force announcement said this information had been discussed on 19th February at an emergency meeting of the JMMC.

'The Angolan/Cuban delegation, however, stated that there was nothing they could do about the matter because, according to them, the jurisdiction of the JMMC stretches only one kilometre on either side of the border of the two countries'.

On the 23rd February it was announced that the JMMC would meet in Luanda later in the week to discuss the implementation of the peace plan. No agenda details were released, but it was expected Angola and Cuba would raise claims that South Africa had been sending troops to help UNITA and South Africa would bring up the thorny question of SWAPO operations south of the 16th parallel.

On the 27th February, Foreign Minister Pik Botha said he would be raising the issue of SWAPO activity south of the 16th parallel directly with the Secretary General of the Security Council.

On the same day at the first substantial session of the five nation Joint Military Monitoring Commission – JMMC, in Luanda, Angola, attended by South Africa, Angola and Cuba, with the United States and Soviet Russia having observer status, South Africa's Director General Foreign Affairs, Neil van Heerden, rejected allegations by Angola that South Africa had breached the peace agreements by sending troops into southern Angola to assist UNITA in their current offensive against the MPLA.

The Angolans said they had confronted the South Africans with proof, but they had rejected it. The Angolans refused to make the evidence public.

There was speculation that the Angolan's allegation arose from the possibility of UNITA having long range G-5 or G-6 artillery pieces, left behind by the South Africans when they withdrew from Angola in 1988.

Dr Chester Crocker, who led the US observers at the talks, told reporters that he believed UNITA did possess long range artillery, but he didn't know if they had G-5s or G-6s. He made the point, though, that the Americans had no 'influence' by which they could substantiate the claim or not.

When discussing a communique issue on completion of the talks, the Russians suggested the phrase,'alleged' South African assistance to UNITA, was too strong a one to use. They preferred the words 'claim' or 'assertion'. This, by all accounts, was not well received by the Angolan/Cuban delegations.

Although the Angolans had agreed in the tripartite agreement to use their 'good offices' to get SWAPO to move north behind the 16th parallel, by the end of the talks the issue remained unresolved.

A SWAPO observer was present at the talks, so that organisation was aware of everything that went on, but they didn't take part in any of the discussions, because there was no provision for it.

General Jannie Geldenhuys, Chief of the SADF, when briefing South African military correspondents in February, pointed out that SWAPO had failed to move their personnel north of the 16th parallel.

He explained that while it was true SWAPO was not a signatary to any of the agreements which had led to the pending implementation of resolution 435, Angola as SWAPO's host country was.

Everything proviso in every agreement was interlocking and a quid pro quo forsomething else, and the movement of SWAPO north of the 16th parallel was one of those provisions.

Angola as a party to the agreements had committed themselves to using their 'good offices' to persuade SWAPO to move north of the 16th parallel.

This had not happened, General Geldenhuys said, which meant the Angolan government should now admit either they 'haven't the political will to get SWAPO north of the 16th parallel, or they haven't got the ability to do so.

He also said there appeared to be an 'apparent unwillingness' on the part of the Angolans and Cubans to investigate the complaint.

The Citizen on the 28th February said that South Africa can soon be expected to take a tough line. According to one source, while no deadlines had been set, 'there could be a lot more jumping up and down in Havana [when the JMMC was scheduled to meet there in March] if SWAPO hasn't complied with the terms of the agreement to which they made themselves a party'.

South African intelligence sources began reporting that SWAPO forces in Angola were being issued with completely new kit issues, starting from their boots and working upwards to their military caps.

Information came in from the local Owambo population, but unfortunately only after the 1st April, that on the 27th March when SWAPO commenced their build up of guerrillas, ready for their border crossing into Namibia, the 'authorities', it is unknown if this referred to the Angolans, Cubans or SWAPO, or all three in combination – but it happened on Angolan national territory , restricted the movement of visitors into the Namacunde area and temporarily prohibited the normal cross-border movement of locals into Namibia.

Civilian aircraft were also prohibited from overflying the border area.

According to South African Intelligence sources, gleaned only after the 1st April, Sam Nujoma paid a personal visit to the Peu-Peu area on the 30th March and addressed SWAPO guerrillas preparing to infiltrate Namibia during the night of the 31st March.

Peu-Peu is south of the 16th parallel.

A significant report would appear in the SWAPO sympathising, *The Namibian,* on Monday 3rd April: 'Addressing a general military ceasefire parade at Okatale near the Namibian-Angolan border attended by more than 9 000 combatants of the People's Liberation Army of Namibia (PLAN), Mr Sam Nujoma, SWAPO President . . .'

A 'ceasefire parade' indicates he had already signed the ceasefire agreement, which shows it was current.

The burning question is, what were 9 000 PLAN guerrillas doing at Okatale near the Namibian-Angolan border, when they were supposed to have moved north of the 16th parallel?

He told his audience that from 1st April some would be ordered to change from uniform into civilian clothes and go to Namibia to carry out 'the political mobilisation of the masses to vote for SWAPO, and thereby consolidate the revolutionary gains which SWAPO had made . . .'

Other SWAPO activities during March were the movement of their 2nd Mechanised Brigade from Lubango to the Xangongo/Techipa area, the concentration of approximately 500 guerrillas in the Chitado area and a substantial but unknown number of conventional/guerrilla forces in the vicinity of Ongiva, and the stockpiling of military equipment, weapons, ammunition and supplies in scattered dumps along the Angolan border with Namibia.

There were also a number of secret infiltrations into Namibia by guerrillas, bringing in ammunition and supplies which they cached in secret dumps in Owamboland.

At the meeting of the JMMC commencing on the 21st March in Havana, Cuba, the question of SWAPO elements being south of the 16th parallel was once again raised by the Director General of Foreign Affairs, Mr Neil van Heerden.

The Angolan delegation apparently gave categorical assurances that SWAPO would be moved north of the 16th parallel before the 1st April commencement of the peace agreement.

5

Friday 31st March 1989

The Regional Commissioner of Police for the northern border area, Major General Hans Dreyer, held little enthusiasm for the morrow, in spite of most people in authority still regarding a SWAPO disruption of the peace process as a remote possibility.

Knowing SWAPO and the way that Sam Nujoma operated from many long years of experience of bitter terrorist warfare, he remained convinced that Nujoma would make a major incursion into Namibia.

He believed it would be a naked grab for power, at the time most favourable to him, without any regard to the peace treaty. This would be when Namibia had been reduced to defenceless and rendered incapable of repulsing a SWAPO attack.

The most propitious time was obvious. This would be once the demobilisation of the SWA Territory Force was complete, after the fangs of the SADF had been drawn by drastically reducing its numbers and confining the remainder to their camps under UNTAG supervision and finally as soon as the SWA Police had been disarmed of their heavy weapons and reduced to carrying sidearms only.

That would be on Saturday the 1st April, the day the peace agreement took effect.

Yet it still sounded a preposterous idea to most, for what would SWAPO gain by breaking the peace?

But in addition to General Dreyer's personal hunch , which fortunately for the peace process ensured the police would be prepared anyway, there was also clear evidence to suggest the straws of war were being gusted about in the wind.

The most important of which was that SWAPO units were still deployed close to the border, having made no effort to withdraw north of the 16th parallel to comply with the peace agreement. And fresh information had been received, indicating that a unit of 150 SWAPO fighters had moved south to a point ten kilometres north of Beacon 4, apparently ready to mount an armed incursion into Owambo.

Making war while acquiescing to peace is not unusual in the history of mankind. The Japanese were talking peace to the Americans in December 1941, when they sent their carrier borne aircraft to smash the US fleet in Pearl Harbour.

So convinced was General Dreyer that SWAPO were coming over on the 1st April, that after discussions with the Commissioner of Police, Lieutenant General Dolf Gouws, himself a redoubtable guerrilla fighter in his earlier days, it was agreed that although his men would remove the heavy armaments from their

Casspirs and Wolves at midnight, they would store them together with the ammunition within the vehicles for the whole of the 1st April, and would only afterwards put them in store.

These intentions were conveyed to Major General Stephen Fanning, the UNTAG Police Commissioner.

General Dreyer had given orders in January for the police under his command to intensify routine patrolling of the border area, to guard against SWAPO infiltrations. This had been carried out to the letter, but in the event things had been fairly quiet.

The Casspirs and Wolves and the Blesbok and Strandwolf transporters, though, had paid a heavy mechanical price for being continually on the go, and few of them were in the best of mechanical condition.

For General Dreyer that was merely unfortunate, because with only thirty police groups under his command, his men were drastically thin on the ground.

At full strength, a group consisted of forty five policemen with four fighting Casspirs or Wolves and a Blesbok logistics vehicle, but groups were never at full strength because of leave, sickness, transfers and so on.

When at maximum possible strength he had a mere 1 350 men manning 120 fighting and 30 logistic vehicles to attempt an effective police coverage of 400 kilometres of hostile and mostly undemarcated border.

It was a border that traversed untamed grasslands, bush, swamps, bleak mountains and a desert so harsh that the Bushmen, who live in conditions of pitiless hardship enough to dehydrate the souls of lesser mortals, believe it was created by God when angry.

That day his men would continue patrolling the border, working at maximum possible strength, prepared for whatever might happen. Units would not return to their bases in the evening, but would sleep out in the bush, ready to check the border cutline for the tracks of possible SWAPO infiltrators at first light.

Ready for the momentous events of the next day, Namibians, were finally able to catch a glimpse of Mr Martti Ahtisaari, Special Representative of the Secretary General, when he arrived by air at Windhoek airport, his main base until the Namibian independence process was over.

Security at the airport was tight and only people with business there were allowed into the terminal building, after being physically searched by UNTAG personnel.

SADF snipers were positioned on the roof to guard against an assassination attempt.

Both Mr Louis Pienaar, who met the Special Representative, and Mr Ahtisaari, addressed a press conference attended by about 200 mostly foreign journalists, at the airport.

Mr Ahtisaari said the 1st April marked the beginning of a new era. He went on to say: 'All Namibian political prisoners and detainees, wherever they are held, must be set free. Those who are in exile must have the chance to come here. Laws which could interfere with the holding of free and fair elections will be abolished. There must be an end to violence and intimidation. When the Namibian people have chosen, the outcome must be accepted and respected by all'.

He mentioned that although 4 650 UNTAG troops would eventually be deployed, only about a 1 000 were in place by that time.

This was, in fact, an over estimation.

'I had hoped,' he said, 'that we would have finished the budgetary and political processing in New York faster than we did – but we did not. We will deploy our people within the means available, but it is important that we have the transportation, communications and accommodation available for the UNTAG forces.'

He said that he and Mr Pienaar would work together with Namibians to resolve situations as they arose.

Mr Pienaar spoke in much the same vein, but warned that the 'intimidation factor' might increase in the next six to nine weeks after certain units of the SWA Territory Force had been demobilised and when SWAPO cadres returned across the border

About 4 000 people, mostly black supporters of the DTA, were waiting outside the airport gates to greet him, but they caught little more than a glimpse as he was whisked away to Windhoek afterwards.

The DTA had trucked, trained and bussed their supporters to the airport from all over Namibia.

The road between the airport and Windhoek had been daubed in dozens of places with road sized DTA slogans in white paint.

SWAPO stayed away from the welcoming saying they wanted to 'avoid any incidents which could mar the commencement of the period leading to independence'.

Finnish by birth, Mr Ahtisaari (52) has been a diplomat since 1965, having served as Finnish Deputy Director Foreign Affairs (1972–73) and Finnish Ambassador to Tanzania (1973–76). He was also accredited to Zambia, Somalia and Mozambique (1975–76).

Martti Ahtisaari has been involved with the Namibian question since 1975, when he served for two years as a member of the Senate of the Institute for Namibia. After that he was appointed UN Commissioner for Namibia (1977- 81), and became the UN Secretary General's Special Representative for Namibia in July 1978.

Martti Ahtisaari has a honourable diplomatic career behind him, and the prospects ahead of him are even brighter. With effect from the 1st January 1987, in addition to his position as the Secretary General's Special Representative for Namibia, he was appointed by Secretary General Javier Perez de Cuellar as the Security Council's Under Secretary General for Administration and Management.

The way his career has progressed, the day could well come, if the opportunity arises, for him to move up the ladder to take the Secretary General chair, provided, of course, he doesn't upset too many members of the UN, and he plays his political cards with the necessary dexterity.

That he is wary of his likely historical image, he showed by becoming the only person of note involved in the Namibian situation to decline an interview with the author , on the grounds that he never gave personal interviews to writers and journalists.

After stepping off the aircraft at Windhoek Airport, he must have favourably compared the nice warm Namibian day to the likely wintery sub zero temperature back in his native Finland.

He might not have suspected it then, but within twenty four hours he would find Namibia even hotter, and his personal position as the Secretary General's Special Representative for Namibia, which from 1978 until the settlement in December 1988 had been little more than a bureaucratic sinecure, had suddenly become a real hot seat.

For Sergeant Wessie Wessels, group leader of Zulu Echo, it was routine police patrolling, but because they were operating adjacent to the Owamboland border with Angola, he had decided to keep his group of four fighting Casspirs and a Blesbok logistics vehicle together for the day, operating them as a single unit.

Although orders were that heavy weapons must be removed from the Casspirs only at midnight that night, to comply with the provisions of resolution 435, he had already instructed they be dismantled and stowed away in the Blesbok, leaving his men with only their personal R-5 carbines and pistols.

Sergeant Wessels for one, was certainly not expecting trouble. Before starting on patrol he had briefed his men to carry out routine identity card checks of locals they might come across, on the off chance of finding an infiltrating SWAPO insurgent in civilian clothes, perhaps an intelligence gathering mission, or maybe a political commissar out to intimidate the locals. There was no thought they could happen on heavily armed SWAPO insurgents.

It was a hot morning and having commenced patrolling early, by about 09:00 most of the men were hungry and thirsty, in need of perhaps a coke and a snack, so Sergeant Wessels ordered they make a refreshment stop at a cuca shop.

In Owamboland cuca shops are native run eating house or restaurants, although perhaps the latter title is too grand a name for most of them, and are places where one can buy anything from bread to cooked food, with either a beer, some tea or perhaps a cool drink to wash it down. At some of them obliging ladies who are more than just shop assistants are in attendance, and a man may partake of other delicacies that may tickle his fancy.

The cuca shop where Zulu Echo stopped for brunch was not one of those more flamboyant establishments. As his Casspir stopped outside the cuca shop, the smell of frying chips, *lekker slap* chips, wafted up to where Sergeant Wessels was standing in the gunless turret.

He remained there looking on as his men dismounted from the cars and wandered into the cuca shop, some yelling out orders for chips to the assistants, whom they knew well from previous visits.

He dawdled idly, intending to go down himself when the rush was over, only half noticing a yellow vanette parked about eight meters away from his Casspir.

Two black policemen, neither of whom were armed, were standing by the entrance to the shop, as two men brushed past them and began walking towards the vanette.

'Hey!'

They stopped and turned around as the policemen walked over to them.

One of the men was fairly elderly, but the other was young, perhaps eighteen or twenty years old. He had on a black jacket, underneath of which he was wearing a shirt displaying the SWAPO emblem.

There was nothing illegal in that, but in the circumstances of the day, they were clearly people who merited an ID check.

The policemen and the two men walked slowly over to the vanette, where the older man, after rooting around in the glove compartment, produced his identification.

The younger one patted his pockets, then shook his head, smiling nervously.

'No, sorry, it isn't with me. It's back at the kraal . . . just down the road.'

'No trouble,' replied one policemen, 'just get in the Casspir and we'll drive there and check it out.'

The young man hesitated as if about to protest, then shrugged in apparent resignation and walked towards Sergeant Wessels' Casspir.

As they reached the open rear door, he quickly thrust his hand into his jacket and withdrew a clearly identifiable oval metalic object.

Grenade!

Sergeant Wessels and his policemen were wise in the ways of war, and hard experience had changed them into men who didn't die easily.

The black policemen, sensibly, ducked and ran, quickly putting cover between themselves and the armed enemy.

There was little else to do, because without guns, tackling a determined enemy brandishing a live grenade, is a game to play only if you have ambitions of ending up as a dead hero.

The unarmed Sergeant Wessels was similarly stuck.

He watched the insurgent helplessly, tensed up and waiting for him to pull the pin and lob the grenade into the rear of the Casspir.

He had decided to escape the blast by throwing himself over the front of the cab, ignoring the long drop to the ground. Still, better some bruises and maybe a few broken bones, than being a corpse in the Oshakati mortuary.

Momentarily the insurgent appeared confused, perhaps undecided.

Then he pulled the pin, but didn't throw it.

The lever spun away and he thrust the grenade downwards, clasping it with both hands between his legs.

He died instantly as the grenade exploded.

They searched the badly mutilated body for identification, the blast had all but severed both the legs, but there was nothing to shed light on his identify or mission.

His older companion was arrested, but he seemed genuine in his protests that he knew nothing about his erstwhile companion, so he was released from custody a few days later.

By arrangement, Lieutenant General Prem Chand's second in command, Brigadier Danny Opande of Kenya, went to SWA Territory Force's headquarters, Windhoek, at 11:00 daily for a briefing by the Chief of Staff (Operations), Brigadier Johan Louw, while each afternoon the Brigadier went to UN headquarters to see General Prem Chand personally.

For some reason or other that Friday's morning meeting was later than usual, taking place at about 12:00 instead.

Brigadier Louw together with Colonel Jan Bierman, briefed Brigadier Opande on Sergeant Wessie Wessels' incident involving the SWAPO insurgent who had blown himself up with a grenade, and also on the information regarding the presence of a SWAPO group ten kilometres to the north of Beacon 4.

Maps were used to assist in the briefing.

'What are the intentions of this SWAPO group of 150, do you think?' Brigadier Opande asked.

'If they come over, it will be to establish a base,' Brigadier Louw told him.

After what was described as a 'stormy meeting' at UN headquarters, New York, all UN aid to SWAPO was cut off with effect from midnight, after a move by Secretary

General Dr de Cuellar, thus ending a decade of SWAPO nurturing by the UN.

The Secretary General made it clear that in terms of agreements made with South Africa, he wanted the UN to steer a strictly impartial course during the election run up.

Separate moves were afoot to deny SWAPO its special observer status at the UN.

Foreign Minister Pik Botha and Defence Minister Magnus Malan, headed the party of South African officials who in the early morning flew to Ondangwa Air base and then on to Oshakati in preparation for the prisoner exchange, scheduled to take place at Ruacana towards lunchtime.

At Oshakati, which until then had been the most important South African military forward base in Namibia, both ministers took the opportunity to make speeches, and talk to newsmen, during which they thanked all people who had been involved in Namibia on South Africa's behalf for so many years, and for their contribution, particularly those who had served in the forward areas.

Minister Botha stressed that South Africa was not just withdrawing, but 'returning home with dignity' after fulfilling all commitments given to it by the people of Namibia and the world.

He pointed out that South Africa had made Namibia one of the best developed countries in Africa. Roads, railroads, airfields, hospitals and schools had been built, mostly at the expense of the South African taxpayer who had contributed billions of rands.

He refuted the notion that South Africa had been raping the country of its minerals, pointing out that the mining industry contributed a mere 10% to the gross domestic product.

Meanwhile, it was only intense diplomatic activity that had rescued the on off prisoner exchange, pending since signature of the tripartite agreement in New York in December 1988.

In the final event, it was only a last minute personal plea written by President P W Botha to Unita leader, Dr Jonas Savimbi, to release two Cuban prisoners held by him, which had allowed the exchange to proceed.

The final deal, only cleared by Jonas Savimbi the previous day, involved eleven Angolan and four Cuban prisoners, one of whom, Domingo Vinez, was the pilot who had distinguished himself by losing his way and eventually crash landing his MIG-21 jet near Otjiwarongo, Namibia, in December 1988.

Rifleman Johan Papenfus, as the Cuban/Angolan's only South African prisoner, was their sole bargaining chip. He was a rarity, too, saying much for South Africa's fighting abilities, for in fourteen years of war he was only the third white prisoner to be taken.

The South African press corps had flown from Pretoria by C-160 transport earlier in the day, and had then been driven by bus to the joint border posts where the exchange was scheduled to take place. Awaiting them was a large party of journalists from Angola, Cuba, Soviet Russia and other communist bloc countries.

The actual meeting at the border, was treated officially as a resumption of the JMMC meeting which had taken place and then been adjourned on the 23rd March at Havana, Cuba.

Leading the military delegations to the JMMC, were Major General Willie Meyer, commander of the SWA Territory Force, for South Africa, and Lieutenant

General Leopoldo Cirtas Frias, a Cuban divisional general, and FAPLA's armed forces chief, Lieutenant General Antonio dos Santos Franca Ndalu, for the Angolan-Cubans.

Before the exchange began, Foreign Minister Pik Botha handed over to the Angolan-Cuban delegation detailed documents supported by maps showing where SWAPO elements were still positioned below the 16th parallel. He also pointed out that the South Africans had information that some 150 SWAPO insurgents were deployed in Angola, ten kilometres to the north of Beacon 4, ready to make an incursion into Namibia.

They were officially asked to look into the matter and rectify it by seeing that SWAPO withdrew in accordance with the agreements already signed.

The protest, the twenty seventh of its kind on the same subject made by the South Africans to the Angolans/Cubans since the signing of the tripartite agreement in New York, was accepted after some non committal diplomatic comments, which amounted to no more than they had said in the past, i.e. that they would look into the question and use their 'good offices' to get SWAPO to move back behind the 16th parallel, although not in any way accepting the validity of the South African allegations.

The prisoner exchange signalled the last meeting of the JMMC, for once resolution 435 was implemented the next day, the purpose for which it had been established fell away. Consequently, the Sector I0 commander at Oshakati, Brigadier Chris Serfontein, was already engaged in withdrawing personnel from the various monitoring points along the border.

In spite of this the South Africans were uneasy, because no easy route of communication to the Cubans and Angolans would remain, if an emergency arose. There was a delay in Rifleman Papenfus being brought down to the border post, caused it was rumoured, by a friendly Cuban officer having a last minute farewell drink with the prisoner before he was freed.

It seemed an unbalanced affair when at 13:00 the Cuban and Angolan POWs formed up in threes facing the border, all wearing South African supplied civilian suits with shirts and ties, while facing them on the opposite side was Rifleman Johan Papenfus, wearing a grey coloured Red Chinese style safari suit.

Then in a manner which has become almost a drill since the Cold War commenced, the Berlin Wall type exchange got into motion with the Cubans and Angolans marching north into Angola, all keeping step in a soldierly fashion, while the more lonely Papenfus, flanked by Angolan escorts, walked in a seemingly more individualistic and relaxed manner south into Namibia.

Rifleman Papenfus looked neither left nor right as he passed the other party, but momentarily he was the focus of all of their attentions, possibly from the curiosity of him being their passport to freedom.

For the historic record, he could claim the dubious distinction and certainly mixed blessing of being the last South African soldier to leave Angolan soil.

As he stepped into Namibian territory, Odette, his six year old niece, raced ahead of his brother Frank and sister Marietha and gave him a quick hug.

Meanwhile, the released Cuban and Angolan prisoners had broken ranks once they were on Angolan soil, and were happily mobbed by their compatriots.

They were allowed to talk freely to the press.

One Cuban soldier, Rudolfo Latingua, complained bitterly about UNITA, saying he had serious paralysis of one hand as a result of his wounds being neglected. He also accused them of trying to force him to betray his cause.

Another Cuban, Luiz Gonzales, on the other hand said he had been well treated by UNITA, receiving medical attention when needed and always being rationed with the best food that was available.

Rifleman Papenfus, though, was at first kept away from the press, but he managed to say before being whisked away for medical examination at the Ruacana army base, that he was well and glad to be home.

Foreign Minister Pik Botha made a speech thanking the Cuban authorities for the good treatment Papenfus had received while in their hands, making particular reference to the medical treatment of his wounds after capture.

'It was a very auspicious event and we were all happy,' said South African Foreign Affairs Director, Derek Auret. 'It was the culmination of months of negotiations.'

After lunching with Rifleman Papenfus and his family at Ruacana, the ministerial party left for Windhoek, to ready themselves for the momentous events of the next day.

Colonel Koos Botha, the commander of Ondangwa Air Force Base, had a nice touch in mind to make the 1st April memorable.

He had arranged for the printing of a special certificate commemorating the first day of peace, copies of which would be given to every man stationed at the air base on that day.

It was intended to be quite a function, for with the winding down because of resolution 435, many of the personnel there, including the Bosbok squadron, would be leaving in the next few days.

Most of the warplanes had already gone, and children were playing in the emptied bomb dumps.

Things could never be the same again for the South Africans at Ondangwa. From the 1st April it would become little more than a civilian airport facility run by the SAAF for UNTAG, with Colonel Botha becoming like the manager, looking after movement control and seeing the grass was cut.

There was also the courtesy of welcoming four senior Polish air officers, who had already arrived there to act as UNTAG observers.

Much beer was expected to flow in a thrash of gigantic proportions, and six sheep had been slaughtered for the braaivleis.

In the event the function still took place the next evening and those present received their 'peace' certificates. It was, however, an understandable anti climax, because instead of peace and lots of beer, the aircrews would be back on a war footing, out in the veld fighting to control SWAPO's invasion.

British Prime Minister Margaret Thatcher, at a press conference held at President Kamuzu Banda's Sanjika Palace, Malawi, on the last day of what had become known as her Africa Safari, during which she had been making clear her open policy towards South Africa to African leaders, said she had not yet made a decision about making an early visit to Namibia.

Later, when speaking as the guest of honour at a banquet hosted by President Banda, Mrs Thatcher said that bringing justice and freedom to the region was one of the world's most pressing tasks, adding:'This is a time of new hope for southern Africa.'

She went on to say that South Africa's assent to the Namibian independence process and the withdrawal of Cuban troops from Angola were encouraging developments.

In spite of Mrs Thatcher's denial that a visit to Namibia was yet on the cards, the newsmen travelling with her were convinced arrangements had already been finalised. They said she was expected to leave Blantyre at 09:00 on Saturday, arriving in Windhoek about three hours later. During her visit she would meet the British troop component of UNTAG, have discussions with Foreign Minister Pik Botha and probably make a flying visit to the British owned Rossing Uranium Mine at Swakopmund.

The pressmen were right in their speculations, as in Windhoek's official circles, both UN and South African, arrangements for her visit had already been finalised.

When the news broke later in the evening that the visit had been confirmed, SWAPO's Secretary for Publicity and Information, Mr Hidipo Hmutenya, said Mrs Thatcher's 'mission to Namibia is just a thinly disguised way of finding a convenient venue to meet with her South African friends'.

Brigadier Johan Louw, Chief of Staff (Operations) and Colonel de Jaager had spent many days burning the midnight oil, working SWA Territory Force and SADF troop strengths as they would be at the various bases on that day around the country and detailed plans of future troop reductions.

Approximations had already been worked out and passed to General Prem Chand ten days before, to allow UNTAG to do its planning, but accurate figures were required that evening.

Everything was detailed there. The residue strengths of the mostly demobilised battalions of the SWA Territory Force, the force levels of SADF personnel at the various bases, when certain numbers of men would be leaving this base or that base to return to South Africa and so on.

In general terms, and this was already public knowledge, the reduction of SADF force levels was being handled in three phases.

Phase 1 – The run up to the 1st April maintaining existing troop levels and keeping to the ceasefire;
Phase 2 – Six weeks after the 1st April troop strengths will be scaled down to 12 000;
Phase 3 – Nine weeks after this troop strengths will be scaled down to 8 000;
Phase 4 – By the 1st November troop strengths will be reduced to 1 500; and
Phase 5 – Between election day and the implementation of independence in Namibia, all remaining SADF troops would be withdrawn.

In spite of this, Chief of the SADF, General Jannie Geldenhuys, had announced in the press as early as the 28th January, that the SADF's withdrawal from Namibia had been accelerated, with the removal by road, sea and air of military equipment and the household effects of personnel.

Many men had also been transferred back to South Africa.

General Geldenhuys had given assurances then that by these movements, the normal troop strengths in Walvis Bay would not be exceeded. He estimated the cost of the withdrawal to South Africa as R146 millions.

By the evening of the 31st March, the once powerful SWA Territory Force had all but disappeared. 101 (Owambo) Battalion was a good example of what had happened to all of them.

This unit, probably more feared by SWAPO than any other in the SWA Territory Force, had been reduced to almost a shadow of its former self. Of its 2 000 men, 1 341 had already been demobilised and sent home. Most of those remaining were administrative and logistical personnel needed to oversee the close down of the regiment. In stages, as the unit's affairs were wound down, the rest would go. 50 were scheduled for demobilisation on the 10th April, another 85 would depart on the 24th April, on the 30th April a further 378 would go and the remainder would leave on the 12th May – and 101 Battalion would remain only in military tradition. The South Africans kept their word and more, meticulously, and force levels were down virtually to the man, to exactly what they had promised UNTAG they would be.

Some would later say the South Africans had bent over backwards to comply with their part of the agreement, but perhaps, in truth, they did a couple of double somersaults as well.

Eventually by 21:30 the paper was finished. It was delivered shortly afterwards by hand to Kenyan Brigadier Opande of UNTAG.

Both Brigadier Louw and Colonel de Jager went home, tired but satisfied the job had been well done.

That evening Advocate Louis Pienaar, the Administrator General of SWA/Namibia, hosted a dinner for the dignitaries, both South African and United Nations', who were in Windhoek to witness the start of the peace process and welcome the British Premier, Mrs Margaret Thatcher.

At the dinner on the South African side, were Ministers Pik Botha and Magnus Malan, Derek Auret of Foreign Affairs, General Willie Meyer, Commander of the SWA Territory Force, General Dolf Gouws, Commissioner of Police, and other dignitaries and personalities.

On the UN side were Martti Ahtisaari, General Prem Chand, Cedric Thornberry, and some of their senior lieutenants.

Naturally, as one might have expected, the dinner turned out to be a working one.

Before it started, Minister Pik Botha saw Special Representative Martti Ahtisaari in private and gave him all information that had been passed to the Cuban/Angolans at the Ruacana meeting of the JMMC earlier that day.

He specifically pointed out the presence of the SWAPO group north of Beacon 4, apparently poised to infiltrate Namibia.

Martti Ahtisaari apparently took note of what Minister Botha had told him, replying in general terms that he believed it would be extremely stupid of SWAPO to cross into Namibia the next day, thereby breaking Sam Nujoma's commitments relating to the settlement proposals arising from the Geneva Protocol.

Much of the discussion at the dinner table afterwards centred around the threat posed by the presence of PLAN fighters just north of the border. It was stated by various people that it was indeed a threat which couldn't be disregarded.

Yet no one for a moment, even suggested that they believed it was a threat serious enough to materialise into reality the very next day.

In general terms, too, there was much speculation as to why the Cubans and Angolans had not managed to move PLAN elements north of the 16th parallel by then.

After the dinner, Martti Ahtisaari, according to what he later said at a press conference, 'immediately contacted New York, the Secretary General's office, and we were in touch with SWAPO (presumably the SWAPO observer still at the UN) and the permanent representative of Angola immediately'.

He did not reveal what transpired.

There is little to be found at Opuwo in the Kaokoveld. It is a government station in the depths of one of the last remaining unspoiled wildernesses in the world, and all the whites who live there, barring one, are employees of the Namibian administration.

The biggest contribution to the little settlement, was made by the white and black soldiers of 102 Battalion of the SWA Territory Force whose home base is at Opuwo, but by the 31st March the unit had been all but completely disbanded in obedience to the terms of the UN peace plan. The next largest contribution was by the black and white policemen of the SWA Police stationed there. When 102 Battalion was finally disbanded, they would become the largest single group there.

That evening at the venue of the Opuwo Police pub, an unusual event was hosted by police commander, Inspector Nick Peens.

The next morning would herald the start of the much publicised Namibia Trek, which would start out at Opuwo. It had not unreasonably been described as the ultimate back packing challenge by its sponsors, the Rhino and Elephant Foundation.

Twelve fairly ordinary people had volunteered to hike the 700 kilometres from Opuwo southwards via Sesfontein, Khorixas, Twyfelfontein, Burnt Mountain, Brandberg, Omaruru, Hentiesbaai and ending at Swakopmund, the old town which had changed little in appearance since the days of German colonialism.

The trek's purpose was to raise funds by sponsorship for 'grassroots' conservation, directly involving the indigenous people in remote areas where the black rhino was in danger of extinction.

Leading the trek was Wim Peters, a veterinary surgeon from Cape Town and accompanying him were Grant Craig from Kempton Park, Marek Patzer, Chris van der Merwe, Frik Olwage, Palma Olwage, Dave Verster, Cathy Odendaal and Frik van Jaarsveld – all from Johannesburg, Johan Bakkes and Kobus Gerber from Pretoria and Celia Spouncer from Great Britain. Everyone going on the trek, the people involved in its organisation and journalists from South Africa and overseas, were in the police pub that night, together with the police and other Opuwo residents discussing the morrow.

From the bar, which is built on the side of a hill, they could look out over a valley and see the rolling arid terrain of the Kaokoveld.

'There is no problem so far as terrorists are concerned,' the police reassured the trekkers. 'Things have been peaceful around here for months ... besides, tomorrow – the day you start the trek, is 435 day'.

It had been a hard day's patrolling for the men of Zulu Oscar, commanded by

Warrant Officer Fanna du Rand, as it was they who had picked up the information from local villagers that about 100−150 SWAPO insurgents had deployed about ten kilometres north of Beacon 4, ready to infiltrate Owamboland.

After reporting the information to police control, they had spent the day systematically checking long stretches of the border, but had found no signs to indicate an infiltration had yet taken place.

The information was highly positive, though, so Warrant Officer du Rand decided not to order the removal of the heavy armaments from his fighting vehicles. Instead they would be left mounted until the following morning, just in case.

Midnight on 31st March not only signified the commencement of resolution 435, it also signalled a handover of responsibility by the Chief of the SADF, who had been responsible for all aspects relating to the border war since September 1977, to the Commissioner of the SWA Police.

It was the end of an era.

Readying for War

The 200 men of SWAPO's PF Detachment, including the secretary of company 3, Albert Nakawa, war name Karate, got ready to move south late in the afternoon.

Nakawa had crossed the border into Angola to join SWAPO in 1978 when he was fifteen. He was sent to Cuba, where after more than eight years of study he passed standard 11, having left Namibia with Standard 5.

On his return to Angola in 1987 he was infantry trained and posted to the mixed SWAPO/Cuban Zebra Battalion, where as a Spanish interpreter he was involved in the training of SWAPO cadres by the Cubans in armoured warfare.

In March the Zebra Battalion was disbanded and he was posted to the PF Detachment.

Each man was unusually heavily burdened, as in addition to the weight of their usual kit, equipment and weapons, they were also carrying additional uniform sets, mostly brand new and still in plastic wrappers. Amongst them were a great variety of uniforms including Russian fatigues, FAPLA, Cuban and Kenyan and other camouflage uniforms, including an unfamiliar one, which when they queried its origins, they were told was a gift from the OAU.

They were not told the reason for the additional uniforms, but it was unusual because normally a man was issued with one set which he put on, underneath of which he wore civilian clothes, probably a shirt and trousers, which was to help him to blend with the local population in case of an emergency.

No one other than the detachment commander was aware of their destination within Namibia. They only knew what they had been told by SWAPO's Regional Commander, who had come down especially to brief them earlier in the day.

'All Namibian people who had left the country, both soldiers and refugees, will be going home,' he said in his address. 'Across in the country [Namibia] there are going to be elections and you soldiers are going back to be monitored in bases by UNTAG. Your only mission is to be monitored by UNTAG and not to fight, lay ambushes or look for people to kill.'

He didn't mention where UNTAG was, nor where they would establish their bases, but Karate assumed the Detachment Commander had his orders. As was usual on SWAPO operations, only the Detachment Commander knew what was going on, for security reasons.

Yet in spite of the mission supposing to be one of peace, they were heavily armed, with cadres equipped with AK-47 or SKS carbines – many fitted with grenade launchers, heavy and medium machineguns, RPG-7 or RPG-75 anti tank rocket launchers, grenades, large quantities of ammunition and at least two SAM-7 ground to air missile launchers complete with missiles.

Also, and this was important because it had not happened before in previous incursions, the group were equipped with high frequency radio communications equipment to enable them to maintain constant touch with SWAPO headquarters in Angola.

They were ordered to cross the Kunene River into Namibia between 16:00-17:00, but they couldn't because there had been heavy rains upstream and the river was in spate and too deep at the crossing point.

Scouts were sent both upstream and downstream to locate alternative crossing points, but by the time they had sorted this out and waded across, it was late at night.

James Sikalungu, war name Lee, was the political commissar of Company 2 of SWAPO's Paratroop Detachment. He was not, in fact, a paratrooper and neither were his comrades, it was just a fanciful name, in the same way that those belonging to SWAPO's Zebra Battalion were not Zebras.

Hailing from the Caprivi, James had left Namibia to join SWAPO in Zambia in 1978. From there he was sent to Cameroon where he studied art subjects until 1983.

After completing his education he returned to Angola where he became a teacher, teaching children, at the Kwansa refugee camp.

In 1985 he was sent for infantry training at Lubango where he was trained to fire the AK-47. In May 1986, he was posted to SWAPO's Moscow Battalion where he remained until 1987, when he was sent to Lubango to attend a political seminar. On its completion he became the political at his present unit.

His job entailed enlightening the soldiers about the 'revolution'.

Every day he listened to the BBC, the SABC and the Voice of America. He knew all about the peace initiatives and lectured his men every day, including telling them they would be going to bases north of the 16th parallel.

On Wednesday 29th March SWAPO's Chief of Staff addressed them, saying they were returning to Namibia. He didn't say exactly what they would be doing in Namibia, but he mentioned they would be seeing UNTAG who would 'ensettle' them.

This was confusing, because James had been expecting to move north of the 16th parallel, but he was a soldier and orders were orders.

The detachment, which consisted of two companies with a strength of 60 men in each, 120 men in all, under the command of Detachment Commander Sanjaba, moved out that night, crossing the border into Namibia in the early hours of the morning.

They were all heavily armed with both smallarms and heavy weapons, and were carrying large quantities of kit and equipment, including many extra brand new uniforms. No one told James the purpose of the extra uniforms.

They also had radio equipment so they could keep in touch with their headquarters in Angola.

Four or five days after entering Namibia, his detachment was involved in a major action with the Security Forces. He doesn't know what happened to the others, but the men on his left and right were shot dead. He surrendered.

To the east and the west, along perhaps 300 kilometres of Angola's border with Namibia, embracing most of Owambo and parts of Kaokoland, other SWAPO detachments, involving more than 1 600 heavily armed insurgents in all, were either infiltrating Namibia that night, or were busily preparing to do so on a phased basis over the next few days.

6

Saturday 1st April 1989

The Namibia Trek

At first light, just after 07:00, accompanied by much back slapping and cheery wishes of goodwill, the twelve back packers of the Namibia Trek set out south from Opuwo heading for the desolate plains, bare hills and mountains that would finally lead them to Swakopmund and the end of their challenge.

The War in the Bush

Constable Sakkie Jooste, group leader of police callsign Zulu 5 Juliet had experienced a quiet night. The evening before he had split his group into small units, operating observation points on the high ground overlooking the Kunene River and known SWAPO infiltration routes to the west of Ruacana, checking for signs of SWAPO. His OPs gave little more than a sketchy coverage to the area between Kunenestein and Okatjene.

There had been no reports of anything heard or seen, which was not surprising, because the night had been dark, with little or no moon.

This all changed when just after first light a radio report came in from one of his teams advising they had found spoor indicating that a group of maybe fifty or more SWAPO had crossed the Kunene River into Namibia during the night.

Constable Jooste found the report difficult to believe, and decided to check out the signs himself before reporting to Ruacana police control. The last thing he wanted was for either himself or Zulu 5 Juliet to look foolish. The police in the northern border area adopt a highly professional attitude towards their work, and tend to look askance at men who are precipitate with their reports, or who give the slightest indication of being jittery. He called up his other cars, instructing that the men still out on OPs be collected from their positions. Once this had been done, they were to rendezvous with him at the suspected crossing point, about fifteen kilometres west of Ruacana.

Once there, it took Constable Jooste little more than a cursory examination to confirm the report. One thing was certain, though, a large number of SWAPO had come in. It was clear he couldn't handle the situation on his own. He needed reinforcements.

At 07:45 the radio at Zulu 6 – the police control room at Ruacana, crackled into life as Constable Jooste called in.

Sergeant Rassie Ras tiredly picked up the handset to reply. He was hoping to be relieved, it had been a long and boring night and he was ready for bed.

Constable Jooste transmitted his report and Sergeant Ras became immediately alert, feelings of wanting to sleep deserted him.

'This is Zulu 5 Tango. We have picked up fifty tracks at [map reference] VL0873. Direction south. Chevron [pattern boots] and barefoot.'

Sergeant Ras acknowledged, then called up headquarter's control at Oshakati and passed on the message for General Dreyer's information.

Inspector Nick Peens, area commander of police in Kaokoland, was at his main forward base out in the bush when the report came in. He spoke directly to Constable Jooste, who was stationed under his command at Opuwo. After satisfying himself as to what was going on, he called Sergeant Ras on the radio and requested he arrange with Captain Keith Fryer, the MAOP – Mobile Air Operations officer based at Ruacana, and arrange for a Bosbok spotter aircraft to be sent to pick him up. He would take over the direction of the operation from the air. He also told him to arrange with Captain Fryer for Alouette gunships to be put on standby.

Sergeant Ras 'phoned Captain Fryer immediately and passed on Inspector Peens' request.

Captain Fryer was astonished, to say the least.

'Why should I put gunships on standby? There's been no infiltration.'

'But there has, pal,' Sergeant Ras assured him. 'There has!' Captain Fryer moved into action immediately, contacting Commandant Church at Oshakati and relaying him full information on the infiltration.

An Alouette trooper, with its pilot Captain Alan Slade, already at Ruacana, was placed on immediate standby. Commandant Church also ordered two Alouette gunships at Ondangwa to be readied for movement to Ruacana.

At 08:15 callsign Zulu Hotel, commanded by Constable Danie Fourie, reported on the radio they had found the tracks of a further three SWAPO insurgents, a short distance farther to the west of the infiltration already being handled by Zulu 5 Juliet. They had begun a follow-up.

At first light the Zulu Oscar group, commanded by Warrant Officer Fanna du Rand, with Sergeant Wayne Prinsloo, Constable Freddie Harding and Constable Johan van Sittert as car commanders, were checking for signs of SWAPO spoor in the border area between Beacons 6 and 7. They were still dealing with the information of the day before, but had found nothing until then.

Warrant Officer du Rand responded immediately to Constable Jooste's call for assistance.

He called Sergeant Dewald Pretorius of Zulu Yankee on the radio and arranged to rendezvous with him. Warrant Officer du Rand knew the mountains to the west of Ruacana well, for he had often worked in them. He planned to combine Zulu Yankee with his own Zulu Oscar and firstly head south, then north, using a little known rough and winding track through the mountains, and attempt to cut off and ambush the infiltrators as they moved south.

He ordered Constable Duppie du Plessis, commander of Zulu Victor, to take his group and rendezvous as soon as possible with Constable Jooste of Zulu 5 Juliet, who was waiting for reinforcements before he began tracking the infiltrators.

After joining Zulu Yankee, Warrant Officer du Rand led a column of both groups south through to Okatjene. From there he took them south along a track meandering between two large rivers and then turned due north into the mountains.

The radio traffic was hot and the messages urgent.

'April fool, April fool . . . the whole lot of us!'

It was someone from a team listening in, but not yet involved in the operation.

'Negative, negative,' Warrant Officer du Rand responded sternly, leaving no one in any doubt. 'This is no April fool . . . this is for real. We are dealing with a serious case here.'

Colonel Koos Botha, commander of Ondangwa Air Force Base was in conference when the first reports came in. There was a visit by Brigadier Hegter and his staff from Windhoek and all air force base commanders in the operational area had come to Ondangwa for the conference.

Commandant Church, the air operations commander, immediately went to the control room.

Major Alan McCarthy was the commander of the Alouettes at Ondangwa. All pilots stationed there did bush tours on a rotating basis from their home squadrons in South Africa.

The strength of the Alouette squadron there, in advance of the scaling down provided for in the peace plan, had been reduced by the 1st April from the normal operational standby minimum of eight helicopters, to five. Of this five only three were at the Ondangwa, with one on routine standby at Ruacana and another at Eenhana.

Within twelve weeks from the 1st April, a further reduction to four aircraft was scheduled, which is very few when one considers the length of the Namibian/Angolan border. What did the reductions matter anyway? The war in Namibia was over and the need for gunships a thing of the past. That was the sentiment generally prevailing at Ondangwa on the morning of the 1st April.

Being a Saturday morning, Major McCarthy was not working, but was pottering around at home on the base.

The 'phone rang and he answered.

It was the control room . . . two Alouettes had been placed on immediate standby to go to Ruacana. On arrival at Ruacana, there was a strong possibility that at least one would be immediately deployed operationally. His first reaction was to smile . . . it was a joke, an April fool's joke.

'You're bloody joking!'

'No, sir, it's not a joke. It's really serious – genuine, sir.'

Not convinced, he still hurriedly dressed and grabbed his kit – silently promising retribution if it turned out to be a hoax. He got into his car and drove to the control room.

Captain Mario Bergottini, the other chopper pilot on call, arrived almost simultaneously.

'April fool, eh?' Mario said wryly.

But they quickly learned from Commandant Church it was no joke.

Unfortunately the three Alouette gunship helicopters available for operational use at Ondangwa, were gunships in name only. Their normal armament – the devastatingly effective 20mm cannons used in ground attack situations - had been stripped from them and transported to Grootfontein the previous day, in terms of the scaling down.

Colonel Koos Botha, the commander of the Ondangwa air base, had fortunately already sent an urgent signal to Grootfontein requesting the immediate return of two 20mm cannons.

Luckily, a SAAF C130 transport aircraft, the only one in Namibia at the time, was readily available and within the hour it touched down at Ondangwa with the cannons aboard. Unfortunately, it brought only a small reserve supply of ammunition.

A Bosbok aircraft was also readied to take off for Ruacana, for use as a Telstar – radio and communications aircraft, and as a spotter if needed.

It did not take long for Constable Duppie du Plessis and his car commanders, Constable Frank Young, Constable Fanie le Roux and Constable Dirk Spies of Zulu Victor, to rendezvous with Constable Jooste and Zulu 5 Juliet.

He was waiting for them with his second in charge, Constable Stony Steenkamp, and the rest of his command who were all black policemen, at the SWAPO crossing point on the southern bank of the Kunene River.

Four hundred meters south of the river comes the high ground, which quickly rises into mountains. It is rugged and inhospitable country, and it was clear the follow-up had to be carried out on foot. The Casspirs were unable to move forward, except to the foothills, because of the absence of roads or even the roughest of tracks.

After joining together, the combined units began following the tracks from the river, the trackers in front and the vehicles behind. After a short distance, someone found a forty meter long nylon rope and a pair of boots concealed under a bush.

SWAPO usually rope their men together for safety's sake during river crossings, because swimming is a rare ability amongst indigenous blacks. Another safety reason is that the Kunene River is infested with crocodiles – and they show absolutely no racial or political preferences when grabbing a meal.

Constable Jooste decided to send a team of black policemen into the mountains to follow the spoor on foot, nominating Sergeant Uapuratena Zaako and eight others for the job.

It must be stressed that all Zulu 5 teams, who are headquartered at Opuwo in Kaokoland, pride themselves on their mountain work and prefer fighting on foot, to fighting from the cars. Sergeant Zaako and his men were well equipped and carrying a radio.

After some time, Sergeant Zaako came on the air to report his team were still on spoor, and about to follow tracks into a huge ravine.

Group leaders Constables Jooste and Du Plessis, decided after a council of war, to ask for the use of the Alouette trooper, which was standing by and immediately available at Ruacana, to leapfrog a second team ten kilometres farther south into the hills. By checking for spoor they could ascertain if the infiltrators had managed to penetrate that far. If they hadn't they would lay ambush and cut them off, otherwise they would follow them up from there.

Sergeant Ras, at Ruacana control, asked Captain Fryer at MAOPs for this assistance. Permission was granted and Captain Alan Slade's Alouette trooper was tasked on the strict understanding it couldn't be used, no matter the circumstance, to assist with supporting firepower.

Shortly afterwards Captain Slade landed his Alouette briefly, where the fighting cars of Zulu 5 Juliet and Zulu Victor had laagered between the river and the mountains.

Constable Duppie du Plessis and two black policemen climbed aboard.

Captain Slade took off and flew due south, heading for a map feature indicated by Constable du Plessis. While in flight everyone aboard kept their eyes down, searching for movement or other signs of SWAPO, but things seemed deceptively peaceful down on the ground.

Minutes later, Constable du Plessis confirmed Captain Slade's navigation with an affirmative nod, and the Alouette dropped down quickly, its rotors generating a wild storm of dust as it neared the ground. Momentarily it seemed caught between landing and hovering, as the three policemen leaped out and took up tactical positions. Then it leapt back in the air and was gone.

The moment they were down, Constable du Plessis and his men began quartering the ground, searching for enemy tracks.

Captain Slade, meanwhile, returned to the vehicle laager, picked up another three black policemen and trooped them to Constable du Plessis' position, giving him an effective strength of six men, including himself.

About this time, Warrant Officer Corrie Prinsloo of Ruacana police was pottering around his house when his brother-in-law called in to see him.

'There's been a major SWAPO crossing in the mountains to the west.'

Warrant Officer Prinsloo, who commanded a team of trackers specialising in mountain work, his brother-in-law worked another team, found it difficult to believe, so he went to the control room to see for himself.

'It's true,' Sergeant Ras confirmed. 'Not only in the mountains either. Other reports have come in from the central and eastern regions, as well.'

Warrant Officer Prinsloo made arrangements to put his tracking team on standby, getting them ready to move out.

Sergeant Zaako came back on the air to report the tracks were very fresh, indicating his team was close to the enemy. He said he was proceeding with extreme caution.

Constable Jooste, waiting with the fighting vehicles in the foothills, decided, once the Alouette had finished trooping the rest of Constable du Plessis' men out to his position, to fly with Captain Slade back into the mountains, to try for a visual sighting of Sergeant Zaako and his trackers, so they could check ahead for signs of an enemy ambush.

Sergeant Zaako, using the radio, talked the Alouette in until it was over his position, repeating that the spoor was fresh and that he reckoned he was close behind the enemy.

There was poor visibility because of thick bush and trees.

Captain Slade flew on ahead of the trackers, when suddenly, to everyone's shocked surprise, they caught sight of many uniformed SWAPO insurgents actually preparing ambush positions on the summit of a flat topped hill overlooking a dry stream bed.

Constable Jooste saw from the lie of the land that the trackers were heading straight for the killing ground of the ambush.

The enemy ignored the helicopter and made no attempt to open fire.

He called Sergeant Zaako on the radio, warning him of the extreme peril that lay ahead of his patrol.

Nothing happened.

He called again.

There was still no reply.

In the worst possible example of Murphy's law, the tracking team's radio had gone on the blink.

'Open up on them,' Constable Jooste demanded.

'I can't,' Captain Slade replied with anguish.

His orders were clear and specific, and impossible to bend. He could operate his Alouette as a trooper or as a spotter, but he couldn't open fire – not even in self defence.

Much was hanging on his actions, maybe the whole peace process. It would have been easy to play Nelson and obey his instincts. All he had to do was give the nod to his engineer/gunner – who was just itching to open fire. But that nod could have caused an international incident.

He spoke to MAOPs Ruacana, demanding clearance to open fire. He had SWAPO insurgents visual. He couldn't say exactly how many because some were in cover, but it could be fifty plus. A police section was down there, out of radio contact and about to walk into am ambush. They could all be killed.

'Negative . . . you cannot open fire,' came the even and apparently indifferent reply from Captain Keith Fryer at Ruacana.

They couldn't know it in the helicopter, but Captain Fryer had been begging and pleading with higher authority for permission, with as much passion as Captain Slade when pleading with him, and Constable Jooste when pleading with Captain Slade.

With added desperation, Constable Jooste tried over and over again to contact Sergeant Zaako on the radio . . . to warn him of the ambush and the massive enemy force that lay ahead.

Frustratingly, not only did the radio stay obstinately silent, but they had also lost visual contact because of the thick bush. They couldn't even drop a warning note.

Eventually, what they had all feared, happened. There was a crackle of gunfire spelling out the springing of the SWAPO ambush. They assumed Sergeant Zaako's patrol had walked right into it.

Captain Slade dropped down and flew low over the contact area, trying to see what was going on, his gunner itching to blast away with his single ,303 machinegun.

Then they dropped too low, became too inquisitive, and there was the punch of adrenalin as the thump, thump of AK fire began and the dirty brown smoke puffs of RPG rockets started skybursting around the aircraft.

'. . . not even in self defence.'

Bastards!

He couldn't defend the aircraft, so he had no option but to fly out fast to where the sky was blessed with a greater tranquility.

Those aboard felt consumed by a deep gloomy frustration and rage as they flew back to Zulu 5 Juliet and Zulu Victor's laager, wondering impotently if Sergeant Zaako's patrol had been wiped out, if any of them were still alive.

A sitrep was passed to Ruacana, and Warrant Officer Prinsloo's tracking team, consisting of himself and nine black policemen, was ordered to the Ruacana airfield, to standby for Puma uplift. They had been tasked to locate and assist survivors of the ambushed tracking team.

They checked and rechecked their kit while waiting at the airfield, eager to be on their way and up in the mountains so they could help their comrades. To their deepest frustration, however, nothing happened. Authority to use the Puma as a trooper had been denied. Without Alouette gunship topcover, the chances were the Puma would be lost to ground fire. Yet the provision of topcover remained impossible, so long as the gunships were denied permission to open fire.

When the ambush report came in, Inspector Nick Peens was already strapped in the rear passenger seat of the Bosbok that had been sent to fly him to Ruacana, and the pilot was carrying out pre flight checks.

Constable Mark Joubert, manning the radio at the Kaokoland forward base, reported to him that the contact was still in progress.

Inspector Peens instructed him to tell Ruacana his Bosbok was taking off immediately.

The Alouette gunships piloted by Major Alan McCarthy and Captain Mario Bergottini were airborne from Ondangwa, just after 10:00.

While in flight Major McCarthy's flight engineer/gunner, Sergeant Bert Steyn, checked out the 20mm cannon. He hoped that if it came to action, there would be enough ammunition to see it through, because they only had about half of what they normally carried.

After landing at the Ruacana airfield – which is some distance from Ruacana itself, they immediately arranged to refuel the choppers.

Once this was underway, Major McCarthy called Captain Fryer on the radio and asked for instructions.

Captain Fryer said they were not to come to Ruacana itself. They were to get airborne again and get out to the contact area as quickly as they could.

He confirmed that Captain Slade was already in the area and had been shot at.

To the south, progress along the mountain tracks has been tortuous for Warrant Officer du Rand and the Zulu Oscar and Zulu Yankee groups.

The roads were unbelievably rough and mostly narrow, with acute sometimes hair raising bends the norm, rather than the unusual. Adopting any formation other than single file was impossible. At some bends the fighting vehicles, because of their length, had to reverse and go forward several times, before negotiating them. This was no easy matter when driving on treacherously loose gravel, or on a crumbling track, with the possibility of a side slip into a deep ravine being a constant danger.

When action began in the north by the Kunene, everyone became consumed with impatience, wanting to get to grips with the enemy. But patience, rather than impatience, was the only way to get that column through the hills.

Yet in spite of the difficulties they made good progress, until eventually they were halted by a washaway, where the road had gone and further progress in the cars was an impossibility.

The ten vehicles of the combined groups were spread out over several hundred meters of mountain road, and because of the terrain, all were out of sight of Warrant Officer du Rand and Sergeant Dewald Pretorius in the first and second cars.

While in this situation of obvious tactical disadvantage, SWAPO compounded their problems by opening fire.

There were between 80–120 heavily armed and uniformed SWAPO insurgents deployed on the mountainside to their left. They concentrated the full weight of their fire on the two leading Casspirs.

It was impossible to turn around, or to go forward, so the only remaining alternative was to fight it out.

'It was one hell of a contact . . . like a small war,' Warrant Officer Fanna du Rand recalled later.

There were at least ten near misses by rifle grenade. Fortunately, SWAPO's aim, was poor, probably because they were ill trained in the skills of firing downhill.

Explosions way up on the mountainside, indicated that some inexperienced SWAPO cadres, carried away by the excitement and heat of battle, had used live ball ammunition instead of ballestite cartridges, when using the grenade launchers on their rifles.

A mistake like that can result in the serious injury or death of the firer. No bodies, however, were picked up afterwards. But because of the emergency situation prevailing, no proper sweep of the area was carried out. Warrant Officer du Rand and Sergeant Pretorius shot back with everything they had, firing their heavy machineguns and using mortars with anti personnel fragmentation bombs to good effect.

The crews of the cars behind debussed and came forward, adding the weight of their personal weapons to the battle.

SWAPO couldn't take what was being dished out to them, and resistance suddenly crumbled and they broke, fleeing up the mountain to get to the safety of the reverse slope. A few braver ones remained, but the enemy fire gradually became more sporadic.

Amazingly, although SWAPO had all the advantages, including surprise, they failed to cause even one police casualty.

Major McCarthy and Captain Bergottini arrived over the contact area some time after noon, joining up with Captain Slade. He gave them a run down on what had happened.

The Alouettes began orbiting the area, staying fairly high, trying to see what the enemy was up to on the ground.

Major McCarthy was literally amazed to see about thirty to forty SWAPO insurgents in a tactical formation climbing a hillside, they were in uniform and carrying kit, equipment and weapons.

It was obvious they had seen the aircraft, they couldn't possibly have missed them, but they took no notice, neither adopting a threatening attitude nor opening fire.

Major McCarthy got on to Captain Fryer at MAOPs, Ruacana and requested permission to open fire. He impatiently explained how the insurgents were deployed in large numbers below him. It was too good a chance to miss . . . it was like Christmas for a gunship crew.

His request was relayed to the main Sector 10 control at Oshakati.

Major McCarthy confidently expected an affirmative reply, but Captain Slade and Captain Fryer knew otherwise, having already been drawn through the grinder themselves earlier.

'Your can fire – but only in self defence – after they have fired first.'

'We must be able to fire, we have 'em visual . . . about thirty or forty of them.'

'Negative, do not, repeat do not open fire.'

Major McCarthy couldn't believe it.

The air waves ran hot and lucid, as arguments with few holds barred raged back and forth.

Experiencing more frustration than they had ever known, the pilots continued orbiting, monitoring the enemy's progress.

The SWAPO below ignored them completely, so long as they stayed high, but when they swooped experimentally low, they immediately scattered and took shelter against and amongst the trees, but still made no attempt to open fire.

'Are we being fired at, Mac?' Captain Bergottini kept asking Major McCarthy. 'Are you sure they're not firing at us?'

'Negative, ' Major McCarthy would reply patiently.

Then when he really became fed up with the question.

'I can't really see ... but I suppose I'm not really looking.'

Major McCarthy was very aware of the situation's sensitivity, and understandably didn't wish to be responsible for initiating an unauthorised ground attack.

Later they pulled Mario Bergottini's leg, saying he had just wanted to start a war.

Inspector Nick Peens, the Kaokoland police commander, arrived overhead in the Bosbok spotter. At first he experienced communications difficulties, because the police and helicopter gunships were working on an unusual radio channel. Eventually he got through to Constable Jooste who briefed him.

He could scarcely believe his eyes, when as they flew over a horseshoe bend of a dried up river, he saw about fifty SWAPO, not even in cover. He could even pick out the leader – a man gesticulating his arms, putting his men into ambush positions.

The choppers were nearby and Inspector Peens asked his pilot why they weren't engaging the enemy, only to be told they had orders not to.

'If the enemy fires on them, they must seek permission and a decision will then be made at high level to see if they can return fire or not.'

'That's bullshit,' Inspector Peens said, outraged.

'That's the right word,' confirmed his pilot.

Inspector Peens spoke to Major McCarthy by radio, begging him to open fire, asking him how he could stand aside while policemen were dying down there.

But the gunship pilots couldn't do anything. They were caught in the same trap as everyone else.

Ruacana then ordered the Bosbok to return there and land.

Inspector Peens was so angry, that after landing he found he was unable to even talk to the airmen there, even though he knew the orders were not theirs.

Warrant Officer du Rand, in the south, had meanwhile organised a pursuit group comprised of men drawn from both Zulu Oscar and Zulu Yankee, and sent them to climb the mountain and follow-up their SWAPO ambushers. 'If we could only have got our Casspirs up the mountain, we would have killed the lot,' Warrant Officer du Rand said later, 'but the terrain made it absolutely impossible'.

The group comprised Sergeant Wayne Prinsloo in command, with Constable Freddie Harding, Constable Theunis Kruger and twenty black policemen. They carried two-way radios for communication purposes.

They organised into a long sweep line and advanced up the mountain, expecting to draw heavy fire from the enemy. It seemed, however, they had taken the opportunity to made good their escape, because nothing happened.

Halfway up there was a tense moment of contact, and a stump which for a fleeting moment had behaved or looked like an enemy, was shot into splinters.

It was not the best of times for anyone, for storming a hill is not the easiest of infantry jobs around. The black policeman behaved with exemplary rock steadiness and determination, not surprisingly, some were veterans of literally hundreds of contacts with the enemy.

For Sergeant Wayne Prinsloo, Constable Theunis Kruger and Constable Freddie Harding, things were different. They had all been infantry trained, taught how to fight on foot, but deployment in a training area even with ball ammunition, is never quite the same as being faced with a real enemy, intent on killing you before you killed him.

And to make it worse ... there was the mountain.

The point of extreme danger was the summit.

The enemy could easily be waiting there, in cover and slightly back on the reverse slope, ready to sock them to eternity at point blank range?

Then they got there ... what a relief ... the enemy had flown!

They had not gone too far, though, because although the slope down and the valley below seemed clear of enemy, there were about eight of them on the slope of the next hill a kilometre away. Some were in trees, apparently watching to see when the police appeared, but others were just lounging around on the grass. None, by their subsequent actions, seemed particularly perturbed.

Sergeant Wayne Prinsloo and the two white constables with him, were all young and keen. The next plan seemed obvious. The enemy were there, so the answer was to go down and scrub them off SWAPO's establishment.

The more experienced black policemen, however, were more cautious. They looked thoughtfully down into the valley, believing SWAPO were waiting in ambush. They had probably set it up in the thick bush fringing the dried up river bed at the foot of the hill. If they took the chance and just rushed on down, they would surely walk into an ambush and suffer heavy casualties.

'No ways,' said Sergeant Wayne Prinsloo. 'There's no bloody ambush down there.'

Constables Theunis Kruger and Freddie Harding agreed.

Let's give it a go.

The black policemen were adamant.

SWAPO were down in the valley ... expecting them to do something stupid.

Sergeant Wayne Prinsloo reluctantly accepted their advice. They wouldn't go down. In the SWA Police the golden rule is never to go against the advice of the black policemen ... not if you have any ambitions of staying alive! Nevertheless, he still discussed the question on the radio with Warrant Officer du Rand.

'Negative ... stay where you are,' Warrant Officer du Rand told him, agreeing with the black policemen.

So the police remained in their position.

'It was the first time I have heard of a unit actually sitting down and keeping a terr unit visual for such a long time. It is unheard of in my experience,' Warrant Officer du Rand said afterwards.

He called Ruacana and pleaded with Sergeant Ras for gunships.

'Negative,' he was told, 'no gunships. Helicopters can only be used for casevacs'.

It was arranged that one would pick him up, so he could check the situation of Sergeant Prinsloo's team from the air.

The approach of the returning choppers was heard as a distant murmur in the air by Sergeant Wayne Prinsloo's men. Others obviously heard as well, for suddenly, about 25−30 well armed SWAPO broke cover from the bushes by the dried up river, and jogged uphill to join their comrades.

They had been in ambush after all.

The police hadn't gone down there, so the SWAPO must have thought they had been seen, and the gunships had been called for to blast them.

The young whites, so keen to rush precipitously into action, were profuse in thanking the black policemen for saving their lives.

The gunships came in and circled, one landed and picked up Warrant Officer du Rand, then took off again.

'I nearly had a heart attack,' Warrant Officer du Rand recalled, 'when I saw the terrs walking around so casually on the ground.

'I begged the pilot to let his engineer open fire with the cannon, but he said they couldn't without permission.'

He demanded to speak to Sergeant Ras at Ruacana control.

'Tell General Dreyer what is going on. Our guys are bleeding down there and the Alouettes won't shoot.'

His eyes were wet with tears of anguish.

'Standby,' said Sergeant Rassie Ras.

He was back in a few moments.

'Roger that,' he said, 'General Dreyer confirms the pilots can open fire at the terrs on the ground. They have his personal authorisation.'

But the air force had a different chain of command, and they wouldn't accept orders from a police general.

The story went back to Oshakati, then to Windhoek.

'Negative the gunships cannot open fire.'

'I was so enraged that although it wasn't the pilots fault, I nearly took out my pistol and made him give the order to open fire. It was touch and go. While my men were being killed on the ground, I refused to accept that any other member of the Security Forces could just opt out.'

For three quarters of an hour an unremitting effort was made on the radio by Constable Jooste to raise Sergeant Zaako's group, but without success.

Then, suddenly, one of his men came on the air. He confirmed they had been ambushed. Three men, Sergeant Zaako, the team leader, and Constables Mathias Lukas and Daniel Sakaria were missing. They were leading the patrol, and when firing commenced two went down. No one knew if they had been wounded or killed. The third man was missing, no one knew what had happened to him.

It seemed likely they were all dead, but there was an offchance they had been captured. There were four men still out in the hills, two of them wounded and needing to be casevaced. Constable Gideon Titus had been shot in the left forearm and Constable Gerhardt had shrapnel wounds in his buttocks.

Two other survivors were making their way back independently to the vehicles on foot.

Constable Jooste and Constable du Plessis discussed things on the radio. Constable du Plessis said that as he was already out in front anyway, the helicopter, when it came to casevac the wounded, should first pick him and two others up and drop them off to beef up the ambush survivors.

Windhoek instructed that when the trooper went in to collect the casevac, UNTAG observers from Ruacana should go with it.

The UNTAG officers at Ruacana were duly invited to join the party.

They said with no pretence of false bravery: 'They're shooting at you . . . no ways!'

Captains Slade and Bergottini landed their helicopters, one at a time, to refuel at the Kunene River laager of Zulu 5 Juliet and Zulu Victor. Police groups always carried emergency supplies of Avgas for helicopters. Unfortunately, there was insufficient there for Major McCarthy's Alouette, so he headed back to Ruacana to refuel.

The trooping and casevac plan went ahead at 13.05 and Constable du Plessis and his men were picked up by Captain Slade's Alouette trooper, while Captain Bergottini's gunship provided top cover.

The ambushed team fired a yellow parachute flare to mark their position.

An RPG rocket air burst near the choppers and there was a sudden crackle of

AK fire. Captain Slade touched down briefly, probably for no more than a minute, while his passengers deplaned and the wounded were put aboard.

Then it was up and off again.

Almost immediately a major attack was launched against the reinforced ground party, by about forty SWAPO insurgents concealed nearby.

The battle raged for what seemed an interminable time, with the policemen shooting back with everything they had.

The SWAPO fire slackened, then eventually ceased, when Sergeant Wayne Prinsloo's pursuit group in the south alarmed the enemy by stonking a barrage of mortar bombs into their positions, thanks to excellent fire control instructions given over the radio by Constable du Plessis. It was immediately obvious the enemy were retreating in disorder, thoroughly worried by the possibility of being caught between the two groups in a pincer movement.

While their confusion reigned, Constable du Plessis withdrew his men about fifty meters, disengaging from the enemy in the process. After Major McCarthy had refueled at the Ruacana airfield, he took off intending to head for the village, so he could discuss the no firing orders with Captain Fryer personally. While on route he heard on the radio that SWAPO had opened fire on the other two Alouettes.

Fire had been returned.

Major McCarthy got clearance from Captain Fryer at MAOPs to return and rejoin Captains Bergottini and Slade.

Just as Major McCarthy arrived overhead, Captain Bergottini, who had only been carrying a reduced supply to start with, ran out of ammunition.

This left him with no option but to return to Ruacana to rearm.

RPG rockets exploded in the air in dirty brown puffs, like ack ack bursts. The shock waves of a near miss are considerable. The rockets leave no giveaway trails after firing, so the short and sharp detonations, which can be heard clearly above the sounds of the aircraft engines, always come as a nasty surprises.

Captain Slade was the next to run out of ammunition, but Major McCarthy told him to stay in orbit, for command and control and mutual support purposes.

Major McCarthy's gunship engaged a group of fifteen insurgents deployed on the side of a hill.

It was impossible to say how many they hit, but they counted five bodies and saw a lot of abandoned rucksacks and other kit scattered beneath the trees when overflying the area the next morning.

The initial part of the engagement, involving only Captains Slade and Bergottini, lasted some twenty minutes. After Major McCarthy picked up the strings of combat, it lasted for another twenty or so minutes.

Captain Bergottini soon got back to the contact area and took over from Major McCarthy, who had to return to Ruacana himself for more ammunition.

The enemy, who must have had enough, suddenly ceased firing at the helicopters.

The pilots asked for clearance to continue shooting at enemy targets of opportunity, pointing out it would be ridiculous to allow them to continue their march south through the bush without opposing them.

'Standby! Standby!' Captain Fryer at MAOPs said, while attempting to get authorisation for the shooting to continue.

The problem was the length of the chain of command. It went from MAOPs Ruacana to Sector 10 HQ at Oshakati, to Western Air Command in Windhoek and from there to the Commissioner of the SWA Police and the Administrator General.

One can be certain that much of it went to the Chief of the Air Force and up to Cabinet level in South Africa, as well.

'No', was the answer which finally came back. 'Only shooting in self defence'.

Inspector Peens went up in one of the Alouettes to check things out on the ground again and was once more astonished to see some fifty SWAPO on the ground, who like before, were not at all bothered by the presence of the helicopters.

After flying across a mountain ridge to check the valley beyond, he was aghast to see another large group of SWAPO, also about fifty strong.

'You must open fire,' he told the pilot. 'What's the use of being a pilot around here, if you can't support our people'.

The pilot declined, much against his will.

Inspector Nick Peens shook his head in disgust.

'Okay, take me back to base. I'm not going to hang around here as a spectator, just to see my guys getting killed.'

They were then ordered to return to Ruacana anyway.

When checked at Ruacana it was discovered that Captain Slade's trooper had sustained battle damage, having been struck by a single AK round. There seemed no critical damage, but in the SAAF no chances are taken, so it was ordered back to Ondangwa for further checks and repairs.

Sergeant Wayne Prinsloo and his team had been moving slowly northwards towards the Kunene River, for most of the day. Finding SWAPO spoor was not difficult, it was everywhere. Sometimes the human tracks seemed like game trails, there were so many of the enemy around.

There had experienced one fleeting contact, but it had been difficult to tell if they had hit any of the enemy.

When fire was opened again, two inexperienced black constables threw grenades, which struck branches and exploded short, fortunately without wounding anyone.

'Hell, we got a fright,' Sergeant Wayne Prinsloo said afterwards. 'We thought they were mortaring us.'

'Any casevacs? Any casevacs?' the shout went up.

But there were no casevacs, and no enemy either.

It was just a false alarm.

Later they saw more SWAPO moving in the distance. They opened fire, but the range was extreme so the likelihood of hitting anyone was remote.

By 16:00 Sergeant Prinsloo was wondering if he should head back for the Casspirs, or whether he should keep the unit out for the night. If they stayed out, he would need to arrange for a gunship to drop off water supplies and rations.

He started discussing this with his men, but was interrupted.

'Ssh,' a black constable held a finger to his lips. Both he and the other black policemen raised their weapons and opened fire.

Sergeant Wayne Prinsloo and the white constables hadn't seen anything. The firing stopped and they walked cautiously forward.

Thirty metres away was the body of a uniformed insurgent, shot through the head. Next to him was an SKS rifle fitted with a rifle grenade, and a pack was on his back. Inside were spare uniforms and tinned food, produce of Denmark and Switzerland, originally supplied as refugee aid.

The insurgent had become separated from his comrades. He probably heard voices and thought it was them, so he made his way towards them. It was a bad and very final mistake on his part.

Constable du Plessis and his two companions had been operating an OP, but during the afternoon they cast around for spoor, eventually finding some which indicated there could well be another SWAPO group in the vicinity.

He called Warrant Officer du Rand on the radio, and arranged for a group of twenty men, drawn from Zulu 5 Sierra, Zulu 5 Echo and Zulu Victor, to be trooped out as reinforcements so he could mount a follow-up.

The difficulty was how to deploy them.

Sending them in on foot would cause too much delay.

A Puma helicopter was needed to troop them out as one load.

A conference took place at Ruacana between the police and the air force on this question.

The pilot of the Puma on standby, Major Willie Ras, was reluctant to endanger his aircraft by going in without topcover, which was in accordance with practise.

The trouble was that topcover had been approved only for casevacs.

Certainly the gunships could go in with the Puma, but this would be of little use if the pilots were operating with hands tied behind their backs, especially if they were the hands with the guns in them!

Eventually after requests and counter requests for more information had kept the radio waves busy for some time, permission was granted for gunships to provide effective topcover for the Puma, while it trooped men forward to Constable du Plessis' position.

Major Alan McCarthy and Captain Mario Bergottini provided the necessary topcover with their gunships.

The additional men were flown in without incident. Warrant Officer du Rand had joined Captain Bergottini in his Alouette as an observer.

Down below Constable du Plessis was finding that tracking in the mountains was not easy, but suddenly his men spotted a group of SWAPO on a hill about 500 meters away. They seemed to be heading in his direction, so he reported it.

'I had no idea how many there were,' said Warrant Officer du Rand afterwards, 'But I was deeply worried it was a large SWAPO party trying to capture them.'

Both gunships flew over the position indicated by Constable du Plessis, and RPG rockets began air bursting around them. Rifle fire was also heavy.

From Constable du Plessis' position, the air bursts seemed right next to the choppers.

The pilots couldn't see the enemy, but Constable du Plessis indicated where they should put in some flushing shots.

Captain Bergottini passed on the order and his engineer/gunner happily obliged, unable to see the enemy, but taking corrections from Constable du Plessis as he did so.

'Okay, bit to the left.'

'A little lower.'

'More to your left.'

'Roger, but a fraction to the right.'

'Super . . . got 'em.'

Warrant Officer Corrie Prinsloo and his tracking team had spent a frustrating afternoon, most of it at the Ruacana airfield.

Three times they were scrambled to be taken into the mountains, but twice the orders were cancelled due to the problem of using the Puma without Alouette topcover. On the third occasion they actually took off, but a Puma couldn't be spared to take them right into the mountains, so they were dropped off at the laager of Zulu 5 Juliet and Zulu Victor near the Kunene River. After that there was nothing more they could do until the next morning.

Constable du Plessis and his men stayed out in the mountains that night, camping on the enemy's tracks, when it became too dark to continue.

Sergeant Lappies Labuschagne, group leader of Zulu 5 Sierra, and his men were operating along the southern bank of the Kunene River in the area of Swartboo-isdrift when the first reports came in.

The ironstone in the mountains around that part of Kaokoland, as well as the distances involved, was causing poor reception and much interference with radio transmissions that morning. There was suddenly an unusually large amount of radio traffic, which he couldn't make out, so he ordered his vehicle column to stop when they reached high ground, so he could listen.

He sat by the radio with car commanders, Constable van Vuuren – the group's second in command and Constable Haasbroek, monitoring transmissions.

It all seemed pretty puzzling. Serious reports like what was coming over, happened only on exercises, not during operations, during the real thing.

'No, man,' Constable van Vuuren said eventually, shaking his head, 'it's just an April fool's trick. It's a pretty good one, though.'

They continued on route for a few kilometres and again stopped to listen.

The reports were baffling.

Fifty spoor or more? That was incredible . . . if true!

Inspector Nick Peens suddenly came on the air and crisply began giving orders. That settled it.

If Inspector Peens was around, it definitely wasn't an April fool's trick.

Heavy weapons had already been removed from the gun mountings of the fighting vehicles and stowed away in the Blesbok. News of the large scale incursion came as a shock.

While the likelihood of SWAPO sending men over had been accepted, they had anticipated infiltrators would come singly or in pairs, probably wearing civilian clothes and lightly armed with pistols and grenades. They would be people like political commissars, coming to politicise or intimidate the tribesmen into support-ing them. They certainly hadn't expected large numbers of run of the mill PLAN fighters.

Sergeant Labuschagne took stock of his group's fighting capabilities, while the heavy weapons were unloaded from the Blesbok transporter and his men got to work remounting them on the fighting cars.

They had little with which to wage war – a niggardly supply of ammunition for the 50 calibre Brownings and only one belt for each of the 30 calibre Brownings. Normally, they carried a minimum of one spare ammunition belt per weapon – three if trouble was expected. For their personal R-5s each man had six full magazines.

Fortunately, they did not become involved in action, but 'contact' was a commonplace word heard on the radio that day.

At 11:13 the radio crackled into life. Police callsigns Zulu Hotel and Zulu Foxtrot

– Sergeant Herman Grobler, reported the capture of a SWAPO terrorist dressed in civilian clothes and armed with a Soviet supplied Makarov pistol.

When interrogated he gave his name as Filipus Hanawa and said he had infiltrated Namibia the previous evening with two others, crossing the border near Beacon 30.

All three crossed in uniform, but when they realised that police teams were active in the near vicinity, they changed into civilian clothes, cached their uniforms and split up in an effort to evade capture.

The spoor of Hanawa's comrades was being followed in a southerly direction.

Constable Claasie Claasens, leader of police callsign Zulu November, had been on the move with his group since first light, routinely checking for SWAPO spoor along the border in the region of Beacon 18.

Groups on routine patrol when checking for spoor generally move slowly, their speed being governed by the trackers on foot in front of the cars. Yet, because progress is constant, with the trackers rotating and riding in the cars when they get tired, a lot of ground can be covered in a day.

The tracks found that morning, though, hardly needed an experienced tracker to qualify them, because they were not the usual faint traces, but amounted to an almost freshly beaten path leading south.

'How many?' Constable Claasens asked his senior black sergeant.

The sergeant shook his head.

'A lot . . . at least fifty'.

Most were wearing the normal issue SWAPO boots, with a chevron pattern on the sole.

There were several kraals nearby, and some of the black policemen hived off to see the villagers and make enquiries. The locals were friendly and cooperative, and willingly volunteered information.

Yes, they confirmed, the spoor had been made by infiltrators. A large formation of PLAN fighters, all wearing uniform, heavily armed and carrying a lot of kit and equipment, had crossed into the country from Angola during the night.

A terse radio message was transmitted back to control, where it was recorded on the log.

'12:00   Zulu November picked up 50 tracks south of Beacon 18, direction south.
           According to the local population they are in uniform and armed.'

It was clear Constable Claasens needed assistance, and he was told to remain in position until reinforcements arrived.

Police groups Zulu 1 Hotel, Zulu Delta, Zulu Kilo, Zulu Mike, Zulu Sierra and Zulu Tango, were ordered to rendezvous with him.

When operating at full strength a police counterinsurgency group, working on the old Koevoet system, consisted of four Casspir or Wolf infantry fighting vehicles and a Blesbok or Strandwolf logistic vehicle, which carried the ammunition reserve, food, water, general equipment and so on.

Each fighting vehicle, in addition to the personal weapons of the crew – an R-5 carbine and perhaps a pistol each, had fixed weaponry aboard. This was sometimes a 50 calibre Browning heavy machinegun or a 20mm cannon, twin 20 calibre Brownings and a MAG mounted to fire through the front windscreen. Many cars were mounted with 60mm mortar tubes and some even had heavier calibres, depending on the individual fancies of the car commanders or group leaders.

The Blesbok or Strandwolf transporters were equipped with machineguns mounted above the driver's cab.

Most of the heavy weapons had been removed from their mountings the previous night, as ordered, and stowed away in the Blesboks or Strandwolves. In other cases, however, heavy weaponry had been taken off earlier to facilitate normal police patrolling. Unfortunately, some of the weapons had been diverted to other purposes, which left five or six of the cars grouping together for the follow-up, with only a basic minimum of firepower.

The groups' vehicles were below strength, due to the intensification of patrolling during March, which had been virtually without respite. This had resulted in a lot of vehicles being off the road for mechanical repairs.

The operation, because his group had found the spoor, was commanded by Constable Claasie Claasens.

About twenty five vehicles settled down for the pursuit, deployed in a tactical formation of two extended lines, one behind the other, the more heavily armed fighting vehicles in front and the rest, together with the logistic vehicles, at the back. The trackers walked in front, protected by the guns of the cars.

Sergeant Piet 'Hand' Cronje, commander of Zulu Mike, was in the rear line, while his second in command, Constable Nick Coetzee, was in front. The tracks were clear, fresh and easy to follow, but the infiltrators kept breaking into splinter groups, each taking different directions, presumably as an anti tracking measure, but after a while they would rejoin the main group again.

Just after 13:00 the trackers warned that the signs on the grounds indicated the enemy were looking for a place to mount an ambush.

They were right and at 13:21 the enemy sprung their ambush, firing a hailstorm of RPG-7 rockets and armour piercing rifle grenades at the police from short range.

The police had been expecting it and they immediately returned fire. In the first few minutes of hell, though, SWAPO knocked out six vehicles causing heavy police casualties. Five of the vehicles were those from which weaponry had been removed to accord with the peace plan.

Had they been properly armed, one can be sure there would have been less personnel and vehicle casualties, for the policemen's trigger reactions, tempered by the steel of long, hard and unremitting bush warfare, was almost immediate. But fast trigger reaction without triggers to pull, made them sitting ducks.

The trackers ducked quickly into the safety of the cars, which drove straight through the ambush, weapons returning fire with a steady tattoo, while riflemen manning the gun ports began calmly calling out targets of individual enemies they spotted, bringing a hail of fire down on to them.

The enemy were strung out in a V shaped ambush formation over a distance of about two kilometres, sheltering behind bushes, tree stumps or whatever other cover they could find.

They fought back hard and strong, the large number of rifle grenades and the rocket fire from RPG-7s and the throw away RPG-75s, directed at the police, testified they had come sufficiently well armed and prepared to sort out the much feared police Casspirs and Wolves.

Once a car got through the ambush, the crew members adopted their normal shock tactic of circling back, then criss-crossing and milling through the ambush area. While the more obvious targets of enemy seen were shot at, shelter of any description that might conceivably be used as cover, was also systematically raked with fire.

The action lasted for more than an hour, by which time most groups had shot out their ammunition, including reserve supplies, so nothing could be done about following-up enemy making good their escape.

The site of an ambush mounted by a group numbering of about twenty survivors was found to the south west of the contact. The tracks indicated that after getting into firing positions, they suddenly thought better of it and fled the area instead. A total of thirty three SWAPO dead were found in the contact area after sweeps made that afternoon and again on the next day.

One prisoner was captured. No enemy dead were removed from the field of battle that day. They were left for possible later inspection by UNTAG observers.

Most of the SWAPO dead, in this and later contacts, and prisoners captured, were found in possession of propaganda leaflets, designed as an intimidatory measure, to be left with the bodies of Security Force members they managed to kill.

None were ever used for this purpose, because SWAPO didn't get the chance, so their actual propaganda value was nil.

Their very possession, however, showed SWAPO had come for war. The suggestion they had come in peace was clearly a lie. One, which is reproduced in these pages, has on one side a cartoon character of a brutal Koevoet policeman happily cutting the throat of a black civilian. On the other it intimates a Security Force member has fallen prey to insurgents. It warned his comrades in crude terms that one day 'the people will decide to hang or put you before a firing squad'.

Beneath this is a SWAPO badge with the comforting words: 'Freedom' and 'Justice' – some freedom, some justice!

The police, although coming out on top, were badly bruised in this action, for besides losing six fighting vehicles – three damaged beyond repair, something unheard of in South West Africa up until then, Constables Uutafehe Tjiposa (27), of Zulu Alpha and Kriston Israel (28), and George Dawid (26), of Zulu 1 Hotel all died later from wounds.

Others wounded and casevaced were Constables Piet Botha, Constable de Swardt (20) – unluckily wounded in his first contact, 1st Sergeant Thomas Khambanza, 1st Sergeant Daniel Naholo, 1st Sergeant Maiuondjo Kazahe, Sergeant Johannes Likuwa, Sergeant Linus Daniel, Constable Wanekeni Fernando and Constable Sakaria Kornelius.

The heat and confusion of battle can well be judged by reading between the lines of the message snatches as they were radioed back to control and typed into the battle log.

13:21 Zulu November has made contact south of Beacon 18.
13:30 Zulu November had three contacts in the area south of Beacon 18. There is no casevac.
13:54 WL7760 [map ref] – four casevacs all lying. One with stomach wound. At [Map ref] WL7169 1 casevac lying.
14:04 4 vehicles shot out in contact south of Beacon 18.
14:17 Swapol report [they] need all types of ammo in the central area. Swapol also has four lightly wounded and score now five vehicles shot out.
14:26 1 Puma airborne to casevac the injured at the area south of Beacon 18.
14:58 Contact at Beacon 18 possible. 9 casevacs.
15:16 20 tracks south of Beacon 18. SWAPO had laid an ambush for Swapol but had moved away. Swapol is following tracks in a SE direction.

Colonel Kotze, the commander of the SWA Territory Force's 101 (Owambo) Battalion, was expecting it to be a quiet Saturday morning. There was little of his once powerful fighting battalion left. The men had been demobilised and sent home, after handing in all their kit, everything right down to their boots, in to the stores.

The only military personnel on the base were a few guards and those officers whose transfers to other units in South Africa had not already been effected

Transport on the base had been reduced to a basic minimum. The fighting Casspirs had been despatched to Grootfontein about a week before, for eventual movement back to South Africa, after first being stripped of heavy weaponry and radios. The unit's basic military equipment, together with weapons and ammunition, was also crated up and ready to go to Grootfontein.

Colonel Kotze was attending an orders group at Sector 10 Headquarters in Oshakati when news came through that police had been in contact with SWAPO near Ruacana.

Permission had not been granted for the regiment's recall, but the Colonel returned to 101's base to alert his officers and oil the necessary machinery in case it came about.

Then, when it became obvious during the course of the day that a recall was all but inevitable, arrangements were made to put the emergency recall procedures into motion.

A message broadcasting the recall over Radio Owambo, on the hour every hour, in Owambo, Afrikaans and English was prepared. But even without that black troopers and NCOs started to drift in, the news of SWAPO's treachery having begun to spread by Africa's bush telegraph.

By that afternoon there were sufficient drivers around to fill a Dakota, which took off and flew them to Grootfontein, so they could convoy back some of the desperately needed fighting Casspirs, loaded to capacity with weapons, equipment and ammunition.

102 Battalion of the SWA Territory Force, home based at Opuwo in Kaokoland, drew its recruits from the Himba and Herero tribes, together with a sprinkling of Vembas and Jembas.

When the 1st April dawned, the main stages of the unit's demobilisation in terms of the peace plan had been completed.

The unit, a far smaller one than 101 Battalion, was composed of four rifle companies and the battalion headquarters with its infrastructure of signallers, clerks, drivers and so on.

The rifle companies had been demobilised the week before, weapons had been put back in the armoury and all personal kit and equipment had been handed in and returned to stores.

Afterwards the men had left and returned to their tribal homes. The peace plan allowed for a time scale of six weeks from the 1st April, for the unit to be completely evacuated and closed down.

Opuwo is a long way from civilisation, even in Namibian terms, but in spite of that a lot had already been achieved, with much of the transport, stores in general and weapons having already been started on its way back to South Africa, via the SADF's main logistical base at Grootfontein.

The unit's white officers, however, with the exception of second in command and logistics officer, Major Theunis van Staaden, were fortunately, still on the base. Major van Staaden, the only married officer with children of school age in the unit, had left on transfer for Pietersburg, RSA, on the 22nd March with his wife and family. He was returning temporarily to the unit on the 3rd April, to assist with the administration involved in the regiment's shut down.

When news of the SWAPO infiltrations came in, all work on the disbandment, needless to say, was immediately suspended. Unlike 101 Battalion, with their broadcasts on Radio Owambo to recall troops, this was impossible with 102. Kaokoland must surely be one of the last really remote places left in the world today, radio transmissions at best are difficult to pick up and at worst impossible, except perhaps for propaganda broadcasting beamed in by such major stations as the Voice of America, the BBC's Overseas Service and Radio Moscow.

An added complication is that the people are appallingly poor, the tribes very backward – some like the Himbas, being judged as the third most primitive in Africa and the seventh most primitive in the world. So, understandably, radios are not, in any case, commonplace amongst a people where many still wear animal skins, instead of cottons, wools and man made fibres.

The plan for the emergency recall of the unit, involved what would once have been called bush telegraph. Messengers were sent out to the various tribal headmen, who in turn would send out their own people to call back men of the battalion living under their tribal jurisdiction.

The native population of Kaokoland, at its most, is less than 20 000, but they had a highly positive attitude towards the battalion, which was the main source of employment and income within the region.

The battalion was just over ten years old, but there had been little wastage caused by men leaving, even fewer deserting. Men tended to soldier on, and most had proudly worn its insignia since the day the unit was formed. The Kaokoland tribes are, in general, anti SWAPO, which they regard as an Owambo organisation. If it should take over in Namibia, they believe it will harshly dominate and oppress them.

At the end of the day, after word came from Windhoek, messengers were despatched to commence the recall to arms. Arrangements were also put in hand to get the unit's transport, weapons and so on back from Grootfontein.

Police callsigns Zulu 1 Hotel and Zulu 1 Mike, under the overall command of Warrant Officer Jackie Grobler, were far south of the border area near Okatopi on the 1st April, operating routine patrols with small detached sections.

General Dreyer's order that all heavy weaponry be removed from all cars as at midnight on the 31st March, did not apply to Zulu 1 Hotel and Zulu 1 Mike, because they had been on extended patrol for nearly a month, and Okatopi was not a place where problems with armed SWAPO insurgents was likely to arise. Consequently, none had heavy weapons fitted anyway, or even stowed away in the backs of the transporters.

So far as ammunition for personal weapons was concerned, it was doubtful if they had more than ten per cent of their normal holding.

When news of the SWAPO crossings reached them, they packed up everything in a hurry and got on the road back to Etale, where they were needed as soon as possible.

They arrived there late in the afternoon and immediately got to work recovering their heavy weapons from the armoury, getting in ammunition and readying their cars for battle.

Unfortunately, they faced an acute shortage of ammunition, as the groups who had been in the fighting, had shot out just about all ammunition in their vehicles, and so had taken just most of what was left as resupplies.

By the time Zulu I Hotel and Zulu I Mike had finished, every last round had been cleaned out of the Etale armoury. Warrant Officer Grobler assumed command as operations officer at Etale, and became responsible for directing all groups operating from that base.

Inspector Chris Ronne, had been sent from the northern border region to Windhoek with 40 white and 200 black policemen as a precautionary measure in case civil unrest developed between DTA and SWAPO supporters when Mr Martti Ahtisaari arrived at Windhoek Airport on the 31st March.

He heard about the incursions at 11:30, and he immediately asked for permission to return to the north, where he and his men were needed urgently to help stem the SWAPO tide.

They drove back almost non stop, eventually reporting at the Eenhana base late that evening.

For their duty in Windhoek all vehicles had been disarmed while the men had carried sidearms only.

There was much to be done.

Men worked late into the night sorting out weapons, drawing ammunition and generally readying the cars for operational use.

Windhoek – The Other Face of War

The hoisting of the sky blue UN flag in Windhoek, formally marked the first day of the implementation of the peace plan for Namibia.

Early on there was a traffic stopping and noisy, although peaceful, demonstration as more than a thousand SWAPO supporters, wearing party t-shirts and waving flags, attempted a celebration march into Windhoek from Katutura Township.

The SWAPO supporting *The Namibian* said afterwards they were 'workers' organised by the National Union of Namibian Workers and their intention was to march on the residence of the Administrator General.

A single line of riot control policemen blocked their way into the city on the Okahanja freeway. A senior police officer ordered them to disperse, which they did cheerfully, peacefully and without incident.

At the black township of Katutura electioneering started early with a well supported meeting of the DTA and affiliated political organisations taking place, with men and women wearing DTA t-shirts in the organisation's red, white and blue colours.

It was a gala occasion providing much colourful background for the photographers and journalists then crowding Windhoek to write about and record in pictures. Whites mingled happily with blacks as the meeting progressed, while bare breasted maidens in tribal garb ululated to the beat of drums, and Herero women wearing full long dresses and heavy headgear in the style of the early German missionaries, looked demurely on.

At 10:00 Brigadier Johan Louw, Chief of Staff (Operations) for the SWA Territory Force was at home passing the time of a relaxed Saturday morning.

The telephone rang and he answered it. It was Colonel Jan Bierman.

'Are you sitting in your chair, Brigadier?' he asked.

'Why?' Brigadier Louw asked.

'We have problems,' Colonel Bierman said.

He gave him sketchy details, all that was then known, about the SWAPO infiltration to the west of Ruacana. At this stage it was still believed to be an isolated infiltration.

At lunchtime Colonel Bierman 'phoned the Brigadier again. There were reports coming in from what seemed to be all over the border area.

Brigadier Louw contacted both Lieutenant Colonel Doyle Raymond and Major Fernandis, both US officers attached to the US delegation to the JMMC, and told them about the SWAPO infiltration as a matter of courtesy.

He told them propaganda suggesting that SWAPO had long held bases within Namibia had begun to surface, but they both apparently dismissed the idea as preposterous.

Both officers and their predecessors, Colonel Jim Mailey and Lieutenant Colonel Jim Myer, had been keen to see as much of Namibia as possible. During their respective tours of duty, they had travelled the country extensively. In addition to their official duties, which included paying regular visits to all JMMC posts along the Namibian-Angolan border, they had, by all reports, made many friends throughout Namibia. They had also gone out of their way to meet and discuss the Namibian situation with prominent tribal headmen in Kaokoland, Owamboland, Kavango and Caprivi.

The Commissioner of Police, Lieutenant General Dolf Gouws, personally 'phoned the Administrator General at about 10:00 and gave him the news.

There were casualties on both sides.

The Commissioner assured him that his police units were in action and fighting to gain supremacy and control in the unexpected situation. He said, however, that he expected them to cope.

General Gouws and Mr Pienaar were to maintain close contact for the rest of the day.

On hearing the news, Mr Pienaar telephoned Mr Ahtisaari and passed it on. They had commitments to meet each other twice later on in the day, in any case. The first time would be at Eros Airport to greet Mrs Thatcher on her arrival. The second would be when Mr Ahtisaari and General Prem Chand came to his official residence later that afternoon, to be present for a courtesy call by the British premier.

They agreed to stay in touch, all the while keeping a close watch on the situation. Mr Ahtisaari, because of the delays imposed by the so called Non Aligned Group at the United Nations – suspiciously led by Zimbabwe and Zambia and including SWAPO as a full member – on the passing of UNTAG's budget, had virtually no men on the ground. Consequently he was completely reliant on the South Africans for information.

Shortly after receiving the first report, General Gouws contacted the Administrator General again, asking for authority to use SADF helicopters for casevac purposes.

Mr Pienaar contacted Mr Ahtisaari about this request, and he conceded the use was necessary.

After 11:00, as a result of another conversation with General Gouws, Mr Pienaar again 'phoned Mr Ahtisaari to establish the principle of self defence. Helicopters had already been shot at from the ground and Mr Pienaar passed on that he had authorised them to defend themselves. Mr Ahtisaari agreed with the self defence principle.

Shortly after midday, the British premier's Royal Air Force VC-10 touched down at Windhoek airport. The Union Jack unfurled and fluttered from the cockpit as the aircraft taxied in.

Waiting at the airport to greet Mrs Thatcher were the Administrator General, Advocate Louis and Mrs Pienaar, the British Ambassador to South Africa, Robin Renwick, the UN's Special Representative, Martti Ahtisaari, Lieutenant General Prem Chand and the commander of the British signals component to UNTAG, Lieutenant Colonel Ian Donaldson.

It appeared that Mrs Thatcher was unaware of the SWAPO incursion. If she had known, Louis Pienaar believed, she would have mentioned it.

From Windhoek Airport, which is 45 kilometres out of town, Mrs Thatcher was flown by an Anglo American executive jet to Eros, a smaller airport for light aircraft in the city itself.

It was a short flight, only ten minutes in duration, and Mr Pienaar and Mrs Thatcher had little time to talk. He made a brief mention of the SWAPO incursion, but Mrs Thatcher appeared preoccupied and didn't seem to take notice. He concluded she was mentally working through the speeches she intended making to the British UNTAG troops, and to dignitaries at the British owned Rio-Tinto Zinc's Rossing Uranium Mine at Swakopmund on the Atlantic coast.

Up until then, the reports – including the last one he had received before leaving for the airport, still tended to indicate the incident as an isolated incursion – certainly not as the outbreak of a minor war. On this basis he decided the information would keep until Mrs Thatcher completed her Rossing Mine visit, and called on him later at his official residence.

At Eros Airport they parted company, Mrs Thatcher leaving with a UN escort for the SWA Territory Force base at Luiperdsvallei, just close to town, which was being shared with UNTAG.

While there she met Lieutenant Colonel Donaldson's British signallers, and took the opportunity of extending her condolences over the deaths of two of their number who had been killed in a road accident. In her speech she told them the work of their unit could help to determine the future of southern Africa, as it stood 'at the gateway to peace, to freedom, independence and justice'.

After lunch she flew by the executive jet to the Rossing Mine.

Foreign Affairs Director, Derek Auret, and the official party he was with, got news of the SWAPO incursions just as they were going to lunch. It delayed their meal. Then as more reports came in, virtually between each course, their lunch became protracted, with starters spoiled and rare steaks becoming well done.

In the early afternoon a SWAPO rally, its start heralded by a column of motor cars all sounding hooters continuously, began in the veld outside Katutura Township.

It attracted a large crowd of several thousand supporters, including a sprinkling of whites, who joined in the clenched fist salutes and the shouts and chants of 'Viva SWAPO' and 'Viva Nujoma' and 'One Namibia, one nation'.

100

Mr Martti Ahtisaari, General Prem Chand, Mr Cedric Thornberry and various members of the Administrator General's staff met at Advocate Pienaar's official residence before 18:00.

Mrs Thatcher was by then some forty five minutes behind schedule, having experienced a few hitches in her program, but this allowed time for the others to compare notes and update themselves on the situation at the border.

The seriousness of the incursion had not been in doubt for several hours, and no one any longer regarded it as an isolated incident.

While the overall picture had still not clarified, there were reports of incursions and spoor being followed over a very wide front.

It had been estimates that over 150 heavily armed insurgents had crossed from Angola into Namibia.

Mr Pienaar made this clear to the officials with him, that the large numbers made it the biggest single SWAPO incursion into the country in the last twenty years of warfare.

They waited for Mrs Thatcher, their faces grim, all pondering the same question. Would the violence signal the end of the peace process?

South Africa's Foreign Minister, Pik Botha, meanwhile, was at Windhoek Airport awaiting Mrs Thatcher.

Mrs Thatcher eventually arrived at the Administrator General's official residence at about 18:45. After the normal pleasantries and greetings had been exchanged, Mrs Thatcher mentioned what a nice thing the whole 435 operation was. What it meant for the future of Namibia, and ultimately, what it would mean for South Africa itself.

When the right moment presented itself, Advocate Louis Pienaar told her that 'unfortunately he had very bad news' for her.

He briefed her on what had happened.

He noticed concern, real concern, passing over her face. It went through his mind what she was probably thinking. She had undertaken an African voyage, visiting several states adjacent to South Africa, and now she was in Namibia. Her main objective, he conjectured, had been to help South Africa get out of its position of isolation.

Mrs Thatcher immediately understood the importance of the incursion, and its likely consequences to the peace issue.

It wasn't said, but Louis Pienaar, an experienced senior advocate, guessed what was crossing her mind. If South Africa jumped the gun, committed all its forces and threw 435 overboard, then all her efforts to help in the region would be for nought.

Mr Pienaar pleaded with her, saying he was sure the police force could manage and cope with the situation. He emphasised that in terms of resolution 435 it was his responsibility, as the Administrator General, to maintain law and order in Namibia, and he accepted that responsibility.

Having made that clear, he pointed out it still wasn't the responsibility of the Administrator General alone, or even of South Africa alone, to redress the situation. The implementation of resolution 435 had come about as a result of international agreements, endorsed by the international community as expressed or identified by the Security Council.

'It was now the duty of the international community itself to address the problem,' he told her.

Mrs Margaret Thatcher grasped the point immediately and began to speak, referring to the SWAPO incursions as 'flouting the authority of the UN'.

The conversation which by then included the senior UN officials, went on for some time. Mrs Thatcher enquired if UNTAG had the ability to deal with the incursion, but was told they had only a few men, virtually nothing on the ground. They really couldn't render assistance.

Afterwards the party went to Eros Airport, from where Mrs Thatcher was flying by the same executive jet to Windhoek Airport.

At Eros she gave a special press conference, saying to newsmen she was calling for an urgent report to be made by the UN Special Representative, Mr Martti Ahtisaari, to Dr de Cuellar on the incursion into Namibia.

She said the Secretary General should, as soon as possible after a period of twenty four hours, call a special session of the UN Security Council to consider Mr Ahtisaari's report.

Mrs Thatcher referred to the incursion as 'a challenge to the authority of the international community'. She said she intended to bring the matter up with Soviet leader Gorbachev, at talks pending in London during the coming week.

During the press conference Mr Pienaar was called away to the 'phone. It was Foreign Minister Pik Botha, at Windhoek Airport, wondering why Mrs Thatcher had been delayed.

Minister Botha had prior to this spoken to the press at Windhoek Airport, saying the State President, Mr P W Botha, had asked him to contact the UN Secretary General, Dr Javier Perez de Cuellar, over 'this most serious development'. He said he had 'irrefutable evidence' to show that SWAPO was responsible for the clashes.

Using the strongest of diplomatic language he said 'that unless the Secretary General makes his position clear on this flagrant violation of international agreements, the South African government will be left with no choice but to require UNTAG to depart from Namibia until SWAPO can be brought to its senses'.

He added that the SWAPO incursion was a clear violation of the tripartite agreement between South Africa, Angola and Cuba, and a repudiation of the approval the Security Council had given it.

'It also means that SWAPO's undertaking to the Secretary General that it would cease all hostile acts as of 1st April was a farce.'

Mr Botha discussed the incursion on the telephone with Mr Louis Pienaar, making it clear he believed South Africa was facing a serious onslaught. As a result he was considering releasing South African forces from their confinement to base, and moving away from resolution 435.

When Mrs Thatcher had finished speaking to the media, Mr Pienaar privately told her of his conversation with Mr Botha.

'I'm not saying this is policy,' he said, 'but this is crossing the minds of the South Africans. It is an option . . .'

He urged her to discuss the matter with Mr Pik Botha, during her meeting with him at Windhoek airport.

Mr Louis Pienaar and the party of senior Namibian and UN officials who were seeing her off, watched anxiously, wondering if 435 would still be on course by the morrow, as the executive jet sped gracefully down the runway and became airborne.

Afterwards they returned to the Administrator General's official residence, where they remained available and on call for the duration of the Botha/Thatcher talks.

Eventually, Pik Botha had managed to get through on the 'phone to UN

Secretary General, Dr Javier Perez de Cuellar. He apprised him of the situation, making the point that the situation was serious. He said the SWA Police needed assistance, and they needed it urgently. The only help available was from the South African controlled military – UNTAG couldn't assist because they weren't geared for it and not even deployed.

Dr de Cuellar agreed that South African military assistance was vital to normalise the situation.

Just as the telephone conversation ended, the aircraft carrying the British Prime Minister touched down on the runway.

Many of the press corps had stationed themselves at Windhoek Airport, instead of at Eros, and others drove out there afterwards, and they began a tense vigil while the critical talks took place within the terminal building.

Earlier, before news of the SWAPO incursion broke, it had been intended the talks would be wide ranging. Great events of the past years would have been recalled and discussed and South African achievements and successes in various fields underlined.

In the event, after the critical happenings of the day, only one subject was on the informal agenda. Mr Botha briefed Mrs Thatcher on what he had done so far. He said he had spoken to Secretary General Dr Javier Perez de Cuellar and explained in broad terms the approval given for South African troops to be deployed in support of, although under the control of the SWA Police.

During the ensuing talks Mrs Thatcher adopted the stance that, in her belief, South Africa should take care of and firmly handle the counterinsurgency situation. She was insistent, however, that they should stay within the framework of already signed agreements, avoiding unilateral action at all costs.

She made her point with crystal clarity.

Until then South Africa had played the game strictly by the rules, consistently abiding by the letter of agreements – often doing even more than was needed.

SWAPO on the other hand, was the guilty party.

They had undoubtedly broken their part of the bargain, seriously flouting international agreements in the process. This made it even more vital that in the delicate international situation pertaining, South Africa didn't succumb to temptation and take precipitate action . . . and end up sharing the guilt.

The point was well taken by Foreign Minister Pik Botha, but it had been decided already, during telephone discussions with President P W Botha, that South Africa would do nothing without UN approval.

For two hours and many cups of tea and coffee the talks went on, with Minister Botha occasionally 'phoning and speaking to Louis Pienaar or one of the other South African officials with him, to get explanations or gain clarification on matters of detail.

Finally, Minister Botha 'phoned the Administrator General and asked what he could arrange within the framework of resolution 435, to get elements of the military released.

Louis Pienaar and Martti Ahtisaari, together with their officials, sat around the table and began negotiating a plan of action to support and assist the hard pressed SWA Police during the time of crisis.

It did not take long and within twenty minutes rough agreement had been achieved. The restriction to base of six battalions and an air force element to lend support, would be lifted immediately. They would be put under police command and work in close cooperation with the SWA Police.

This, to make the point clear, released the SAAF helicopter gunships for offensive action.

Of vital importance was the principle thereby established that although the SWA Police, elements of the SWA Territory Force and the SADF were not donning blue berets, they would be working with the direct authority of the Secretary General's Special Representative.

They were *de facto* UN troops for the duration of the operation – a definition which will surely be unpopular with certain countries. One wonders what their attitudes will be towards awarding the South Africans, who thereafter took part in operations, the UN campaign medal for peacekeeping!

On Wednesday 5th April, at a press briefing, Mr Cedric Thornberry spoke of that critical night.

'The situation which the UN faced was one which was totally without precedent. We had the alternative of accepting a decision by the RSA to decide that it could no longer be bound by resolution 435, and the settlement proposal and [for them to] deal with what they perceived to be a major threat, with what that decision would entail, or for [UN to agree to] a controlled move out of bases, on a strictly interim basis . . . while it was being assessed.

'I think that must have been one of the most difficult decisions that any Secretary General of the UN can ever have taken.

'And I would not like it misunderstood what those circumstances were.'

The terms of what had been agreed and arranged was conveyed to Foreign Minister Botha at Windhoek Airport at about 22:30.

There was a general feeling of intense relief, knowing that Foreign Minister Botha and British Prime Minister Thatcher had found common ground. It was particularly good news for the South Africans, because the strength and international influence of Mrs Thatcher, who so fortuitously had been on the spot, ensured that recommendations she agreed with would not lightly be gainsaid.

Before leaving, Mrs Thatcher reiterated her advice that South Africa must be careful to remain within the bounds of agreements and that none of its commitments should be dishonoured.

The press had been hoping for a further statement from Mrs Thatcher, but they were unlucky. Photographers dashed after her as she walked briskly towards the RAF VC-10. She paused briefly to allow photographs, then continued on to the aircraft.

UN Secretary General, Dr Javier Perez de Cuellar, had meanwhile made a statement, confirming he had been in contact with Foreign Minister Pik Botha, and saying he would take immediate steps to prevent a recurrence of the incident, in which 38 SWAPO insurgents and two SWA Police members had died in skirmishes in the north of the country on the first day of the UN supervised transition to independence.

Dr de Cuellar said the armed incursion was a severe violation of the Security Council resolution agreed to by South Africa, Cuba and Angola.

Foreign Minister Pik Botha told the press after Mrs Thatcher's departure, that Dr de Cuellar had agreed that because there was a real danger of more SWAPO incursions during the next few days, South African troops should be used to assist the police in 'guarding the border and ensuring the safety of the people of the region'. In terms of the agreement the movement of SADF troops would be subject to 'continuous review and monitoring by UNTAG.'

He mentioned that the Secretary General would be making immediate contact with General Prem Chand.

Asked if the agreement reached with the Secretary General meant his earlier threat to demand the withdrawal of UNTAG had fallen away, he said the agreement was a 'practical and realistic assessment of the situation as it is now. The question of whether the UN resolution 435 independence plan for the territory would continue, will be determined within the next 24 hours'.

Meanwhile, at Louis Pienaar's official residence, hurried plans were finalised and arrangements made for a SAAF Dakota to be put on immediate standby, ready to fly an UNTAG fact finding mission under the leadership of Mr Cedric Thornberry and Brigadier Daniel Opande, the Kenyan deputy commander of UNTAG troops, and two other officials, and a South African team of four officials, led by Police Commissioner General Dolf Gouws and SWA Territory Force commander, General Willie Meyer, up to the border that night.

The Dakota was airborne before midnight.

The office of the Administrator General issued the following official statement:

Border Incursion – According to information received a group of terrorists crossed the Angolan border into Owambo during the night of 31st March-1st April.

One group of between 40–50 insurgents entered Owambo south east of Ruacana, a second group of about 50 at Beacon 18 and a third group of three at Beacon 30 5.

The SWA Police are in pursuit of the insurgents and active contact has been made with all three groups. Casualties have been reported.

The Administrator General said the events were viewed with grave concern, following so closely on the hour of implementation of the independence plan.

Both the South African government and the Special Representative of the Secretary General of the UN have been fully informed.

The Administrator General has personally kept Mr Ahtisaari abreast of the events. The Secretary General has also expressed his serious concern and offered his cooperation by sending a team of observers to the areas concerned.

After consultation with Mr Ahtisaari, the Administrator General arranged for the removal of casualties by Air Force helicopters, despite the restriction to base of Defence Force personnel as from today.'

Special Representative Martti Ahtisaari, made a statement saying Mr Pik Botha and the Administrator General had drawn his attention to 'certain incidents on the northern border of Namibia involving armed incursions and clashes with local police resulting in a significant number of casualties.

'The Special Representative considers this is a very serious development and is giving it the highest priority'.

He said a UN team was being sent to the border, and he expected to have their report by the next day.

The most interesting and revealing words of that dramatic day, however, came from SWAPO leader, Sam Nujoma, when during an interview of Zimbabwe Television that evening he condemned the visit of British Premier Margaret Thatcher to Namibia as 'most unfortunate'. He said Mrs Thatcher should have waited until Namibia had been 'liberated' before visiting the territory. He advised her that 'she should leave immediately'.

Sam Nujoma well knew that only 'negotiating' processes surrounded resolution 435. 'Liberation' processes concern the use of force and armed men and he had only two days before signed the solemn pledge of a ceasefire for the Security

Council of the United Nations. This slip of a word reveals the precise intentions behind him ordering large scale incursions of heavily armed PLAN guerrillas into Namibia on the 1st April.

It appears as if on that critical Saturday evening Nujoma believed his 'armed struggle' and the 'liberation' of Namibia was within a whisker of success and the SWA Police, his only possible stumbling block, was by then on the brink of annihilation.

Perhaps he even confidently expected his unleashed guerrillas to storm southwards so fast and irresistibly that the safety of Margaret Thatcher in Windhoek would be threatened.

Well, if he expected all that, he was directly in line for a sharp and bitter disappointment.

7

Sunday 2nd April 1989

The War in the Bush

After spending the night at the Ombulantu base, Sergeant Fires van Vuuren, group leader of Zulu Tango, led his group along the main Ruacana road until they reached the intersection where the Calueque road heads north to the border and then on into Angola.

This is near where Concor, who were involved in the construction of the Ruacana Dam, had a camp. His car commanders were Constables Derek Kumst, Kobus van Loggerenberg and Kalfie Gouws.

They drove up the Calueque road until they reached the border and then deployed eastwards, seeking enemy spoor.

At about 09:40 Constable Gouws' trackers discovered the spoor of about 40–50 SWAPO insurgents, moving in a south westerly direction.

Assistance was called for and Zulu 1 India, commanded by Sergeant Neil Vincent, with car commanders Constables Willie Meyer, Theunis Kruger and Sol soon made rendezvous with them. Other help came in the person of Warrant Officer Geys of the Security Branch, who brought three Casspirs with him, one commanded by Constable Jakes Jacobs.

They formed a fighting line and with the trackers on foot in front, they began following the spoor.

The trackers believed the infiltrators were about eight hours ahead, which meant they had come in about 02:00 that morning.

After being on spoor for some time, the tracks were joined by those of another group, which was also estimated at being 40–50 strong. This meant there were a hundred, maybe even more, PLAN fighters ahead of them.

Soon afterwards the trackers reported it had become too dangerous to continue following-up on foot, as the enemy were near.

They got into the cars and the fighting line moved forward again.

A lot of men had passed that way and the tracks were easy to follow. Suddenly the spoor split , some tracks going in one direction and others in another. Suddenly there were tracks everywhere, some almost like footpaths or heavily used game trails.

Reports began coming in from cars along the fighting line.

'Another path in front over here.'

'Over here, as well.'

Sergeant van Vuuren knew the SWAPO group ahead was big, so he asked

107

Sergeant Rassie Ras, still manning the control at Ruacana, for gunship support.

The answer was negative, for the moment – the gunships of Major Alan McCarthy and Captain Mario Bergottini were assisting Zulu 5 groups way over to the west of Ruacana. They were ordered to return to Ruacana, refuel and then go out to assist

Zulu Bravo, commanded by Constable Werner Mouton and Zulu Victor, commanded by Constable Duppie du Plessis, were already on their way to reinforce Sergeant van Vuuren.

Inspector Jumbo de Villiers was at Ruacana control when he heard radio reports of what was happening. He decided that as soon as a helicopter gunship became available after refueling, he would fly out with it and act as air to ground coordinator.

He drove to the airstrip.

The police on spoor, still advancing slowly in line, were suddenly ambushed.

Using their new tactics which had become apparent since the day before, SWAPO opened up with a barrage of RPG rockets, rifles grenades and smallarms fire.

'Contact! Contact!'

It was Sergeant Fires van Vuuren on the radio.

While he was speaking, people listening in at Ruacana control, could hear his words being punctuated by the rattle of AK fire and the boof, boof, boofing short bursts of return fire from the police heavy machineguns.

Within the first few seconds, a bomb from a British manufactured 2 inch mortar of World War-2 vintage, scored a direct by the turret of Constable Derek Kumst's Casspir, inflicting serious shrapnel wounds on him and knocking out the car.

A hit on a Casspir of Zulu I India by an armour piercing rifle grenade, killed Constables Josef Andreas and Aktoffel Silvanus.

Others wounded and requiring casevacs were Warrant Office Thomas Nangombe of Zulu Bravo, Constables Dawid Albin and Hidinifa Ndakolo of Zulu Victor, Constable Oscar Hanai of Zulu Oscar and Constable Moses Kaimbi of Zulu 1 India.

Fortunately, the Alouettes of Major Alan McCarthy and Captain Mario Bergottini, had just finished refueling at Ruacana, only ten minutes flying time away, and they were scrambled immediately.

'How about me coming with you?' Inspector de Villiers had asked Major McCarthy.

Well, there was a seat to spare, so why not.

Major McCarthy, however, had underestimated the load capability of his Alouette. He had particularly overlooked that the tanks were brimming with seven hundred pounds weight of fuel and there was also a capacity load of ammunition aboard. Those factors alone, though, wouldn't have mattered, what did was that Inspector de Villiers hadn't been nicknamed Jumbo without reason.

Major McCarthy's Alouette gamely but protestingly laboured its way into the air at about 13:00, struggling to attain an air speed of thirty knots.

Captain Bergottini's chopper, being unencumbered, began running away from his leader, creating a certainty he would soon be left far behind.

Major McCarthy tried desperately to gain height, but he began to realise that with the weight the aircraft was carrying, he was fighting a losing battle.

The policemen down there, to make matters worse, were having a rough time.

They needed air support and they needed it in a hurry. They weren't prepared to exercise patience either.

'Where are those bloody gunships?' an exasperated voice on the radio asked for what must have been the fifth time.

Sorry, guys, I'm coming, Major McCarthy thought under his breath.

'I'll have to drop you off on the road,' he told Inspector de Villiers apologetically..

He gestured at a group of police Casspirs, travelling east on the main road towards the battle.

'I'll drop you by them ... they'll pick you up, okay?'

'Fair enough,' the Inspector acknowledged.

Major McCarthy called up his half section.

'The guys are screaming ... give me minute and I'll be with you.'

He dropped down to the road and Inspector de Villiers deplaned. Lightened like it couldn't believe it, the Alouette leapt back in the air.

The two gunships swept in and across the general area of the contact, while the by now familiar dirty brown puffs of RPG rocket bursts began hunting them around the sky.

Major McCarthy decided a fast climb to a thousand feet would get them away from the main danger and both Alouettes moved quickly to gain height.

Captain Bergottini circled the central contact area in the south on the lookout for targets, while Major McCarthy hunted the outskirts.

Both pilots saw the white trail, but neither knew what it was. It first followed a flat trajectory, then suddenly spiraled upwards as it sensed the heat coming from the power unit of Captain Bergottini's Alouette and greedily reached out to lock on. Fortunately, it missed, probably because the Alouette was too low for the missile to settle down.

Then came another, this time the backblast picked up the aircraft and threw it about violently, so near was the miss. This was their first taste of the Soviet supplied SAM-7, the Strella, a weapon the Russians had supplied to Joshua Nkomo's ZIPRA during the bloody war years in Rhodesia, and which he used to blast two civilian airliners from the sky, murdering many innocent civilians in the process.

Police group Zulu Yankee was racing to the area to throw its weight into the battle. Constable Johan de Lange watched a flare, signalling the presence of friendly forces, shoot into the air and he pointed it out to Sergeant Pretorius.

'About eight hundred meters to go, I reckon.'

Major Alan McCarthy at first saw about twenty insurgents on the ground, then there were more, maybe thirty to forty altogether, all running for cover.

It was a mutual viewing experience, proven by the RPG rockets sky bursting in the vicinity, and the unfriendly zing-zinging of AK rounds really trying not to miss.

Sergeant Bert Steyn, Major McCarthy's engineer/gunner, began selecting targets with a singleness of purpose, dealing with them fully and efficiently, then switching his attention to the next unlucky recipients of his marksmanship.

The gunships orbited the target area, cannons hammering, pilots and gunners working as the most complete of teams, concentrating on the job in hand almost to the exclusion of anything else, but always aware that inevitably, as they circled, they were losing height, making themselves better targets for the RPG rockets.

At 500−600 feet, when the enemy's return fire started becoming uncomfortably accurate, they disengaged and the pilots clawed their Alouettes skywards to regain lost height.

The gunships were devastatingly effective and many of the enemy, who had been caught in the sights of the merciless cannons, sprawled smashed and bloodied on the sandy soil of the bushveld.

Captain Bergottini's gunner had shot off all his ammunition, but his Alouette remained in the area, acting in a supporting role for Major McCarthy.

For the police it was the usual chaos of a contact, the organisation of which, as always, became progressively better the longer the contact lasted, with the insurgents eventually beginning to crumble and bombshell in different directions.

Cars wheeled and circled the contact area, milling back and forth across the veld with guns blazing.

The cars of Zulu Yankee wheeled into the contact area and their guns joined the fray.

Gradually the firing slowed and then began to diminish, until finally it was only sporadic.

Then the checking on who was okay and who wasn't began.

Sergeant Fires van Vuuren called up each of his cars in turn.

'Any casevacs?'

'Negative,' said Constable Kalfie Gouws.

'Negative,' confirmed Constable Kobus van Loggerenberg.

He called up Constable Derek Kumst.

'Zulu Tango Two . . . Zulu Tango One.'

One of Zulu Tango 2's black constables, nicknamed Spinnekop – the spider, came on the air.

'Hey, Sarn't, the commander is hurt . . . really badly hurt. Someone must come and fetch him as we can't drive the car – it has two flat tyres.'

Other group leaders were calling for sitreps and the toll of police casualties gradually became known.

'Two dead over here!'

'When is the Puma coming in to casevac the wounded?'

'There is a real urgency here. Let's get a move on!'

Major McCarthy had kept the Puma holding just to the north of the tarred road, until a safe area could be secured for landing, and the casevacs had been brought in to one spot.

A smoke signal was fired by one of the Casspirs, and Major McCarthy thinking it was an urgent casevac, provided topcover while Captain Bergottini landed his Alouette nearby. In the event, it was a misunderstanding, there was no casevac, so Captain Bergottini took off again. Eventually, once things had been sorted out on the ground, and with the Alouettes providing topcover, the Puma landed. With a hurried efficiency eleven of the wounded were gently, but quickly, loaded aboard.

All the casualties still hadn't been brought in, but the doctor on board the Puma said that some already there were in a very serious condition, and had to be flown to Ondangwa immediately.

The Puma had brought cannon ammunition for the Alouettes to rearm with, but because of the medical emergencies they were only able to dump a couple of cases on the floor of the veld before taking off again.

Major McCarthy decided not to rearm in the area. There was too much sand and dust which could get in the belts and cause jams, so they flew back to Ruacana, which after all, was only ten minutes flying time away.

With the intensive fighting of the past two days, stocks of cannon ammunition held at Ruacana had been reduced to a critical level. On top of that, much of that which had been available was ball ammunition, which is nowhere near as effective as the high explosive variety.

Then an unsung hero, Captain Chris de Beer at Ondangwa, stepped into the breach and on his own initiative overloaded a Kudu fixed wing light aircraft up to its gills with nine cases of 20mm ammunition, taking it far over its weight limit. This created a real danger of it crashing, either during takeoff or while landing.

The groundcrews doing the loading, tried to dissuade him from taking so much, but he insisted that the guys in the field needed it, and needed it desperately, and that in any case, they were all, including himself, flying under operational conditions.

Thankfully he made it, filling the critical resupply breach, and making ammunition shortages at Ruacana a thing of the past.

Back at the contact area, there was no time for niceties, no time for a sweep, the slack for routine things like that would have to be taken up later. There was no time even to count and draw satisfaction from the number of SWAPO casualties – a quid pro quo for their own comrades killed and wounded. But whatever they were, they at least knew SWAPO had taken a severe pasting.

Of more immediate importance was the spoor found – the spoor of SWAPO survivors escaping south.

Police teams Zulu Yankee, Zulu Bravo, Zulu Oscar, Zulu Victor and Zulu Delta, all by then under the command of Inspector de Villiers, regrouped for a follow-up. Wearily they formed up the cars, many of them battle damaged and scarred by bullet strikes, into their usual tactical formation.

Then with the trackers on foot out in front, they set off in hot pursuit.

It did not take long.

'Contact!'

Sergeant Dewald Pretorius had seen an armed enemy in cover behind a tree.

The guns of Sergeant Pretorius' and Constable Zeelie's Casspirs clattered briefly and the insurgent died.

Constable Johan de Lange saw something and was about to bawl 'contact', when he realised it was merely an abandoned pack, together with other things. A black constable jumped down and scooped up the stuff, tossing it into the rear of the Casspir. Constable de Lange's eyes widened more than a little when he saw an unfired SAM-7 launcher together with its ground to air missile amongst the gear.

'Careful, guys,' he warned the rest over the radio. 'It looks like they've still got some big stuff with them.'

The battle line advanced at a steady twenty kilometres an hour. The trackers were back aboard the fighting cars, because were clear easy to follow.

Occasionally, just to ensure they were not being fooled by anti tracking, they jumped down from the vehicles and made confirmatory checks.

They knew some insurgents were hiving off, but they kept to the main spoor. It was impossible to follow everyone, and splitting forces would have been foolhardy.

Then it was back into the Casspirs and off again.

Time was important, time was of the essence. The enemy were fleeing. They had to be caught before they could reorganise, rearm and resupply themselves from hidden caches.

Constable Werner Mouton, Zulu Bravo's group leader, caught a momentary glimpse of movement a hundred meters ahead. It was another armed insurgent.

'Contact!' he bawled and opened fire, killing the enemy with a short burst.

Constable Theunis Kruger of Zulu 1 India, saw another enemy at what seemed eyeball to eyeball range, but before he could trigger and shoot, the insurgent slipped from view as one of the Casspir's monstrous front wheels rolled forward, drew him down, and crushed him to death.

The gunships returned and during their first swing out in front of the cars, Major McCarthy's gunner, Sergeant Bert Steyn, shot dead another insurgent.

They reported to the ground forces that another was waiting in a clearing ahead, his weapon on the ground and his hands raised in a clear gesture of surrender.

'Contact!' another shout came from along the line.

The guns in Inspector de Villiers' and Sergeant Wayne Prinsloo's cars fired briefly, almost perfunctorily, and another two SWAPO were added to the score.

This obviously frightened off the surrendering insurgent, for before a car could reach him, he had snatched up his weapons and fled.

Fifteen minutes later another insurgent was seen.

He slipped the pack from his shoulders and let in drop. Retaining only his personal weapon, he ran for his life, zigzagging and shucking of anything hampering his flight, a trail of kit marking his progress.

But he stood no chance.

He zigged and then zagged, but then zigged back into a short but wicked burst of fire which ripped him apart.

The trackers jumped down and examined the spoor remaining.

A sergeant raised two fingers as a signal.

'Only two left!' he yelled back to the cars.

As he did this, something seemed to happen. It was obviously a combination of the excitement of the chase, the pumping of adrenalin and the successes they had achieved. But whatever it was it caused the trackers to cast aside their normal caution, borne of hard experience.

'Come on!' the sergeant yelled, gesticulating wildly ahead with his R- 5. He started to run, and those on the ground raced after him.

Car commanders shouted out words of caution, but it didn't stop other black policemen, infected by the excitement, from leaping off the Casspirs and joining the wild and headlong hue and cry.

Within moments they were lost to sight in the thick bush.

'Get after them,' came the order.

But, fortunately, they needed no Casspir back-up.

Distant shouts echoed back.

Then a tense yell.

'Contact!'

A rip of AK fire on automatic.

A few short tat, tat, tats bursts of R-5 rifle fire, and then silence. It was 16:30, and the last two insurents had been accounted for.

There was time for only a short and not particularly effective sweep, which makes it probable some enemy bodies were not found.

In fact, according to intelligence sources, SWAPO sympathising villagers buried some of the dead themselves. Yet despite this, the bodies of 27 SWAPO dead were recovered.

Much SWAPO war material was recovered. This included a large quantity of packs containing sets of new uniforms, many AK and SKS rifles, two RPG-7s and a generous supply of rockets, one 2 inch British made mortar tube, twenty 82mm mortar bombs but no tube, and a great variety of other stuff, including ammunition, grenades, webbing, equipment, and so on.

A few days later, Constable Werner Mouton, Zulu Bravo's group leader, captured the commander of this SWAPO group. He said he had brought in 65 men on the Saturday night.

He had expressed disappointed in his ambush, which he had expected would be more effective. According to him, his problems began when the gunships arrived overhead, as this signalled the departure of most of his men, who immediately broke and ran.

After sleeping on the tracks leading from the scene of the previous day's action, Sergeant Piet 'Hand' Cronje, group leader of Zulu Mike, early that morning, sent two fighting vehicles and the Strandwolf supply vehicle back to Etale to collect a much needed resupply of ammunition.

He remained at the contact scene, thinking the arrival of an UNTAG observer team was imminent, but no one came.

Eventually Warrant Officer Jackie Grobler, running the control room at Etale, confirmed that UNTAG weren't coming 'yet', and said that Sergeant Cronje should return with the rest of his men to base. While they were restocking and rearming the cars at the Etale base, Warrant Officer Grobler called Sergeant Cronje into the control room.

He said the combined groups of Sergeant Scheepers' Zulu X-Ray and Sergeant Sarel van Tonder's Zulu Kilo, only seven cars in total, had found the spoor of between 20—40 SWAPO insurgents, which they had already started to follow up. Neither Sergeant Scheepers nor Sergeant van Tonder had much experience, so he instructed Sergeant Cronje, an experienced and capable group leader, to take his Zulu Mike group out to assist, once they had taken on their re-supplies.

Warrant Officer Grobler called Zulu X-ray and Zulu Kilo and said they could continue the follow-up, but they should take it slowly and proceed with caution, until Sergeant Cronje and Zulu Mike caught up with them. At 11h50, before Zulu Mike arrived, SWAPO sprung their ambush at a place about twelve kilometres south east of Etale.

The seven police vehicles were advancing cautiously in a fighting line, when a volley of RPG rockets and armour piercing rifle grenades was blasted at them.

Three vehicles were knocked out almost immediately.

Sergeant Sarel van Tonder's Casspir was hit with a rifle grenade on the front passenger side. It killed the front gunner, and ripped open the driver's face.

The vehicle, in flames and out of control, continued until it crashed into a tree, and ground to a standstill.

The driver, although wounded and dazed, managed to escape and jump aboard a passing Casspir.

The four surviving cars fought their way through the ambush with a dour determination, every gun blazing.

Sergeant Cronje and Zulu Mike were ten kilometres away, when thick black smoke spiraled into the sky, marking the position of the blazing Casspir of Sergeant Sarel van Tonder.

Sergeant Cronje moved Zulu Mike into a fighting line, then bundu bashing at maximum possible speed, they advanced towards the contact area. When they were nearby, Sergeant Cronje called Sergeant van Tonder on the radio, asking for a sitrep.

Sergeant Toti, whose car was amongst those knocked out, replied.

'Sarel is not answering his radio . . . it's his car that's burning.'

The Zulu Mike cars swept in with guns blazing, killing five SWAPO insurgents almost immediately.

Resistance suddenly crumbled, and the ambushers bombshelled in virtually every direction.

Poor Sergeant Sarel van Tonder was found dead close to his burning vehicle.

The criss-crossing jumble of tracks in the vicinity told the experienced black trackers the story of what had happened, as clearly as if it had been filmed.

The enemy had dragged Sarel from his Casspir, although he had resisted and fought back strongly, obviously aware that SWAPO took no prisoners. After a bitter struggle he was finally overwhelmed. They threw him to the ground and battered him to death with their rifle butts. But even after he was dead, they still shot him in the head, just to make sure.

Sergeant van Tonder (24), by becoming a policeman, followed in the footsteps of his father, Major Sarel van Tonder, who is a serving officer in the South African Police. The body of a black crewman lay nearby. He had also been captured, then thrown to the ground and a burst of automatic fire shot into his head.

In addition to Sergeant van Tonder, others killed were Constable Leon Thorne (22) of Nigel, Special Constable Abiatal Nambahu and Special Constable Thomas Johannes.

Wounded and requiring casevac were Sergeant Fernandu Abner, Constable Kankameni Shahange, Constable Shiningweni and Constable Jacob Jolonimo.

When the fighting had died down, a sweep was mounted and the bodies of five dead SWAPO were found. Unfortunately, there were neither the men nor the time to carry out a proper sweep, so it is possible the enemy lost more dead.

By the time the area had been swept, the casualties casevaced and tows put on two of the battle damaged Casspirs, it was late afternoon.

Nothing could be done about Sergeant van Tonder's car, which was still burning furiously, so it was left for later recovery. Sergeant Piet Cronje, from long experience, knew it would have been unwise, because of their depleted numbers, to sleep on the spoor until the next morning, as SWAPO were likely to return during the night and investigate the contact area. So he gave orders for all teams to return to Etale.

The follow-up would have to wait until the next morning.

Early in the morning, just after first light, a force of twelve fighting vehicles and three supply vehicles, drawn from Zulu Golf, Zulu 1 Hotel, Zulu 1 Delta, Zulu Sierra and Zulu 1 Mike, under the overall command of Sergeant Wouter de Kok, headed north from Etale for the border.

The information they were working on was specific.

A prisoner captured on Saturday, had given information that a group af eight SWAPO, based at Umakundi in Angola, had either infiltrated or were about to. He also knew of another 40 strong group who would be crossing into Namibia in the same border region.

At about 10:00 the trackers picked up the spoor of about forty SWAPO heading south.

It was easy to follow, with no signs of anti tracking.

The trackers said it was from the previous night, which was confirmed by tribesmen living nearby. The locals, however, were nervous, because they said the infiltrators were still around in the area.

Alouette gunships were called for.

Sergeant Wouter de Kok and Sergeant Koos Swart were in joint command of the operation.

The cars were formed into two fighting lines, with the supply vehicles in the rear line and the trackers on foot in front.

The lines advanced slowly but steadily across the flat but heavily shrubbed veld.

By 11:50 the spoor had led by them to a stream in the centre of a shona. From there it turned left, going between two kraals. There was thick bush and shrub, with the occasional tall tree, in the vicinity of the kraals. It was apparent SWAPO could be around, because the villagers were not in the kraals although the ashes of the cooking fires were still warm.

This is often a good sign of a SWAPO presence in the vicinity, because the local population, to avoid being caught in the grinder between SWAPO and the Security Forces, invariably run away and hide in the bush.

The fighting line halted and a Casspir on each flank raced to leapfrog ahead a few hundred meters, to see if they could cut the spoor ahead to save time. SWAPO were in ambush, deployed in one long line, immediately ahead of the advancing police. The commander of one of the leapfrogging cars, suddenly spotted the enemy and opened fire.

The ambushers replied with rifle and machinegun fire, mortars, RPG-75 rockets and rifle grenades.

A rifle grenade decapitated poor Warrant Officer Leonard Benjamin, an experienced black group leader, who was on foot in front of the cars with the trackers. He didn't stand a chance.

At the same time two projectiles struck his Casspir. One smashed the diesel tank, severely damaging the transfer case, and the other blasted out a rear wheel.

Another projectile knocked out the car of Sergeant Wouter de Kok, but fortunately he escaped injury.

The moment firing began, Sergeant Koos Swart manning the gun in his car's turret, opened fire, directing short bursts into cover of any description which could even remotely conceal an enemy.

Suddenly, and too late, he saw an insurgent about to fire an RPG-7 rocket.

The projectile exploded car with a roar, but the Casspir didn't stop. Sergeant Swart knew he had been wounded, for he could feel an odd sort of warm sensation in his legs. He dismissed it as minor shrapnel wounds – thanking his lucky stars it wasn't serious, then carried on firing. His driver had also suffered shrapnel wounds, but he fought the wheel, managing to retain control of the Casspir. He glanced back at his commander in the turret, and was amazed to see that Sergeant Swart's right leg had been amputated below the knee and the calf and fibula of his left leg was also gone. He was still manning and firing the gun, completely oblivious to the fact that the missile's core had cleaned off his right leg and nearly amputated his left.

Fortunately, there was little or no bleeding because the projectile's searing heat had cauterised the wounds.

'It could only have been survival instinct,' he said later.

The driver pulled him down inside the Casspir, and made him aware he had been seriously wounded.

Before telling anyone he needed a casevac for himself, Sergeant Swart first called Sergeant de Kok on the radio, telling him to take complete control of the operation, and only then mentioned he had been badly wounded.

The driver drove the car from the immediate contact area to where the Puma would be coming in for the casevacs. Not surprisingly, Sergeant Koos Swart was in deep shock, feeling certain his left leg would have to be amputated as well.

Two months later, Sergeant Koos Swart was eagerly looking forward to getting his artificial right leg. He still had his left leg, the calf of which had been amazingly reconstructed by specialists at 1-Military Hospital, Pretoria, using muscle grafted from his hip.

Sergeant Wouter de Kok's Casspir had also been knocked out, a mere seven metres from the ambush line. Coolly and with commendable bravery, he insisted on retaining command of the combined group. In spite of a constant danger of his Casspir being stormed by the enemy, he remained on the radio for the duration of the contact, brilliantly directing operations and at all times keeping his command under strict control.

Known as a calm and objective group leader, Sergeant Wouter de Kok excelled himself that day.

After the first onslaught, the surviving police fighting vehicles fought their way through the ambush, then turned and began milling and circling around the contact area.

Mortar bombs began exploding at random, fortunately doing no damage. This SWAPO unit had a number of mortars, mostly the 81mm of Soviet origin, and the old British two inch – designed for holding against a solid object, like a tree, and fired at an almost flat trajectory.

Constable Steff Leppan, while under fire, picked up Constable Oppie Opperman, of Volksrust, and other wounded, and took them to the Puma helicopter which had landed to pick up casevacs.

After the casevacs had been flown out, Sergeant de Kok ordered a sweep of the area. This was by no means a routine exercise, as the enemy were still offering substantial, even if erratic, resistance. Some SWAPO elements had taken perches in trees, from where they continued shooting, until they were eventually spotted and shot from their snipers' nests by the Casspirs' heavy calibre machineguns.

In one kraal, four wounded insurgents, asking no quarter, carried on shooting, until, eventually, they were killed.

Although the enemy concentrations of the initial SWAPO ambush and the immediate after fighting were broken up fairly rapidly, sporadic contacts between the police and the insurgents continued over a wide area for the next two hours, as the enemy who had survived, tried to make good their escape.

The sweeps of the area finally ended after 17:00.

The tracks of three insurgents escaping the field of battle, were relentlessly pursued by Zulu 1 Mike, but they were fortunate and escaped capture or death by a hair's breadth, crossing the border into the safety of Angola, only just ahead of their pursuers.

Much booty was captured. There were two Soviet SAM-7 ground to air missile launchers, one recovered from the battlefield and the other from a cache within the base area, a morse transmitter, for communications back to Angola, together with a code book and excellent medical kits containing everything from penicillin to Russian condoms.

In the cache, which the trackers estimated had been there a month, were many brand new uniforms, most still in original wrappings.

There was a large variety, including Red Chinese rice fleck, Kenyan camouflage labelled Made In Kenya, uniforms of Soviet Special Forces, FAPLA and Cuban camouflage and many labelled Contitrades manufactured from Rhodesian camou-flage, overprinted with an additional black pattern. This material must have originated from bulk stocks held in Zimbabwe, surplus left over from the war. Some Soviet pattern fatigue caps had 'Joseph Stalin' badges on them.

The bodies of twenty two insurgents, which included the commander, Oompie Gorbachev, were found at the scene.

The police casualties, other than those already mentioned, were Constables L Sam M Gotlieb and Mwetusa Hishidivali wounded.

In the early morning, the combined groups of Zulu 1 Juliet – commanded by Sergeant Kok, and Zulu Quebec – commanded by Constable Duffield, were seeking enemy spoor in the border region, working on specific information volunteered by a prisoner captured the previous day.

The information proved correct, for at about 10:00 the tracks of some 50−70 insurgents were discovered. They were heading south from Beacon 29, following an old but clearly defined footpath.

Assistance was called for, but initially, groups throughout the border area were fully extended following spoor, some were on the brink of contacts. Gradually, as groups became free from follow-ups, they were sent to join Zulu 1 Juliet and Zulu Quebec.

By 13:00 the follow-up group had swollen to about thirty fighting vehicles. Reinforcements were made up of Zulu Lima – commanded by Sergeant Zeelie, Zulu Foxtrot – commanded by Sergeant Herman Grobler, Zulu 4 Echo – commanded by Constable Drom van Rooyen, Zulu 4 Foxtrot – commanded by Constable Peet Nel, Zulu 4 Hotel – commanded by Constable Boetie Badenhorst and Zulu 1 Sierra.

They were organised into two fighting lines, those in front being the more powerfully armed cars mounted with 50 calibre Brownings or 20mm cannons and those in the rear, which included the Blesbok and Strandwolf transporters, with the lesser armaments.

More tracks led in from other places, merging with the original 50−70 they had been following. Eventually the trackers estimated the combined SWAPO groups ahead numbered well over a hundred.

Eventually, the need for trackers to be on the ground out in front fell away, for the spoor was easy to follow and the enemy had made no effort to conceal their progress by back tracking.

The police stopped at every kraal they passed and spoke to the locals.

They confirmed there were many SWAPO ahead. Some reckoned they were as much as three hours ahead, others thought it was only two.

'Go back, go back,' villagers at one kraal told them in alarm. 'There are not enough of you. You must go back and get more policemen.'

Most were openly hostile and resentful towards the SWAPO incursion, and unhesitatingly provided information to the police.

At about 14:00 disagreement emerged amongst the trackers regarding SWAPO's intentions. The tracks seemed to indicate the enemy had lost common purpose. They were splitting up with people heading off in different directions, which was confusing.

The science of tracking can never be an exact one, even though experienced trackers are often amazingly correct.

Some argued that the enemy were close by, but others, because of estimations regarding the age of a urine patch found, reckoned they were still at least two hours ahead.

The time differential was crucial. If SWAPO were nearby and a contact imminent, then gunships had to be called immediately. On the other hand there was no point making a premature call. Hanging around awaiting a contact that never happened, squandered fuel and valuable flying time – crucial when real action occurred.

The very experienced Warrant Officer Attie Hattingh of Zulu Uniform, and Inspector Chris Ronne, were on their way to join the follow-up force, but were still some fifteen kilometres out.

It was decided to slow down the pursuit until they caught up, for it was evident they were going to need every bit of help they could get. After progressing another fifty metres, a police tracker of Zulu Foxtrot noticed something unusual and asked to his group commander, Sergeant Herman Grobler, to call for a halt.

Sergeant Grobler spoke briefly on the radio and the fighting line stopped.

Both he and the tracker got down from the vehicle and examined the ground. The tracker had noticed donkey spoor. After examining it, they concluded SWAPO had been utilising donkeys for the transportation of heavy weapons and ammunition.

They climbed back in the car and progress resumed. Fifty metres farther on, Sergeant Grobler's car crashed through thick bush into a clearing and was confronted by a SWAPO insurgent, no more than ten metres ahead.

He was holding an RPG-7 rocket launcher at the aim.

It was an ambush.

SWAPO initiated the action, opening up on the fighting line from both flanks, using RPG-7s, RPG-75s, 60mm mortars, 81mm mortars and rifle launched armour piercing and anti personnel grenades.

Six cars were knocked out in the first minute of the contact, two burst into flames.

One of cars that caught fire and subsequently burned out, was commanded by Warrant Officer Epaffra Yambu of Zulu 4 Foxtrot. Before baling out with his crew, he grabbed a 60mm mortar tube and ammunition which he set up in front of his burning car. Within minutes he was pasting the enemy with mortar bombs, which did a lot to turn the tide of battle in favour of the police.

The Casspir of Constable Boetie Badenhorst (24) from Secunda, group leader of Zulu 4 Hotel, was hit by several projectiles, killing him and wounding other crewmen.

The car of Constable Danie Fourie, group leader of Zulu Hotel was another one shot out. Tragically, Constable Fourie (22) of Ladysmith, Natal, was to die of wounds the next day in 1-Military Hospital, Pretoria. His family had a police tradition and his father, Detective Warrant Officer Danie Fourie, is a serving officer in the South African Police.

Constable Kobus Theron's Casspir of Zulu 4 Foxtrot was in the forward fighting line. Everything seemed a kaleidoscope when he thought back later. The first he knew of the ambush was when the Wolf next in line to him opened fire, but he had no idea of the target. Then an insurgent ran across the clearing to his front.

He triggered the 50 Browning, but an RPG-7 rocket struck his car simultaneously. He was thrown back into the interior by a violent combination effect of blast and shrapnel. He had been badly wounded by something passing between his elbow and his ribs.

A second missile blasted the engine compartment and the vehicle shuddered to a halt.

Although unaware of it then, he discovered later his Wolf had been struck by a total of seven projectiles. It is a tribute to the robustness of the Casspir that this fighting car was back in the bush, on operations, only two weeks after this.

He shouted to Constable Martin, manning the calibre 30 Browning that fired forward through the front windscreen, to get up in the turret and take over the 50 calibre Browning.

Every crew member, to a lesser or a greater extent, had suffered shrapnel wounds. Fortunately, most could continue to take part in the battle, firing at the enemy through the car's rifle ports with their R-5 carbines. Constable Martin fired only a few rounds with the 50 calibre Browning, before he, too, was wounded, almost identically to Constable Theron – between his elbow and his ribs.

After some time, it seemed like hours to Constable Theron, a Wolf with an army medic aboard, Corporal Bernard Brumloop, halted next to them.

The badly wounded were taken from the vehicle and given medical attention beneath a tree. Resistance by the enemy was still lively and there was much gunfire, but Corporal Brumloop, in the finest traditions of the South African Medical Service, ignored the happenings around him and concentrated on caring for the wounded. The crew members still capable of it, together with the crew of the assisting Wolf, maintained a steady fire into the surrounding bush, preventing the enemy from storming the cars.

The moment the situation allowed, an Alouette gunship dropped down and casevaced Constable Kobus Theron and Constable Martin, the most seriously wounded, away from the immediate battle area. They were picked up later by a Puma and casevaced to Ondangwa.

Sergeant Herman Grobler knew his car had been hit by a rocket fired by the SWAPO RPG-7 gunner.

He didn't actually register what had happened, but his car had stopped and the interior was a chaos of electric blue flames and choking grey smoke.

Returning fire was a trained instinct.

The twin 30 Brownings were cocked and ready, so he immediately opened up at whatever could be enemy positions.

Luckily, although the smoke hung in the air for a while, the flames had apparently originated from some sort of electrical damage, and the vehicle did not catch fire.

Feeling dizzy, Sergeant Grobler slumped down from the turret into the body of the vehicle and was shocked to see his right leg was almost severed below the knee.

It had probably been struck by the core of the rocket projectile. He took stock of what was happening in his car. It was a bloody shambles, with the crew sprawled about, either wounded or dead.

His black group leader, Sergeant Daniel Teteiko, and Constable Thomas Kandjala had been killed, while Sergeant Linus Nghipandulwa had lost a leg. Many had shrapnel wounds, two had serious eye injuries.

He caught the arm of his driver, Sergeant Daniel Mangala, who was struggling to get through to the rear of the vehicle.

'Where are you going?' he asked. He had thought for a moment the sergeant was trying to escape from the vehicle, but this was certainly not the case. There was a lot of fight left in Sergeant Mangala. All he needed was an R-5 rifle, because his own had been damaged. Grabbing a spare, he climbed to the top of the car and opened fire on the enemy.

The firing intensified and Sergeant Grobler realised the battle was not over. As a group leader he still had responsibilities.

He somehow clambered back into the turret, cocked the action of the 20mm cannon and reengaged the enemy. He fired several bursts, consisting of no more than twenty rounds in all, before the radio cable twisted into the ammunition belt, jamming the weapon.

He attempted to free it, but when he failed he grabbed the twin 30 calibre Brownings, and began firing bursts until the ammunition ran out.

When the battle moved away from his immediate vicinity, he dropped back inside the Casspir and asked Sergeant Mangala for the first aid box. He attempted to stem the bleeding by applying a tourniquet to his grossly injured leg, without much success. He then bandaged it as best he could.

Sergeant Herman Grobler is a trained medic and he made the decision, correctly as medical opinion confirmed later, that his leg was beyond saving. It was badly shattered and much of the bone and living tissue was missing. If he took it off, he stood a better chance of stopping the haemorrhage.

He ordered a constable to pass over his bush knife.

Divining his commander's intentions, the constable refused point blank. Sergeant Grobler was not a man to take no for an answer. He made the request a direct order saying if he didn't obey, he would draw his pistol and shoot him.

The constable reluctantly unsheathed his knife and handed it over.

Sergeant Grobler then amputated his own leg below the knee. He staunched the bleeding, dressed the wound and inserted the needle for a drip.

Having treated himself, he turned his attention to the crew.

He knew the importance of having casualties' blood groups immediately available. It might mean the difference between life and death during a casevac. As group leader he had comprehensive records of this in his car. Despite his wounds, he got down to sorting this out, writing down everything needed, ready for when medical assistance came.

There can be no doubt his clear thinking actions contributed much to the ultimate recovery of his wounded subordinates.

It is doubtful if the actions of this amazingly brave, heroic and modest police sergeant, would have even come to light had his amputated lower limb not been found on the battlefield. Being white and bandaged, it naturally excited some curiosity.

His story was later related in awe by his black police comrades. Men whom he had unselfishly helped, despite being more badly wounded than they were.

Sergeant Herman Grobler didn't believe he had done anything special. To him it was his routine duty as a group leader and as a medic. It was certainly nothing worth making a fuss about. It is of such stuff that the heroes of legend and history are made, but there can be only an elite minority whose bravery matched that of Sergeant Herman Grobler, South West Africa Police.

Despite the initial disaster, the surviving cars maintained discipline and went right through the ambush, their guns hammering out retaliatory fire.

Once through they wheeled, circled and milled around the battle area.

It was a hard fight, but as time wore on, they gradually attained supremacy in what mostly became scraps fought out at point blank range. Then the enemy began to bombshell and try to escape in all directions.

A seriously wounded prisoner, said before dying that he had infiltrated with a 100 strong unit of SWAPO's Far East detachment. Once within Namibia they had joined forces with SWAPO's Alpha Group, which had come in separately.

They were busily entrenching and preparing their base when the police arrived.

Other police casualties were Constable Joseph Fillipus, killed in action, and Warrant Officer Daniel Uyepa, Sergeant Hafeni Neliwa, Sergeant Gabriel Moses, Constable Fillipus Shilongo and Constable Abed Ita, all wounded and casevaced.

The Zulu 4 Foxtrot group – commanded by Constable Peet Nel, suffered nineteen men wounded altogether during this action.

Puma pilot, Major Willie Ras, managed to cram an amazing twenty one casevacs into his aircraft for one flight back to Ondangwa.

A sweep resulted in the discovery of twenty dead insurgents. Much equipment was captured, including 70 backpacks, 30 fired and 20 unfired RPG-75s, 80 anti personnel and 60 anti tank rifle grenades and 30 AK or SKS rifles.

Shortly after first light, Sergeant Wessie Wessels, group leader of Zulu Echo, operating out of Ombulantu, decided to take his group to the border, in the region of Beacon 10, to check for the spoor of infiltrating SWAPO.

His car commanders were Dawie, Morne and Bertus – all constables.

At about 08:00 he deployed the cars into a tactical line, with all available trackers in front, and began working westwards, staying just south of the border but keeping it in sight.

When they were halfway between Beacons 11 and 12, Sergeant Wessels ordered his group to halt, so he could remove a large branch that had jammed beneath his Casspir.

While doing this, the police trackers, impatient to carry on, spread out on foot to enlarge their field of search.

Unexpectedly, Dawie's trackers found enemy spoor, heading south. The tracks were checked by Warrant Officer Emanuel, the senior blackpoliceman, and he confirmed the spoor had been made by ten men. Two were wheeling bicycles. He reckoned the tracks had been made during the night.

Sergeant Wessels reported it to Sergeant Rassie Ras at Ruacana control.

It was clear assistance was needed, and after telling Sergeant Wessels to standby, Sergeant Ras checked around and ascertained that Sergeant Andre Meyer's Zulu Whisky group, was only three kilometres away to the west.

Sergeant Andre Meyer asked for a thousand foot flare to be fired into the air, to mark Zulu Echo's position, and after seeing this, he set out to join them.

'Do you have anyone else in the area?' Sergeant Wessels asked Ruacana control.

'Yes, Pierre, with Zulu India ... he's about eight to ten kays south of you.'
'Roger, I need him as well.'
'Roger.'

Zulu Whisky soon got there, and a quarter of an hour later, Zulu India commanded by the group's second in command, Pierre – a constable, arrived as well. Sergeant Wessels deployed the cars into a fighting line and with the trackers in front, they moved out in pursuit of the infiltrators. The spoor was relatively easy to follow, and by continually leapfrogging the flank cars ahead to cut the spoor, good time was made.

It was, as Sergeant Wessels described it, 'like a hot knife going through butter'.

In spite of this they twice lost the spoor in areas where the ground in the shonas was hard. But after searches, they always found it again. Finally after being on spoor for several hours, they reached a huge shona at about 10:00, it was all of three kilometres long.

The two command cars of Sergeants Wessie Wessels and Andre Meyer, leapfrogged ahead on the flanks to try to cut the spoor ahead, stopping near a large kraal complex. Here the spoor turned due east.

The trackers readied to get back into the two cars, so they could leapfrog ahead again.

Without them realising it, though, SWAPO insurgents had set up an ambush on the far side of a fence that joined the two kraals, only eight meters in front of them.

A tracker suddenly spotted the ambushers. He yelled a warning and it became a mad rush as everyone scrambled to get back in the Casspirs.

'Terrs to my left front,' Sergeant Meyer warned over the radio.

Both Casspirs opened fire. There were two tremendous explosions as RPG rockets or rifle grenades near missed the Casspirs.

Guns began blazing on all sides, as the rest of the cars made a racing advance to catch up with the lead vehicles.

Sergeant Wessels ordered his driver to take the car left, so they could get out of the enemy's field of fire, but they ran into some other insurgents instead, who commenced a hot fire on the car.

Sergeant Wessels ordered the driver to crash through the fence, behind which the enemy were positioned, registering that the fence had been reinforced as a precaution against that happening. But neither the fence the nor its strengthening was a match for the rampaging Casspir, which crashed through it with ease.

Yet such was the confusion reigning, that no one could afterwards say if they had run down any SWAPO cadres or not.

Once through, the driver turned left, smashed through some bushes, went across a muhango land and then turned into a clearing in the bush.

More SWAPO were waiting there, all guns blazing.

'It reached a stage,' said Sergeant Wessels, 'when I didn't know if they were in front, to my side or behind me. I kept firing then ducking into my turret, then firing again. To complicate things, the other cars came in late so I didn't know where they were either, so there was a danger of catching a "friendly" bullet as well. I don't mind admitting, I was really shit scared!'

Soon, though, the battle began to settle down and Sergeant Wessels began regaining control of the situation, allocating sectors to the various cars.

The cars began criss crossing the battle area and milling in the time honoured fashion. Sergeant Wessels' car drove into a muhango land. Standing there by himself was an armed enemy.

The Casspir's guns blazed and he died.

The driver wheeled the car and unwittingly drove straight into and up a large mopani tree stump, which left it helplessly suspended above ground.

The driver tried to reverse and then go forward, but the wheels spun helplessly.

It was not the best of times to be caught like that, because all around was a hell of gunfire as everyone else got on with the contact.

Nearby a Zulu Whisky car, commanded by Constable 'Faan Cubaan', had driven into a huge concealed hole. It was stuck at an angle of 45 degrees and impossible to move out.

Sergeant Wessels knew there was a real danger of the enemy storming his car and killing them all, so he ordered the crew to keep a sharp look out and to continue shooting.

He defended the front, using the twin 30 calibre Brownings.

He tested it experimentally, and was left aghast with the discovery that in the heat of contact, he had expended all rounds. He changed to the 50 calibre Browning, but after firing only two rounds it jammed.

Undefeated, he grabbed his personal R-5 carbine.

He noticed Constable 'Faan Cubaan' gesticulating wildly at him from the turret of his car, which was stuck only eight meters away.

He guessed, correctly, 'Faan Cuban' was worried that some of the enemy might be hiding nearby, out of his vision, readying to storm the car. Sergeant Wessels obliged him by shooting at any cover that might be within blind spots of the other car.

Then he ran out of R-5 magazines, so he unholstered his personal pistol and continued shooting with that.

During a lull, he rooted about inside the car and discovered an ammunition belt for the 30 Browning, so he reloaded that and resumed firing.

Smallarms fire sometimes rattled against his turret, but he didn't know if it came from friend or foe, as police fighting vehicles were shooting and milling around in the vicinity.

He decided to play safe by firing then ducking, firing then ducking.

His radio was unserviceable, probably damaged from the impact, so he had no means of communicating with anyone, and in a broad sense, knew nothing of what was going on.

He discovered a smaller radio, and between bursts fiddled to connect it, finally regaining communications with the other cars towards the end of the contact.

'Okay, guys, let's not go mad,' he said coming back on the air. 'Let's clear the area nice and easily without taking risks. Get the trackers to check for spoor while you are doing it.'

It was thick bush and little was openly visible, so everyone was amazed when a total of twenty five enemy dead were found. One prisoner was captured.

Sergeant Wessels' car remained well and truly stranded – a wrecker was eventually sent for and used to coax it off the stump.

Sergeant Wessels ordered a 360 degree check to be made for spoor around the contact area.

Zulu Whisky and Zulu Juliet found the tracks of two survivors, which indicated they had first crawled, and then got up and ran in an effort to get away. Unluckily for them, they were no match for the cars which quickly caught them up and killed them.

This raised the total of enemy dead to twenty seven.

Remarkably, the police casualties were light, which only two men suffering minor shrapnel wounds. Large quantities of SWAPO kit and equipment was recovered from the contact area. There were several SAM-7s, 2 RPG-7 and many RPG-75 rocket launchers, a large quantity of AK rifles, a British mark vii mortar tube, three 60mm mortar tubes and many armour piercing and anti personnel rifle grenades. There was a multitude of packs, some contained up to three sets of different patterned brand new uniforms still if their original wrappers.

At 14:00, which was the earliest a Puma could be spared, Warrant Officer Corrie Prinsloo and his tracking group of nine men, were airlifted into the mountains and dropped in the area where Sergeant Zaako and his men were ambushed on Saturday. Their orders were to find the three missing policemen.

Inspector Ben Vermaak, flew as an observer in a Bosbok spotter aircraft, but because of the rugged terrai below he was unable to be of much help.

Such was the terrain, that considerable difficulty was experienced in locating the actual contact area and after searching for two hours nothing had been found.

Eventually, after a thorough coverage downwind of the area where it was suspected the contact had taken place, the searchers located the bodies of two of the missing policemen by smell.

It was easy to see what had happened. They had been in the lead when the group walked into the ambush. The ambushers had selected an almost perfect position, it was on high ground with the sun behind them and shining directly in the eyes of the approaching policemen.

They hadn't stood a chance.

Fire had been opened at almost point blank range.

SWAPO had stripped the bodies of their webbing equipment and had taken their R-5 rifles.

From the signs it was possible to read what had happened. When the ambush was sprung, the six police survivors immediately returned fire, causing the ambushers to split into two groups, one lot escaping to the west and the others to the east.

The was no trace of the third missing policemen.

Fanning out from the contact area Warrant Officer Prinsloo's men began checking for blood spoor. They suspected their comrade had been wounded, but had managed to get clear of the contact area.

They finally found some blood flecked leaves, indicating someone had fled in a northerly direction.

Four hundred metres farther on, they discovered some items of abandoned SWAPO webbing.

They spread out and began a detailed search of the vicinity.

It was not long before a tracker found an unarmed insurgent hiding in the grass. He surrendered immediately. He had been wounded in the leg during the engagement with Sergeant Zaako's group.

He told how his comrades had abandoned him in the veld, taking his AK, his webbing and even his food and water with them.

They had left him to die because he needed assistance to walk.

Not surprisingly he was suffering from a raging thirst.

After this had been satisfied, he was helped to a LZ where he was casevaced by helicopter.

On interrogation he revealed his group had been told before infiltration they were going to a base within Namibia. The commander didn't say where, but mentioned he would consult with UNTAG who would advise him what to do and where to go. He mentioned a group of 80 SWAPO, based at Umakundi, just inside Angola, and another unit of 40, and said both had either infiltrated already or were on the verge of it.

From there SWAPO tracks heading out of the area were followed. These led to where the gunships had seen action late on Saturday where they found the body of an insurgent. According to papers on him, he was a detachment medical officer.

He had with him two AK carbines, an R-5 rifle and a SAM-7 complete with missile. One AK was apparently his own, while the other was probably that of his wounded and subsequently callously abandoned comrade. The R-5 belonged to one of the policemen killed in action the previous day.

The body of the remaining policeman was found a few days later, about 400 metres away from where the others had been discovered. The signs indicated that he became separated from the rest during the ambush. Unfortunately for him, it seemed the SWAPO escaping the contact area had bumped into him and shot him dead.

The bodies of five insurgents, who probably numbered amongst his killers, were located deeper in the mountains, together with a lot of kit, arms and equipment.

They were gunship kills from the previous day.

Because of the emergency situation prevailing along the border, this remote and difficult contact area wasn't properly swept during April, so it is probable the bodies of other SWAPO casualties were not found.

Constable Chips Bosman really couldn't believe his bad luck.

Sure everyone stationed at Opuwo had to take their turn on the roster as canteen and pub manager. It was fair, and anyway he didn't really mind. He was young and it was something new to learn. As a career policeman the more experience he gained in administration the better.

But why Friday 31st March?

What a day to post him in from Constable Jimmy Botha's group, Zulu 5 Echo.

He had heard about the incursions on Saturday morning from Lance Corporal Jose Saayman, a SAMS medic attached to SWA Police, who had sought him out and told him.

'It sounded like the whole of SWAPO had come in, from what he told me,' he said later.

He spent the rest of the day alternating between the canteen and pub – where his duties lay, and the radio room listening to ongoing operations – where his heart lay.

He just couldn't handle being in the quiet backwater of Opuwo, when all his mates were operational out there in the bush.

He had been in the operational area since June 1988 – a whole ten months. Since then he had been highly trained in counterinsurgency. All those hours, days, weeks and months preparing for when SWAPO came. Now they had come, but instead of being out in the bush, he was back at camp planning meals and checking to see there was enough beer around to wet the throats of the others, when they came back to tell him war stories.

He could hardly contain himself until Inspector Peens returned that evening.

'Sir,' he said, 'this bloody canteen aint so important as what is happening out there.'

Inspector Nick Peens, a seasoned warrior himself, understood his feelings.

'Okay, I'm returning to Ruacana tomorrow. You can go with me.'

'I was in my seventh heaven,' Chips Bosman recalled afterwards.

Six battalions of the SWA Territory Force were reactivated for service by agreement between the Administrator General and the Special Representative of the UN Secretary General.

The numbers of many battalions were bandied about in the press and elsewhere in the first few hot days of war in April, and much confusion was created as a result. Many overseas journalists, eager to file a story showing that South Africa was cheating on the arrangements, began adding up numbers and decided a lot more than six battalions had been reactivated.

The confusion was caused a lack of understanding of the nature of the 5 series battalions, 51 based at Ruacana, 52 based at Oshakati, 53 based at Ondangwa, 54 at Eenhana and 55 at Napara in Kavango.

These battalions were, in effect, front line headquarters, rather than battalions of troops in the true sense. Troops to man them came in rotation from various sources in the SWA Territory Force and also from the SADF. They had no soldiers, however, who would have called them 'home.'

The effect was that when in terms of resolution 435 troops were confined to bases, the 5 series bases were emptied of troops who returned to their various home bases, wherever that might have been, for confinement or demobilisation, depending on the unit in question.

When the 5 series battalions were reactivated, five companies of troops had to be found for each, and found in a hurry, and a greater mixture of units resulted than there had ever been before.

51 Battalion, for instance, found itself staffed by a company from 911 Battalion, two companies from 201 Battalion, a company from 102 Battalion and two companies from 101 Battalion. In support they had a combat team and an armoured car squadron from 61 Mechanised Infantry Battalion.

The other 5 series battalions had similar personnel makeups during the April emergency period.

To achieve this companies were drawn from various battalions almost at random, but most of them, except for 101 and 102, remained with most of their men still subjected to confinement to base, as demanded by resolution 435.

The battalions of the SWA Territory Force, are mainly tribal in foundation. 101 is principally Owambos, 102 consists of the Kaokoland tribes, 201 and 203 is made up of Bushmen, 911 is a mixture of all eleven population groups and 202 consists principally of Kavangos.

All day appeals for the recall of 101 Battalion were broadcast by *Radio Owambo*, and men began drifting in and reporting for duty, first in dribs and drabs, then in ever increasing numbers.

By Sunday morning they had fourteen Casspirs back from Grootfontein, and every man who could be spared was engaged in refitting weapons. After that they were taken to Oshakati, where radio technicians got down to refitting radio equipment.

126

Finally, after the guns had been test fired, four tracker teams were deployed into the bush, two to eastern Owamboland and two to the west, to assist the police in the hunt for SWAPO insurgents.

The tempo at the base didn't slow down, if anything it quickened, as more vehicles and equipment began to roll in from Grootfontein.

When a man reported in for duty, he was immediately sent to the Quartermaster's stores. The only kit available was that which had been handed in when the unit was demobilised, and this lay around the stores in great unsorted and untidy heaps. They rummaged amongst this, sorting themselves out with basic issues of uniforms, collecting webbing sets and taking footwear from a mountain of boots, until finally, they drew their personal issue R-5 carbines.

On this day alone the hospital at the Ondangwa air base handled fifty seven battle casualties.

There was a desperate need for blood and a call was made for donars, virtually everyone volunteered. This, of course, is normal in the front line, because men feel very close to the war. The problem was that blood couldn't be taken from everyone. Pilots, for instance, had to maintain a high state of readiness, and giving blood degrades them for some hours. The same applied to men on base security duties.

Ondangwa itself could easily have been under threat, and if a man was on his feet, the giving of blood adversely affected his alertness.

There was a unit of Parabats on the base, a small reaction force, they were there for emergency tasks like search and rescue. Their services were utilised to unload casualties from the Pumas and take them into the wards, because the medics were fully occupied either in the hospital or out in the field with the casevacing helicopters.

Every available man on the base who could be spared from his normal duties, was diverted to the prime task of helping the wounded.

Service wives were roped in to help with casualties, and assist those giving blood. Others volunteered to look after the children of the wives working at the hospital.

At times it was chaos, with men lying on stretchers on the hospital lawns being given initial treatment. When darkness fell, emergency lighting was rigged up to illuminate the general area.

The majority of casualties were seriously wounded, having fallen victims to SWAPO's heavy weaponry, like RPG rockets, rifle grenades and mortars.

The intention was to treat and stabilize them, then where possible, fly them out that evening to 1-Military Hospital, Pretoria, so the hospital was free, cleaned up and ready for the next day's casualty intake.

The casualties for Saturday had been flown out to South Africa by a Flossie C-130 transport, at 02:00 that morning.

All day the aircraft that could be spared, flew topcover over the base keeping a watchful eye for insurgents, in case they were in the area, shepherding in and protecting aircraft as they landed or took off.

A black policeman was sitting quietly on a stool, a hand holding his bandaged face. He had lost an eye and was in pain.

There was the wap, wap, wapping of rotor blades as a Puma came in to land.

It was more casualties, they seemed endless.

The Parabats ran out carrying stretchers to bring them in. It was not what they had been trained for, but they had proven that above being the toughest of fighters, they ranked amongst the most gentle of men. A white policeman was stretchered in, there was no question of it, he was very badly wounded.

He opened his eyes and saw the black policeman.

'Piet!' he called out hoarsely.

His face adopted the broadest imaginable smile, reflecting relief that no one could misunderstand.

The black policeman returned that broad smile.

They just stayed where they were, he on his stool and the white man on his stretcher, laughing and grinning at each other, each of them so glad the other was still alive.

Yet, in spite of the seeming chaos of casualties, the one organization fully prepared and ready to meet any emergency, by reason of their organisation in Namibia and the Republic of South Africa, was the South African Medical Service – SAMs.

In medical parlance there is a term known as the 'golden hour'. When a man is wounded, an imaginary clock begins ticking away the precious seconds and minutes of what could well be his last hour of life.

For 90% of those who die, do so within sixty minutes of being wounded.

It is within this vital time span that most lives are saved, when medical competence and know-how count for more than anything else. Get a patient past that first hour, and it is probable he will recover and live on to a ripe old age.

This chain of recovery and procedures to prolong the life of a wounded man beyond the golden hour, begins with every fighting man in the field. Each has been trained in basic first aid, or as it is better called, buddy aid. First aid, as a term, can sound unimportant, even boring, to a recruit who is in a lecture room far from the strident clash of battle. Buddy aid, however, impresses that if he doesn't pay attention to lectures, he could end up responsible for a buddy dying from his wounds.

'Medic!' is the first call a man makes when his buddy is wounded.

While awaiting the medic, he will be capable, on his own, of stopping bleeding, maintaining an airway and immobilising the patient.

He will be entrusted with the first five minutes of the golden hour until the medic arrives and takes over.

The field medic, or to give him his full title, operational medical orderly, is the next and perhaps the most vital link in that chain of casualty survival. By agreement with UNTAG, SAMS medics were supplied to police sections, although the police also had some of their own.

They are highly trained in buddy aid procedures and much more. They can give resuscitative life saving procedures, administer drips and perform minor surgical procedures, like a tracheotomy, or others of a life saving nature.

If a patient is suffering from a thoracic wound, leading to a tension numothorax, then he will die unless immediate remedial action is taken. To meet this emergency, medics are trained to insert a needle into the patient's chest cavity and drain off air and blood trapped inside. This is done via an underwater system, which prevents air being sucked back in.

Medics can administer drips into venous or arterial systems in both upper and lower limbs, and inject pain killers and other substances.

The medic's sacred trust is restricted to treating the patient for fifteen minutes of that golden hour.

The next link in the life saving chain is a doctor, in all probability a young national serviceman. He will have completed his medical training and spent a year or two working in advanced emergency type situations, probably a casualty department. In addition he will have completed a military medical course, where the foremost medical experts in South Africa, will have trained him on the treatment of high velocity and explosive's injuries, as well as on things like trauma and shock. Some will have taken courses in aviation and diving medicine and maybe a few on the medical aspects of psychological warfare.

This doctor will go with the helicopter, usually a Puma, when it flies in to casevac the patient. This happens within twenty minutes of the patient being wounded.

While en route to the contact scene, he will establish radio contact with the medic on the ground who will brief him on the kind of injury he is dealing with. It might be a chest wound, a head injury, the amputation of a limb or anything else. The doctor will advise the medic to stem bleeding, check blood pressure or assist with whatever other medical support is called for in the circumstances.

The doctor will also be relaying information back on definite surgical procedures, blood groups and so on, to assist in the preparation of a theatre for surgery. This might be to a base hospital, or otherwise to a field hospital at a tactical base, set up in a forward area to retain medical care within the golden hour's time limitations.

Having picked up the casevac, the doctor continues treatment in the helicopter, doing whatever can be medically done to help the patient before he is actually wheeled into the operating theatre, after which the surgeon takes over.

To maintain this high level of doctor availability in the field, the South African Medical Service works on a ratio of at least one, although it is usually two, per company of troops. In remote areas where distances are extreme and troop dispersal scattered, doctors are often maintained at a level as high as one per platoon of thirty men.

Their positioning in any operational area is carefully calculated, so a wounded man, no matter where he is, can be placed safely in a doctor's hands within the mandated twenty minutes.

When looked at in isolation, this is no mean achievement for there must be many people falling victim to road accidents in South Africa, who remain without medical attention for periods much longer than that.

Of course, and this must never be overlooked, this high degree of medical attention given to casualties in the field, would have been impossible but for the high degree of efficiency and dedication of the SAAF helicopter pilots actually doing the casevacs.

Once at a base hospital like Ondangwa, or even at a forward base hospital, the most sophisticated medical facilities are available. Available, too, are some of South Africa's most eminent medical specialists, who as Citizen Force volunteers, make up medical teams there.

To give an example of facilities available, Ondangwa Hospital has two fully equipped surgical theatres, two wards and a large facility able to deal with any laboratory situation, electrolyte balancing, cross matching etc.

Whole blood, no matter how extreme the emergency, is routinely checked for venereal diseases, hepatitis and aids, so no hangover tragedies can occur as a result of battlefield exigencies.

This, it must stressed, was until relatively recently, a calculated risk which had to be taken during times of war. A risk which is undoubtedly still omnipresent in many countries of the world.

Once a patient had been stabilised at Ondangwa Hospital, or its equivalent elsewhere, they were normally flown by C-130 transport aircraft to 1-Military Hospital, Pretoria, under a doctor's supervision if deemed necessary. This hospital is recognised as being amongst the most advanced in the world, so far as military medicine is concerned.

When the massive SWAPO incursions occurred on the 1st April, fully manned medical facilities in Sector 10, the military area in Namibia facing the onslaught, were in operation at the Ondangwa and Oshakati base hospitals. With UNTAG's permission this was quickly expanded.

Six battalion size sick bays were activated at Opuwo, Ruacana, Ondangwa (two), Eenhana and Otjivelo, together with fourteen company size sick bays.

Doctors and medics staffed the company clinics. But other than in remote areas, as has already been explained, platoon and section level medical facilities were manned by medics.

When things blew up, 6 National Service doctors and 20 operational medics, and 28 doctors and 62 operational medics from Citizen Force battalion groups, were placed on standby.

Five doctors and ten medical orderlies were flown in from South Africa on the 1st April, to reinforce Ondangwa's medical staff.

The first medical reinforcements were drawn from the more readily available Permanent Force and National Service doctors and medics.

Two Citizen Force battalion group surgical teams on routine standby were deployed shortly afterwards. Teams are always on standby in South Africa and available on 24 hour call to be flown out in an emergency. A surgical team is made up of a surgeon, an anaesthetist and sometimes an orthopaedic surgeon.

Of those remaining, some were deployed in the operational area as the needs of the developing situation dictated, and some were not. Some were posted to 1 Military Hospital, Pretoria, to assist. With the inflow of battle casualties, the staff at that establishment were working under tremendous pressure.

Going hand in hand with treatment of the trauma of physical injury, are preventative rehabilitation measures in the physicological and welfare fields. Wives and parents are notified as soon as is possible, for it is now accepted as vital that the family and next of kin be involved in the treatment and rehabilitation process.

When considered necessary, families are flown to Pretoria and accommodated, so they can be at a patient's bedside.

The Goebbels' Factor – SWAPO's Propaganda War

In a statement issued in Luanda, SWAPO denied that PLAN fighters had 'launched a military raid on South African troops'.

It said clashes had been 'initiated by the SADF' which had been engaged in hunting down SWAPO guerrillas ... before the beginning of the confinement to bases of SWAPO and South African forces ... SWAPO forces fired only in self defence after being hunted down and attacked'.

The statement said SWAPO forces were under 'strict instructions not to initiate any act of military hostility in violation of the ceasefire agreement which came into effect on April 1 ... It is the ernest desire of SWAPO to scrupulously observe the terms of the ceasefire agreement'.

It continued by saying that UNTAG should move swiftly to 'demobilise and confine to base the former warring troops'. It added SWAPO had already invited an unnamed 'UNTAG force commander' on 22nd March to discuss the demobilisation and confinement to bases of troops.

The statement was referring only to Namibian Security Forces, and not to SWAPO.

It said, and here was the catch, that 'SWAPO was ready to play its part' to avoid more clashes by 'moving all armed PLAN combatants inside Namibia to places or bases of confinement'.

The statement, according to *The Namibian*, confirmed that on Friday 31st March, Nujoma 'had visited the border area to issue ceasefire directions to combatants'.

In an obvious move to blacken the Namibian Security Forces, the statement claimed that 'eight civilians were shot [dead] and several injured by shots fired from SA military helicopters'.

It then had the gall to stress that this underlined 'the urgency for UNTAG to supervise the ceasefire agreement with seriousness and a sense of urgency . . . The military skeleton of 1 000 UNTAG troops is far from being adequate to deal with the situation'.

Sam Nujoma, shedding crocodile tears while addressing west European parliamentarians in Harare for a conference on Namibia, said SWAPO was 'shocked and dismayed' that Mr Martti Ahtisaari had permitted the use of 'the very forces [101 Battalion] against which we asked UNTAG to protect our people from – to once again kill and main our people'.

He demanded an explanation from the UN Secretary General.

He confirmed his actions in voluntarily ordering a ceasefire in September 1988, and said his undertaking in this respect had been 'honoured to the letter'.

Sam Nujoma confirmed that after receiving his part of the identical letter relating to the ceasefire from the UN Secretary General on the 29th March, he had addressed SWAPO combatants on the subject, which as has already been indicated, probably took place below the 16th parallel.

He said 'SWAPO is committed to honour the letter and spirit of that ceasefire. However, we are aware and we have . . . evidence that South Africa has her own schemes. We have already warned the international community about these schemes'.

He spoke of 'the schemes' mentioning South Africa had often said they would not allow the 'red flag' to fly over Windhoek. He said South Africa's strategy was to 'engineer and set off events that will lead to the abrogation of the transition process, but without appearing to be the culprit'. He suggested they would use Koevoet and the SWA Territory Force to 'prevent SWAPO from forming a government'.

He described Pretoria's allegations that SWAPO had violated the ceasefire as a 'figment of its imagination . . . SWAPO forces are strictly ordered to observe the ceasefire. In this case, they were attacked inside Namibia and only responded in self defence'.

He repeated his denial that SWAPO forces had crossed into Namibia and accused South Africa of 'massacring SWAPO supporters'.

The BBC London, however, didn't add to the propaganda war and got it right in their 11:00 news in brief which said: 'Senior Police officers in Namibia reported that fighting between special forces and SWAPO guerrillas is continuing. It has been reported that more than 400 SWAPO entered Namibia. Mortars, AK-47s, SA-7 missiles have been captured. No SWAPO statement has been released. A UN team has been flown to the contact area. It was agreed that SWAPO and RSA troops would be confined to bases as from 1st April. As a result of the situation UN and RSA have agreed that SA army units would be allowed to leave bases to assist police. 40 people have been killed so far in the fighting'.

The United Nations and UNTAG

The UN team of four officials, headed by Mr Cedric Thornberry and Brigadier Daniel Opande of Kenya, and accompanied by SWA Police Commissioner, General Dolf Gouws, SWA Territory Force Commander, General Willie Meyer and two other Namibian officials nominated by the Administrator General, landed back at Eros Airport just after midday, where they were besieged by journalists.

Sources at the border told the author afterwards that the teams had arrived early in the morning on Sunday, in time to question two prisoners and examine the bodies and weapons of the SWAPO dead.

It was said that Brigadier Opande, understandably, showed a high degree of embarrassment when it was pointed out that some of the SWAPO dead were dressed identically to himself, in Kenyan camouflage.

It was unfortunate for the Kenyan image, that Brigadier Opande, as the deputy to General Prem Chand and responsible for deciding which areas the various nationalities of UNTAG troops should be sent, had allocated the central area of Namibia – Windhoek and places far removed from the border, to the Kenyan detachment.

If they had been allocated the border area, one can imagine the confusion that would have been faced by the police and those helping them, every time they spotted someone wearing Kenyan uniform.

Was he SWAPO, or was he Kenyan UNTAG?

Unavoidably, the reasons behind Brigadier Opande allocating his troops areas well away from the border, and as a consequence the fighting as well, becomes a matter for conjecture as do other matters which came out later.

The intriguing question of how and why SWAPO possessed any Kenyan uniforms at all, has never been satisfactorily explained. A Kenyan lieutenant colonel, a staff officer at UNTAG's Windhoek headquarters, told the author that Kenya was proud of its camouflage uniforms, so consequently, they were sold to many countries.

This does not ring true, however, because states normally, and for self evident reasons, make every effort to keep bulk stocks of their uniforms away from other countries. For instance, what would the likely reaction of Britain or Soviet Russia be, if either put in an order to the other for the supply of enough uniforms, to equip, let's say, a battalion of troops.

Africa with its history of coups, counter coups and double cross coups, is even more sensitive to uniforms being freely available.

132

The Kenyan lieutenant colonel couldn't say, and it is a pity the Kenyan government hasn't been officially asked by the UN in the interests of UNTAG impartiality, exactly which countries they have supplied their uniforms to.

Cedric Thornberry, described by one newspaper as grim faced, when asked about the situation, replied: 'Hmm ... it's dark but I can't qualify that now'.

When pressed by reporters he said impatiently: 'Come on, give me a break, I have to report this to the Special Representative'.

The Other Face of War

Late in the day, the Administrator General issued a statement:

> The investigating teams, consisting of four representatives each from the Administrator General and the Special Representative of the Secretary General of the United Nations, returned from the border areas in the afternoon.
>
> Later the Administrator General and the Special Representative, accompanied by their aides, held discussions. The Administrator General will now report to the South African Government.
>
> Meanwhile the Administrator General remained in close liaison with the Special Representative.
>
> The Administrator General gave the assurance that appropriate steps were being taken by SWA Police, supported by army units released from base, as agreed with the Special Representative, to control the situation.

First thing that morning, Mr Botha despatched an urgent letter to UN Secretary General Javier Perez de Cuellar regarding SWAPO's violation of the ceasefire agreement. It read:

> With reference to our telephone conversation of 1st April 1989, I have to inform you that a grave situation has arisen on the northern border of Namibia as a result of continued and escalating violence by SWAPO of the agreement signed in New York on 22nd December 1988 by the Peoples Republic of Angola, Republic of Cuba and the Republic of South Africa.
>
> The incontrovertible facts are:
>
> (i) During the night of 31st March 1989 and on 1st April 1989 an estimated 600 to 800 SWAPO elements crossed the border from Angola into Namibia. This figure could be as high as 1000 men. They are heavily armed with AK-47 semi automatic rifles, mortars and even ground to air missiles. These elements entered the territory in their uniforms.
>
> (ii) On the basis of information obtained from those captured, SWAPO elements were ordered to cross the border into Namibia in uniform and under arms, inter alia, in order to establish bases in Namibia. They claim that their commanding officers informed them that as a ceasefire was in existence they need not fear resistance. Should resistance be encountered the UN would take care of them.
>
> (iii) Reliable information indicates that between 4 000 and 5 000 SWAPO elements are presently below latitude 16 degrees south.
>
> Mr Secretary General, this inexplicable action on the part of SWAPO constitutes a clear violation of agreements reached between South Africa, Cuba and Angola.
>
> These agreements were endorsed by the Security Council.
>
> We are clearly dealing with a situation where SWAPO is flouting those agreements and is defying the Security Council.
>
> In addition SWAPO has of course violated the written undertaking it gave to you to cease all hostilities as of 1st April 1989.

I trust that you will agree that this is an intolerable situation.

The RSA has acted strictly in terms of its commitments and will continue to do so.

It is significant Mr Secretary General that at the time of writing no statement has yet been made by the leadership of SWAPO on this crucial disregard of its obligation to you, the Security Council, and the international community at large.

One cannot help to feel compassion for such unnecessary carnage of SWAPO elements who could have reentered Namibia, quite legally to participate peacefully in the political process according to the agreed procedures of which they had obviously not been informed.

The leadership of SWAPO will have to account for their callous disregard for human life and contempt for international agreements.

They will have to explain their action and its dire consequences to the people of Namibia.

SWAPO's leadership should urgently be brought to its senses.

 (i) As you are aware SWAPO was required by this time to have all its personnel confined to bases north of latitude 16 degree south. These bases should, in terms of agreement be monitored by UNTAG.

(ii) I should be grateful to learn whether UNTAG is in fact monitoring such bases and to enquire whether the monitoring reports could be made available to me.

The Administrator General will continue to act in concert with your Special Representative regarding any steps considered necessary to deal with the situation.

I was in the territory on 31st March and 1st April 1989 where I met with your Special Representative and his staff.

I have a deep understanding of the onerous task assigned to them, particularly at this time of such threatening crisis.

I trust, Mr Secretary General, that you and the Security Council will make it possible for my government to cooperate and fulfill its commitments in terms of the agreements.

I appeal to you and to the Security Council to take a firm and clear stand on this act of defiance by SWAPO.

8

Monday 3rd April 1989

The War in the Bush

In the early morning, a much strengthened combined police/army strike force, under the overall command of Zulu Mike's commander, Sergeant Piet 'Hand' Cronje, left Etale Base.

There were 25 fighting cars from police callsigns Zulu Mike, Zulu Alpha, Zulu Kilo, Zulu X-ray and Zulu 1 Delta, together with nineteen Ratels from the SADF's 63 Mechanised Battalion.

They planned to return to the contact area south east of Etale, where the late Sergeant Sarel van Tonder's Zulu Kilo group had been so badly mauled on Sunday.

They would cast around, find tracks and follow-up the enemy as a complete group.

The formation adopted by the police/army groups, was three battle lines, one behind the other, covering a total front of some 800 metres.

In the leading line, Ratel 90s (Ratel armed with 90mm guns) alternated between two fighting Wolves or Casspirs, making some sixteen vehicles in all. The composition of the second line was similar, but with Ratel 20s on the flanks. The Blesbok and Strandwolf supply vehicles took up the rear line.

At the contact scene, the police trackers got to work. They discovered tracks indicating, as Sergeant Cronje had suspected, that SWAPO had returned in force during the night.

The spoor of what seemed to be about a hundred infiltrators was found.

A cursory examination indicated that while there, SWAPO had buried some of their dead, missed by the police during their sweep.

The spoor of the enemy led south east away from the scene.

With trackers checking the ground in front for spoor, the Security Force formation set off after the infiltrators.

At 10:00 the trackers warned that signs indicated the enemy were preparing an ambush somewhere up ahead.

Sergeant Cronje called Etale control on the radio, and asked for gunships to be scrambled.

When the approach of the gunships was heard as a distant high pitched hum in the sky, a red smoke signal was fired high in the air, to mark the ground forces' position. This must have signalled to SWAPO that a contact was imminent, for they opened up with mortars of all calibres, RPG rockets, rifle grenades and rifle fire.

The enemy were in entrenched positions, laid out in a half circle and extending along a front of several hundred metres.

The vehicles returned fire on the SWAPO positions, the Wolves and Casspirs with heavy machineguns and cannons and the Ratel 90s with anti personnel fragmentation shells.

The area was generally flat, but was blanketed with a dense growth of low bush, which gave the enemy cover and hampered visibility.

The helicopter gunships went in, fired off all their ammunition and withdrew.

Sergeant Cronje ordered the fighting formation to advance. SWAPO had bombshelled after the hammering administered to them by the gunships, but the usual police tactics of circling and milling couldn't be used, as this was impossible with a large number of vehicles.

In the first place they followed the spoor of three escaping insurgents.

They quickly caught up with and shot them. After wheeling they trundled off after another four, whom they also found and shot.

Working in this manner, and retaining strict formation, they fought a series of running actions over an area of about 20 kilometres. This kept them busy for most of the day.

17:00 signalled the last contact, after which no more spoor was found. No proper sweeps were carried out after this operation, so only seven definite kills were confirmed.

For the police it had signalled a radical change of tactics. Although some had feared the formation might prove unwieldy in the field, the successes achieved proved it to be an efficient and versatile method of operation.

The use of Ratels certainly restored the advantage to the Security Forces.

In the east, south of Beacon 29, during a follow-up by Zulu 4 teams supported by SADF Ratels, under the overall command of Inspector Chris Ronne, Kashima, commander of SWAPO's Alpha Detachment which had been badly mauled the previous day, was killed during a contact.

His diary indicated he had brought in 85 men from Angola. Kashima, a senior member of PLAN's military hierarchy, had recently moved from SWAPO's 8th Brigade, which had spent most of the past year helping the Angolans in actions directed against UNITA.

First thing in the morning, four Alouette gunships, piloted by Captains Pierre Steyn, Kobus Swart, Jamie Burger and Chris Opperman, were deployed from Ondangwa to Ruacana, to relieve Major Alan McCarthy and Captain Mario Bergottini, who had been involved in the fighting the whole weekend.

A fairly routine movement, one might think, until one learns the story behind it.

Captain Steyn, of 17 Squadron based at Pretoria, first became aware of the possibility of an emergency situation, when his telephone rang at home at midnight on Saturday 1st April.

He and five other pilots had been placed on a twelve hour standby.

'What for?'

'Some flap in South West.'

On Sunday 2nd April at 08:45 the 'phone rang again.

'Get all your kit together ... the aircraft will be ready to leave for Ondangwa at 14:00.'

Then at 09:30 it rang again.

'Forget the last story ... the aircraft is leaving at 11:00, okay!'

Meanwhile at the air base, engineers had been working feverishly. There was a desperate need for Pumas at the border for casevacs and trooping, but the priority requirement was for Alouette gunships to support the ground forces. They would be airlifted there by C-160 transports, but before loading them, their rotor blades and tailplanes had to be removed.

After that, transportation was simple. A C-160 could take only one Puma at a time, but two Alouettes, top and tailed snugly to fit, could be airlifted as one load, together with crews, guns and so on.

Three C-160s, carrying a total of six Alouette gunships were airborne promptly at 11:00, landing at Ondangwa at about 15:45.

It took twelve hours to reassemble, flight test and have the Alouettes operationally ready. Altogether, including loading time in Pretoria, it took eighteen hours in total to disassemble them, airlift them the best part of 2 000 kilometres, reassemble them, flight test them and have them ready for war.

It was an achievement many top air forces would regard with envy, if not incredulity.

The first six for this special tour, were drawn from 17 Squadron in Pretoria for reasons of convenience. This was so because the C-16Os of 28 Squadron, the transfer squadron, were readily available in Pretoria as well.

The next group of seven Alouette gunships to come as a special tour, which arrived at Ondangwa on the Monday 3rd April, was made up from aircrew and aircraft drawn from other squadrons based at different centres around the country.

A villager living in the mountainous country around Okakjene, reported that five SWAPO insurgents had spent the night at his kraal, leaving in the early hours of the morning.

Sergeant Lappies Labuschagne, commander of Zulu 5 Sierra, and Constable Assie van As, commander of Zulu 5 Tango went to the village and examined the spoor indicated by the villager.

It was clear and relatively easy to follow, the trackers reckoning it was probably eight to nine hours old.

In this difficult mountainous country, it was only possible to follow the spoor on foot, so Sergeant Labuschagne and Constable Tertius Haasbroek of Zulu 5 Sierra, together with twenty black policemen set in pursuit. Constables Assie van As and Willie Hough remained with the fighting vehicles, following behind by various tedious routes and trying to stay as close to the follow-up group as the rugged terrain allowed.

Constable Mike Maree's car, of Zulu 5 Tango, developed mechanical problems and was forced to remain behind until something could be arranged about its repair or recovery. Shortly after this, having been on spoor for about three hours, Sergeant Labuschagne reported on the radio that he thought a contact was imminent.

Two Alouette gunships, piloted by Captains Jamie Burger and Kobus Swart, standing by at Ruacana and ready for such an eventuality, were soon overhead and ready to lend support.

'Contact!'

There was the sudden brief chatter of guns fired at point blank range and the blast of an exploding rifle grenade, and after what seemed little more than a few seconds, it was all over.

Five insurgents were dead, while the rest had fled into the mountains.

'Casevacs!' came the call over the radio.

The jet turbines of the Puma helicopter on standby at Ruacana, roared into life, while the doctor on board made a routine check of his medical equipment.

'We'll go along with you,' Inspector Nick Peens told the pilot.

He had arrived at Ruacana from Opuwo only shortly before, and was anxious to get out in the field with his men.

He nodded to Constable Chips Bosman, medic Lance Corporal Jose Saayman and some black police reinforcements and they got aboard.

The doctor, meanwhile, had established radio contact with the group on the ground. The casualties, all wounded by shrapnel when a rifle grenade exploded against a rocky face next to them, were Warrant Officer Matirepo Tjiraso, Sergeant Tjope Kawedo and Constable Rutjani Kengamise, all of Zulu 5 Sierra. Although not seriously hurt, they had suffered multiple wounds not only from shrapnel, but from rock splinters as well.

Constable Chips Bosman would freely admit later on, that he was nipping when he flew into the contact area. He was likely to be going into action for the first time, and his mind was beset by conflicting emotions.

He leapt from the Puma as it landed, his R-5 cocked and ready to use.

Where are the bodies? Where are the bodies? were his first thoughts.

He certainly couldn't see any.

What's more, amazingly, no one seemed concerned about the bodies either.

Those not helping with the casualties, were having a smoke or a drink. A few were having a bite to eat from their ratpacks. He began to feel foolish and he forced himself to relax.

Then, at long last, someone decided to do something about the bodies.

Men went out and dragged in the corpses of the five known SWAPO dead to a central area. Kit and equipment was stripped from them and searched for documents.

A sweep line of men on foot was formed. They began working their way through the contact area, looking for although not finding any further bodies, but picking up bits and pieces of SWAPO kit and equipment as well as weapons.

Constable Chips Bosman happily grabbed his first souvenirs.

Constable Mike Maree, forlornly waiting back on the road with his disabled Casspir, achieved a capture effortlessly.

He was talking to his men and monitoring the radio to see what was happening, when someone hiding in the bush fairly close by, began shouting and hollering.

There was a quick grab for weapons.

'What the hell is that?' Constable Maree asked in alarm.

'A SWAPO wants to surrender,' one of the black sergeants said.

'I've dropped my rifle. I've really dropped my rifle,'the insurgent screamed.

'Well, bloody come out then.'

'Don't shoot me.'

'We won't. You'll be okay.'

A man stepped gingerly into view, his hands held nervously high. He limped up to the Casspir and was taken into custody.

He pointed into the bush, indicating where he had left his personal weapon. A constable went there and found an AK-47.

The prisoner was badly wounded.

While his wounds were being treated, he said he'd had enough of war to last him a lifetime.

Inspector Peens and some black policemen, in the meantime, had been casting for spoor around the edges of the contact area. Suddenly a speck of blood was discovered. They looked around carefully and found another. It was the blood spoor of two wounded survivors heading out from the contact area.

Inspector Peens formed a follow-up group of himself, Constable Stephan Wilken of Zulu 5 Tango, medic Lance Corporal Jose Saayman and fifteen black policemen.

They set off through the hills in pursuit.

The spoor was difficult to follow and shortly after starting out they lost track of one insurgent. They continued their pursuit of the other one for the rest of the afternoon.

At 16:00 someone glimpsed movement by a tree growing next to a dried up water course.

'Contact!' he bawled.

The enemy, however, opened fire first.

He probably got off two shots, before almost every gun in the police patrol opened up and the hail of bullets slammed him from his cover.

He was still alive when they got to him, but only just.

Lance Corporal Jose Saayman took out his medical kit to help, but Inspector Peens shook his head. He was too far gone for that. In fact it was truly amazing he was still alive because his body, almost literally, had been shot to pieces. His stomach began swelling rapidly and visibly from massive internal bleeding.

'Who are you?' Inspector Peens asked.

'Shikol . . . Regional Headquarters Commander . . . from Paraforces.'

He then died.

The score stood at six killed and one captured.

Early in the day, police groups Zulu Bravo – commanded by Constable Werner Mouton, Zulu Juliet – commanded by Constable Velle Schlachter and Zulu Tango – commanded by Sergeant Fires van Vuuren, who was the overall commander of the combined unit, located the spoor of about sixty SWAPO insurgents.

This was about thirty kilometres south west of Beacon 8, to the south of the Onkandjera road.

Because of the intensive fighting since the 1st April, it was quickly cleared by control for fifteen Ratels from the SADF's 61 Mechanised Battalion, to be placed under police command to lend additional firepower to the follow- up group.

Police groups Zulu India – commanded by Sergeant Botes, Zulu 1 India – under the acting command of Constable Theunis Kruger, and Zulu Yankee – commanded by Sergeant Dewald Pretorius, were also ordered to assist.

By 09:00 the various units had locked on, giving the follow-up group a total fighting strength of about forty vehicles, including the army Ratels.

A tactical formation, with the Ratel 90s interspersed between the police fighting vehicles was worked out, which capitalised on the former's powerful 90mm guns. It was planned that in the event of a contact, the Ratels would fire one 90mm round each, and then drive through the contact area, maintaining formation with the police vehicles. Once through, the police fighting vehicles would wheel around and return, criss crossing and milling through the contact area killing any enemy survivors.

The tracks were easy to follow.

At 17:00, after being on spoor for some hours, the police trackers, who were riding on the Casspirs, warned that the signs had begun to indicate that SWAPO were readying to set up an ambush ahead.

Helicopter gunships were asked for and two Alouettes, piloted by Captains Pierre Steyn and Chris Opperman, were scrambled, but before they arrived overhead, SWAPO sprang their ambush, initiating it with a volley of RPG rocket projectiles, rifle grenades and rifle and light machinegun fire.

Exactly according to plan, the Ratels fired their one round each, then drove through the contact area, maintaining formation with the fighting Casspirs and Wolves, all of them blazing away with their lighter weapons.

Once through, the police vehicles wheeled and went back in, all guns blazing.

Enemy fire had been heavy, but little had been seen of them because of thick bush cover. In fact, the only man able to positively confirm a kill was the major commanding the Ratels.

Army Lieutenant Chris Els (20), from Welkom, suffered a head wound during this action. Regretably he died from wounds after being casevaced.

At the end of this action, the Ratels of the 61 Mechanised Battalion returned to base, leaving the police elements to follow the spoor of seven SWAPO insurgents trying to escape the area.

Police, with the support of the Alouette gunships, eventually caught up with them, and after a brief contact, they were all killed.

Ex-members of both SWA Police COIN and Koevoet began to 'phone in from all over South Africa, once the signal calling for volunteers had gone out.

Sergeant Nati, who was back in South Africa performing routine police work after a long and exciting time with SWA Police Coin, 'phoned the moment he reached work on Monday.

When could he be on his way?

A telex confirming his move back to South West came hours later.

Some members of the South African Police Task Force, men experienced in counterinsurgency work, were nominated to go as well.

A harassed senior police officer was checking and listing volunteers on a parade in Pretoria, men who would be leaving for Owamboland the next day.

A tall man, well dressed in a dark suit and carrying a briefcase, walked on parade.

'Hello, Oom (uncle),' he said, 'I'm going with them'.

'And who the hell might you be?' the exasperated officer asked.

'I'm a *haas*, a rabbit (police slang for an ex-member). I've been selling insurance since I left the police three months ago ... now I'm going back up there.'

The officer looked him up and down and nodded.

'Okay, come back tomorrow morning at eight o'clock. We'll take you back in the Force.'

And so a few days later, Warrant Officer Gene Roos, looking straight out of the box with a new issue of uniform, was back in a Casspir leading a SWA Police group in the hunt for SWAPO insurgents.

140

Monday was not the best of days for Sergeant Rassie Ras at Ruacana. He had hardly had a wink of sleep since taking over the control room on Friday night.

There was a war on, and because of it the language on the radio waves, particularly when a contact was in progress, was often punctuated with expletives not normally heard in the Monday to Friday offices of polite and civilised Pretorian society.

But to the sleep starved, unshaven, hungry and often bandaged policemen fighting from there, whose friends and comrades were being killed and maimed, Ruacana had nothing to do with polite and civilised society.

It was so far removed it could have been on the moon.

Ruacana at that time was a fighting man's world, where life and death balanced precariously, as if on a razor's edge.

Consequently, it was perhaps understandable, if they overlooked that in far away Pretoria, people were officially monitoring transmissions.

During one cliff hanging contact, when the action could have gone either way, and radio silence, except for tactical necessity, was being strictly maintained, someone made a terse comment which rippled the tranquility in Jacaranda City.

'Don't you men know there are women here. Watch your *taal*, do you hear? Don't use swear words on the air, or I'll make a report.'

What he overlooked was that no one at Ruacana cared a damn.

'F... off, man,' Rassie answered bluntly but concisely, 'there's a war on here, even if there isn't in bloody Pretoria!'

To make matters worse, two chaplains came in the control room shortly afterwards, by which time neither Rassie's language nor the situation out in the bush had shown any improvement.

He looked at them wearily, but very patiently.

'Please, gentlemen, please, chaplains. No disrespect meant, but there's a war on. Would you oblige me by f...ing off as well!'

They did.

There was still a flurry of activity at 101 Battalion's base, and by this morning their were enough men back for them to paraded and addressed en mass by their commander, Colonel Kotze.

He told them that the political situation had changed, that SWAPO had mounted a massive infiltration and with UNTAG's permission they were to assist the police.

'Now, instead of peace, we must fight SWAPO again.'

The men on parade went wild, and began cheering and shouting.

Two full companies were deployed that morning.

By evening the whole unit had been deployed, with three companies in central Owamboland attached and working with the SADF's 62 Mechanised Battalion, two companies in the east attached to 62 Mechanised Battalion, another in the main urban areas of Oshakati and Ondangwa and the Recce company available for any tasks that UNTAG might need to give it – remembering there were no UNTAG units available for deployment in the border areas.

In another contact during the course of the day between police groups Zulu

Foxtrot, Zulu 4 Foxtrot, Zulu Uniform, Zulu Quebec, Zulu Hotel, Zulu 1 Sierra, Zulu Lima and Zulu 1 Juliet, south of Beacon 29, another three armed SWAPO insurgents were killed.

No one up at the border had any doubts about it, a *de facto* state of war existed. Men might have postulated, theorized, posed and downright lied in Windhoek, at the UN and elsewhere, but if you were in areas where the thick of the fighting was taking place, then you knew what SWAPO had done.

Yet the start point for most members of the international media set, was that South Africa was in the wrong, because that was the way they tended to look at things.

There were a lot of journalists at Oshakati, many foreign and many local, and on this Monday there were fifteen civilian light aircraft parked on the apron at Ondangwa Air Base, some with single engines and others with two, all chartered by the press.

Helicopter pilot, Major Wimpie Kruger, being ferried in to Ondangwa for flying duty by a C-130 Flossie, looked down at the assembled aircraft in amazement as they came in to land.

'Looks like the boys have started a civvy flying club for us,' he quipped wryly.

Having got to the border, a large number of the international press corps settled down in the bar at the Guest House at Oshakati, where they did most of their news gathering by collecting press releases, reading the local newspapers and incestuously swopping rumours between rounds of drinks.

Although the Security Forces were more than willing to cooperate, they didn't get much cooperation in return. Those unfamiliar with Africa tended to favour the propaganda pushed out by SWAPO, and it was only after the first bodies of insurgents were brought in for them to examine, and after they had seen for themselves they were fully uniformed, and had noted the quality and quantity of their heavy armaments, that some began to believe that maybe South Africa might be just a little bit in the right.

Many were flabbergasted.

'Jeez,' said one previously very hostile American, 'so they are wearing uniforms!'

Others saw signs which weren't there, indicating the Security Forces had murdered them – shot them in cold blood.

It became apparent most preferred to do their news digging at third hand, when immediately after a major contact, a group were offered a Puma flight out to the battleground to see things for themselves at first hand.

There were no takers!

It seems times have changed from the days when men like Papa Hemingway fought to control his sea sickness from the well of an LCI in rising seas off the Normandy beaches on D-Day, 6th June 1944.

During the day a squadron of Impala ground attack aircraft returned to the Ondangwa Air base from Grootfontein. They were ordered to standby and be ready to support the police and those units helping them should they be needed.

This was announced in the press in Windhoek.

142

The Goebbels' Factor – SWAPO's Propaganda War

Certainly Dr Paul Joseph Goebbels, Hitler's suave Propaganda Minister, knew what he was talking about when he said 'the bigger the lie, the more readily it is believed'.

He could have added that 'the more often a lie is repeated, the quicker will be its acceptance as the truth'.

He would have been proud of the world wide campaign launched virtually immediately by SWAPO's propagandists, to show the innocence of that organisation and the culpability of the SWA Police, the SWA Territory Force and the SADF.

The 3rd April edition of the pro SWAPO, *The Namibian*, under its main headline, '435 IN PERIL', said: 'Reports from the far north last night indicated that pitched battles were still raging along a 300 kilometre front between South African Security Forces and SWAPO fighters'.

It went on to say civilians were fleeing from the fighting areas.

No one could take issue with much up to there, except to nit pick by saying the fighting was between SWAPO fighters and the SWA Police – not the South African Security Forces. Even though there was an important difference, because the SWA Police were operating with the authority of the United Nations in terms of resolution 435, while the SADF were confined to their bases.

It continued: 'Villages were reported to be ablaze as 101 Battalion was released from its confinement to base and deployed widely in the region.' Not so good, because to the reasonably uninitiated, the linking of villages being 'ablaze' with 101 Battalion being 'deployed widely' insinuated, to the author at least, that the unit was involved in the arsons, which was palpably false. It then reported that 'an Oshakati resident [unnamed] told *The Namibian* last night that the police involved in the contact were members of the Koevoet unit, which was supposed to have been disbanded three weeks ago.

'He said: "It is the same faces, the same Casspirs, the same uniforms. The police involved in the fighting are from the Koevoet unit."

'He added that residents had heard "with horror" over state controlled radio yesterday that the UN's Mr Martti Ahtisaari, acting under instructions from the UN Secretary General, had given approval for 101 Battalion to be released . . . and deployed to assist police.

'"The people are shocked and very unhappy that the UN has done this. Almost everyone in the north has felt the brutality of 101 Battalion, and now the UN allows them out to work with Koevoet and carry on just as they have in the past," he said.

'He added that to many people it proved that the UN was "working for South Africa".

This was clearly designed to throw any self respecting UN official with promotion ambitions into nervous convulsions.

The Namibian also reported that Angolan government officials and Cuban officers, speaking from Cahama in Angola, had denied SWAPO had made large scale border crossings into Namibia.

A Cuban spokesman said : 'there is [sic] no SWAPO down here'. He went on to say that in terms of the peace plan 'SWAPO fighters had been moved north away from the border to positions around Lubango, about 240km from Namibia'.

Another report in the same newspaper said that a contingent of journalists, photographers and church officials flew to 'the scene', whatever that might have meant, to assess . . . reports that members of the Security Forces have gone on the rampage and were 'harassing residents and assaulting them'.

Other stories relating to the implementation of resolution 435 from Friday 31st March and on, were well covered, but nowhere in this issue was there even an implied criticism of SWAPO for sending its fighters on an armed incursion into Namibia. Frighteningly for the cause of press objectivity and truth, many of the reports in this newspaper were picked up and repeated in newspapers around the world.

The United Nations and UNTAG

The press were quick to notice that UNTAG were vacilating and revealing little of their attitude towards the situation.

Gradually, as time progressed, it would become obvious.

UNTAG's official spokesman in Namibia, Fred Eckhard of the US, reportedly said in was unclear in terms of the peace agreement, whether the SWA Police were entitled to act against SWAPO insurgents crossing from Angola into Namibia.

Chief Inspector Kierie du Rand, the SWA Police's Chief Liaison Officer, publicly took sharp issue with him, pointing out that it was routine maintenance of law and order for police to guard against border violations by people not carrying identity documents and armed for obvious offensive intentions.

Mr Eckhard also said UNTAG was investigating the 'possibility' that SWAPO had been 'misinformed' about the terms of the ceasefire and resolution 435 and had believed they were entitled to bring in armed men to assembly points inside Namibia.

A news report said the UN Under Secretary General in charge of peacekeeping operations, Mr Marrack Goulding, was flying to Luanda urgently to discuss the deteriorating situation with the Angolan government.

The Secretary General, Dr de Cuellar, gave an oral report to the Security Council on the situation, based on information supplied by UNTAG's four man enquiry team led by Cedric Thornberry, which had visited the border to investigate the situation.

The Other Face of War

Mr Botha told pressmen that both he and Defence Minister, Magnus Malan, would be reporting to the South African State Security Council during the day.

He said that South Africa is trying to establish a 'ceasefire within a ceasefire' in an effort to stop the fighting. He described the situation as 'grave' but said 'it can be overcome if South Africa continues to act correctly'.

He mentioned that the SWA Police would not fire on SWAPO unless they were fired at first.

The Administrator General issued the following statement regarding the border incursion:

1 On Saturday evening 1st April the Administrator General and the Special Repre-

144

Above – Sam Nujoma believed that with the SWA Police disarmed of their heavy weapons, the SWA Territory Force demobilised, the SADF reduced and confined to bases and UNTAG's arrival deliberately delayed by the Africa Group of the Non Aligned Movement, the time was ripe for a coup de main. On the 1st April 1989 he launched 1 600 heavily armed PLAN fighters into Namibia from Angola.

2. Above – Maj Gen Hans Dreyer, Regional Commissioner of Police for the northern border, and his black and white policemen, beat them hands down.

Below – British Premier, Mrs Margaret Thatcher, fortunately for the peace process, was in Windhoek when it all happened. Her unequivocal condemnation of SWAPO caused a reluctant UN Security Council to act.

4. Below – SA Foreign Minister, Mr Pik Botha, broached no nonsense. Either the UN acted against SWAPO and allowed a limited number of SA military to leave their base restriction to assist the SWA Police, or UNTAG could pack its bags and get out.

5. Above – UN Special Representative, Mr Martti Ahtisaari (lt) and South African Administrator General, Adv Louw Pienaar, in the front line of efforts to get the peace process back on course.

7. Left – Brig Daniel Opande of Kenya, 2 i/c to Gen Prem Chand.

6. Below – Gen Jannie Geldenhuys, Chief of the SADF (lt) and Lt Gen Dewan Prem Chand of India, the UNTAG Force Commander, both distinguished general officers found they had much in common.

8. Above – SA had bent over backwards and more to stick to the peace agreement. Here men of the crack 101 Battalion hand in their equipment during the demobilisation process.

9. Below – Gen Prem Chand (cent) led a joint UNTAG-SADF team on an extensive tour of the border in mid March. He confirmed there were no SWAPO bases inside Namibia. Many traditional leaders asked him for UN protection against SWAPO after the SADF's withdrawal.

10. Above – UNTAG mounted a massive campaign to publicize 'Free and Fair' elections. They forgot to tell SWAPO.

11. Below – Certificates commemorating the peace for issue to those at SAAF Base, Ondangwa, on the 1st April were printed. Instead Operation Agree became Operation Disagree.

12. Below – The innocent bystander. This Himba tribeswoman belongs to the 7th most primitive tribe in the world.

Air Force Base Ondangwa

SEMPER PARATUS

Operation Agree

This certificate is handed over at AFB Ondangwa

on ....

to

No .... Rank .... Name ....

commemorating the implementation of the negotiated
settlement plan for the independence of S.W.A.

Thank you for your contribution towards the success
achieved on the Base.

As our fathers trusted humbly,
teach us, Lord, to trust Thee still :
Guard our land and guide our People
In Thy way to do Thy will

OFFICER COMMANDING AFB ONDANGWA .... DATE ....

13. Above – SWAPO invariably initiated the contacts. In this contact Alouette gunships were in support of police.

14. Below – 21 police fighting vehicles were knocked out by SWAPO's many anti tanks weapons.

Namibian Citizens In SWATF

You Fell Prey To PLAN Combatants. Why?

BECAUSE

1. You are traitors, betraying your own land and people.
2. You agreed to fight us on behalf of the racist white foreign colonialists from South Africa and delay freedom and independence of our people.
3. You are killing our people, burning their houses, destroying their crops and stealing their cattle;
4. You are raping our mothers, sisters and women of old age;
   As a rule, rest assured, you shall have to pay the price for your evil deeds.

REMEMBER

To be a traitor, as you are, you are assured of a shadowed future. There is no hope for a happy life. As you know, one day, the people will decide to hang or put you before a firing squad. So much for a traitor...

****

15-16. Above – SWAPO hardly came in peace as they now say. Each fighter carried copies of this crude propaganda leaflet (back and front shown) to pin to the bodies of members of the Security Forces they killed. They didn't get the opportunity to use them.

17. Below – Police groups form into a fighting line on a dirt road, ready to sweep through the bush in search of SWAPO.

18. Above – After the battle, the sweep . . . and the SWAPO
dead.

19. Below . . . and their weapons of 'peace'.

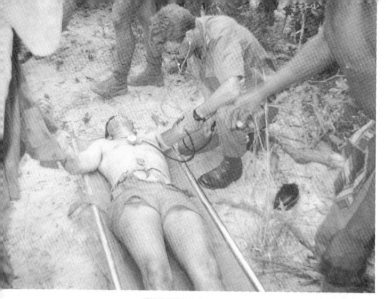

20. Left – No matter how remote the contact area, the South African Medical Service ensured casualties were tended by doctors within 20 minutes of wounding.

21. Right – SWAPO dead being brought into base on a Casspir. Much criticism of this practise has been levelled at the police over the years. There is, however, no satisfactory option as there is no space for bodies in a fighting vehicle when operational.

22. Left – A Police Casspir, battle damaged hut still fighting.

23. Above – Alouette gunship brings SWAPO prisoner in to Etale base. Note the 20 mm cannon, which so often proved itself the king of battle.

24. Right – All SWAPO units were well equipped with radios for communications with their Angolan HQ. This set is one of many captured during the April incursions.

25. Left – The unexplained mystery as to why SWAPO brought in Kenyan camouflage, identical to that worn by the Kenyan contingent of UNTAG.

26. Left – SADF Ratel 90 and crew, acting in support of the SWA Police, stand by for patrol at Etale base.

27. Below – SADF Ratel knocked out by SWAPO in a battle on Thursday 6th April.

28. Above – Joint patrol of army Ratels and police fighting vehicles on the move.

29. Below – Army Ratels and police Casspirs, with an Alouette gunship overhead, advance towards contact.

30. Above – Police group leaves Etale base for patrol at first light.

31. Below – Officer of 101 Battalion SWA Territory Force, examines yet another Soviet supplied SAM-7 captured from SWAPO.

32. Below – SA Army National Servicemen standing by, ready for call out, at Ehomba base in Kaokoland.

. Above – Pilot's eye view of
wambo from a Dakota. An alti-
de of no more than 50 feet was
aintained as a precaution against
AM-7s. Owambo is like an endless
at savannah, punctuated by
etch marks of hundreds of water
led shonas.

. Right – Puma helicopters of the
AF standing by at Ehomba base
Kaokoland.

35. Left – Going up with the
rations on the Dakota 'rum
run' from Windhoek to On-
dangwa.

OSHIKANGO
HOLIDAY/BEACH
RESORT
24 HR FRIENDLY SERVICE (8 DAYS A WEEK)
FREE BOARD & MEALS
NO JOINING FEE
DAY TRIPS ACROSS BORDER   TBA

APPLY POST 19(½) OR ANY
FRIENDLY UNTAG PERS.

PROMOTED BY AUST-BRIT TOURS
(YOUR FRIENDLY TRAVEL AGENTS)

5. Page left – Police patrol asks Owambo villager if any SWAPO were in the area.

7. Above left – Paul Balko-Mertz, with British Royal Signaller, Captain James Dakin, commanding the mixed British-Australian unit manning UNTAG assembly point at Oshikango.

8. Above right – In spite of the British-Australian 'promotional' efforts, the SWAPO infiltrators obeyed Sam Nujoma and stayed away.

9. Centre – Consignment of vehicles, gift of West Germany, shipped in for UNTAG via Walvis Bay.

10. Right – In spite of many negatives before arrival, UNTAG personnel were soon refusing to move outside bases in northern border area without South African mine protected vehicles. They got some Buffels and then some Casspirs, which they preferred.

41. Above – War birds of the SAAF. Bosbok spotters and Alouette helicopter gunships, recalled from RSA to act in support of police, at Ondangwa Air Force Base.

42. Below – Nearby the blue UN flag flies by an UNTAG chopper, painted in stark white, signalling that Ondangwa will never be the same again.

sentative of the UN Secretary General agreed that certain specified units, to be agreed, would be released from restriction to base to provide such support as might be needed by the existing police forces, in case they could not handle the situation by themselves. The situation would be kept under continuous review and the movement out of existing bases would throughout be monitored by UNTAG military observers.

2 On Sunday morning April 2nd, in the light of the situation then prevailing, it was agreed that the minimum units of the SWA Territory Force could be released from restriction to base in order to provide the necessary support to the SWA Police in accordance with the understanding reached between the Administrator General and the UN's Special Representative.

It was reiterated that the situation would be kept under continuous review.

3 The latest position can be summed up as follows:
   (i) Six battalions of the SWA Territory Force have been activated and the restriction on confinements to base for these battalions lifted. By this morning three of these battalions had been deployed to assist the SWA Police.
      They are accompanied by UNTAG observers.
  (ii) The latest casualty figures are as follows:
      SWA Police -19 killed, 41 wounded.
      SWAPO- 143 killed, wounded unknown, 4 captured.
 (iii) The Administrator General has also been informed by the SWA Police that the Regional Chief of Staff of PLAN, one Heidongo, had been identified amongst the casualties in western Owambo.

4 The Administrator General wishes to give his full assurance that the situation was under full control. Advocate Pienaar calls on all citizens to remain calm and to afford him and the Special Representative every opportunity to diffuse the situation in the manner and along the procedural lines as agreed upon by him and the Special Representative.

Of Monday's press reaction, the most memorable was undoubtedly by the *Windhoek Observer*, whose highly individualistic proprietor/editor, Hannes Smit, was the only local pressman of note to head straight for the border, the moment the guns began to shoot, to see for himself what was happening.

The result was an impressive special edition packed with photographs taken in the 'front line'. Its banner headlines read: 'WAR ERUPTS'.

The *Times of Namibia*, which started going on the streets five times a week instead of weekly on that very day, chose as its headline: '140 killed in bloody clashes'.

The *Windhoek Advertiser* chose 'A Bloodbath' as its headline.

The *Citizen*, Johannesburg, used its whole front page to cover Namibian events, headlining it: 'BIG SWAPO TOLL IN NEW CLASHES'.

The *Star*, Johannesburg, devoted most of its front page to the Namibian situation, and included a large picture of Sam Nujoma with the caption: 'It can't be true ... Its headline read: 'Heavy fighting along border'. The story, as it first broke, was dealt with the day before in the *Sunday Star*, under the headline 'Crisis hours for war or peace.

The *Sunday Times* of the 2nd April had frontpaged the story under the headline, 'Namibia on knife edge'.

9

Tuesday 4th April 1989

The War in the Bush

During the course of the morning, Constable Assie van As, commander of Zulu 5 Tango, worked his group southwards searching for SWAPO spoor.

While checking around the vicinity of a kraal three kilometres north east of Etoto, trackers discovered the spoor of five SWAPO insurgents. They reckoned the track were a day old.

They followed them for two kilometres and found the place of where the enemy group had slept the night.

According to the signs, like patches of urine and faeces found nearby, they had only left their camp about 3–4 hours before.

Their spoor led away in a south easterly direction. It seemed as if they'd had enough of the mountainous and inhospitable country west of Ruacana and were trying to get back into the familiar and more friendly home territory of western and central Owamboland.

Constable Assie van As called for assistance and Zulu 5 Sierra, commanded by Sergeant Lappies Labuschagne, Zulu 5 Echo, commanded by Constable Jimmy Botha and Zulu 5 Juliet, commanded by Constable Sakkie Jooste, joined them on the tracks.

Inspector Nick Peens also arrived to lend assistance.

The cars were deployed into a fighting line, and with the trackers working in teams and on foot ahead of them, they set off in pursuit.

The fugitives were highly skilled in the arts of anti tracking and they led the police a merry dance for the whole day.

For one particular period, the spoor became unexpectedly easy to follow and they made good time. Then suddenly the trackers came to the realisation they had been tricked – somewhere back on the trail, one of the insurgents had slipped away. Now, instead of five, they were following four. Determined not to be caught like that again, they continued the hunt. An hour farther on, though, it had happened again. Another insurgent had slipped away.

Then there were only three! In the late afternoon, two Alouette gunships joined them to provide topcover, but they couldn't assist as spotters, because their instructions were to stay high and out of range of the enemy's RPG rockets.

The insurgents used every trick in the book, and many that weren't, creating as much doubt and confusion as they could. Sometimes the tracks were made by bare feet, sometimes by shoed feet, as they fought a grim and silent war to shake the police from their tracks.

But the police clung doggedly to their heels, determined to catch them before night fell.

By late afternoon they had caught up with them.

But they still couldn't catch them. When flank cars leapfrogged ahead in an attempt to cut their spoor, the insurgents were somewhere between them and the main party, doubling back and out to the flanks, concealing themselves in the thick bush, mixing the spoor of the hunted with the spoor of the hunters, creating maximum confusion.

They were master backtrackers indeed, but in spite of their every ruse, the police stayed tenaciously on their trail.

But the clock inexorably began to tick away the daylight hours.

Then as light was fading, Inspector Peens, Constable Wilkin and medic Lance Corporal Jose Saayman, who had been in front with the tracking team, began changing over with reliefs to maintain freshness. Constable Chips Bosman took the weight of the radio pack from Lance Corporal Saayman.

Sergeant Lappies Labuschagne of Zulu 5 Sierra, frustrated at their continued lack of success, decided to leapfrog ahead on the flank, in a last chance bid to flush out their wily foes.

He yelled for Constable Bosman and some of the trackers to jump aboard. As the Casspir moved forward, the sharp eyes of Constable Scooterfoot Bell, nicknamed way back after losing a part of his leg during a contact, saw an insurgent dive into a bush.

He immediately opened fire.

All cars followed suit, as did the helicopter gunships.

It was Constable Chips Bosman's first contact, and the highly experienced black sergeants and constables with him in the car, knew it. He remembers with gratitude how they tactfully nursed him through it, ensuring he took the right action at the right time and that he shot at the right places.

The insurgent had to be dead – no one could have survived the devastating hail of fire directed at him – but he had two companions.

The cars began milling around the area, blasting every bush, stump or other cover which could possibly have been used as a place of concealment, in an effort to kill or flush them out.

'I remember thinking,' Constable Bosman said afterwards, 'how difficult it must be to get everyone to cease firing once a contact has begun . . . but you soon learn!'

The insurgent killed had almost made it.

An AK rifle and a medic's pack was found with his body. The trackers cast around for the spoor of his comrades, but there was nothing. Anyway, by then they were safe. Even if tracks had been found, it was almost dark and too late to follow-up. By using truly excellent, almost out of the textbook anti tracking skills, they had evaded the dragnet.

There were three other major contacts between the Security Forces and SWAPO on this day.

South of Beacon 29 police groups Zulu Uniform, Zulu Quebec, Zulu Lima and Zulu 4 Delta were in contact with armed SWAPO insurgents, killing two and capturing another.

South of Eenhana police groups Zulu Papa, Zulu Sierra and callsign Victor

163

Tango were in contact with armed SWAPO infiltrators, killing twelve and capturing one.

After a follow-up, police groups Zulu Papa, Zulu Sierra and Zulu 1 Sierra, killed another armed SWAPO infiltrator, some ten kilometres farther south than the last contact.

Sergeant Thys de Jager, when he left Opuwo less than a month before, had not expected to see the wilderness and desert of Kaokoland again in his life.

It wasn't that he hadn't liked it, it was just that enough was enough.

Since then he had been on honeymoon, enjoying sands of a different kind, the sands of Durban beach.

On the Sunday morning he had been sunning himself on the beach, a last sunning before he and his new wife got into their car to drive to Pretoria, where with his leave over, he would commence duty with the Police Dog Section.

His wife, who had been packing, came down to the beach. Her face reflected concern.

'There's something on the news saying there was a big contact with SWAPO in South West.'

'No,' he said, 'couldn't be. That's nonsense. It's all over, there's peace now.'

'That's what it said.' They listened to the radio continually, moving from station to station, but as luck would have it they couldn't pick up another news broadcast.

Eventually, he couldn't contain his curiosity any longer, so he 'phoned Namibia and was fortunate enough to speak to Inspector Ben Vermaak.

'Sorry, Thys,' he told him, 'but I am too busy even to talk. All hell has broken loose up here.'

They drove back to Pretoria, their conversation centred on one subject and one subject only.

What was happening over there? What had happened to his friends? Were they all right?

The next morning he reported for duty at the Dog Section in Pretoria.

His feelings were mixed, as only a man who is at peace, while his friends are at war, will understand.

A telex arrived during the course of the morning.

Volunteers with experience in the SWA Police's former Counterinsurgency Unit, or in Koevoet, were urgently required.

He went to speak to Captain Jacobs of the Special Task Force and narrated details of his experience.

'But do you want to go back up?' the captain asked him.

Sergeant de Jager was in two minds. It was not that easy. He was newly married and, as his wife had said, he had done his bit already. Perhaps it was the turn of others.

Besides that, how long would it last?

Perhaps it was just a flash in the pan.

He really didn't know.

He shook his head doubtfully.

The Captain understood.

He asked who had been killed and who had been wounded.

The dead had all been his friends.

He looked anxiously through the list of wounded.

From there he went straight to 1-Military Hospital, spending an hour or so talking to Sergeant Kokkie de Kock, Constable Jasper Genis, Sergeant Herman Grobler and Sergeant Koos Swart.

He listened to their stories, hearing how SWAPO had treacherously swept over in force, and without warning.

They discussed the large numbers of RPG-7s, the RPG-75s and the rifle grenades.

And they spoke of other things, laughing over older but happier times.

That was it.

He went straight from the hospital to Police Headquarters. He saw General Bert Wandrag, and volunteered in person.

'You've just got married . . . are you sure you want to go?'

'Yes, sir.'

'You must be bloody mad,' the general said approvingly.

Shortly afterwards he boarded an SAAF C-130 transport and by midday on Tuesday 4th April he was back in Owambo.

The Goebbels' Factor – SWAPO's Propaganda War

The Namibian devoted a large part of its Tuesday's paper to subtle and blatantly unsubtle salvos of propaganda fired at or in the general direction of the SWA Police, the SWA Territory Force and anything else which could vaguely be put under the South African umbrella.

Again, there was not even an oblique hint that could vaguely be interpreted as a criticism of SWAPO.

It started with an almost half page picture of dead bodies placed above the headlines, the caption of which read : . . . The bodies of 21 dead SWAPO fighters, 'already in a state of decomposition' . . .

The significance of the passage marked with quotes would only become apparent later on.

Beneath that the headline: 'US BLAMES SWAPO', with the sub head 'but some claim there was "no invasion"'.

After dealing briefly with US accusations, it went on to say that unnamed 'sources' in northern Namibia contradicted South African claims of SWAPO border crossings, saying they had been there 'at the time Security Forces started to hunt them out,' and had been attacked just after they 'had dug up their arms caches and were preparing to cross back over into Angola to be confined to base there'.

Under a heading 'UNTAG under fire', the UN role was attacked by a 'resident' who said reports had been made to two Malaysian members of UNTAG at Oshakati of the fighting 'and the fact that bodies remained on the battle scene for longer than 24 hours', but they 'revealed an attitude of indifference to the matter, and continued reading their novels . . .'

It also said that 'Namibians in the area were further especially annoyed at the fact that Koevoet, which allegedly was disbanded, but in fact incorporated into the SWA Police force, reportedly fired first at groups of SWAPO combatants who had "earlier" been operating in the area, but were busy regrouping to be eventually demobilised and confined to base . . .'

It mentioned that several 'concerned civilians' were accusing UNTAG of possible "collaboration with the Boers" and said 'angry civilians' were 'expressing their disappointment at the way UNTAG has thus far conducted its monitoring of the transition,' and have 'appealed to the UN body to seriously and immediately reconsider its role in the territory, and to reverse its decision to allow the redeployment of certain of the SADF's units, including Battalion 101'.

On page 2 under 'Weaknesses of Resolution' appear quotes from Zimbabwe's Foreign Minister, Nathan Shamuyarira, in which he says: 'We do not believe it would be in the interest of SWAPO to violate the ceasefire. It is the South African regime that had an interest in doing so'.

Then under 'SA wants to destroy 435' appears a joint statement by SWAPO front organisations National Union of Namibian Workers – NUNW, and the Namibia National Students Organisation – NANSO, in which they spoke of 'clear and deliberate strategies of South Africa to undermine and destroy' the implementation of resolution 435, condemned the 'deliberate provocation' by South Africa to reverse the independence process and demanded that UNTAG 'effectively monitor and restrict South African forces to base'.

It also complained that 'Koevoet members were secretly rearmed' which was 'tantamount to collusion between the UN and South Africa to effectively suspend the independence plan. The people of Namibia demand an explanation from the Secretary General of the UN . . .'

On page 3 under 'In Kavango 202 [Battalion] back to bases' is a report saying the unit was never properly disarmed and the start of the peace process 'was marred by incidents of violence.' It then listed eight alleged assaults allegedly committed by members of the unit on innocent civilians.

Then came 'War Stories', a report by Chris Shipanga, who visited the border to 'interview witnesses and ascertain the "facts" of the situation'.

The article's tone gave the impression he was interested only in 'facts' indicating wrongful action by the SWA Police. On his visit to a battlefield he wrote the mind boggling 'there were, however, bloodstains everywhere, indicating that bodies had been dragged around'.

For those interested in the protection of the bushveld environment he said that 'the natural vegetation of bushes and trees were damaged by heavy armoured vehicles used by Security Forces during the bloody clash . . .'

From an 'eye witness' came: 'While my brother was fetching them some water, the man told me that they were regrouping themselves, and were not here to fight . . . suddenly the combatants were caught under heavy gunfire coming from the Casspir vehicles . . . Another eye witness, Mr Junias Wedeinge, also confirmed that Security Forces were first to open fire after having surrounded the place . . . Black members of the Security Forces were reportedly also not allowed to inspect the bodies [of PLAN fighters]'.

The last sentence, with its racial overtones, is pure and simple disinformation. 90% of policemen fighting on the border were black. Having accounted for a large proportion of SWAPO's casualties themselves, why would anyone have stopped them from inspecting the bodies?

The pro SWAPO Council of Churches for Namibia – CCN, added its voice to the propaganda war with a statement by General Secretary Dr Abisai Shejavali, who urged that the number of UNTAG troops be reinstated from 4 650 to the original 7 500 because the reduction would hamper the peace process.

A ten man delegation from CCN had been to the border to investigate. Dr Shejavali asked for SWAPO prisoners and the bodies of their dead to be handed over to UNTAG. He also asked why the South Africa forces had not 'first' informed UNTAG of the presence of SWAPO guerrillas.

He added his 'shock and distress' at hearing that 101 Battalion 'should regroup and work with the South Africans to help with law and order'.

The delegation reported having found that 'it was the SADF that surrounded the place and started to shoot,' and that there had been 'considerable damage [the insinuation being it was done by the Security Forces!] to personal property'.

They also said: 'Helicopter gunships have been unleashed on civilians and Namibian soil now bleeds when it should be rejoicing.'

Impartially, he added, 'this is unnecessary death on both sides'.

At a news conference in Harare Sam Nujoma urged the UN Security Council to immediately bolster the strength of UNTAG from the 4 650 approved by the Council to 7 500 as had been demanded by the African countries.

He let it be known that he had already made this plea earlier at a joint ninety minute meeting with the British, Chinese, Soviet and US Ambassadors.

Mr Nujoma repeated his denials that 1 200 of his PLAN fighters had infiltrated from Angola saying 'our people have been fighting inside Namibia for the past 20 years . . . have we had no troops there for the past 23 years?'

During a lengthy tirade he expressed 'utter disgust over the killing of innocent Namibians, some of whom were celebrating the ceasefire.' He urged the Security Council to stop the South Africans 'from butchering Namibians and confine the South African army to their barracks

Asked if he would be returning to Namibia, Nujoma replied, 'Yes, very soon.'

A SWAPO official, who asked not to be named, said it would not be Sam Nujoma's first visit home.

'He has been in and out with his men quite often.'

He should have tried that one on the UN Secretary General – for as will be seen by events later in the day, he seemed to believe anything.

The Other Face of War

Mr Botha said plans were being made to reactivate the tripartite Joint Military Monitoring Commission – JMMC, of South Africa, Cuba and Angola, at Angola's suggestion, to deal with the crisis situation. He hoped this would be achieved within 48 hours. He insisted that any peace plan would have to involve the return of all SWAPO forces to Angola, where they would be monitored by UNTAG.

He also said the report to the Secretary General of UN Special Representative, Mr Martti Ahtisaari, had confirmed South Africa's version of events and shown that 'SWAPO leader, Mr Sam Nujoma, lied when he claimed SWAPO forces had not crossed the border'.

It had also confirmed that up to 1 000 SWAPO guerrillas had infiltrated from Angola.

General reaction confirmed that this was the version accepted by the international community.

Mr Botha also said his government had earlier asked the UN to immediately deploy all available UNTAG forces on the Owambo-Angola border to patrol the area. In addition to patrolling they should 'determine at first hand the situation on the ground and the extent of SWAPO's illegal infiltration of the territory'.

Administrator General Louis Pienaar, Special Representative Martti Ahtisaari and General Prem Chand flew together to the border area to make a first hand assessment of the situation there.

While there they held lengthy talks with police and army chiefs.

At a press conference in the evening, Mr Pienaar urged the international community to pressure SWAPO to assist South Africa in getting resolution 435 back on track.

He strongly emphasised that South Africa would never allow SWAPO to operate bases inside Namibia.

The United Nations and UNTAG

UNTAG's Brigadier Daniel Opande of Kenya, Mr Edward Omotose and Lieutenant Colonel Klaas Roos of the Netherlands, were scheduled to meet in Luanda today with the UN official in charge of Peacekeeping operations, Mr Marrack Goulding, a former British Ambassador to Angola.

Mr Goulding was touring the Gulf area, when he was ordered to Luanda to confer on the Namibian crisis.

It was revealed by UNTAG spokesman, Mr Cedric Thornberry, that the decision to allow South African forces to leave their bases to engage SWAPO was made by General Dewan Prem Chand of India, the UN force commander.

Mr Thornberry agreed the general situation was 'deplorable' and begged understanding from those of the press corps who suggested the UN had poured petrol on the flames by releasing units of the SWA Territory Force from restriction.

Thornberry said the UN had found itself 'in a dilemma' over the last few days. They had faced the task of assessing the embattled situation and taking 'decisions, however painful those may be' to release SADF units from base restrictions.

'We had a situation which the authorities were incapable of dealing with in the frame work of the existing forces,' he said.

He said UNTAG had been monitoring the movement of those units in and out of their bases, but 'if we go beyond that and accompany military or police on their missions, it would certainly take us well beyond the mandate we have at this stage.'

Mr Thornberry's statement must be considered as very odd, even though the Administrator General's press release on the 3rd April did say 'the movement out of existing bases would throughout be monitored by UNTAG military observers'. This indicated that UNTAG had declined to send observers out with SWA Police and supporting military. By the use of the phrase 'existing bases', one can see they had also declined to place observers at forward operational bases.

The author was assured by high authority that the South Africans would have welcomed observers accompanying them.

Mr Thornberry's contention that UNTAG lacked a mandate is also puzzling. In paragraph 9 of the Western Five's letter of the 10th April 1978, which formed the basis of resolution 435, it says: 'The Special Representative shall make arrangements when appropriate for UN personnel to accompany the police forces in the discharge of their duties'.

168

The military units operating in the field were operating under police command – in support of the civil power as it were – so they would undoubtedly be considered police officers by any international legal definition.

The phrase 'UN personnel' is used, so by that definition the observers could be soldiers, policemen or even civilians.

The only other problem for the Special Representative to overcome would be the phrase 'when appropriate'.

Well surely, even when viewed by a layman, the time when all hell is breaking loose between two warring parties, must be the most appropriate time imaginable for UN observers to deploy.

But perhaps, to be truly impartial, the last thing needed by UNTAG's leadership, was the embarrassment of having observers at the sharp end of conflict, sending back blow by blow reports of what SWAPO was doing, confirming the South African versions of what was happening.

But, whatever, UNTAG until that time, certainly showed promise of becoming the most expensive provider of gate guards in history.

One American behind the TV crews at this briefing asked: 'How many SWAPO members must die before UNTAG gets its act together.'

According to the *Star's Africa News Service,* there was much nodding of heads by media veterans.

Which just goes to show it was a lot easier, and a lot less dangerous, to nod one's head wisely in Windhoek, than it was to go out in the bush oneself and see at first hand what was going on.

UNTAG's job wasn't made easier when Dutch Foreign Minister, Mr Hans van den Broek, who anxiously sought assurances from UN Secretary General Dr Javier Perez de Cuellar, that Holland's 33 soldiers assigned to Namibia wouldn't get caught up in hostilities there.

To compromise the Secretary General made them part of the 'civilian component', so, presumably, this made them safe from pulling duty even as gate guards.

According to early in the day news reports, a UN spokesman in New York, Mr Francois Giuliani, blamed the Security Council for not having enough UN troops available in Namibia when the crisis arose. He said the secretariat had warned repeatedly that the delaying of an enabling resolution to finalise the budget for UNTAG, would create problems.

As a result, instead of having six weeks to mount the operation, a minimum set by the Secretary General, he had to settle for four.

The result was that when the crisis came, there were only 100 UN troops positioned in northern Namibia, most of them logistical and communications staff.

When pressed by reporters to say which side was responsible for the clashes, SWAPO or South African led forces, he said: 'I am not going to take sides on this issue unless I have firm guidance, which I do not have.'

In a rare South African-Soviet meeting, Mr Jeremy Shearer, South Africa's Ambassador to the UN, met with the Soviet President of the Security Council, Mr Aleksandra Belanogov, and discussed the Namibian crisis.

Reporters noted that Mr Belanogov was afterwards 'notably restrained' in his comments about Namibia.

Probably even he was bemused by what was going on.

With the urgency for an early meeting of the Security Council, created by British Premier Mrs Margaret Thatcher, who was directly responsible for Special Representative Martti Ahtisaari sending his enquiry team, headed by Mr Cedric Thornberry, posthaste to the border at midnight on Saturday 1st April, and with the submission of their report to the Secretary General for the meeting of the Security Council on Monday 3rd April, everything moved really fast.

Then, inexplicably, things slowed right down.

No formal public meeting of the Security Council was held, only an informal one in private behind closed doors.

Nothing but rumours, a certain amount of squirming and a distinct air of embarrassment emerged from the Security Council, until late on this day. It was as if they were wondering what to say. How they should handle a situation where the feet of their heroes had turned out to be made of clay.

The South Africans had been told, as was revealed by Foreign Minister Botha earlier in the day, that the Brigadier Daniel Opande-Mr Cedric Thornberry's investigation team's conclusions had coincided with the South African version of events.

But suddenly they didn't.

Or did they?

The Secretary General's statement to the informal meeting was later made public by South Africa. Part of it read:

In being interviewed, the two prisoners stated to the UNTAG team that they were the persons reported to have been captured by the Security Forces on the previous day. According to the report that I have received, they stated that they belonged to SWAPO armed units and that they had been told by their regional commanders to enter Namibia. Each said that said that he had been instructed not to engage the Security Forces, even if he saw them, because a ceasefire was to be in effect and there was to be no more fighting. The unit to which each belonged was, however, to carrying with it all their arms, even rockets and anti aircraft devices. One had entered alone: the other in a group of between 40−50 personnel. One said that he had been told by his detachment commander that he would be instructed, in Namibia, where he should go, so that the Un could supervise him and his colleagues. The other said that he had been sent to find out whether the Security Forces SWAPO fighters, or were observing the ceasefire. His commander was to join him in Namibia. Their purpose was then to come and establish bases inside Namibia. The team asked the detainees if the bases were for 'fighting or for peace'. He replied that it was necessary to have a base inside Namibia and that UN personnel would then come and take care of them. Each reiterated several times that they had been told that the war was about to be over, and that they were to enter Namibia and help to establish a base which would then be under the UN . . .

'In the light of the seriousness of the situation and the disparity between the objectives of the captives, as conveyed by them, on the one hand, and those attributed to them by the Security Forces who had seen their intention as aggressive and hostile, on the other, the team immediately called on the Security Forces to exercise the maximum possible restraint, while immediate efforts were made to resolve the situation.'

This was the closest he came to offering a conclusion as to which side fired first, which seems, in fact, to favour the SWAPO version.

According to news reports originating from UN circles, De Cuellar based his ultimate conclusions on consultations with three people, Foreign Minister Pik Botha, Special Representative Martti Ahtisaari and SWAPO's Representative at the United Nations, Theo-Ben Gurirab.

Knowing the result, backtracking on the Secretary General's thought process is simple. Botha believed SWAPO started it, Gurirab hotly denied it and Ahtisaari either came down on the latter's side, was ignored or was pressured by his boss into being either sensibly 'impartial', or to shut up.

He must have been furious at Ahtisaari's error of judgement in saying too much to the South Africans about the conclusions of the Opande-Thornberry report!

The ridiculous thing is that de Cuellar shouldn't even have asked Gurirab, because he wasn't supposed to have been there, as SWAPO were deemed to have lost all UN privileges with effect from the 1st April, to demonstrate UN 'impartiality'.

Dr de Cuellar also explained to the Council that he had authorised a 'strictly limited and temporary suspension of the requirement for some units of the South African military to be confined to base'.

After the informal meeting, the Security Council let it be known they fully supported the efforts of the Secretary General to resolve the crisis.

If Secretary General de Cuellar thought South Africa would let the matter rest there, he was mistaken. Foreign Minister Pik Botha riposted a letter back immediately, saying:

With reference to my letter to you of 2nd April 1989, I regret to inform you I have how now received further disconcerting evidence to the effect that:
  (i) Over 1 000 SWAPO (PLAN) forces have now infiltrated into Namibia;
  (ii) Over the period 21−30th March 1989, SWAPO forces of the 1st Mechanised Brigade redeployed from Lubango to locations at Xangongo and Techipa (i.e. from 300 kilometres north of the Namibia/Angola border to approximately 70 and 50 kilometres from the border, respectively);
  (iii) SWAPO tank elements were moved from Luanda to the border area during the same period to be deployed for offensive action against Namibia;
  (iv) Approximately 4 450 SWAPO forces are now deployed south of the 16th parallel;
  (v) Two mixed PLAN/Cuban semi conventional battalions of a strength of 450 each are positioned 600 metres north of Beacon 12 on the border and at Ongiva airfield respectively; and
  (vi) SWAPO elements inside Namibia are in continuous radio contact with their command posts in Angola.
It is my duty to bring to your attention that unless active and effective measures are taken to stem the rapid deterioration of the situation, the whole peace process in Namibia is in danger of collapse.

The President of the security Council, Ambassador A Belanogov, yesterday stated inter alia:

"In my view, the interests of independence of Namibia require full cooperation of the parties with the Secretary General and his Special Representative and scrupulous respect for the agreements relating to the settlement plan".

There can be no doubt as to what the agreements referred to by Ambassador Belanogov, and endorsed by the Security Council, require of each of the parties. What are the obligations undertaken by SWAPO under these agreements?

(a) On 12th August 1988, the President of SWAPO informed you by letter that SWAPO had agreed to comply with the commencement of the cessation of all hostile acts, in accordance with the Geneva agreement. He also stated that SWAPO would be ready to abide by that agreement until the formal ceasefire under resolution 435/1978 (para 10 of your report S/20412 of 23rd January 1989 to the Security Council);

(b) Paragraph 5 of the Geneva agreement referred to provides that Angola and Cuba "shall use their good offices so that, once the total withdrawal of South African troops from Angola is completed, and within the context also of the cessation of hostilities in Namibia, SWAPO's forces will be deployed to the north of the 16th parallel";

(c) Various of the relevant agreements affirm the principle of abstention from the threat or use of force against the territorial integrity of states; and

(d) On 18th March 1989, in a letter to you, the President of SWAPO confirmed SWAPO's agreement to abide by the ceasefire from 1st April 1989 and reconfirmed SWAPO's acceptance of the de facto cessation of hostilities "in and around Namibia between South Africa and SWAPO, in accordance with the Geneva Protocol of 5th August 1988.

Since the above obligations were endorsed by the Security Council, the South African government would be grateful if you would as soon as possible confirm that the Council is willing to do everything in its power to secure SWAPO's compliance with them. If not, must the South African government assume that the Council is now of the opinion that SWAPO is no longer bound by its obligations?

The facts of the developments over the past three days speak for themselves. Heavily armed SWAPO personnel crossed the Namibian-Angolan border in large numbers on the 1st April 1989. They carried with them not only semi automatic rifles but also mortars, anti tank weapons and ground to air missiles. On their own evidence they were instructed to enter Namibia and establish bases inside the country. These facts are borne out by the report of the Special Representative.

You will realise, Sir, that the South African government cannot be expected to implement its undertakings under the relevant agreements while SWAPO continues to act in flagrant violation of the provisions of those agreements with the acquiescence, tacit or otherwise, of the Security Council. In such circumstances South Africa has the undoubted right to suspend its compliance with its obligations. If, on the other hand, it is alleged that South Africa is in breach of its own obligations under the agreement, I shall be glad to learn which they are and how they have been breached.

In conclusion, SWAPO must now face up to the realities. Effective and immediate steps must be taken to ensure its compliance with all its obligations. Otherwise, in the exercise of its rights, the South African government will have no option but to consider its reciprocal obligations suspended until such time as UNTAG is in a position to ensure SWAPO's scrupulous observance of the provisions of the relevant agreements.

Washington wasn't exactly delighted with the Secretary General' conclusions either. The US State Department announced it was holding urgent consultations with the Soviet Union, Cuba and Angola to prevent the unravelling of the UN sponsored accords for Namibia's independence.

It urged SWAPO to halt their cross-border forays and for South Africa to exercise restraint.

A spokesman, Ms Tutwiler, said 'SWAPO had mounted a 'major infiltration' of Namibia in violation of UN Security Council resolution 435 and related accords.

She accused SWAPO of violating the agreements saying 'SWAPO appears to be taking advantage' of the ceasefire and the vacuum created by only about 1 000 of the projected 4 650 UN troops having been deployed so far.

'This serious incident must not be allowed to derail the process of decolonisation which so many have laboured so long and hard to achieve. The UN Secretary General and his Special Representative have the responsibility for maintaining the ceasefire in Namibia and for preventing infiltrations across Namibia's borders,' she told a press briefing.

Ms Tutwiler said the US would support any steps taken by the Secretary General to speed up the deployment of the remaining UN peacekeeping units, but Washington would continue to oppose an increase in the numbers of UNTAG.

Great Britain wasn't impressed with Dr de Cuellar's conclusions either.

Mrs Thatcher in a hard hitting statement pointed out that his report 'specifically confirms there had been a large scale incursion from Angola to Namibia by armed SWAPO personnel'.

Repeating condemnations of the infiltration expressed in Windhoek, she said: 'It is a most serious challenge to the authority of the UN and the internationally agreed arrangements for Namibian independence.

'There's no place in the UN plan for SWAPO to have bases in Namibia. Indeed, SWAPO have committed themselves to the Geneva accord under which they're required to stay north of the 16th parallel in Angola.

'It's the breach by SWAPO which has led to the most regrettable fighting and loss of life. I would emphasise the South African units involved are acting with the authority of the UN. It's now important that the authority of the UN is upheld and the agreements implemented in full.'

It caused little surprise when the Africa Group of the Non Aligned Movement took a different angle, issuing a communique on OAU notepaper accusing the UN of 'betraying' the Namibian people, and denouncing Special Representative Martti Ahtisaari, saying they had learned 'with utter disbelief' that he had allowed South Africa to use 'notorious murder squads' to 'kill and maim Namibians.'

It said: 'The UN must now explain why UNTAG was not fully operational on 1st April and is still not today.'

The explanation was simple, although everyone at the UN seemed too bound up in diplomacy to give it, the Africa Group themselves had deliberately created the delay by refusing to pass UNTAG's budget, probably in collusion with SWAPO, so they could mount their armed bid for the control of Namibia without opposition.

The documents cited 'eye witness accounts', asserting that the South Africans had attacked elements of SWAPO who were assembling for monitoring by UNTAG.

'SWAPO's long standing invitation to the UN,' it continued, 'to discuss the confinement of its combatants to bases inside Namibia should be addressed immediately, if future conflicts are to be avoided.'

It said that Mr Ahtisaari's 'ill conceived' decision' to release South African troops from base confinement would have 'far reaching consequences because it not only places the UN on the side of the South African colonial regime of illegal occupation, but also betrays the Namibian people and violates the letter and spirit of' resolution 435.

'The decision further displays a serious lack of judgement and an incredible insensitivity to the oppressed people of Namibia.'

It drew attention to a report by Secretary General Waldheim of the 26th February 1979, which said that ' any SWAPO armed forces in Namibia at the time of the ceasefire will likewise be restricted to base at designated locations inside Namibia', and said it 'is these SWAPO forces that are being attacked in northern Namibia.'

It insisted SWAPO had not infiltrated, but had always had combatants in 'their country of birth.'

The African Group conveniently overlooked that it was South Africa's refusal to allow SWAPO bases within Namibia, an argument eventually resolved in South Africa's favour, which had delayed the settlement plan's implementation for more than ten years.

10

Wednesday 5th April 1989

The War in the Bush

Zulu 5 Tango, commanded by Constable Assie van As, and Zulu 5 Sierra had combined and were working their way along the bank of the Kunene River, downstream of Swartbooisdrift, searching for SWAPO spoor.

A report came in that a Himba youth living locally, had reported seeing a group of more than fifty SWAPO heading southwards, to the northwest of Swartbooisdrift, the previous day.

The information was considered sufficiently reliable to justify the informant being picked up by helicopter and flown out to see Inspector Peens, who was operating out in the veld with Zulu 5 Tango and Zulu 5 Sierra, so he could be questioned.

He confirmed his earlier report, and guided the police to where he had seen the infiltrators.

Police trackers said that signs on the ground indicated that at least fifty, but maybe as many as eighty, SWAPO infiltrators that had passed that way.

Assistance was called for and Zulu 5 Echo – commanded by Constable Jimmy Botha, and Zulu 5 Juliet – commanded by Constable Sakkie Jooste, rendezvoused with the others in the veld.

The fighting cars of the combined groups, totalled a mere eleven out of what should have been a strength of twenty Casspirs or Wolves, plus four Blesbok logistic vehicles.

Certainly battle damage and rough handling occasioned by operational conditions had contributed much to their dwindling numbers, but mostly it had been caused by fair wear and tear, the vehicles having been constantly on patrol, virtually without let up, for the whole of March, in terms of General Dreyer's orders.

Most had been subjected to running repairs, but few, if any at all, had luxuriated in the clean oil and grease of a recent service.

The cars deployed into a fighting line, and with the trackers on foot in front, they set off in pursuit of the infiltrators.

After a few kilometres they came to a kraal, where they enquired from villagers if they had seen any SWAPO in the vicinity.

'Yes,' said a villager, 'there are many near here.'

He went on to explain, while other villagers interjected excitedly, that six SWAPO infiltrators had asked for water at the kraal only a short time before.

The leader had left a message for the Security Forces.

'If the Kovoets or soldiers come,' he had said, 'you must show them our spoor. Tell them we'll be waiting for them'.

Inspector Nick Peens discussed the matter with Inspector Ben Vermaak, who was acting as operations officer at Ruacana, and asked him to come out in a Bosbok spotter aircraft, so he could control the operation from the air and maybe see what the enemy were doing on the ground.

The ground forces waited until Inspector Vermaak was overhead in the spotter, and then began following the enemy's tracks.

Inspector Nick Peens was in front of the cars on foot, working with the trackers.

Inspector Vermaak broke in on the radio and said it looked to him as if the spoor was heading towards some broken hills and kopjes, marking the start of the foothills of the Zebra Mountains, the main range of which commenced about ten kilometres farther on.

He reckoned that from what he could see, they would have to leave the cars and continue on foot on reaching the high ground, as he didn't believe the Casspirs would be capable of making it.

After circling the ground forces for a while, the pilot, on Inspector Vermaak's instructions, flew his aircraft straight ahead of the police groups, over the hills ahead, to see what could be seen.

There was a sudden sharp explosive crack somewhere, causing Inspector Peens to pick up the radio handset.

He felt sure it was a grenade, believing someone in the combined groups had got jumpy and thrown one.

'Who threw that?'

The answer came from Inspector Vermaak in the Bosbok. 'The bastards just fired an RPG at us.'

Later, when the battle was over, he told Inspector Peens that it had been a SAM-7 missile, not an RPG at all. When it had sped past, rocking the Bosbok with its violent and stormy backblast, the pilot, Captain Derek McNamara, asked what it was.

Inspector Vermaak, determined to stay in the battle area at all costs, said it was an RPG.

He was concerned that if the pilot reported to MAOPs Ruacana that a missile had been fired at him, he might well have been ordered to clear out of the area for safety's sake, because Bosboks weren't armed.

He certainly didn't want that.

Albert Nakawa, secretary of Company 3 of SWAPO's PF Detachment, who was on the ground with the enemy forces, confirmed it was a missile fired at the Bosbok and not a RPG rocket.

Inspectors Peens and Vermaak discussed the situation over the air, deciding on a plan of action.

It was likely the enemy were in force, undoubtedly heavily armed and probably occupying entrenched positions in the high ground, only twenty kilometres away, where he would explain the position to the air force representative in person, and request an air strike by Impala jets from Ondangwa.

The target, generally, was the high ground, but Inspector Vermaak could be fairly specific on the location of SWAPO's positions, thanks to the SAM-7 ground to air missile used in their attempt to shoot him down.

He briefed the air force representative at Ehomba on the situation. He thought it might have worked, and recommended through channels back to command in Windhoek that they give it a try.

UNTAG, however, when approached, refused to sanction an air strike.

Instead four Alouettes, three gunships and a trooper, which didn't require UNTAG's approval, were made immediately available to lend support.

Two of them, one piloted by Captain Jamie Burger and the other by Captain Kobus Swart, were out assisting police teams following up SWAPO in the Ombulantu area.

Captain Pierre Steyn, piloting an Alouette trooper, and Captain Chris Opperman, piloting a gunship, both on operations elsewhere in the veld, were also diverted to assist.

Having established their fuel state, Ruacana directed them to fly to Ehomba, where after refueling, they would be briefed on the operational position.

Once there, Inspector Vermaak briefed the pilots on what had happened, mentioning an 'RPG-75 rocket' had been fired at his Bosbok spotter earlier.

By 16:00 the Alouettes were airborne.

Inspector Vermaak in the Bosbok arrived overhead first.

The police groups on the ground, while awaiting the arrival of the helicopters, took the opportunity to redeploy.

Five cars from Zulu 5 Tango and Zulu 5 Echo, under the command of Constable Jimmy Botha, were sent to a position north west of the target koppies to act as a stopper group.

Inspector Peens with the remaining six cars, from Zulu 5 Tango and Zulu 5 Sierra, together with their commanders and crews, and Constable Raymond Archer, medic Lance Corporal Jose Saayman and ten black policemen from Zulu 5 Echo, deployed to the eastern side and made ready to advance.

The normal practise when contact is imminent, is for ground troops to advance with gunships flying overhead, trigger ready to lend support and deal with situations as they arise.

This time, however, because the police were few on the ground and the terrain so rugged and inhospitable, the gunships went in first to give flushing fire to roust the enemy from their positions, and with luck, get them running, which would make things easier for the ground forces.

Captain Pierre Steyn, flying an Alouette trooper armed with a single machine-gun, was in command in the air.

The enemy had made no further hostile moves since blasting off the SAM-7 at the Bosbok earlier.

The helicopters went on ahead and began orbiting the area, directing flushing fire into the bush and at any possible enemy positions in the hills.

There was no reaction from the enemy down below, although aircrews reported catching occasional glimpses of military packs strewn at random and apparently abandoned.

The ground troops of Inspector Peens in the east, had formed into a fighting line, and with men on foot in front, they began advancing on the enemy held koppies.

When within sight of a dried up stream bed at the foot of the high ground, an insurgent unexpectedly broke cover on the side of the hill, and began sprinting away in panic.

Then he was joined by another and then another.

Suddenly the whole hill seemed to be alive with SWAPO, all trying to make good their escape.

One Alouette pilot reported counting at least forty, but another believed their numbers were closer to fifty.

There was certainly no shortage of targets, the enemy seemed to be everywhere. The engineer/gunners on the choppers had a field day.

It soon became clear, though, that not all the enemy had broken and ran.

RPG rockets began airbursting around the aircraft.

Captain Swart's helicopter collected four hits from enemy AK fire, one striking only a few centimetres from his head and another just missing his engineer/gunner, Sergeant Frans Schutte.

After completing some five orbits of the area, during which time their cannons had scarcely paused, one helicopter after another reported having run out of ammunition.

This left them with no option but to break off the fight, and return to Ehomba to rearm.

Captain Pierre Steyn, piloting the command and control Alouette, remained behind to give assistance and direction to the ground troops.

It had been the worst of times to run out of ammunition for his engineer/gunner, Sergeant Jacques Grobelaar, because there were still an abundance of SWAPO targets down there.

Forced by the undulating ground below to maintain a height of 1 100 feet rather than the safer 800 feet, they became the next members of the SAM club when a ground to air missile whooshed up and past them, its backblast shaking and throwing the helicopter about as if it had been grabbed by a giant hand.

Constable van Vuuren on the ground watched it miss by what he thought was no more than two meters. He was awed by its tremendous speed and the enormous smoky backblast which, momentarily, the Alouette's rotors seemed to chop up and disperse, as Captain Steyn fought to regain control.

'I thought he'd had it,' said Inspector Peens. 'I called him on the radio to sak if his chopper was okay, but he said he was fine.'

Things on the ground were just as hot for Inspector Nick Peens and his men. 'Contact!'.
'Contact!'.
'Contact!'

Resistance had certainly not ceased.

The right of the fighting line drew the first fire, which was RPG rockets, rifle grenades, mortars and AK fire.

It was a kaleidoscope of personal impressions.

For Constable Assie van As, it was a hell of weapons firing, grenades exploding.

An insurgent was firing a mortar at low level, like an artillery piece.

Constable Raymond Archer of Zulu 5 Echo was advancing on foot with his section of ten black policemen.

Sergeant Lappies Labuschagne stopped his car, and shouted for them to climb aboard.

Moments later Sergeant Labuschagne opened fire on the enemy, hammering away at them with his main armaments.

Constable van Vuuren's car developed a flat tyre about a kilometre from the base of the koppies. He had no spare wheels left aboard, so he couldn't continue. He deployed his men around the Casspir to prevent the enemy from storming it, and spent a most uncomfortable time until the battle was over, blinded by the thick bush and thus unable to add the weight of their firepower to the fight, while both

178

enemy and 'friendly' bullets, often uncomfortably close, zinged past constantly.

Other cars were milling the area at the base of the koppies, all guns blazing, ducking and diving amidst the enemy fire.

Many mortar bombs exploded amongst the cars, but fortunately there were no hits. The ground was very rocky and punishing on the cars, but it was not a time to worry about things like that.

Constable Assie van As' car smashed into something and stopped. He couldn't go forward and he couldn't go back, so he continued to fight the car from a standstill.

SWAPO fighter Albert Nakawa remembered the confusion.

'I saw four helicopters and then I heard some cars also, they were coming. From there they start shooting also, mortars. One man with a Strella shoot at the helicopters – the helicopters came from the east. I just ran away on my own. I didn't fire any bullets. I just ran with my gun and my bags. I joined about eight to ten other fellows, I didn't count. We went south direction, we went west.'

Constable Mike Maree had the medic, Lance Corporal Jose Saayman, in his car. It struck against and slid over, with an unhealthy grinding of steel, a huge rock which had been covered by a bush and unseen by the driver.

'The whole car lifted and I thought, well, that's the diff gone,' said Lance Corporal Saayman afterwards.

Astonishingly, though, the amazing Casspir played at being a tank, somehow clambered across, then continued on its way.

There was much shaking of heads and swearing at the workshops later on, though.

'You are never scared,' Lance Corporal Saayman said afterwards, 'because these police guys work like professionals. The way they operate behind their guns is amazing. They are so experienced, they seem to know everything, especially the blacks. Some have been involved in this since the beginnings of Koevoet. And then the way they drive. When you hit contact, they always do the right thing. You just feel safe with them. It is difficult to explain'.

As the return fire of the enemy became more random, police got out of their cars and set up mortars, and began pounding suspected enemy positions.

A few of the cars, because the action had been so intense, had used up all the ammunition for their main armaments, necessitating them collecting resupplies from the Blesbok and Strandwolf supply vehicles.

The enemy somehow completely avoided Constable Jimmy Botha's stopper group, comprising Zulu 5 Echo and Zulu 5 Tango, so he was ordered to return and rejoin the main group to assist with the sweep.

There was not much time left as darkness was fast approaching.

Two cars stopped next to Constable van Vuuren's car and helped him fix his wheel. Afterwards, they carried out a westerly sweep together, finding several SWAPO bodies and one badly wounded survivor, who died before he could be casevaced. He held no rank, being only an ordinary cadre, but he said there had been 150 heavily armed SWAPO in the hills, immediately facing the advance of the police, with another 75 in some other koppies nearby.

Inspector Peens took a small foot group into the high ground.

An insurgent with an RPG-7 concealed in a crevice, tried to bring his weapon to bear, but he was shot dead by a policeman nicknamed Gadaffi.

Constable van Vuuren with Lance Corporal Saayman and some others saw a pair of feet protruding from beneath a rocky shelf. Not sure if the owner was dead or alive, they shouted for him to surrender. When the feet didn't even twitch, Lance Corporal Saayman fired three shots beneath the ledge. Immediately the feet exploded into activity, and the insurgent crawled out and surrendered.

Altogether eleven bodies of SWAPO dead were found that evening.

Another eight, bringing the total to nineteen, and much in the way of weapons and equipment, including two fired and one unfired SAM-7, was found during a sweep the next morning. There were rumours later on that tribespeople found and buried another seven as well. It is understood, too, that even more bodies were found when another sweep was conducted some weeks later, once the war had quietened down.

Remarkably, considering the fierceness and the extent of the battle, the police suffered no casualties whatsoever and neither were any vehicles knocked out, indicating that those members of SWAPO responsible for inviting them to battle, had committed a major error of judgement.

The police groups camped out for the night on the tracks, ready to continue their hunt for SWAPO the next morning.

Commandant Jaco Kruger of 101 Battalion was in overall command of four groups operating to the south west of Ombulantu. Two of the groups were under his direct command while the commanders of the other two were Major Ben Venter and Captain Njoba.

The teams spread out over a wide area to look for spoor.

At 09:00 a team reported finding the tracks of some 30−40 SWAPO heading south. They were old, estimated as having been made on Sunday 2nd April.

The unit regrouped at the spoor and a more extensive examination was made.

Interestingly enough, amongst the old tracks, the fresh spoor of another five insurgents was found, indicating they were following and trying to find the earlier group.

Commandant Kruger deployed a total of twenty one Casspirs with crews amounting to more than 200 men for the follow-up.

Although only following the spoor of five insurgents, there was a strong possibility they had joined up with others, so there was a distinct possibility of them being ambushed by anything from 30−40 SWAPO.

At 11:10, as the groups approached the open ground of a shona, smallarms fire was directed at them from the right.

They replied with the combined and devastating fire of all vehicles, and enemy resistance ceased virtually immediately.

The bodies of two SWAPO insurgents were found, as well as the blood spoor of a wounded survivor who was attempting to escape the area.

The two dead, who had paid the highest of prices for standing and fighting it out with the Casspirs, were young, probably no more than fifteen or sixteen, as were so many of the SWAPO infiltrators sent in on this April incursion.

Some of the ex-SWAPO fighters serving in the ranks of 101 Battalion, were very upset about this, accusing Nujoma of being little less than a murderer. They said a child would accept anything his leaders said. He would believe he could tackle experienced fighters like the police and army head on, not thinking for a moment that he and the rest would end up dying like flies, and for nothing. But Sam Nujoma would have known all about that.

The spoor of the wounded survivor was handed over to Sergeant Botes, group leader of Zulu India, who was in the vicinity, to follow-up.

After each contact the Security Forces had to pick up the bodies of the SWAPO dead and return them to base for examination by UNTAG, because they refused point blank to accompany the policemen or soldiers in the field.

Later that day, working with six groups in combination, Commandant Kruger decided to check the Ongulumbashe area. This was where SWAPO had established a base in March 1966, 23 years before, and where all their men were either wiped out or captured. Obviously, both Commandant Kruger and the police reasoned, if SWAPO's intention was to establish bases, then what better place than somewhere where they could pretend they had been ensconced for two decades.

Also working the same area were police groups Zulu India – commanded by Sergeant Botes, Zulu Echo – commanded by Sergeant Wessie Wessels, Zulu Whisky – commanded by Sergeant Andre Meyer, Zulu Juliet – commanded by Constable Velle Schlachter, Zulu Oscar – commanded by Warrant Officer Vanna du Rand and Zulu Yankee – commanded by Sergeant Dewald Pretorius.

At 16:00 one of the police teams made contact with SWAPO. Various units, including 101 Battalion teams led by Commandant Kruger, Major Venter and Captain Njoba homed in to join the fight.

It was a similar story to the earlier one. Four young and inexperienced SWAPO cadres had decided to ambush a complete police group. One died immediately and the three survivors fled, only to run into the path of the incoming 101 Battalion teams, who shot them dead.

Other than one RPG rocket launcher, only AK and SKS rifles were recovered at the scene of this action.

Commandant Kruger's trackers found the spoor of three insurgents leading south from the contact scene.

They got back into formation and commenced a pursuit of the enemy.

Eventually the spoor split, with one man going off on his own, while the other two stayed together.

Knowing from experience that when men went off on their own, they were inevitably of command rank, Commandant Kruger and Lieutenant Eloff took their units in pursuit of the single man.

Realising he was going to be caught no matter what he did, the insurgent waited until the Casspirs were no more than six meters away, and then opened fire with his AK.

It was a hopeless gesture, and he was shot dead immediately.

The soldiers retraced their footsteps to where the spoor and split earlier, and set off after the remaining two.

The insurgents, hearing the growl of engines approaching, attempted to evade the Casspirs, first running across a shona, then through a kraal, until finally, they took up positions in the cover of some thick bush.

As the fighting cars began crossing the shona, the enemy opened up with inaccurately fired armour piercing rifle grenades, followed by a few short bursts of AK fire.

They were killed, literally seconds later, by the concentrated return fire of the fighting Casspirs.

Although not documented in detail here, there was a another contact during the day to the east of Oshigambo between SWAPO and police groups Zulu Papa, Zulu Sierra and Zulu 1 Sierra, during which one infiltrator was killed.

It is, in fact, almost impossible to recreate the pressure the Security Forces were facing over that trying period, because the contacts resulting in enemy being killed, was only part of the story.

Altogether on this Wednesday, which was certainly not the busiest of those nine days of war by a long way, there were 55 entries in the Security Force's war diary. Some entries, naturally, involved the contacts and incidents already detailed. But amongst the rest were fifteen reports relating to the possible or alleged presence of SWAPO infiltrators at various places along the Namibian-Angolan border region, eight reports of SWAPO spoor being found – some of which were followed and lost and six aircraft deployments to deal with reports, most of which turned out to be 'lemons'.

Everything, whether it was obviously true or probably false, clearly real or remarkably remote, had to be dealt with by police or by the military units assisting them, with a painstaking attention to detail.

Any of the reports could have been true, and all had to be looked at and investigated in that light.

The strain on the men involved, and their work load, can just be imagined.

The Goebbel's Factor – SWAPO's Propaganda War

SWAPO's internal wing, represented by its acting president, Mr Nathaniel Maxhuilili, launched an action against the Administrator General, Mr Louis Pienaar, in his capacity as the representative of the South African government and head of the SWA Police, to order him to comply with the provisions of the Inquests Act, in respect of the bodies of SWAPO fighters killed in recent clashes.

The application would be heard in the Windhoek Supreme Court on the 6th.

It asked that all such bodies, obviously of people who had died of unnatural causes, which had been buried in mass or unmarked graves, should be exhumed, identified and properly examined in terms of the Inquests Act and other laws which require the police to properly and 'fully investigate crimes or alleged crimes.'

He stated he was 'shocked' to read in newspapers that the SWA Police were disposing of the bodies of members of PLAN who had died in the confrontation in hastily dug mass graves, or by leaving them lying exposed to the forces of nature.

The custom of the police when dealing with major armed incursions in remote areas, had been to bury the bodies in mass graves, dispensing with post mortems because the causes of death were usually self evident, although if doctors were available they did examine the bodies.

The situation, for right or for wrong, was treated as if a state of war existed, which during the first week of April, most certainly did.

SWAPO's Secretary of Defence in Luanda, Mr Peter Mueshihange, rejected the Administrator General's surrender ultimatum saying they were ready to call for a ceasefire, but their fighters had to be confined to bases within Namibia.

'Our combatants have been operating inside Namibia for more than 22 years,' he said.

'SWAPO will not accept their fighters being escorted back to Angola because it is an attempt to humiliate Namibian patriots who made supreme sacrifices for their country,' he insisted.

He added, with a note of disbelief, that South African losses were far higher 'than the 20 they have been claiming.'

Which just goes to show that the best laid plans of mice and men ...

Two Windhoek lawyers, Mr David Smuts and Ms Michaela Clayton, attached to the Windhoek Legal Assistance Centre, submitted a seven page report to Mr Martti Ahtisaari, alleging police were not taking prisoners during their confrontations with SWAPO.

They said they were acting on behalf of 'various individuals, organisations and mass movements' who had briefed them to carry out an investigation at the border.

They said they had found various battlefields which had been strewn with tinned food, spent SWAPO and Security Force cartridges, medical supplies and the bodies of several cadres indicated by villagers, missed by the police during their sweeps.

They interviewed three tribespeople who had been in the vicinity when contacts had taken place. One said he didn't know who was shooting at whom, another said he had seen bodies on the battlefield which the Security Forces prevented him from examining and another who said the guerrillas had been 'resting and eating' when the shooting began.

They asked the police at Oshakati for permission to interview two prisoners, but this was refused, because they were detained in terms of emergency regulations.

They said they were obliged to infer from the fact that as only two prisoners had been taken, the police were following a policy of not taking further prisoners.

The lawyers also called on the police and military to comply with the provisions of the Inquests Act, and to observe the 'basic demands of human decency ...'

They commented on the lack of UNTAG presence at the border, and expressed concern that UNTAG observers were not accompanying the Security Forces in the area and properly monitoring their conduct.

Strangely enough, there was not even a suggestion by either of these lawyers, that the police had at any time or in any way acted correctly. Neither did they advance any of their own constructive ideas as to how they thought masses of armed insurgents, equipped to shoot down aircraft and destroy tanks, should be dealt with.

Their report, according to what was written in the SWAPO supporting, *The Namibian*, consisted only of carping criticism, seemingly designed to boost SWAPO and denigrate the image of the Security Forces.

Surely, to any reasonable person, they were protesting too much!

Robert Hughes, Chairman of the British Anti Apartheid Movement, in a letter to the British Prime Minister, registered 'deep distrust and strongest protest' saying the actions of herself and her ministers 'can only undermine the prospects of resolving the current situation.'

'The result of your intervention,' he went on,' is that South African forces are now operating with the authority of the UN, and there have been extensive reports from church and other independent sources that these forces, which included the notorious Battalion 101 and Koevoet, have committed numerous acts of intimidation and murder of civilians'.

He refuted the British government's contention that there is no provision in the peace plan for SWAPO to have bases in Namibia, and quoted provisions cancelled by agreement as long ago as 1980.

He ended by saying: 'All available evidence from independent sources indicates that it was the South African Security Forces . . . which started the current conflict by launching unprovoked attacks on SWAPO forces in northern Namibia.'

The 'independent sources', of course, comprised a daisy chain of conspiracy of flimsy foundation indeed.

SWAPO's Information Secretary, Mr Hidipo Hamutenya, called for the sacking of Mr Martti Ahtisaari, saying: 'SWAPO will find it extremely difficult to cooperate and work with such a person'.

He said the Special Representative's actions in authorising South African troops to go into action had 'aggravated' the fighting.

Instead, he should have 'separated the rival sides, gone on radio to appeal for calm and ordered them to cease fighting and remain in their positions while UNTAG restored peace'.

He said PLAN's military commanders were waiting in Luanda to be placed at UNTAG's disposal.

Hamutenya said they were ready to broadcast instructions to combatants, on both the Angolan and Namibian radio, telling them to end the fighting. '. . . we believe this can be done in a matter of hours, but we have had no response as yet from UNTAG'.

He said Mr Ahtisaari should have sent a 'skeleton force' of UNTAG troops to the scene of the fighting, and raised the UN flag in order to separate the two sides.

A senior SWAPO officer, Commander Uuno Shaanika, added: 'We are ready to announce a cessation of hostilities and together with UNTAG forces, to go to the area of conflict to issue instructions to our combatants on the battlefield to end the fighting'.

SWAPO's Windhoek branch, issued a statement demanding the immediate resignation of Special Representative Martti Ahtisaari, accusing him of being unable to exercise 'any meaningful authority over the South African colonial structures in Namibia'.

It accused the 'colonial government' of 'attempting to derail the peaceful implementation of the UN plan' and 'attacking combatants of SWAPO while they were trying to regroup and hand themselves over to UNTAG'.

'As a result of the South African provocative military attack, PLAN combatants were left with no alternative but to defend themselves.'

It also condemned UNTAG's decision to deploy the 'notorious, 101 and 102 Battalions in order the fight the SWAPO combatants.

It said that Mr Pik Botha's threat to pull out of the peace process was a 'clear indication of South Africa's original planned intentions'.

The National Union of Namibian Workers, a front organisation for SWAPO, held a meeting attended by an estimated 1 000 people at Katutura Township, Windhoek.

Mr Ben Ulenga of the Mineworkers Union of Namibia, canvassed as a future SWAPO labour minister, criticised the UN for not having the wherewithal to control the situation.

'They are actually not here. We cannot rely on them. We must stand up and do what has to be done.'

By any definition UNTAG, had they been so minded, could have investigated this veiled threat as intimidation, or at the least, as incitement.

The next speaker, CCN General Secretary, Dr Abisai Shejavali, launched an attack on the Security Forces, saying he couldn't understand 'why South African soldiers and Koevoet must still attack others in a time of peace.'

'I expected that if South Africa knew of the presence of PLAN,' he continued, 'they would have had to report it to UNTAG so UN representatives could deal with the matter'.

He recklessly defamed the UN representative at Tsumeb, saying a group of pastors found him drunk when they went to see him.

The Other Face of War

The Administrator General, Mr Louis Pienaar, issued the following appeal to SWAPO combatants operating in Owambo:

> You are illegally within Namibia in contravention of the UN independence plan.
>
> As such the SWA Police will have no alternative than to continue to pursue and arrest you.
>
> A large number of your comrades have already unnecessarily lost their lives. By your action you are endangering the process of free and fair elections under UN supervision, to which your leaders had agreed.
>
> To stop further bloodshed, I call on you to lay down your weapons and surrender to the police. I, as Administrator General, who is responsible for the maintenance of law and order, guarantee your safe conduct back to your bases in Angola.
>
> If you choose not to surrender, turn northwards towards Angola with your weapons. Tracks leading northwards will not be pursued aggressively by the Police.
>
> If you do not respond to this plea before noon on Saturday, 8th April 1989, the police will have no other option than to pursue you with all means at their disposal.
>
> I make this appeal to avoid unnecessary bloodshed.

Advocate Bryan O'Linn, Chairman of the Namibia Peace Plan – NP435, said at a Windhoek press conference that SWAPO's explanation that its combatants were regrouping within Namibia is 'not very convincing'. He added that even if true, there didn't 'appear to be sufficient excuse for such behaviour because there is no provision for such a move in the peace plan'.

He stressed that UNTAG was had not been ready to handle the crisis on the 1st April because of 'infighting at the UN', which had left them little time to prepare for their task.

He said the time had come for all parties, the UN, the South African government, SWAPO, the DTA and so on, to address the real issues, to establish the truth and put their points of view forward in a responsible manner.

Mr Pik Botha, South African Foreign Minister, sent the following letter to the Secretary General Dr Javier Perez de Cuellar:

Further to my letter of 4th April 1989, I wish to inform you that the South African government feels encouraged by the firm and positive reaction of various governments endorsing the provisions of the Geneva Protocol including the obligation of SWAPO to remain north of latitude 16 degrees south in terms of paragraph 5 of the Protocol.

I would like to repeat my urgent appeal to you to bring influence to bear on the SWAPO leadership to cease the senseless course on which it is embarked. The SWAPO leadership must be persuaded immediately to call a halt to the continuing illegal armed incursions of its members into Namibia which is the cause of the needless human carnage taking place at the moment. I have been informed that a further 300 SWAPO armed personnel crossed the border from Angola last night. A captive today disclosed to the police that he was on the border on 3rd April 1989 with his group awaiting instructions. They received orders by radio to cross the border on the same day.

In an effort to relieve the situation, the South African government has requested the Administrator General to broadcast a message to the northern region of the territory. His message will contain an appeal to the infiltrators to surrender and to lay down their arms or to withdraw northwards to Angola. He will explain that it is unnecessary to return to their own country to die in this way when they could return to vote and to live in their land in a peaceful way as provided for in agreements to which SWAPO has subscribed. Whoever gave the order for SWAPO members to infiltrate into Namibia in uniform and heavily armed to establish bases and caches of arms, misled them as this action is in violation of the agreements for a peaceful settlement reached by Angola, Cuba and South Africa which were endorsed by the United Nations and accepted by SWAPO.

The message will add that the decision to return in peace and to work for progress in Namibia is in the hands of the people of Namibia. SWAPO members who lay down their arms in peace will be given a guarantee that no steps will be taken against them and they will be given safe conduct to assembly points under UNTAG supervision from where they can be transported safely to suitable points north of latitude 16 degrees south with the cooperation of the Angolan authorities. Further, SWAPO members who wish to return northwards into Angola, are assured that the Namibian police force will not pursue them.

This appeal will also be broadcast by the Administrator General on television. The radio broadcast will be repeated at regular intervals for the next week or more. It would be helpful if the United Nations as well as all government members of the United Nations could assist in this effort to save human lives.

The United Nations and UNTAG

At an UNTAG press briefing in Windhoek, Mr Cedric Thornberry revealed that Mr Ahtisaari and his staff were having a meeting of 'considerable importance' with 'a number of bishops and other senior members of the Council of Churches for Namibia – CCN, with whom 'Mr Ahtisaari and a number of us in UNTAG, have had long and very fruitful contacts ... and for whom we have the very highest respect'.

This made it clear to everyone that UNTAG was accepting without reservation the blatant pro SWAPO propaganda originating from that body of hopelessly biased churchmen.

He announced that a number of governments had come to UNTAG's assistance and the airlifting of personnel, equipment and supplies into the country would be accelerated.

186

He pointed out that it was no good bringing in and deploying a battalion of UN troops or police observers, if they couldn't move around, they had nothing to eat and couldn't communicate.

He said that 'essentially, you know, an army marches on its stomach. These days an army marches on its four wheeled drive'.

When he mentioned that some 400−500 vehicles were being shipped from Japan, he was asked why they could not be airlifted. He asked the questioner, not unreasonably, what it would cost for a person to fly from Japan to Namibia, and suggested he relate that to the cost of flying in a large number of vehicles.

When asked about the question of SWAPO being granted bases in Namibia he replied: 'It was brought up most frequently between 1979−1982, because at that time SWAPO claimed the right to be able to establish bases inside Namibia, and then to have them monitored by the UN. As I think I said yesterday, that claim was never accepted by any of the other parties to the settlement proposal, which as you know was a kind of treaty, was a consensus, arrived at by a very painful process of negotiation and compromise. So that all the other parties in the settlement agreement said, no that isn't part of the settlement agreement.

'In the end, in 1982, the position I think, was made really clear beyond any shadow of doubt, that this was something additional to the settlement proposal and that if SWAPO wanted that as well, then it would have to be negotiated as an additional element in the settlement proposal.'

An UNTAG press release announced they had 921 personnel deployed in Namibia as at that day.

The twenty one countries which had supplied military personnel included Australia (96), Bangladesh (25), Canada (60, Czechoslovakia (20), Denmark (132), Finland (43), India (20), Ireland (20), Peru (19), Poland (32), Spain (49), Sudan (20), Switzerland (46), Togo (25), United Kingdom (79) and Yugoslavia (25).

Radio France Internationale reported Secretary General Dr Javier Perez de Cuellar as saying he intended allowing SWAPO to establish bases inside Namibia.

He said he would submit his proposal to South Africa for consideration 'because unfortunately they are obliged to accept it'.

This was contrary to South Africa's position, supported by Great Britain, the United States and Canada, that under the peace protocols SWAPO was obliged to withdraw to its bases north of the 16th parallel in Angola.

It was reported that South Africa was seeking urgent clarification of the Secretary General's statement.

11

Thursday 6th April 1989

The War in the Bush

Picking up from where they had left off the previous evening, the Zulu 5 teams led by Inspector Nick Peens, tracked some thirty survivors from the contact area in the foothills right into the Zebra mountains.

They were aware that at least a hundred insurgents, although it was probably many more, had escaped into the mountains.

Alouettes piloted by Captains Pierre Steyn, Kobus Swart, Chris Opperman and Jamie Burger, were scrambled to lend support.

A major ambush by the retreating insurgents was anticipated, so the gunships provided flushing fire ahead of the ground forces, as they moved slowly and cautiously through the broken valleys and bushy plains before the mountains began.

SWAPO fighter Albert Nakawa and seven others, including the Detachment Commander, were out ahead of them. All were very thirsty, having only drunk water once since yesterday's action.

'The helicopters came from the east and started shooting in the area. They were shooting, shooting, shooting. The Detachment Commander and other fellows went one side, while we four went west.'

For Nakawa the war was reduced to the sole task of looking for water. They found water later that day, but he was tired so the others abandoned him. He lost track of time, wandering alone in the harsh environment of the Zebra Mountains for more than a week, the last four days without food and a minimum of water, until eventually he was captured by soldiers. He still had his AK and pack with him.

The police couldn't get their fighting vehicles into the mountains and a request for Puma helicopters to troop the men deep in, so they could work at outflanking and outwitting the enemy, by laying ambushes and generally harassing them on foot, was refused because of an aircraft scarcity.

It was also decided the threat posed by the insurgents, because they had scattered into the mountains, which were remote and far from centres of population, had diminished.

It was not considered wise, particularly at that time of crisis, for police units to become tied down in what would inevitably become a wearing campaign of attrition.

It was decided instead to hand the situation over to the army, for them to mop up the stranded insurgents.

Various military units, including the SADF's Parachute Battalions, 201 Bushman Battalion and 102 Battalion of the SWA Territory Force, were brought in.

They mounted observation posts, laid ambushes and followed-up spoor, capturing or killing many of the enemy during the next few weeks.

SWAPO's original target area, it was learned later, had been the administrative centre of Opuwo, where the police Zulu 5 teams and 102 Battalion were home based.

102 Battalion based at Opuwo, was back to full strength, and operating from its forward base at Ehomba in the Kaokoland bush.

Callsign 10 Mike Delta, consisting of twenty two soldiers commanded by Sergeant Pekaha, followed SWAPO spoor by the Kunene River, north west of Swartbooisdrift.

They made contact, killing two armed infiltrators and capturing another.

Captain Sys Prinsloo, commander of 101 Battalion's 904 company, was operating with his company and police groups Zulu Papa and Zulu Sierra, south of Beacon 24.

At about noon on Wednesday 5th April, the police teams had picked up the fresh spoor of some forty infiltrating SWAPO, who were heading in a southerly direction.

They had followed the tracks, the fighting vehicles of the police groups on the left and the twelve 101 Casspirs on the right, until darkness fell, and the combined units had then camped out for the night on the spoor.

In the morning they resumed the follow-up, maintaining the same formation as the previous day.

After going for no more than a kilometre, the spoor swung north east on to what was almost a footpath.

From here on the spoor was easy to follow and the enemy, who were all wearing boots, had made no effort to conceal their spoor by anti tracking.

The trackers who had been walking in front of the vehicles, got back aboard and the pace of the follow-up increased, with the vehicles, which had been deployed into two lines, making between 20−30 kilometres per hour.

At about 11:00 they reached a kraal. Here the spoor looped off to the right, then abruptly made a ninety degree turn into the bush.

They crashed through the bush for about a kilometer until they reached a bush road, crossing directly ahead of them.

As the front line of Casspirs reached the road, SWAPO who were lying in ambush ahead, opened fire with mortars, RPG rockets, rifle grenades and light infantry weapons.

It was estimated that at least fifteen RPG rockets were fired in the first few minutes of the contact.

Four police Casspirs were shot out at this stage.

The surviving Casspirs then stormed through the enemy positions with all guns firing. The enemy were well dug in, with a ragged line of one man foxholes spread over an area of about 150 metres. Behind those positions were two well dug in 60 millimetre mortars.

The driver of 101 Casspir, callsign 14 Charlie, while milling around the contact area, turned his car ninety degrees after seeing three insurgents running, putting himself side on to an RPG position. The rocket struck the car in its diesel tank, knocking it out.

It began to burn.

The car commander, Corporal Stony Steenkamp, manning twin Brownings in the turret, saw two insurgents ducking away and shot them.

Meanwhile, the rest of the crew began baling out to escape the fire, but as they did, an insurgent concealed nearby opened up with his AK at almost point blank range, killing three troopers.

Corporal Steenkamp, who had left his Brownings and jumped down into the body of the vehicle to bale out as well, suddenly realised that something was terribly wrong out at the rear of the vehicle. Ignoring the fire, he checked out the lie of the land through a rifle port in the side of the car, and saw the insurgent who had killed his crewmen, in his foxhole, AK at the ready, waiting for those still alive to bale out.

Corporal Steenkamp fired through the rifle port, killing him.

The rest debussed and Corporal Steenkamp, keeping strict control over his crew, put them into defensive positions around the knocked out Casspir, while all around them fighting vehicles, guns blazing, milled back and forth across the battle area.

Lieutenant Rassie Erasmus, a team commander, had the tyres of his Casspir shot out, and was unable to move his vehicle either forward or back.

The front gunner firing the 30 calibre Browning forward through the windscreen, saw an RPG gunner at the aim loom up no more than ten metres in front of the bonnet. The driver triggered first and the insurgent died.

Another RPG gunner stood up in front of Captain Prinsloo's Casspir, but he also fell victim to the front gunner's Browning.

Captain Prinsloo's Casspir, by then, had five wounded crewmen aboard.

Alouette gunships were called for and four, piloted by Major Wimpie Kruger, and Captains Eugene Viljoen, Mark Hill and John Barnard were scrambled.

Other help in the form of police groups Zulu Foxtrot, Zulu Hotel and Zulu 1 Sierra and a 101 Battalion company commanded by Major van Niekerk, was also on its way.

Many of the cars which had taken the brunt of SWAPO's first onslaught, had tyres shot out, but those able to, together with the reinforcements as they arrived, fought their way through the SWAPO positions and began milling and criss-crossing the battle area.

The insurgents decided they had had enough and began to bombshell.

Two more Alouette gunships were scrambled at Ondangwa to lend assistance.

Things were serious for the ground forces, as there were four dead and seventeen casevacs, of which four were serious.

A Puma was desperately needed for casevacs, but it wasn't even airborne by then.

Major Wimpie Kruger decided that so far as the four seriously wounded were concerned, there was a definite time crisis, so he ordered that two be loaded aboard his aircraft and two aboard Captain Viljoen's aircraft, so they could be flown to the sickbay at Eenhana, from where they could be picked up by the Puma and flown on to Ondangwa.

This was done, and within fifteen minutes of the contact commencing the patients were undergoing treatment by the doctor at Eenhana. They were not taken into the sickbay, but retained on the flightline, ready to be picked up by the Puma as it doglegged to Eenhana on route back to Ondangwa.

190

One casualty, Medic Corporal Bernard Brumloop, a brave man attached to police, who until then had himself been treating wounded while under fire with no thought for his own safety, was in a serious condition. The doctor at Eenhana suggested to Major Kruger that he chopper him direct to Ondangwa, rather than wait for the Puma, because that would get him there five minutes ahead of time, a factor likely to prove crucial in saving his life.

The surgeons confirmed later that it did.

For most of the chopper pilots this and similar battles over the same period, were a new experience and they learned a lot. There had never been contacts of this magnitude in Namibia before where, large units of insurgents had fought back with heavy armaments from well entrenched positions.

It reminded the more salted pilots of the major air to ground battles they had fought in during the last three years of the Rhodesian War, ten years before.

The SWAPO group commander was discovered mortally wounded in a trench. Before dying he confirmed that his group, callsign Group 4, had been forty strong.

He said they had been lying in ambush, awaiting the Security Forces, for nearly twenty four hours.

The final count of enemy dead at the contact scene was twelve.

A large quantity of weapons, equipment and ammunition was recovered from the battlefield.

In the central area, after a night camped out in the bush, Zulu 1 India – commanded by Sergeant Neil Vincent, Zulu Whisky – commanded by Sergeant Andre Meyer, Zulu Juliet – commanded by Constable Velle Schlachter and Zulu Yankee -commanded by Sergeant Dewald Pretorius, cast westwards just after first light. Shortly afterwards the trackers discovered the spoor of SWAPO infiltrators. It was fresh, clear and easy to follow. It led south in the general direction of Tsandi.

Adopting their usual tactical formation, the follow-up team began making excellent progress.

While the main body remained on the spoor, cars on the flanks raced ahead for two, three and sometimes even four kilometres. The trackers would then debuss and walk towards the centre, searching for the tracks of their quarry.

Once found, they sent up a smoke shell, sometimes a red, sometimes a yellow and sometimes a green, depending on the group.

On sighting the smoke signal, the other units would race forward and catch up. After confirming the spoor they would go on track again. The whole leapfrogging process then being repeated.

In this way they stayed on spoor for maybe 25–30 kilometres, until reaching the outskirts of Tsandi, a tribal township and business centre.

There, because of the large number of locals around, they lost the tracks.

After much casting about and checking of the ground, the trackers were unable to find them again.

The men were tense, tired, thirsty and hungry.

Much of the tension was caused by the ever proximate danger of stumbling into a SWAPO ambush.

Constable Willie Meyer, a car commander with Zulu 1 India, explained.

'In any follow-up you are full of butterflies, like nobody has ever experienced – it's nothing like even the tension before a big rugby game. You are always aware of what could happen if you don't see the enemy . . . if he sees you first!'

It was decided to stop by a cuca shop in Tsandi. Everyone ordered cool drinks and hot *slap* chips, everyone that is, except for Constable Kallie Smit, a car commander with Zulu Whisky.

Constable Smit remained obstinately on the outskirts of the township with his trackers, casting about to find the spoor the others had give up on, willingly relinquishing his chance of chips and a cool drink in the process. Grimly determined the enemy, whose tail they had doggedly clung to all morning, wouldn't escape that easily.

Then he found the spoor.

Meanwhile, the others were anticipating their chips, by then bubbling merrily in hot oil on the cuca shop's stove.

Constable Smit called them on the radio.

He had found the fresh tracks of two SWAPO insurgents in a shona and was following-up in a north easterly direction.

He needed assistance – urgently.

'Hold on, Kallie,' he was told. 'We're on our way.'

Then, with scarcely a backward glance of regret at the pans of frying chips, the men ran outside and mounted their Casspirs and Wolves.

The teams were racing from the village in the best of possible US cavalry styles, when Constable Werner Mouton – commander of Zulu Bravo came on the air.

He asked their position.

He was close by and following SWAPO spoor in a south westerly direction towards Tsandi.

They compared notes over the radio.

There were definitely two SWAPO groups. Coincidentally they were on reciprocal courses – heading for each other. They couldn't be more than a few minutes apart.

Constable Mouton's trackers insisted a contact was imminent.

'Stay in position,' he asked the others. 'If you carry on, you'll ruin my spoor.'

It was highly frustrating to call a halt, particularly for Constable Smit, whose determination and perseverance had brought the combined groups to the brink of success, but there was no alternative.

Constable Werner Mouton, as hot as he was on the tracks of his enemy group, had to be given first crack.

They weren't in competition. Their objectives were the same. Still . . .

They waited for the sound of shots.

Nothing happened.

Perhaps Werner's bloody missed them! Then he came on the air reporting the capture of three SWAPO, one a commander. They were from both groups, caught just as they joined forces.

A two for the price of one situation.

The combined groups of Zulu India – commanded by Sergeant Johan Botes, Zulu Echo – commanded by Sergeant Wessie Wessels, Zulu Delta – commanded by Sergeant Dean Viljoen and Security Branch unit Zulu 21 Alpha – commanded by Constable Johan Jacobs, were operating in much the same vicinity.

Shortly after 09:00, they found the spoor of four SWAPO insurgents heading in a southerly direction, and began a pursuit.

Not long afterwards, the tracks of another three joined the originals, bringing the enemy's strength to seven. The trackers estimated the trail to be about a day old. It was difficult to follow because of weathering. After a frustrating period of losing it, then casting around and picking it up again, losing it then picking it up again, the tracks swung east. After another three painstaking kilometres, they lost the spoor altogether. Sergeant Johan Botes, hearing on the radio that Zulu 1 India, Zulu Whisky, Zulu Victor and Zulu Yankee had just come free and were only five kilometres away, decided to enlist their assistance.

'Come on Sarge,' Constable Willie Meyer, was meanwhile saying persuasively to his group leader, Sergeant Neil Vincent, of Zulu 1 India, 'what about a beer at the cuca shop? We already missed out on cokes and chips earlier.'

'Okay,' Sergeant Vincent eventually relented, 'but one beer each and no more. A job might come in.'

Smiles all round were the order of the day.

They parked the Casspirs outside the cuca shop. The crews went inside, one man remaining on the radio to monitor transmissions.

A few bought cokes, but most gladly ordered their one beer. Soon they were sitting outside in the sun, sipping drinks contentedly, while a few tackled delayed meals of Russian sausages and *slap* chips.

Perhaps the guys had simple tastes, but at the time it tasted better than French champagne and caviar.

Then reality rudely returned.

The radio operator leaned down from the door of his Casspir.

'Sergeant Botes of Zulu India wants help.'

'Oh, my indigestion,' sighed a policeman, stuffing the rest of his Russian sausage in his mouth, and washing it down with a last swig of beer.

It just wasn't a day for leisurely lunches.

Within twenty minutes Sergeant Neil Vincent's teams had locked on with those of Sergeant Johan Botes.

While awaiting their arrival, Sergeant Botes' trackers had been fruitlessly casting around to regain the spoor. It was a particularly densely populated area and the many tracks of locals moving about in the vicinity made success remote.

It was decided that all vehicles, there were 26 altogether, would be formed into a long fighting line. They would then advance eastwards -the last known heading of the spoor, in the hope of cutting it again.

After a few kilometres they discovered suspect tracks, which they followed for a short distance.

There was a sudden startling glimpse of someone ducking for cover. Fortunately, although a few rounds were loosed off, firing ceased immediately when it was realised it was only a scared villager.

Fortunately, no harm had been done, but it must be appreciated that in bush war close encounters, a surplus of trigger hesitation can cost a man his life. But in spite of this, the danger of an innocent being hurt is always in the forefront of an operator's mind.

It was this caution, born from a high degree of training, that saved the villager's life.

After pointing out to him that running from a Security Force patrol in times of an emergency can be more than just dangerous to one's health, the cars resumed positions and the line moved on.

They progressed about ten kilometres.

It was beginning to look like a lemon.

To the front of Sergeant Wessie Wessels, group leader of Zulu Echo, was a large muhango land and beyond that an extensive kraal complex.

Before reaching the land, a jackal, disturbed by the Casspirs, leapt from a clump of thick bushes and began running evenly along in front of his Casspir.

More for a diversion than anything else, Sergeant Wessels unholstered his 9mm pistol, already loaded with a full magazine of fifteen rounds, and cocked the action.

'Listen, guys,' he called over the radio, 'there's a jackal to my front and I'm going to shoot it. When you hear firing, it will not, repeat not, be a contact, so don't open fire.'

Constable Willie Meyer of Zulu One India manning the twin 30 calibre Brownings in his Casspir's turret, misheard and shook his head. Why would somebody want to shoot a donkey at a time like this?

Satisfied he wouldn't cause a general alarm, Sergeant Wessels promptly opened fire with his pistol, blasting away a fusillade of all fifteen rounds.

The jackal, however, bore a charmed life, and was still bouncing cheekily along in front of the Casspir when the magazine was empty.

Thoroughly put out by his poor marksmanship, Sergeant Wessels discarded his pistol and grabbed his R-5 carbine.

Switching the change lever to automatic, he again opened fire.

Suddenly, Constable Johan Jacobs in his Security Branch Casspir, saw three armed SWAPO break cover in the muhango field and run for the shelter of the nearest huts.

He opened fire, killing one, but the two survivors dodged amongst the huts and were lost from view.

They worked out later that four insurgents had been in concealment to the left of the muhango land, while another three had been in the centre towards the huts.

When Sergeant Wessels began shooting at his jackal, the three, not unreasonably, had assumed their four comrades were being fired on.

They broke cover and this cost them their lives.

Cars began shooting and machinegun fire rippled up and down the line.

There are fortunes of war, misfortunes of war and things that work out all right in the end.

Constable Meyer didn't open fire.

'It's a contact,' his driver, Sergeant Ysterface, yelled.

'Bullshit, no,' said Constable Meyer, 'I don't know why, but it's some arsehole killing a donkey.'

'No, sir, no, sir,' said Sergeant Ysterface. 'It's contact ... open fire!'

'Negative,' said Constable Meyer, 'there's buggerall happening.'

'Contact! Contact!' his battle experienced black crewmen bawled. In the heat of the action Constable Meyer was ignored. 'Go right! Go right!' the crew instructed Sergeant Ysterface excitedly.

He reacted and swung the Casspir violently right.

Constable Meyer, who still hadn't seen anything and who was by then thoroughly annoyed, bent down to speak to Sergeant Ysterface.

'Bear – bloody – left!' he ordered.

There was no reaction and Constable Meyer was suddenly kept busy ducking up and down in the turret, to avoid overhanging branches.

He was absolutely livid.

He came upright as they came out of the trees, suddenly saw a black man ahead.

He had on a white shirt and black trousers and was running furiously, his arms pumping up and down, as he raced for cover.

A villager, was Constable Meyer's first reaction.

'There he goes! There he goes!' the black policemen howled in excitement.

'You can't bloody shoot . . . he's a bloody civilian,' Constable Meyer yelled back. Then he blinked and did a quick double take.

Civilians didn't carry Russian AKs!

When they checked afterwards, there were no villagers around anyway because, as normal, they had cleared out when SWAPO arrived.

The Casspir charged at the enemy, while Constable Meyer and everyone else in the car opened fire.

They paused briefly, picked up the body and an AK rifle fitted with a grenade launcher and some rifle grenades, then carried on.

A burst of return fire starred the bullet proofed front window of a Zulu 1 India car. It didn't do much good for the enemy, two of whom were shot by Sergeant Johan Botes and another by the crew of Zulu I India's Blesbok supply vehicle.

Alouette helicopter gunships appeared overhead, but they took no part in the action.

The running spoor of two SWAPO insurgents heading north west were located by the trackers of Sergeant Wessels of Zulu Echo.

Cars set off in pursuit.

Sergeant Johan Botes' car was immobilised with two flat tyres, so he remained behind. With him was a car of Zulu 1 India, with two wounded crewmen aboard.

Two cars on the flanks of the pursuit group, leapfrogged ahead to cut the spoor.

An insurgent broke cover and was shot.

Another kraal complex lay ahead.

The fighting line became disrupted when some of the Casspirs, including those of Sergeant Dewald Pretorius and Constable Johan de Lange, found themselves faced by a large ditch which they couldn't negotiate.

They kept watch over their gunsights on possible escape routes from the kraals, in case any of the enemy tried to run for it.

The rest of the line, which was unimpeded, wheeled around to cover the village area.

Constable Meyer who had become detached from the rest, called Sergeant Wessels on the radio, asking him to fire a thousand footer parachute flare as a signal, so he could see where he was and rejoin him. The signal shot into the air and burst high up.

'There,' Constable Meyer indicated to Sergeant Ysterface.

They set off ploughing through the bush, heading in the general direction.

'Left, left, left . . . now right and straight ahead,' Constable Meyer directed.

He suddenly realised that because of the thick bush, they had passed Sergeant Wessels' position.

He ordered Sergeant Ysterface to do a U turn.

'There he goes!' two black policemen in the back of the car yelled.

Constable Meyer was talking on the radio, asking Sergeant Wessels for another signal.

'Wait one,' he said. 'My guys have spotted something.'

He was surprised the black policemen hadn't opened fire. They were highly experienced and invariably quick on the trigger when sighting an enemy.

'Where is he?'

They pointed at a large tree.

He was hiding in that.

The tree was too large for the Casspir to push down and overrun, so Constable Meyer told the driver to circle it so he could check it out.

'Shoot! Shoot!' the black policemen yelled, almost jumping up and down. 'Shoot!'

'I would if I could see something,' Constable Meyer replied scathingly.

There were many cars in the general area, so shooting without a definite target would have been irresponsible. It would likely have caused casualties in the other cars.

'He's there . . . shoot him!' his crew were yelling.

He couldn't see anything but he obliged his crew fired a quick squirt into the tree. Then as the Casspir passed by, he swung the turret, keeping his guns on target. There was a sudden movement and he fired instinctively, as did everyone else in the fighting vehicle.

An insurgent toppled out from behind the tree, dead.

He was wearing chest webbing and was armed with an old British two inch mortar, together with bombs.

When the Casspir had circled, so had be, keeping the tree between himself and the car.

He might have succeeded in getting away, but for the sharp eyed Owambo policemen.

By the action's end seven SWAPO had been shot dead and much kit, equipment, weapons and ammunition captured.

One of those killed had an old bullet wound, with an entrance and exit, which showed early signs of sepsis. This indicated he was a survivor from an earlier contact.

From all reports, Wessie's jackal survive!

Warrant Officer Jackie Grobler, Ops officer at Etale Base, had spent much of the previous evening questioning a SWAPO prisoner. He said he had been a member of a SWAPO group, estimated at about 200 strong, that had crossed into Namibia in the general area of Beacon 22. Once inside he became separated from the others. He had no idea of their ultimate destination.

From what he said, Warrant Officer Grobler, concluded this was the first information police had received of this particular SWAPO unit's move across the border.

He briefed Sergeant Piet 'Hand' Cronje – commander of Zulu Mike, on what he had discovered, and instructed him to go out and search for tracks in the general area of Beacon 22.

Major Oberholtzer, of the SADF's 63 Mechanised Battalion, with his command of nineteen Ratels, was still attached to police at the Etale Base.

Sergeant Cronje divided the Ratel strength into two parts, attaching half to his own force of three police groups and detaching the rest to Sergeant Johan Bosch, commander of Zulu Kilo and two other groups.

The reinforced groups went off in different directions to check for spoor.

Constable Nick Coetzee's trackers were the first to report success, finding the spoor of fifteen infiltrators south east of Ehoma.

After this initial trace, trackers cast around in the general area and eventually found what were almost paths, freshly well trodden paths, set about fifty metres apart, and leading south. Each track, in the tracker's opinion, indicated the passage

196

of about fifty insurgents. They reckoned they had been made about mid morning the previous day.

Sergeant Cronje knew from experience, that when SWAPO operated in large groups they seldom marched long distances. He believed they had most probably, established a base of some sort in the immediate area. They could easily be nearby, maybe within a few hundred metres, despite the age of the spoor.

In view of this, he decided it would be unwise to continue on spoor until he had recombined all forces as one group.

He called Sergeant Bosch of Zulu Kilo on the radio and asked him to bring his groups in.

It was 12:00 before the units had regrouped.

The police fighting vehicles, from Zulu Mike, Zulu Alpha, Zulu 1 Delta, Zulu X-Ray, Zulu Kilo and Zulu Charlie and the army Ratels, adopted the same formation they had already successfully used on Monday 3rd April. The vehicles were formed into three lines, covering a front of 800 metres. Sixteen cars, composed of Ratel 90s alternating with two Casspirs or Wolves, were put in both the first and second line. The rear rank consisted of the more lightly armed vehicles, like the Blesbok and Strandwolf transporters.

Sergeant Cronje felt positive it would not be a long trail, that they would soon come to contact. The experienced group commanders with him agreed. The tracks were clearly visible, so he put only three trackers on the ground in front.

The formation set off slowly but steadily across the veld.

After two kilometres the tracks changed direction abruptly.

Sergeant Cronje ordered the formation to wheel, an intricate exercise to perform with so many cars and in such rough country. SWAPO chose the moment to initiate an ambush with a bombardment of RPG rockets, armour piercing and anti personnel rifle grenades, mortar bombs and machinegun fire.

Two RPG rockets struck home on Major Oberholtzer's Ratel-90 with deafening roars, there was black smoke and then flames, as the car began brewing-up.

The crew baled out in an extraordinary hurry and scrambled for safety, fortunately unharmed except for some relatively minor wounds.

For the rest of the battle the Ratel burned furiously, emitting clouds of black oily smoke, while shells inside the hull intermittently exploded.

Sergeant Cronje, in the turret of the command Wolf, was struck on the head by shrapnel, which belted him down into the vehicle's well. He experienced a momentary welter of pain and confusion, and clearly remembers thinking: Oh, my God, I'm dead!

He shook himself together, got back in the turret and began calling for gunship support on the radio.

Two Alouette helicopters at Eenhana, a trooper piloted by Major Wimpie Kruger with Sergeant Gary Brocklebank as his engineer/gunner, and a gunship piloted by Captain Eugene Viljoen, scrambled and were soon hastening to the battle.

All around Sergeant Cronje, cars were returning fire, throwing everything they had at the enemy, whose fire was intense.

He began stonking the enemy with his personal 60mm mortar, which was mounted on his Wolf, quickly expending the nine bombs he always kept readily to hand.

Sergeant Renate Esalungu, fortunately, had anticipated this, and had already prised open another case of bombs. The moment Sergeant Cronje's private store had been used up, he began passing shells up to him, ensuring that between them the hollow rhythm of the mortar didn't miss a beat.

Rifle bullets dinged against Sergeant Cronje's gunshield, gouging scars in the paint. He caught a glimpse of an insurgent in a foxhole. He was aiming and about to take another potshot at him with his AK.

Before he could even attempt to engage him, Constable Nick Coetzee's gunner shot him dead.

It was Sergeant Cronje's lucky day, for just after that, an RPG-7 rocket failed to detonate after striking his Wolf full on the side.

The enemy's powerful 82mm mortars contributed to the battle, but although many bombs burst amongst the cars, none, quite amazingly, hit target. The battle carried on for about an hour without respite, with both sides slugging it out.

Being well entrenched, the enemy were difficult to winkle out.

Because the Security Forces were engaged in an intensive mortar bombardment of the enemy held area, which consisted of extensive trenchworks, the Alouettes, when they arrived, held off to the north until the firing died down.

They began orbiting the area, attracting an enormous amount of ground fire from SWAPO, who seemed to be loosing of everything they had at the choppers.

No SAM-7 missiles were fired, but RPG fire was intense. The next day during a sweep, five RPG-75s were found in one trench alone, laid out next to each other in a neat row.

Two gunships at Ondangwa had also been scrambled, but had not arrived, and Major Kruger began asking over the radio where they were.

Sergeant Brocklebank used three packs of ,303 ammunition while shooting at enemy positions.

The helicopters withdrew partly from the battle area and began giving fire control orders to the ground force's mortars, but this didn't achieve much in the way of results.

Sergeant Cronje suggested an air strike be put in by Impala jets based at Ondangwa.

Major Kruger decided the burning Ratel made an excellent target marker and approved the call for a strike.

Thinking their arrival overhead was imminent, Sergeant Cronje ordered the ground forces to slowly retire. The vehicles began reversing slowly, maintaining formation and continuing to mortar the enemy. When sufficiently far back from the firing line, he called a temporary halt so the punctured tyres on the police fighting vehicles could be changed or repaired.

Once done, this was a practised drill that took only a few minutes, the move continued until they reached the original start point where Sergeant Bosch's command had locked on earlier.

The helicopter gunships, meanwhile, had kept the well dug in SWAPO busy with cannon fire.

There was a delay committing the Impalas, though. Local permission was readily obtained, but they were held on Ondangwa's apron, armed and ready for takeoff, awaiting UNTAG's final clearance from Windhoek.

It was forty minutes before they finally arrived.

The two delayed gunships from Ondangwa arrived first and joined the battle, having experienced a problem with the chat frequency on the radio.

While awaiting the arrival of the ground attack aircraft, Major Kruger landed his

Alouette trooper and picked up the two casevacs, collecting a couple of rounds through the rotor blades in the process.

As they drew near target, the gunships gave the Impala commander a last minute target briefing, and then veered off to get out their way.

The Impala flight of four aircraft, led by Major Jan Minnie and Captain Mark Barker, streaked in low from west to east, ensuring the sun was dazzling the eyes of the enemy, using the blazing Ratel as their principal target marker.

Unfortunately, it was not the best of days for the Impala boys, one bomb load fell bang on target, but two aircraft had hang-ups preventing the release of their bombs, while another stick fell short.

There can be little doubt that because of the early withdrawal of ground forces, some of the enemy succeeded in slipping away from the battlefield.

Officers of the UNTAG air element at Ondangwa, then senior Polish air officers and some Italian chopper pilots, displayed considerable professional interest in the bombing up and preparation of the Impalas for the raid. Like most air forces nowadays, while flyers are highly trained in amazingly sophisticated aircraft, the majority of pilots go from flying school to retirement without dropping a single angry bomb.

They were, it was said, even more professionally interested when they saw two of the aircraft land back at Ondangwa with their bomb racks still full.

They enquired why, so the story goes, and were highly impressed when a tongue in cheek South African officer insisted that as they had achieved their objective with two bomb loads, they had brought the rest back.

After the Impalas' departure, 63 Mechanised Battalion bombarded the target area with 81mm mortars, with the choppers giving target directions, after which the combined ground forces, still retaining formation and led by Sergeant Cronje, fought their way through the base from west to east, avoiding the many bomb and mortar craters as they progressed.

Afterwards, an infantry platoon from 63 Mechanised Battalion went back in to clear the trenches the only really effective way ... the PBI (poor bloody infantry) way – on foot with personal weapons and bombs.

The policemen, whose training in such matters was sketchy, but who by reason of their job were used to occasionally grabbing sticks by the sticky ends, looked on with admiration as the boys in brown got to work.

Unfortunately for the infantrymen, while technicalities of war might have progressed by leaps and bounds, winkling an enemy from a trench has changed little from the way their grandfathers tackled it during World War-1.

While the trench clearing progressed, the crews of the police fighting vehicles together with the Ratels, kept a wary watch on the flanks with their heavy machineguns, but all resistance in the enemy base had disintegrated.

The battle was over by 18:00.

Seventeen of the enemy had been killed, most by shots from above, while another was slain the next day during a minor skirmish in the immediate vicinity.

Reports which drifted in from the local tribal population afterwards, painted a depressing picture of terrible suffering for SWAPO. Many who escaped this battle with their lives, had suffered grotesque wounds caused by the effects of the Security Force's powerful weaponry.

It was said that some died of wounds afterwards, while an unknown number were put out of their misery by their comrades, and buried out in the bush. Rumour had it that this accounted for at least another seven.

Some of the more senior policemen in Owamboland felt certain after this particular action, that former SWA Police Inspector Michael Hadengwa, who defected to SWAPO in Angola in 1988, taking a Casspir with him as a bonus for the Reds, was responsible for the initiation of the new conventional war type tactics used against SWA Police units.

In fact, it is obvious he gave SWAPO, FAPLA, the Cubans and most importantly the East Germans and Soviets a complete rundown on SWA Police tactics, which were then analysed in fine detail and methods worked out to combat them.

They must have reasoned that the police would crumble when faced with a conventional attack. After all, they must have thought, they are bush fighters, very good maybe, but only trained to skirmish with small guerrilla units and certainly not soldiers in the conventional sense.

What they failed to take into account, however, was the guts potential and *esprit de corps* of those truly remarkable bush fighting policemen, and how adaptable they were to changing circumstances.

'They came in fully expecting to kick our arses,' Sergeant Piet 'Hand' Cronje told the author with no little pride, 'but we kicked their's. Would you like to know why? It's because as fighters, no matter what the Russians or Cubans do, we are still far too bloody good for them.'

In another contact sixty kilometres south of Beacon 3I, police groups Zulu 4 Foxtrot – commanded by Constable Peet Nel, and Zulu 4 Delta – commanded by Sergeant Tekkies le Roux, killed another SWAPO insurgent.

In the area 10−20 kilometres south of Beacon 29, Zulu Uniform – commanded by Warrant Officer Attie Hattingh, Zulu Quebec – commanded by Constable Duffield, Zulu Lima – commanded by Sergeant Zeelie, Zulu 1 Juliet – commanded by Sergeant D B Kok and Zulu 4 November – commanded by Constable Sampie Potgieter were involved in two separate contacts with SWAPO.

In the first contact two SWAPO were killed and in the second another who had been on his own.

Corporal Herman Carstens (20) of Warmbaths, died in 1-Military Hospital, Pretoria.

He had been wounded in action on Tuesday 4th April.

The Goebbels' Factor – SWAPO's Propaganda War

The Secretary of the South African Council of Churches – SACC, Rev Frank Chikane, in a statement issued in support of the Council of Churches of Namibia – NCC, alleged the 'carnage of the last few days in Namibia could have been prevented if SA forces had exercised restraint in the handling of the matter, and if Mr Ahtisaari ... would not have allowed the SA Army to leave their bases to be involved in this fighting.

'We believe that this action of Mr Ahtisaari was amongst other things influenced by the failure to deploy UNTAG forces on time and the reduction of those forces by the UN.

'We do not believe the appeal by the Administrator General to SWAPO to surrender to the SA forces will solve the problem.

'The only way to resolve this problem is for the UN Representative to call on all SA forces to return to their bases and for the SWAPO forces to hand themselves over to the UNTAG forces.'

SWAPO front organisation, The National Union of Namibian Workers – NUNW, issued a press statement saying the crisis started when 'SA led military forces attacked PLAN combatants without provocation'.

It also warned of collusion between South Africa and the Special Representative saying: 'We have demanded a forthwith explanation for the authorisation of redeployment to which no response has been forthcoming'.

It said SWAPO insisted on having bases on Namibian soil and said they had never agreed to move their forces north of the 16th parallel.

It described the calls for SWAPO combatants to withdraw from Namibia as absurd and asked: 'Who are the foreign occupationist forces and who are the Namibians?'

It spoke of PLAN fighters being 'callously murdered' and asked what right Mr Ahtisaari had to authorise the redeployment of 'SA murder squads'.

It made five demands:

(i) That the UN Secretary General's Special Representative be replaced;
(ii) That SA troops are confined to bases;
(iii) That UNTAG be effectively deployed;
(iv) That PLAN combatants presently in the country be confined to bases within Namibia; but that
(v) SWAPO is nevertheless prepared to enter into ceasefire negotiations immediately.

The leaders of the six Frontline States, Angola, Mozambique, Zambia, Zimbabwe, Botswana and Tanzania in a joint statement said they were ready to accept UN Secretary General Dr Javier Perez de Cuellar's proposal that SWAPO insurgents be disarmed after a ceasefire and allowed to remain in Namibia.

'The SWAPO forces once disarmed could be confined to one area under the protection of UNTAG forces and they would stay put there until the time comes when the entire SWAPO leadership returns home,' Zambian President Kenneth Kaunda, the current chairman, told a news conference.

'We are not interested in apportioning blame, we are interested in stopping the carnage.'

Angolan President Jose Eduardo dos Santos, however, rebuked SWAPO, saying: 'Angola regrets the SWAPO leadership could not exercise total control over its guerrillas at the critical moment of the start of resolution 435 by stopping anyone from crossing the Angola/Namibia frontier.'

Dr Kaunda said the Frontline States were willing to provide a battalion of troops each to boost the UNTAG forces.

'They would be on site to assist the UN and not SWAPO,' he said.

One could scarcely imagine less impartial troops to boost the strength of UNTAG, than those from the Frontline States, especially Angola.

The police, in reply to a report prepared by lawyers Mr David Smuts and Ms

Michaela Clayton of the Legal Assistance Centre in Windhoek, which alleged police had adopted a policy of not taking prisoners, denied the allegations.

Spokesman, Chief Inspector Kierie du Rand, said it was police policy and laid down in the Police Act, that the 'first action is to apprehend a suspect'. Shooting, he said was a last resort, but 'these people have no intention of being apprehended'.

He said they had ambushed the police and 'thereby initiated the firefight . . . and were well trained, heavily armed and aggressive'.

The Other Face of War

A spokesman in London said both the Soviet President, Mr Mikhail Gorbachev, and British Premier, Mrs Margaret Thatcher, had agreed they would press for a 'cooling' of the situation in Namibia. Both leaders stressed the importance of supporting the UN's efforts to bring about a ceasefire.

Mrs Thatcher raised the matter with Mr Gorbachev when he arrived in London on Tuesday night, because 'she felt it was a matter that should be dealt with urgently'.

The US State Department rejected SWAPO's bid to obtain a military foothold in Namibia.

In a hard hitting legal analysis sent to Pretoria, they said Nujoma had affirmed his acceptance of the peace plan in letters to UN Secretary General Javier Perez de Cuellar in August 1988 and again in March.

'The UN plan contemplates no SWAPO bases in Namibia either before or after April 1st, implementation date . . . the infiltration of armed SWAPO personnel is prohibited'.

Foreign Minister Pik Botha announced there would be a special meeting of the revived Joint Military Monitoring Commission – JMMC, consisting of South Africa, Cuba and Angola – with the USA and Soviet Russia as observers, on Saturday 8th April at a to be disclosed later venue in Namibia.

The South African delegation would be led by Ministers Pik Botha and Magnus Malan.

In a brief statement Mr Botha said: 'Recent diplomatic exchanges have confirmed that Cuba shares the SA government's preoccupation about the seriousness of the situation on the Namibian-Angolan border.

'Cuba has reiterated that it remains committed to a peaceful settlement. Allegations of Cuban involvement in the present hostilities in northern Namibia are denied.

'There is also objective evidence that the Cuban troop withdrawal is continuing.

'This indication of the Cuban government's position is timely, coming as it does on the eve of the ad hoc meeting of the Joint Commission . . .'

It was also announced that Mr Botha, General Malan, and Foreign Affairs Chief, Neil van Heerden, would be meeting Mr Ahtisaari in Windhoek on Friday 7th April.

Intelligence from various reliable Security Force sources, suggested that 250 of SWAPO's PLAN fighters at Itufa base, just north of Senanga, in Zambia, had begun moving southwards towards Sesheke, opposite Katima Mulilo in the Caprivi Strip. Some delay, it was reported, had been caused by fifty of them being drowned while negotiating some swamps, but the survivors were on their way.

The Security Forces in Caprivi were thin on the ground and there was certainly not enough of them to handle a major armed incursion.

This was by reason of the resolution 435 confinement of troops to base, aggravated by the pressure of operations in the central area of Owamboland and in the west.

General Willie Meyer, the commander of the SWA Territory Force, ordered Brigadier Johan Louw to see General Prem Chand, brief him on the situation and seek authorisation for the release of further companies of troops from base restriction, as an urgent precautionary measure.

General Prem Chand seemed to appreciate the importance of the information, but wouldn't make an immediate decision, wanting the matter to be first brought to the attention of Special Representative Martti Ahtisaari.

He was 'phoned and Brigadier Louw went to see him.

The Brigadier explained the position only to be told, quite adamantly, by Mr Martti Ahtisaari, that there weren't any SWAPO bases in Zambia.

This surprised Brigadier Louw because SWAPO bases had been in Zambia since the earliest days of SWAPO, and it had never been regarded as or kept a diplomatic or a military secret.

After a courteous discussion about the general situation in Namibia, during which it became obvious the Special Representative was a worried man, he asked for the South African allegations and requests to be put in writing.

That evening General Meyer, Brigadier Louw and Intelligence Officer Commandant du Toit, went to see Mr Ahtisaari, this time with full reports and written requests.

The Special Representative, although he didn't say it in so many words, had by then fully accepted there were SWAPO bases in Zambia, the officers gaining the impression he had checked up and confirmed this with New York.

He didn't want to make an outright refusal to the request for the release from their bases of more troops, but begged them instead to appreciate that a meeting of the UN Security Council was imminent. He asked them to please exercise restraint until after that had taken place.

General Meyer and his staff officers agreed, but only with reluctance, pointing out that, meanwhile, he would have to carry the full responsibility if an invasion occurred, and for any consequent loss of life.

In the event SWAPO didn't make a border crossing in that area. This doesn't mean they were not there and ready. It was probably because they were forced to abandon their plans due to world pressure.

The interesting aspect arising from this, is that Special Representative and chief of UNTAG, Mr Martti Ahtisaari, who had a clear responsibility to monitor not only the bases of the Security Forces in Namibia, but also those of SWAPO in Angola and Zambia – Zambia having been particularly specified in various protocols, didn't even know SWAPO bases in Zambia existed.

This explains with devastating logic why less than 100 UNTAG monitors were based outside of Namibia, and 4 650 soldiers and 1 000 policemen were based within the country.

The reason can only be that the UN never, at any time, intended to monitor SWAPO bases.

Maybe if they had begun putting UNTAG monitors in place in Angola before the 31st March, the whole SWAPO invasion of northern Namibia could have been prevented.

12

Friday 7th April 1989

The War in the Bush

In the early morning units were sent from Ruacana to check the border area for SWAPO tracks, either coming in or going out of the country, but nothing was found.

It was the seventh day since SWAPO's armed border incursions had commenced and most police fighting vehicles were in a bad state. Many were off the road after mechanical breakdowns, while others were battle damaged.

Mechanics had been working virtually around the clock to keep them on the road.

Because of this, and because things were quiet, the patrols from Ruacana were allowed to return to base to rest.

It didn't affect their readiness, because they remained on call, but rest was what they needed most.

Most changed into civilian clothes, the first time they had put them on for more than a week.

Some laid on their beds to catch up on lost sleep, while others sat around waiting for the fires to be ready for a braaivleis. Everyone was sick and tired of living on ratpacks and stews.

Then Constable Theunis Kruger, acting group leader of Zulu 1 India, called in from an old contact area twenty three kilometres east of Ruacana,the place where 27 SWAPO had been killed on the 2nd April.

He had been routinely checking the area, which hadn't been properly swept until then, and reported finding much stuff which had remained undiscovered since the battle. This included kitbags, mortar bombs and ten bicycles. SWAPO had obviously utilised the bikes as man made donkeys to transport their heavier weapons and war material.

Of more pertinent interest, though, was the fresh spoor of a single insurgent.

He asked for assistance to mount a follow-up.

Inspector Jumbo de Villiers agreed it wasn't advisable for Constable Kruger to conduct the follow-up alone, because Zulu 1 India had been reduced to a low of two fighting cars and a Strandwolf supply vehicle.

Makeshift crews for two fighting cars were hurriedly assembled.

Sergeant Neil Vincent, Zulu 1 India's group leader, and Constable Johan Zeelie took over one car and Constables Johan de Lange and Dirk Spies got aboard the other.

They paused briefly at the cookhouse, picking up volunteers, most of them wearing civvies, to crew them.

It took about half an hour to join up with Constable Kruger and Zulu 1 India.

They formed the cars into a tactical line, and with the trackers deployed on foot in front, they set off in pursuit of the lone insurgent.

A Zulu 1 India car suffered a mechanical breakdown, so it was left on the main road with its crew.

The gunships were scrambled and they quickly arrived overhead.

Minutes later a pilot spotted the quarry.

He called Constable de Lange on the radio, warning him the insurgent was almost directly in front of his car.

Constable de Lange couldn't see, his vision being obscured by the thick bush.

Trackers working one of the flanks, however, spotted the enemy and fired across the front.

Constable de Lange's driver, unable to stop in time, crashed through the bush and ran over the enemy, killing him.

Found with the body was an AK rifle, a mortar tube and two bombs.

Because of the emergency situation, many policemen inexperienced in counterinsurgency work except for basic training, were committed to combat from sheer necessity.

It was a question of learning fast.

One policeman, who had been stationed at the border for only a few weeks, and whose experience was limited to general duties at a large police station in a South African city, continually badgered Warrant Officer Fanna du Rand to allow him to join his crew for a patrol.

Eventually, he relented.

He was short of personnel and besides that the man was as keen as mustard.

'Have you had any counterinsurgency training at all?' he asked.

Well, yes, he had. Not much it was true, and he hadn't attended a COIN course at Maleeuskop. But, rest assured, he knew what he was doing.

'Okay, have you got a sleeping bag? You'll need one because it gets bloody cold out in the bush at night.'

He didn't, but he would soon borrow one.

Much pleased with himself, the new man grabbed his kit and joined the crew of Zulu Oscar 1.

While patrolling, Warrant Officer du Rand and the new man spoke a great deal. His main ambition was to lay his hands on a Russian compass, the type that SWAPO are equipped with, as a souvenir.

'Do you find many around?' he asked anxiously.

'If we have a contact and find one, it's yours, I promise.' Warrant Officer du Rand reassured him.

During the day they became involved in following up a group of about thirty SWAPO insurgents, reportedly moving south west near Tsandi, about fifty kilometres south of Beacon 5.

Five police groups took part in this exercise, the others being Zulu Victor – commanded by Constable Duppie du Plessis, Zulu Whisky – commanded by Sergeant Andre Meyer, Zulu Bravo – commanded by Constable Werner Mouton and Zulu Juliet – commanded by Constable Velle Schlachter.

206

The new man, as befitted his inexperience, was armed only with his personal R-5, and manned a gunport in the Casspir's side.

'If we hit contact, just keep shooting and keep your head down, okay?' Warrant Officer du Rand had briefed him.

The new man said he understood.

'Contact!'

The first time is always the worst, but in spite of everything the new man performed well.

Warrant Officer du Rand's group killed three SWAPO near a large tree, during the first few minutes of battle.

He paused his car briefly, to glance down and confirm the three were dead before claiming the kills, because up there on the border, the making of inaccurate claims was not highly regarded.

Well, they were dead all right.

There was a temporary lull in the shooting, but the new man thought the contact was over. All he could think about was the likelihood of a Russian compass being down there with those dead SWAPO.

No one would beat him to it, he was determined about that.

He opened the rear door of the Casspir and jumped to the ground.

Warrant Officer du Rand chose that moment to order his driver to continue.

He did, stranding the greenhorn by the enemy dead.

Then the firing recommenced, seeming as if it was all around the new man.

Thoughts of the compass deserted him, as he began wildly leopard crawling after the receding rear end of the Casspir.

Fortunately for him, some of the crew had seen him get off, so they shouted out for the driver to stop.

The much chastened new man hurriedly climbed back aboard, suffering a much deserved dressing down in the process.

This didn't mark the end of his suffering, though, because just as he resumed firing at his gunport, something wacked his neck and he experienced a dull and hot pain there.

So this is what its like to die, he thought, clutching his neck. His knees crumpled and he collapsed into the well of the car.

There was an abrupt ceasefire in the back of the Casspir.

The black policemen started laughing. In fact, their laughter became so intense it rendered them incapable of firing their weapons.

When had they seen anything so funny?

This inexperienced white man had been struck by a cartridge case ejected by one of the R-5s . . . and he had thought he was dying!

The bodies of four well armed SWAPO insurgents were found in the contact area.

In a contact some thirty kilometres south of Beacon 22, police groups Zulu Mike, Zulu Alpha, Zulu 1 Delta, Zulu X-ray, Zulu Kilo, Zulu Charlie, Zulu Victor Tango, with army Ratels in support, killed another SWAPO insurgent.

The Other Face of War

The South African Foreign Minister, Mr Pik Botha, sent an excellent letter, spelling out the Namibian position in succinct almost nursery terms, to Secretary General Dr Perez de Cuellar:

I wish to refer to my letters to you of 2nd, 4th and 5th April 1989. I arrived in Windhoek some 5 hours ago and on a basis of a briefing on the latest developments in the northern part of Namibia, it is with great dismay that I must report to you that the situation has deteriorated further.

I attach the latest information supplied to me as well as to your Special Representative and General Prem Chand. Even if all the information cannot as yet be confirmed conclusively, I am satisfied that on the basis of that information which can be confirmed, the general pattern of developments since 1st April 1989 is persisting, namely that continued orchestrated SWAPO incursions into Namibia from Angola are still occurring. The groups are in uniform. They are heavily armed with lethal weapons of war including semi automatic rifles, anti tank rocket launchers, mortars and surface to air missile.

It is manifestly preposterous to suggest that this amounts to peaceful regrouping. Mr Secretary General, what is beyond dispute is that:

(a) SWAPO undertook to be confined to bases north of latitude 16 degrees south at least from the 1st April 1989 where they would be monitored by UNTAG;

(b) SWAPO is not confined to base in Angola north of latitude 16 degrees south and is not being monitored by UNTAG;

(c) SWAPO is accordingly violating the following obligations:

(i) It is not confined to bases north of latitude 16 degrees south;

(ii) Its forces are in areas in Angola south of latitude 16 degrees south;

(iii) It has crossed, and continues to cross, the border into Namibia under arms.

SWAPO commanders are regularly in radio contact with the groups which are still in Angola and also those that have already crossed the border. The SWAPO leadership need only issue an instruction to its commanders that SWAPO lay down its arms and return to Angola. Instead of doing this, the SWAPO leadership encourages more SWAPO groups to flout the authority of the Security Council.

There is at the moment one SWAPO group heading for farming districts south of Owamboland.

On my arrival in Windhoek the Chief of the South West Africa Police appealed to me to urge you to ensure that you and the members of the Security Council are apprised of the seriousness of the situation. He has asked me to invite the Security Council to despatch immediately a fact finding mission which can accompany the police in order to verify the situation on the ground. The Chief of Police has requested the Administrator General and Mr Ahtisaari for minimum additional assistance required to counter the growing threat of SWAPO incursions and to relieve forces which have been operationally engaged for almost a week. He assured me that any action taken will be carried out in terms of the injunction of the President of the Security Council that maximum restraint be exercised.

As you know, Mr Ahtisaari and General Prem Chand are simply not in a position to supply the additional assistance and the Administrator General has accordingly, in the exercise of his responsibility to ensure law and order in the territory, agreed that the Chief of Police may call upon such resources as he may reasonably require from immediately available Security Forces.

As regards the farming districts in the far northern area mentioned earlier, the district civil guard units have now been reactivated to ward off possible attacks on the population on isolated farms by the SWAPO group heading in that direction.

SWAPO incursions are assuming such proportions that in the words of General Prem Chand, no UN force would have been able to handle the situation in any event. Although the South African government appealed to you and the Security Council to speed up the arrival of the full component of UNTAG, this has not happened. I must inform you that unless the Security Council takes steps to stem the SWAPO incursions, the contingents of UNTAG will be incapable of monitoring the restriction of SWAPO troops to base in Angola and Zambia, or keeping the borders under surveillance or of preventing infiltration.

While I stress the necessity for expediting the despatch of UNTAG forces, I am aware of the danger of creating the impression that a larger UN presence in the territory would provide a solution. I do not believe that UNTAG contingents alone could prevent further infiltration and, as necessary as it might be, it would be undesirable to raise expectations only to have them subsequently frustrated. This might further delay implementation of UN Security Council resolution 435 in all its aspects.

The root cause must be addressed and you, Mr Secretary General, and the Security Council know what this is. I assure you that the South African government, for its part, remains committed to UN Security Council resolution 435, the trilateral agreement of 22nd December 1988 and all commitments we undertook in various other agreements and undertakings enumerated in your report of 23rd January 1989.

I am sure that if requested, General Prem Chand would confirm that South Africa has fully complied with its commitments as of 1st April 1989, on which date SWAPO commenced violation of all the obligations undertaken by its leaders. SWAPO had no military bases in Namibia on 1st April 1989.

There is only one solution: SWAPO must undertake to implement its obligations. South Africa remains prepared to comply scrupulously with its obligations.

A meeting of the Joint Commission consisting of representatives from Angola, Cuba and South Africa is scheduled to take place tomorrow in Namibia with observers present from the USA and the USSR. We shall endeavour on our part to consider what practical steps might be taken to save the peace plan signed in New York on 22nd December 1988. We shall let you know of any developments which may result from our meeting.

In the meantime, please ensure that the Security Council is informed of my appeal that pressure be brought to bear on SWAPO's leadership to give the necessary instruction to its commanders to end their illegal operations immediately. There is simply no other practical way to stop the senseless killing of people.

In terms of the settlement plan, SWAPO members can of course return to their country anyway to participate peacefully in the democratic determination of their future.

I would be grateful if this letter, together with my previous communications mentioned above, could be circulated as documents of the Security Council.

Attached was the following document:

Situation regarding the SWAPO infiltration: 7th April 1989
1 Total strength. Latest intelligence reports which have not all been confirmed, indicate between 1 800 and 1 900 SWAPO have infiltrated to date of which approximately 350 infiltrated in the past 24 hours.
2 Distribution. The infiltrators are distributed in groups as follows:
(a) Kaokoland ± 350
(b) Western Owambo ± 450
(c) Central Owambo ± 600 (includes the latest infiltration of 200 at St Mary's Mission)
(d) Eastern Owambo ± 500 (includes a group of 100 which is reported to be on their way to the northern farming areas)
3 Groups not yet in:
(a) Ruacana area. Information received indicates a group of ± 150 SWAPO north of Beacon 3 has the intention of attacking Ruacana. The presence is confirmed;
(b) Namacunde/Oshikango area. Various unconfirmed reports were received of a

mixed PLAN/Cuban battalion which redeployed from Ongiva to the Oshikango area. The battalion has tanks and artillery. Although tanks have been spotted it could not yet be confirmed whether it belongs to this unit. This matter had previously been raised at the Joint Military Monitoring Commission and was not denied by either Cuba or Angola. Cuba has subsequently indicated that it no longer acts jointly with SWAPO;

(c) Central Owambo. A group of 50 heavily armed SWAPO was reported six kilometres north of the border by 08:00 on 6the April 1989. Other reports of SWAPO groups in the Chiede/Oshikango areas could not be confirmed, but reports from different sources will probably confirm this presence;

(d) Eastern Owambo. At various locations ranging from as near as one kilometre to thirteen kilometres north of the border, SWAPO groups have been reported (and some already confirmed). Total strength could be as high as 500; and

(e) Caprivi. Several reports have been received in the last 48 hours that a group of 200 PLAN fighters have been moved to Sesheke (Zambia) just north of Katima Mulilo and that this group is ready to infiltrate the Caprivi.

4 The present situation as compared to 4 April 1989. The latest infiltration into Kaokoland means that the distance over which the infiltration is taking place is now more than 500 kilometres.

(a) Western Owambo. The strength of SWAPO in this area has increased by 350. The group that infiltrated at Swartbooisdrift intends to move to the Opuwo area in order to maintain a presence in Kaokoland. SWAPO groups of 150 at Beacon 3 and 300−450 north of Beacon 12 pose a threat

(b) Central Owambo:

(i) a battalion supported by tanks in Namacunde/Oshikango area have offensive capability and poses a direct threat to central Owambo;

(ii) the heavily armed SWAPO group as well as the SWAPO group which infiltrated at St Mary's Mission is an indication that SWAPO have increased force levels in central Owambo; and

(iii) actions by SWAPO groups indicate offensive aggressive actions. Examples are the laying of deliberate ambushes (which include trench systems) and firing at aircraft and casevac helicopters

(c) Eastern Owambo. The SWAPO groups which have infiltrated to areas south of the Oshakati-Otjivelo road have not yet been located due to the limited numbers of Security Forces available. These groups are a direct threat to the farming areas south of the operational area. Due to the terrain vegetation and the sparse population these groups may be farther south than is presently appreciated.

5 Despite the repeated calls for the maintenance of the ceasefire by several countries, SWAPO (PLAN) continues to increase force levels inside Namibia. The redeployment of the semi conventional battalions and the mechanised brigades (unconfirmed) to the border areas are a further indication that SWAPO does not only intend establishing bases in Namibia. There has been no indication to date of any northward movement of groups.

Members of the population have reported that SWAPO in Owambo have said the following:

(a) SWAPO intends occupying Owambo. SWAPO will then fight to free the whole of Namibia;

(b) SWAPO waited until implementation of resolution 435 because the South African Defence Force would have withdrawn;

(c) SWAPO (PLAN) will not return to Angola. They will fight to the end; and

(d) There are still a large number of SWAPO waiting to infiltrate.

At a press conference in Windhoek Mr Botha revealed the contents of his letter to the Secretary General of the Security Council. He spoke of the SWAPO infiltrations and of their units being south of the 16th parallel, saying there was 'no way that any of you here present can deny it ... There is no responsible government that can deny it. There is no newspaper in the world of influence, that hasn't written. I am aware of editorials in the *New York Times, Times of London,* even liberal newspapers that we regard as anti South African, came out with this firm point of view, because that is the simple truth'.

The Administrator General released a statement saying that as a result of 'the continuing incursions from Angola by heavily armed members of PLAN, it has become impossible to contemplate such elections under the prevailing circumstances.

'One is therefore faced with a *de facto* suspension of the application of that resolution.'

He said that he and Mr Ahtisaari would soon begin discussions on 'practical issues'.

He said reports indicated that SWAPO infiltrations were threatening the safety of farming communities in the districts of Outjo, Tsumeb and Grootfontein. As a result he had reactivated Area Force Units (home guard type units) of the Citizen Force in those districts.

Reports coming in from the Outjo, Tsumeb and Grootfontein farming areas, indicated that farmers had gone back to carrying guns, while radio systems linking isolated properties for use in the event of a SWAPO attack, had been brought back into operation.

A convoy system had been instituted between Oshakati and Otjivelo.

Despite the bloody clashes between the Security Forces and SWAPO, the SADF's main withdrawal program back to South Africa had continued without abatement.

Trains pulling flatbed trucks loaded with armoured fighting vehicles and artillery pieces, and similar road convoys, were seen heading southwards daily.

The Goebbels' Factor – SWAPO's Propaganda War

SWAPO's 'shadow' foreign minister, Mr Theo-Ben Gurirab, spoke on television in Washington, saying Mr Pik Botha had 'invented' the theory about a SWAPO infiltration because not a single SWAPO fighter had crossed the frontier'.

13

Saturday 8th April 1989

The War in the Bush

102 Battalion's callsign 13, operating in the mountains to the south west of Swartbooisdrift, were following the tracks of two SWAPO infiltrators. Eventually, they brought them to contact, killing one.

The survivor was found and killed later in the same day by 102 Battalion's callsign Romeo Mike Charlie, commanded by Sergeant Jippo Kukuba.

Zulu 4 Juliet – commanded by Sergeant Mac McMaster, Zulu 4 Delta – commanded by Sergeant Tekkies le Roux, Zulu 4 Hotel – commanded by Sergeant Peter Marx, all under the overall command of Warrant Officer Herman Havenga, were working in the central region, south of Beacon 30.

They were checking information which said a large SWAPO group had crossed the border and were cautiously making their way south.

According to one source, the insurgents were so thick on the ground they looked like a muhango field just before reaping.

It was a large scale exercise involving cross-grain patrols and searches for spoor over a wide area.

Other units involved were Zulu Uniform – commanded by Warrant Officer Attie Hattingh, Zulu Quebec – commanded by Constable Duffield, Zulu Lima – commanded by Sergeant Zeelie, and Zulu 1 Juliet – commanded by Sergeant Kok.

At 09:00 the signs of old spoor were picked up near some kraals. The trackers spread out to search over a wider area and one discovered the fresh running tracks of three insurgents trying to escape the area.

It seemed they had seen or heard the Security Forces and were still only a few minutes away.

The police gave chase, spread into a tactical line, with trackers on foot in front. In an effort to catch up quickly, Casspirs from both sides of the tactical line leapfrogged ahead constantly.

It was, however, to no avail.

The spoor split, with two insurgents going one way and the third man on his own, going in the opposite direction.

It was decided to pursue the single spoor, banking on the almost certain knowledge gained from experience that when things go against them, SWAPO's

212

officers invariably abandon their men and head off on their own, believing it likely the Security Forces will grab the option of following the majority.

In this case SWAPO's officer training was faulty.

For seven hours the insurgent managed to stay ahead of the police groups, while they doggedly clung to his heels.

They caught fleeting glimpses of him on several occasions, but each time he managed to dodge the bullets and duck away in the thick bush.

And so the chase went on.

The fugitive showed much determination and discipline. Normally, when people on foot are pursued by vehicles, they begin lightening their load early in the chase as an almost inevitable desperation sets in, and discarded items like packs and so on are found early in the chase.

In this case, however, the insurgent dropped nothing for many hours.

At 15:30 the first items of discarded kit were found, then more after that.

He had displayed amazing stamina, but the experienced policemen knew that like a gutsy stag being coursed by hounds, they had at last got his measure. They would soon have him at bay.

There was a sneaking admiration for the enemy, a half hope that perhaps he would make it and get away, but it was war – not a game of rugby.

Maybe he would surrender.

But he was not the surrendering kind. By 16:00 it was all over.

There was a sudden sighting of his running figure, followed by a quick rattle of gunfire, and this time he didn't make it.

He was a young, probably under twenty, but there was no identification on his body. He still had his AK rifle, his webbing – with a full issue of ammunition in the pouches, and his ration packs.

He had obviously been determined to fight another day.

During the morning Warrant Officer Fanna du Rand's Zulu Oscar and Constable Duppie du Plessis' Zulu Victor, were checking for SWAPO spoor in the area about thirty kilometres south of Beacon 4.

Warrant Officer du Rand told his new man to sit in the front passenger seat and man the 30 calibre Browning, which fires forward through the windscreen. Feeling wary, in view of the difficulties he had already experienced with his new man, he made a point of asking if he was familiar with the weapon.

'Of course, I promise I won't let you down again.'

The groups were working in a fighting line, sweeping in a northerly direction, with trackers deployed on foot in front of the formation.

Sergeant Wayne Prinsloo, a car commander of Zulu Oscar, stopped his car at a kraal, and sent in some black policemen to ask the villagers if they had seen signs of SWAPO operating in the area.

He watched a man, some distance to the north, walking unhurriedly away from the kraal.

He was carrying a rifle, but this didn't particularly concern Sergeant Prinsloo, because many villagers had old ,303 rifles, issued to them by the government to protect themselves against marauding SWAPO dissidents.

Somehow, though, something about him didn't gel. There was something irritatingly wrong.

213

The black policemen returned to the Casspir from the kraal. 'What about that guy over there?' he asked

'He looks suspicious,' they confirmed.

'Get back in the car and we'll check him out.'

Warrant Officer du Rand, meanwhile, purely on a whim, told his driver to move out of his seat as he wanted to take over the driving.

He hadn't done this for three years, because he liked to remain free in case of a contact.

When the man saw Sergeant Prinsloo's Casspir coming after him, he began walking faster, but soon he was running.

He seemed to be fiddling with something. Sergeant Prinsloo suddenly woke up to what it was he was fiddling with. He was fitting a grenade to his rifle while running.

That was no old ,303 rifle . . . it was a Russian SKS. He was a terr!

Sergeant Prinsloo cocked the action of the right hand 30 calibre Browning and triggered.

It didn't fire . . . the round ejected harmlessly. He cocked it several times, but each time the cartridges ejected.

Stoppage!.

He grabbed the left hand weapon and cocked that.

It fired.

'The terr saw I was shooting at him, he started running for a kraal which was about thirty meters away in a north west direction. My finger was on the trigger. I fired more to the left. He turned around and with a fluke shot I nailed him through the neck.'

Warrant Officer du Rand took the wheel of the Casspir and accelerated, changing gear – from second – then to third . . .

Tat, tat, tat . . .

'Contact!'

The yell followed the sounds of weapons firing.

Oddly enough the 30 calibre Browning next to him, which should have been pumping rounds at any cover capable of concealing an enemy, was strangely silent.

He glanced sideways and he almost despaired when he saw his new man struggling to cock the weapon.

He saw at a glance it was the first time he had handled it.

'Get out of that bloody seat,' he snarled, 'let's get an Owambo cop in it who can shoot!'

By the contact's end, a second armed insurgent was dead.

The insurgent killed by Sergeant Prinsloo, had a full set of webbing and several rifle grenades. His water bottles were empty, indicating he had just got there and hadn't even had time to refill. Although without identification papers, he wore a metal dogtag, numbered Z34, around his neck.

Warrant Officer du Rand's Zulu Oscar group, stayed out in the bush for the night.

He awakened with a start late at night, hearing strange and very penetrating noises.

Listening intently it came to him what it was.

It was the sound of someone's teeth chattering.

He stared into the darkness, realising it was the new man's teeth.

What's the matter?' he called to him in a whisper.

'It's so bloody cold, I think I'm going to die!'

This puzzled Warrant Officer du Rand.

Sure there was a chill in the air, but to be that cold was ridiculous.

'You've got a sleeping bag?'

'Yes.'

Warrant Officer du Rand wriggled from his own and crawled over. He was amazed to see his only bedding was a thin groundsheet, which he had wrapped around him, and a thin foam biscuit, on which he was lying.

'I told you to bring a bloody sleeping bag.'

'I thought that's what you used,' the new man replied apologetically.

'Come on then,' Warrant Officer du Rand said in resignation, 'you'd better share mine, otherwise you'll bloody die from exposure.'

Then, as they say in Afrikaans, they lay together *lepel* – like spoons, for the rest of the night.

During the course of the day police groups Zulu Papa and Zulu 1 Hotel, working in combination, killed another insurgent approximately twenty seven kilometres south of Beacon 24.

The Other Face of War

A meeting of the reconvened Joint Commission, consisting of a South African and a joint Angolan/Cuban delegation, with observers from the United States and Soviet Russia, got under way at the Mount Etjo Safari Lodge of big game hunter, Jan Oelofse.

The remote bushveld venue was chosen for practical reasons, and not for reasons of secrecy, as was suggested by some fed up members of the press, because with the influx of UNTAG personnel into Windhoek, locating accommodation for the delegates, as well as finding conference facilities in Windhoek, had become a virtual impossibility.

The South African delegation was led by Ministers Pik Botha and Magnus Malan, the Soviet delegation by Deputy Foreign Minister Anatoly Adamishin and the US one by Assistant Secretary of State, Dr Chester Crocker.

The United Nations and UNTAG

It was reported that the political future of Mr Martti Ahtisaari had been temporarily secured by a vote of confidence in Secretary General de Cuellar, which by implication included Mr Ahtisaari as well, during an unannounced and secret meeting of the Security Council's five permanent members.

This was a major setback for SWAPO, whose friends and allies in the Non Aligned Movement and elsewhere had been calling for Ahtisaari's head, because he was blamed for unleashing the South African military forces against SWAPO's infiltrators.

The Soviet Union's participation in the vote of confidence was significant, because it publicly marked that Moscow's unquestioned backing of SWAPO against South Africa had ended, leaving the movement and its allies perched out on an unfamiliar limb.

The Goebbels' Factor – SWAPO's Propaganda War

At a meeting of the National Union of Namibian Workers – NUNW, Ben Ulenga, General Secretary of the Mineworkers Union of Namibia – MUN, said that 'when PLAN combatants were murdered callously the war resumed' and SWAPO had 'every right to send in reinforcements'.

He insisted it was South Africa who broke the ceasefire agreement by its forces opening fire on PLAN fighters who were already in Namibia at the time of the ceasefire.

Ulenga demanded the 'replacement' of Mr Ahtisaari, asking what right he had to 'authorise the redeployment of South African murder squads'.

'The claim,' he said, 'that SWAPO has at any time agreed to the withdrawal of combatants behind the 16th parallel, is a figment of imagination.'

He said quite baldly that the Geneva Protocol was between South Africa, Cuba and Angola, and had nothing to do with SWAPO.

SWAPO's front organisation with the high sounding name, the National Communications Centre – NCC, after a lengthy analysis and much pontificating, intellectually concluded that SWAPO certainly hadn't broken the ceasefire – South Africa had.

SWAPO's London office issued a press release insisting the UN plan 'does allow SWAPO to have bases within Namibia'.

It concluded with the classic: 'The least we could have expected of the Secretary General's Special Representative, Mr Martti Ahtisaari and his senior officials, is that they familiarise themselves with the UN plan and honestly pursue its implementation'.

Sam Nujoma agrees to SWAPO's withdrawal

In a statement released in Luanda Sam Nujoma said: 'We have taken a decision to order all PLAN troops inside Namibia to stop fighting, regroup and report to the People's Republic of Angola within 72 hours'.

He said they should be escorted from Namibia, with their arms, by UNTAG.

'We have come to this difficult decision because we are aware of the historic responsibility that we have to our people and to humanity as a whole and the collapse of the UN independence plan for our country.'

He stressed that although the UN plan allowed for the confinement of SWAPO to assembly points within Namibia, 'we have decided to make a concession on this issue because we realised that South Africa fears that such assembly points will make SWAPO win the planned UN supervised elections.'

216

14

Sunday 9th April 1989

The War in the Bush

Most infiltrating SWAPO groups had been broken up and severely mauled in contacts with the Security Forces, during the nine days since the 1st April.

Many SWAPO commanders, both at detachment and at section level, had been killed. Others, as well as ordinary cadres, both wounded and unharmed, had decided they'd had enough and set off north for Angola, home and safety.

Some had deserted, abandoned their weapons and uniforms, and headed for their tribal areas, where they intended to lie low until the 'peace' was over.

The more hardcore survivors, however, and there were many, had cached their weapons and merged with the local population, while awaiting instructions from SWAPO's leadership in Angola. This was achieved via the radio communications equipment they had brought in, and with which they stayed constantly in touch with SWAPO in Angola, or by messengers using established links with SWAPO contactmen, if their radios had been damaged or captured.

It must be remembered that none of the ordinary PLAN fighters had received operational briefings before infiltrating Namibia. Only their leaders had known what to do and where to go. Consequently, after bombshelling during a contact, many had lost touch with their comrades, ending up directionless and going hither and thither around the Owamboland bush, like the proverbial chickens without heads.

For this reason, many hardcore SWAPO fighters, who had no intention of returning to Angola, had been looking for and following up tracks as eagerly as the Security Forces, hoping to find and be reunited with their comrades, which explains why fresh tracks were so often found on the old.

Zulu 4 Juliet – commanded by Sergeant Mac McMaster, Zulu 4 Delta – commanded by Sergeant Tekkies le Roux, Zulu 4 Sierra – commanded by Sergeant Johan Marais and Zulu 4 November – commanded by Constable Sampie Potgieter, all under the overall command of Warrant Officer Herman Havenga, were checking for SWAPO spoor some forty kilometres south of Beacon 29.

At 10:00 they arrived at a kraal and were told two insurgents had been there earlier, enquiring if any other SWAPO groups were in the vicinity.

The police picked up the spoor where it left the kraal, and set off in pursuit.

After some hours it became obvious the insurgents had tumbled that the police were in hot pursuit behind them, because they split up, each taking a different direction.

The police chose one set of spoor and set off after the owner, catching him up and shooting him dead about an hour later.

An SKS rifle was found with the body.

Afterwards they backtracked to where the spoor had split, and set off after the second insurgent, eventually catching up and killing him some ten kilometres away from the scene of the first contact.

He had been armed with an RPG-7 rocket launcher.

Later in the afternoon they discovered more spoor, this time of an insurgent on his own. They again followed tracks until he, too, was found and shot.

He had been carrying an SKS rifle.

The men of 102 Battalion's callsign 23 were acting as stopper groups and ambushing areas on the southern bank of the Kunene River, to the north west of Swartboo-isdrift, when four heavily armed SWAPO insurgents walked into the killing ground.

The troops opened fire, killing one.

The other three bombshelled, fled into the thick bush and escaped.

Abandoned at the ambush scene was an RPG-7 rocket launcher, a 60

Two of the escapers stayed together.

The soldiers followed their spoor, staying close on their heels, until they eventually reached the Kunene River.

Signs on the bank indicated they had roped themselves together for protection, and then entered the water in an attempt to swim to the Angolan bank.

To the eyes of the experienced trackers, it seemed they had gone in the water only minutes before the Security Forces arrived. They looked out in the river, but there was no sign of anyone swimming there.

They waited for a long time, but the enemy made no reappearance in the shallow water on the opposite side, so it was finally presumed they had either drowned or been dragged under water and taken by crocodiles.

As has been mentioned before, few SWAPO are able to swim, and it was not a subject bothered with on the training program set by their Soviet, Cuban and East German instructors.

Late in the afternoon the police groups from Opuwo, Zulu 5 Sierra – commanded by Sergeant Lappies Labuschagne, Zulu 5 Juliet – commanded by Constable Sakkie Jooste, Zulu 5 Echo – commanded by Constable Jimmy Botha and Zulu 5 Tango – commanded by Constable Assie van As, led by Inspector Nick Peens, the Kaokoland police commander, returned home to base to rest.

They had been the first to be engaged in the fighting on the 1st April, and had remained in the thick of it ever since.

The convoy of bullet scarred fighting Casspirs and Wolves stopped just outside Opuwo, to reform and reorganise in accordance with time honoured custom.

Where they had them, captured SWAPO flags were tied to the radio aerials, and where they hadn't red material was tied on as a substitute.

Then, with the Himba policemen singing stirring and robust songs of victory, songs from days before the white man, whose origins had been lost in the sands of antiquity, the long column slowly wound its way into and through the village in a proud victory march.

Crowds of tribesmen, waving and shouting, their faces wreathed in smiles came running out to greet them.

Smoke grenades were thrown and thousand footer parachute flares of varying colours burst high up in the air.

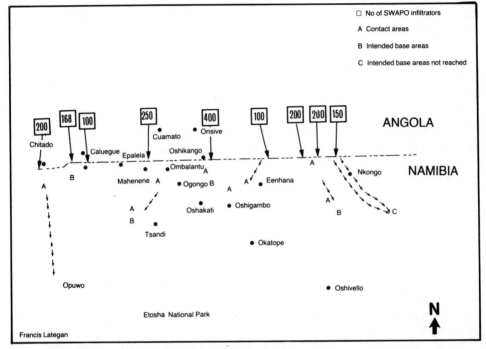

Map showing SWAPO's April infiltration routes from Angola and their intended base areas in Namibia.

Captured AK and SKS rifles, SAM-7 missile launchers, mortar tubes, RPG rocket launchers, SWAPO caps and Jackets – all won at the cost of much blood spilled in the bitter fighting, were vigorously pumped up and down in the air by the crews aboard the fighting cars.

As usual they had taken on and defeated forces far stronger than themselves. An enemy who had targeted Opuwo as their destination, but who instead had died in the Zebra Mountains, or in the bush or desert, or who were wandering around in small broken up units, many of them completely demoralised, after being defeated in battle.

With an overwhelming pride, which no one can attempt to deny them, the policemen of Zulu 5, who in the old days of Koevoet had proudly worn the insignia of a raging wild dog on their uniforms, once again returned home victorious from the wars.

Constable Wynand Bezhuidenhout, stationed with the South Africa Police COIN unit in Pretoria, had served as a volunteer with the SWA Police Counterinsurgency Unit for seven months in 1988.

He first heard news of the SWAPO incursion on Sunday 2nd April.

He spent the whole of Monday listening to every news broadcast and scanning every newspaper as it was released, anxiously devouring every scrap of information relating to Namibia that he could get hold of.

The call for volunteers to serve in South West went out, and he immediately handed in his name.

Another who answered the call, was Constable Danie Nortje. He had never served in Namibia, but he was a member of the SAP's Special Task Force, so he was fully trained in counterinsurgency.

On Sunday the 9th April, both Constable Bezhuidenhout and Constable Nortje, together with eighty four other volunteers, arrived by road at Namibia's northern border area. They brought with them enough Casspirs to replace those which had been knocked out during the fighting.

Up to and including Sunday 9th April, 282 SWAPO had been killed and 12 captured in a total of 63 contacts since the 1st April.

During the same period the Security Forces suffered 125 casualties. Of those the police lost twenty and the army five men, either killed in action or died of wounds.

21 fighting cars were knocked out.

Mount Etjo

According to high diplomatic sources, the Cuban representatives at the Joint Commission's meeting appeared to be genuinely 'livid' as regards the SWAPO infiltrations, while the Angolans were 'less so'.

Both the Angolans and the Cubans insisted they hadn't known SWAPO was going to infiltrate Namibia.

While this might sound incredible in a democratic state, particularly when one considers the logistics and the transport movements required to mount a cross border invasion by some 1 600 men, it is possible, although unlikely for the same reasons, in a totalitarian state like Angola.

What cannot be denied, however, is that it would have been impossible for the Angolans and Cubans to have escorted all SWAPO units to camps north of the 16th parallel in terms of the agreements, only to have had them sneak back on the 31st March and mount an armed invasion of Namibia.

Joining the other delegates at Mount Etju were Administrator General Louis Pienaar and Special Representative Martti Ahtisaari, and their staffs.

It had become clear the UN couldn't and wasn't capable of producing a workable plan, only the parties directly involved – Cuba, Angola and South Africa, could lay down the ground rules.

Although not stated officially by any of the parties, Sam Nujoma's announcement of an immediate withdrawal from Namibia came as a bombshell, because although everyone pretended to laud it for reasons of diplomacy, everyone accepted it was a propaganda move and not a diplomatic one.

If it had been otherwise, Nujoma would have chosen a diplomatics forum, instead of making the announcement unilaterally on a political one.

He should have approached the problem by entering into direct negotiations with the parties involved, or by utilising the Secretary General as an avenue for arbitration.

Before making an announcement, he should have ensured specific arrangements for a truce or a ceasefire had been arranged to facilitate the withdrawal.

This would have allowed time for all parties involved in the conflict, particularly the troops in the field, to be properly notified of the arrangements.

When this isn't done, chaos results and men die, usually those aware of the ceasefire – at the hands of those who don't!

This creates real dangers of the exercise breaking down.

The situation was further aggravated by Nujoma mentioning only once in his announcement, that UNTAG should assist his returning fighters.

No one else in SWAPO's political or military hierarchy mentioned it either. In fact, on the contrary, a senior commander afterwards gave specific orders during a broadcast on *Radio Freedom* in Luanda, saying cadres were to make their own way's back, and not to report to UNTAG.

At the conclusion of the meetings, the following declaration, known as the Mount Etjo Declaration, was issued:

> The Joint Commission created by the Protocol of Brazzaville of 13th December 1988, met at Mount Etjo, Namibia, on 8th-9th April 1989 in an extraordinary session.
>
> Delegations of the People's Republic of Angola, the Republic of Cuba and the Republic of South Africa, parties to the New York accord of 22nd December 1988, attended this meeting.
>
> Delegations from the USA and the USSR participated in their capacity as observers.
>
> (a) The parties reaffirm their commitment to fulfil the obligations undertaken in the accord of 22nd December 1988 for the peaceful resolution of the conflict in the southwestern region of Africa and in conformity with UN Security Council resolution 632 of 16 February 1989.
>
> (b) In order to facilitate the restoration of peace and to promote the full application of resolution 435/78 of the Security Council of the UN and the subsequent agreements subscribed to by the parties, as well as the restoration of the situation in existence on 31st March 1989, and taking into account in this regard the declaration by the leadership of SWAPO on 8th April 1989, the parties agree to a package of recommendations which are reflected in the attached annexure.
>
> (c) The parties urge the Secretary General of the UN to urgently adopt all the necessary measures for the most rapid and complete deployment of UNTAG so that it can fully and effectively carry out its mandate. They likewise urge all member states of the UN, particularly those who are members of the Security Council, to extend to the Secretary General their full cooperation with the carrying out of UNTAG's tasks.

> *Annexure – Principles*
> 1 The withdrawal procedure has as its purpose the restoration of the situation in existence on 31st March 1989.
> 2 The Administrator General and UNTAG shall verify the departure of SWAPO troops from Namibia.
> 3 The security and protection of the SWAPO elements and of the security forces in Namibia enjoy the highest level of importance.
> 4 A period will be established during which SWAPO forces will be granted free

passage to the border assembly points and those assembly points south of the border which are contained in the annexure to this document.

5 As of the signing of this document, it will be considered that the SWAPO forces will be able to deploy with full safety to the established assembly points.

6 The procedure will be simple and practical to allow its implementation in the shortest time possible.

7 This procedure will be executed under UNTAG supervision.

Sequence

1 The People's Republic of Angola commits itself to receive on its territory the forces of SWAPO which leave Namibia and to ensure that these forces and others on its territory are confined north of latitude 16 degrees south under UNTAG's supervision.

2 As of 9th April 1989 SWAPO troops who are still in the territory of Namibia should present themselves to the border assembly points or to the assembly points south of the border herein established, enjoying the right of freedom of passage.

3 All assembly points shall be under UNTAG supervision and shall contain personnel drawn from UNTAG and personnel authorised by the Administrator General. SWAPO shall utilise the normal chain of command for the communications as well as broadcasting on commercial networks to notify its members of said arrangements.

4 The Joint Military Monitoring Commission shall be temporarily reactivated without Cuban representation, unless requested by both parties, until the situation existing on 31st March 1989 has been reestablished.

At the border assembly points which appear in the annexure to this document, joint border control posts manned by forces of Angola and South Africa will be established with the presence of UNTAG to guarantee the control of the crossing of SWAPO forces.

5 The terms of this agreement, the assembly points on the border as well as the assembly points south of the border herein established shall be communicated to SWAPO forces by all means possible.

6 SWAPO forces which turn themselves over to the custody of UNTAG shall lay down their weapons with UNTAG.

7 SWAPO members who present themselves to the assembly points south of the border shall be transferred by air to north of latitude 16 degrees south by UNTAG, or by Angola under the supervision of UNTAG.

8 SWAPO members who present themselves to assembly points on the border will be transferred to bases north of latitude 16 degrees south by Angola under the supervision of UNTAG.

9 The Administrator General and the Special Representative shall be notified as to the number of SWAPO forces which return to the bases north of latitude 16 degrees south from the territory of Namibia.

10 By 15th April 1989, the Special Representative will be informed by SWAPO about the conclusion of the removal of its forces from the territory of Namibia.

11 The end of this process will be based on two essential points:
  (i) Information provided by SWAPO to the Special Representative upon the conclusion of the removal of its forces from Namibian territory; and
  (ii) Joint verification by the Administrator General and the Special Representative of the exit of all SWAPO forces from Namibian territory.

Once these two conditions are met, the situation existing on 31st March 1989 will be considered to have been restored.

12 Having agreed to the foregoing principles and procedure the three Governments take note of a press release by SWAPO leadership announcing the withdrawal of SWAPO forces from the northern part of Namibia to Angola. The three Governments recommended that the Administrator General and the Special Representative of the Secretary General give immediate attention as to how SWAPO's decision can be put

into effect within the framework of the agreed withdrawal procedure with a view to ensure that lives are spared.

Annexure – Proposed assembly points within Namibia
1 Opertti (near Oshivelo)
2 Nkongo
3 Eenhana
4 Okankolo
5 Ondangwa
6 Ombulantu
7 Ruacana
8 Opuwo
9 Ehomba
10 Okangwati

Border Assembly Points
1 Epupa
2 Swartbooisdrift
3 Beacon 1
4 Beacon 7
5 Beacon 14
6 Beacon 19
7 Beacon 25
8 Beacon 34

UNTAG made the following press release with regard to their military arrangements arising from the Mount Etjo Declaration:

The military component of UNTAG is making arrangements to ensure that the initial assembly points will be ready and operational by noon on 11th April.

In these positions, signals personnel as well as engineers, electricians and officers will be working to ensure that all the facilities are in place.

Arrangements are now being made to transport flags, generators and other materials to these positions.

The policy is to make these UNTAG assembly points highly visible with a significant and easily recognisable UN presence.

Continuous announcements will be made in local dialects.

UNTAG has received assurance of full cooperation from UNAVEM in assisting SWAPO personnel, once they cross the border, to be conducted to their bases in Angola.

The military does not have an estimate of the number of SWAPO personnel that might turn up at the assembly points, but UNTAG will be fully prepared to receive them, with the assistance of the churches and medical personnel as necessary.

There are also no accurate figures of the number of wounded.

Finnish troops will arrive in Namibia in the next 3 days for deployment. Kenyan forces will arrive on 13th-14th and 17th-18th April, and Malaysian forces on 16th-18th and 20th April.

Structure of UNTAG Assembly Points

At each assembly point there will be 5 UNTAG monitors and 10 UNTAG soldiers. The soldiers will be Australian engineers and British signalers. The monitors will be officers from various countries. All the UNTAG personnel concerned will be deployed to northern Namibia today. They will move to the various assembly points tonight or early tomorrow morning, in order to be fully operational by noon.

UNTAG personnel are expected to be self sufficient at the assembly points.

The following joint statement by the Administrator General and the Special Representative of the UN Secretary General was released during the evening:

After the statement of Mr Sam Nujoma, President of SWAPO, ordering his troops to withdraw from Namibia to Angola, the Administrator General and the Special Representative have established procedures to facilitate the safe passage of such personnel from Namibia to Angola. These will be carried out under UNTAG supervision.

SWAPO forces are being granted free passage to border assembly points, and to assembly points south of the border. Measures have been taken to ensure their safest possible movement to such assembly points. These points will be clearly identified with UN flags and will be operational under UNTAG at noon local time on Tuesday 11th April. There will be a UN military presence, a presence of the Security Forces in Namibia, as well as a presence of the Security Forces of Angola, at each of the above assembly points, except at those at Okankolo and Nkongo, where there will be no Angolan presence.

At Epupa and at Beacon 25 Angolan presence will, for logistical reasons, be established by noon local time on Wednesday 12th April.

It has also been agreed that the Security Forces in Namibia will not act againstl PLAN members congregated in the immediate vicinity of church premises so that, under UNTAG supervision, they may be escorted from there to assembly points.

From such assembly points PLAN members will be escorted across the border and transported to their bases in accordance with agreements reached at Mount Etjo within the tripartite process.

15

Whatever Happened to SWAPO?

10th April – The prevarication and backtracking by SWAPO began almost immediately, with Sam Nujoma telling BBC's *Today* program that his guerrillas were 'scattered all over Namibia' without communications.

Radio broadcasts to SWAPO cadres in the field were, according to him, pointless.

'Of course, they will not hear this, because they don't have radios,' Nujoma said. 'Besides, SWAPO freedom fighters will not accept in any circumstances orders coming from the so called South African Administrator General, "or from anyone else"'.

He said they would only accept orders given to them personally by their commanders.

He repeated his denial that his fighters had crossed into Namibia on the 1st April, describing the battles as 'a plot very well worked out by Pretoria in order to create this crisis'.

In one fell swoop Nujoma had laid out his future plans.

His men would not be moving back into Angola because they would only accept direct orders from their commanders, they had no radios (although they had) and wouldn't accept orders 'from anyone else'.

On top of that there hadn't been an incursion in the first place.

No one could deny him his consistency.

Neither SWAPO nor Nujoma would change in the coming months.

11th April – Lieutenant General Prem Chand, the UN Force Commander, confirmed that his troops had successfully established a 'highly visible UN presence' as specified in the Mount Etjo agreement.

This presence consisted of nine assembly points spread over an area of some four hundred kilometres.

The personnel used to man them were British signallers, Australian engineers and three Pakistani officers from the observer force.

They were about the only men that could be scraped together from UNTAG's sketchy ground forces then in Namibia.

With a great holding of breath, the great wait for SWAPO fighters to come in and give themselves up for escort back to Angola, began.

By the end of the first day, no SWAPO fighters had reported in.

According to police the situation was relatively calm, but groups of insurgents had been seen ten kilometres south of Oshikati, more east of Ondangwa, a group of a hundred near Oshikango and another fifty near Nkongo.

Information from the local population was that they were caching their weapons and uniforms, and hiding out with the local population.

The Administrator General announced that UNTAG and the SWA Police had agreed that fighters handing themselves in at UNTAG assembly points, would be interrogated.

The purpose was to verify the numbers of infiltrators, to identify the where-abouts of wounded and identify the positions of arms caches.

April 12th – SWAPO's mouthpiece in Namibia, *The Namibian*, under the headline 'FIGHTERS WON'T GO' said no fighters had handed themselves in so far.

They said the fighters objected to Security Force personnel, 'which far outnum-bered' UNTAG personnel, being at the assembly points. They added that an 'unconfirmed' report suggested members of 101 Battalion would be used as interpreters.

They also carried a report from SWAPO's London office saying 'Koevoet units were deployed at dusk on Monday in the bush near Okankolo assembly point, at the time the curfew was reimposed ... Observers have reported that they had obviously been deployed for the purpose of ambushing members of PLAN as they approached the assembly point.'

It also said the Mount Etjo agreement was ambiguous and suggested there were two versions available. 'It was impossible for SWAPO to issue concise orders to its forces while this confusion prevails.'

In a report from Luanda, SWAPO's Information Secretary, Hidipo Hamutenya, had said the 'guerrillas would remain in the bush until all uncertainties were removed.'

The Administrator General announced it had been agreed by the Special Representative that joint SWA Police/UNTAG patrols would check the border daily to identify tracks of PLAN fighters, who had crossed back into Angola without using the reporting points.

When it came to it, UNTAG refused to supply men to accompany the police patrols. The police continued to patrol the border as a routine.

Mr Louis Pienaar said he wanted all the PLAN fighters out of the country by Saturday 15th April.

He said the Security Forces would track and attack any SWAPO units heading south into Namibia, but would leave alone those heading towards assembly points. When asked about a ceasefire, he said:

'We had a ceasefire that was not respected by a certain party, so we are not going to concede a ceasefire until we are satisfied that it is being respected now.'

Special Representative Martti Ahtisaari said although the Mount Etjo Agree-ment had named 18 assembly points it was only a recommendation, and no more than the nine already established would be set up. He said the guerrillas would have about ten days to leave the country.

Mr Ahtisaari, when asked about a report that SWAPO wanted a 'new ceasefire' before their forces reported to UNTAG, said: 'We are not dealing with a complete ceasefire ... that was not agreed. What was agreed was that SWAPO forces would have a free passage to assembly points'.

By the end of the second day, four SWAPO fighters had handed themselves in to UNTAG.

One suffering from shrapnel wounds, arrived at a Lutheran Mission station early that morning and told UNTAG personnel he had three comrades who wanted to come in.

The UN man called the UN monitoring post at Oshikango, then drove into the bush, returning shortly afterwards with three guerrillas, one of them badly wounded.

All had abandoned their weapons and were wearing civilian clothes.

They were taken to the Oshikango assembly point.

13 April – *The Namibian* called the exercise 'Plan No Go'.

It reported that Sam Nujoma had confirmed 'that guerrillas were returning to Angola, but were avoiding the UN monitored assembly points agreed to by South Africa, Cuba and Angola'.

Angola's chief spokesman, Paulino Pinto Joao, said Angola would 'do its best' to ensure guerrillas withdrawing from Namibia would be confined to bases to bases north of the 16th parallel, but they were 'counting on SWAPO's cooperation to achieve this'.

He said it was difficult to control every inch of the border, as there was no cordon sanitaire.

When asked if SWAPO could be trusted to withdraw he said: 'Why shouldn't we have confidence in SWAPO?'

UNTAG's spokesman Mr Cedric Thornberry said: 'We understand very well the reluctance of SWAPO personnel to approach bases where there is a visible, even menacing South African presence ... It may very well be that the church sanctuaries might turn out to be places most used by SWAPO personnel to present themselves'.

He pointed out that the four insurgents who had so far handed themselves over to UNTAG, had not directly reported to assembly points, but had gone to a mission first.

14th April – In a joint statement issued by the Administrator General and the Special Representative, it was announced the deadline for SWAPO fighters to leave Namibia or report to UN assembly points inside the territory, had been extended until Friday 21st April.

'A prolonged stalemate in the affected areas is in no one's interest,' the statement said.

In clashes between the Security Forces during the week, another five SWAPO were killed, while two policemen were wounded.

More bodies from earlier contacts had been located at the contact scenes.

Foreign Minister Pik Botha said SWAPO's April incursion had been reestimated at about 1 600 insurgents. About 900 were thought to be still in the territory.

Mr Botha agreed that the Security Forces would not interrogate SWAPO fighters handing themselves in at reporting points.

16th April – *The Sunday Star* reported that SWAPO's Information Secretary, Mr Hidipo Hamutenya, speaking by telephone from The Hague, Holland, said:

'At least fourteen of our people have been shot by South African troops as they tried to cross the border in the past two days.'

'In no instances have our people initiated the fighting.'

He insisted SWAPO could easily meet the new deadline of 21st April for all of its guerrillas to be out of Namibia, provided South African troops were not patrolling the border trying to intercept them.

'South Africa must decide whether it is going to help or hinder the withdrawal.'

This report was pure propaganda.

From it, though, Mr Hamutenya clearly implied he knew exactly what was going on with the PLAN fighters still inside Namibia.

He didn't say if SWAPO in Luanda had been kept informed by bush telegraph ... or whether it had been by two way radios – which Sam Nujoma had said they didn't have, in spite of the Security Forces having captured several.

It was announced that two more SWAPO insurgents had reported to UN assembly points.

Two more insurgents had been killed and another six captured in fighting with the Security Forces.

UN Under Secretary General, Mr Marrack Goulding, accompanied the Angolan Defence Minister, Colonel General Pedro Maria Tonha, on a tour of bases where SWAPO insurgents were being confined.

Mr Goulding said he hadn't established yet how many had returned to Angola.

Earlier, General Tonha told reporters they had already moved 500 insurgents north of the 16th parallel, in terms of the Mount Etjo Agreement.

He said SWAPO fighters were continuing to cross.

Mr Goulding said he had seen 'several hundred' armed and uniformed SWAPO fighters at Chibemba, a village in the Huila province some 30 kilometres north of the 16th parallel and 180 kilometres north of the Namibian border.

Some, he said, had come from northern Namibia and 'others had been moved north from positions inside southern Angola'. Those coming from inside Namibia appeared to have avoided UN assembly points set up inside the country to receive them.

According to *Sapa-Reuter*, UN sources had said 'it was clear that the bulk of SWAPO had not been north of the 16th parallel on April 1st as they were meant to be under the peace accords ...'

What remained unclear, was whether Mr Marrack Goulding was capable of telling the difference between a FAPLA soldier and a SWAPO fighter, particularly if they were wearing identically patterned uniforms, and had been ordered to regard the truth as unimportant.

Goulding could probably tell the nationalistic differences between most troops of Caucasian origins, providing they were in large numbers and didn't originate from the central European states, but detecting the differences between black troops of central, southern and east African origins, unless he could interrogate them in their own languages, which he couldn't, must surely have been beyond his capabilities.

The point being that while the integrity of Mr Goulding is not doubted, it shows something in the UN system in Angola was badly lacking, if the checking had to be done by the 'boss' during a hurried visit. Surely the whole operation should have been properly controlled by a full staff on a day to day basis, with proper documentation of each PLAN fighter and not just a one, two, three, four business of counting heads.

Like justice, it needed to be done ... and seen to be done.

17th April – The SWAPO supporting Council of Churches for Namibia – CCN, warned UNTAG their delay in sending guerrillas who had reported to assembly points back to Angola 'will cost the UN credibility with the churches in Namibia and also with the people.'

UNTAG demanded the South Africans hand over all SWAPO prisoners captured in the fighting, so they could be repatriated back to Angola.

SWAPO, through its surrogate organisations, cleverly switched the accent from their own fighters still illegally within the country, by producing a petition allegedly signed by 4 300 'war weary' people 'from across Owambo' describing themselves as the 'mothers, fathers, sons and daughters residing in the far north of Namibia'.

Needless to say, it spoke of atrocities by Koevoet, 101 Battalion and South African forces; vague unsubstantiated stories of civilian casualties and civilians who had been forced to flee their homes as 'Security Forces once again roam the north'; how UNTAG was at fault for not deploying earlier and how they should consult 'community, church and other recognised' leaders in the region.

The CCN was obviously standing by ready to be consulted.

Reports of 'atrocities' by the Security Forces would now escalate.

18th April – Mr Louis Pienaar and Mr Ahtisaari agreed they would jointly look into allegations of intimidation by the Security Forces in the far north.

SWAPO's Foreign Affairs spokesman at the UN (whatever was he still doing there?) said that Secretary General Perez de Cuellar should visit Namibia to restore the UN's 'tarnished image' as a result of its shortcomings in carrying out its peacekeeping obligations.

It was announced that representatives of the SWAPO supporting Council of Churches of Namibia – CCN, had been allowed to interview three PLAN combatants in the custody of the UN pending repatriation to Angola. One of them, a church representative said later, 'was still suffering pain from having been knocked down by a Casspir'.

The press were not allowed to interview them.

The three crossed the border into Angola under UNTAG escort at Ruacana at 16:00.

Brigadier Opande of Kenya was there to witness the event and record it on video.

He told reporters they would first be going to Chimbembe and from there to Lubongo. He also said 'one guerrilla I spoke to said he had been here for nine months. Others, I am sure, did cross after 1st April'.

20th April – Three SWAPO insurgents were killed in a clash with Security Forces in northern Namibia.

The Joint Military Monitoring Commission consisting of South Africa, Cuba and Angola, with observers from the USA and the USSR, met at Ruacana.

It was agreed that proposals accepted by the JMMC would be communicated to SWAPO by Angola and Cuba.

21st April – South African Defence Minister, Magnus Malan, revealed details of the JMMC's proposals to Parliament during a defence debate.

1 Angola and Cuba would obtain a tape cassette from SWAPO with a message directing their fighters still within Namibia to return to Angola immediately;
2 The message would not be allowed to contain political propaganda, nor give the impression the SWAPO commanders were in Windhoek;
3 South Africa would vet the message;
4 The message would state that SWAPO forces in Angola were being moved north of the 16th parallel;
5 They would be told that at 18:00 on Wednesday 26th April, all Security Forces would withdraw to their bases for 60 hours to create a 'safe passage' period, during which all armed SWAPO elements could withdraw to Angola;
6 A period would follow for verification as to how many had left; and
7 The length of the verification period would depend on how many SWAPO insurgents had left, and the success or otherwise in locating arms caches.

The South Africans had pointed out that this verification period could be shortened considerably if SWAPO provided information as to the location of the arms caches.

Needless to say, they didn't.

Verification to see how many had left during the period of grace would be conducted by the Security Forces, who would 'at all times', be accompanied by UNTAG observers.

The taped messages to SWAPO would be broadcast over commercial radio stations.

The period of grace was considered a major concession by South Africa, who said they regarded it as a last effort before resolution 435 would have to be renegotiated.

23rd April – *The Africa News Service* revealed SWAPO's reaction to the period of grace. Deputy Information Secretary, Mr Hinananye Nehova said in Luanda: 'we are waiting to see on the ground if that is what really happens'.

'As long as there are no obstacles created by the South African Army to impede our troops, we could successfully complete our withdrawal by Friday.'

He alleged that so far 800 guerrillas had crossed back into Angola and been confined above the 16th parallel – leaving 518 still in Namibia.

24th April – Hidipo Hamutenya, SWAPO's Information Secretary speaking in London where he had gone for talks with Minister of State, Mrs Lynda Chalker, said: 'Before the ink was dry [on the Mount Etjo Agreement] the South Africans were already sending their troops to encircle all the assembly points which were agreed upon.

'Eighteen SWAPO guerrillas were "shot in the back" as they tried to cross the border.'

According to *The Guardian* of London, he appealed to the British to intervene and 'persuade the South African Army to observe the Mount Etjo Agreement'.

Commercial radio stations in Namibia began broadcasting appeals by SWAPO commanders calling on their guerrillas to return to Angola.

26th April – In a news release the Administrator General advised that 35 SWAPO prisoners captured by the Security Forces since the 1st April, had been offered an amnesty for their actions during the incursions.

Four accepted the amnesty and were released and allowed to return to their families in Namibia.

The remaining 31 were handed over to UNTAG for movement back to Angola.

Amongst those returning to Angola were James Shikalombo and Albert Nakawa, who had been interviewed by the author.

Nakawa told a press conference he had crossed the border on or after the 1st April. Although armed, he said, they intended to hand themselves and their weapons over to the UN.

He insisted they had no hostile intentions.

It had obviously slipped his mind telling the author that the opening shot in the battle in which he had taken part on Wednesday 5th April, had been a SAM-7 missile fired by his group at an unarmed SAAF Bosbok spotter aircraft.

Captain Derek McNamara, the pilot, and Inspector Ben Vermaak, the passenger could have reminded him.

Inspector Nick Peens in command of the ground forces, could also have jogged his memory about the message left by his group with local villagers.

'If the Koevoets or soldiers come, you must show them our spoor. Tell them we'll be waiting for them.'

28th April – A two day meeting of the JMMC with South Africa, Cuba and Angola in attendance and with the USSR, the USA and UNTAG present as observers, began in Cape Town.

South Africa put their estimations of the current PLAN position in Namibia as:

Infiltrated on 1st April:	1 619
Infiltrated since 1st April:	57
Total :	1 676
Killed by Security Forces since 1st April:	314
Captured by Security Forces since 1st April:	38
Estimated as exfiltrated:	1 050
Estimated as still in Namibia:	274–300

South Africa told the JMMC that by their Intelligence estimates, substantial numbers of PLAN fighters were still south of the 16th parallel.

Also, that a unit 350 strong was waiting in Angola, near the Namibian border, ready to infiltrate on the night of the 3rd-4th May.

This was, needless to say, disputed by Angola and Cuba.

No infiltration, however, took place.

It was agreed by all parties that South Africa be granted two weeks ending on the 13th May, during which time the Security Forces would be allowed to verify the numbers of SWAPO who had returned to Angola, and to search for arms caches.

29th April – Some 4 500 South African troops were released from base restriction to assist the police in their search for SWAPO insurgents and arms caches.

Despite past promises and their clear duty in terms of the peace plan to do so, no UNTAG forces accompanied the Security Force's verification patrols.

2nd May – It was announced that Security Forces had killed three SWAPO insurgents in two separate contacts on Sunday 30th April. In one of the incidents, SWAPO ambushed the Security Forces.

Six arms caches had been found in various parts of northern Namibia.

In response Mr Ahtisaari said he was 'deeply concerned and saddened' by reports of renewed clashes between SWAPO and the Security Forces.

He said SWAPO's leadership had instructed all its forces to return to Angola and South Africa had undertaken to facilitate this.

'The events which began on the 1st April have already led to bloodshed on a tragic scale and further deaths or injuries must be avoided.'

4th May – UN Secretary General Javier Perez de Cuellar officially called on South Africa to withdraw its Security Forces to their bases.

Responding to this call, Foreign Minister Pik Botha said the appeal ran contrary to the agreement in Cape Town between Angola, Cuba and South Africa, which allowed the Security Forces to operate outside their bases until the 13th May, to verify that SWAPO had returned to Angola.

He said the UN had tried before at Mount Etjo to 'allow SWAPO to get away with the violation'.

'The position,' he said,' is quite clear. SWAPO must be north of the 16th parallel in Angola by the 13th May.

'If the Security Council makes any decision that alters these agreements they must accept full responsibility for the interruption of the whole proceedings.'

He accused the Secretary General, by his attitude, of encouraging SWAPO to make another incursion into Namibia.

The Administrator General, Mr Louis Pienaar, announced he would not confine the Security Forces to their bases before they had completed their checks, in terms of international agreements.

8th May – Security Forces discovered another SWAPO arms cache in northern Namibia. It was the largest found until then, and contained 5 mortar tubes, 221 mortar bombs, 88 rifle grenades, 64kgs plastic explosive, 37 assault rifles and SAM-7 missile launchers and missiles – marked '1988' as the date of manufacture in the Soviet Union.

12th May – It was announced, after a closed doors meeting of the Security Council, that Secretary General Dr Javier Perez de Cuellar had recommended the UN police force in Namibia be doubled in size to 1 000 men.

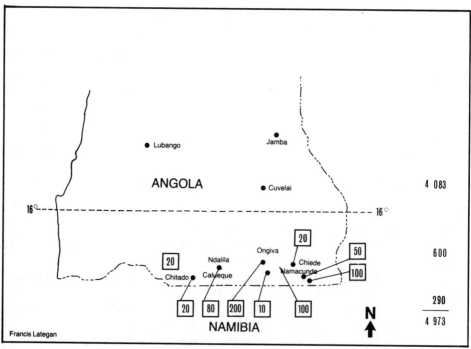

Map showing plan disposition of PLAN fighters, returned to Namibia as refugees, who have reformed into their Units in CCN controlled secondary refugee camps. Numbers shown are minimums.

He said he was also considering strengthening the position of the Special Representative by naming a deputy, probably from an African state (to appease the Non Aligned Move of which SWAPO is a full member).

The Secretary General then lauded the UNAVEM force of 70 military advisers and 37 civilians headed by Brazil's Brigadier General Gomes in Angola, saying 'It will be evident from ... this interim report that UNAVEM is effectively carrying out the tasks entrusted to it by the Security Council in December 1988'.

He said they had recorded the departure of 4 624 Cuban military personnel between 10th January and 31st March and another 2 261 in April.

Strangely enough, the Secretary General felt the need for another 500 policemen in Namibia, to bring police/military personnel totals to nearly 5 500, to supervise the South Africans.

A country which had scrupulously obeyed every protocol.

While his 107 men were considered as adequate for Angola, where SWAPO had broken every protocol with the connivance of Cuba and Angola.

12th May – Security Forces announced another SWAPO insurgent had been shot dead in the northern area of Namibia.

13 May – All units of the SADF and the SWA Territory Force were restricted to bases with effect from 06:00.

This did not include the SWA Police, who in terms of resolution 435 had the primary responsibility of maintaining law and order.

15th May – A further meeting of the JMMC took place at Ruacana.

At this meeting the Cuban and Angolan delegation insisted all SWAPO fighters had been moved north of the 16th parallel.

South African Intelligence sources, however, indicated there were at least 600 PLAN fighters still south of it, mostly in the area of Ongiva, Namcunde and Chiede.

There were said to be SWAPO tanks and artillery at Ongiva.

The differences between the South African and the Cuban-Angolan delegations regarding this matter was not satisfactorily resolved.

UNTAG, who were supposed to be monitoring SWAPO north of the 16th parallel, maintained there were 5 162 plan fighters deployed there.

South African Intelligence, which had proved its remarkable accuracy during the April incursions, insisted there were only 4 083.

Considering the pathetically small number of UN monitors in Angola, and their record when dealing with SWAPO, it seems unlikely the South Africans were wrong.

South Africa asked for the right to have her own monitors stationed in Angola, but this was not accepted by Angola and Cuba.

Plus or minus 300 PLAN fighters were still in northern Namibia.

Not unreasonably, South Africa demanded the right to use troops, presently subjected to base confinement, to respond to any further SWAPO infiltrations.

South Africa indicated that the question of her keeping to the program of troop withdrawals, was linked to a categorical assurance being obtained that all parties, including SWAPO, would thereafter stick to the spirit and letter of the various accords.

If they didn't, South Africa warned, the peace process was in danger of mortal collapse.

The meeting was adjourned. It was scheduled for resumption at Cahama, Angola, on the 18th May.

UNTAG's estimate of SWAPO guerrillas confined to bases north of the 16th parallel, had been based on information provided by Major John Ryan of UNTAG, who said he had visited the SWAPO camp at Chibemba.

He said 5 166 PLAN fighters were paraded and counted by UN officials.

Like the question posed earlier about Mr Marrack Goulding, how did Major Ryan know they were SWAPO and not FAPLA?

To the surprise of no one, Mr Hidipo Hamutenya, SWAPO's Information Secretary, insisted: 'Our fighters are all out'.

18th May – The meeting of the JMMC took place at Cahama, Angola.

The question of PLAN fighters being south of the 16th parallel remained unresolved, because of a flat denial by the Angolans and Cubans that this was so.

Finally, it was agreed South African forces would remain confined to their bases, and that a *de facto* cessation of hostilities existed in the northern area of Namibia.

It was agreed the various parties would proceed with the implementation of resolution 435.

Foreign Minister Pik Botha wrote immediately wrote to the UN Secretary General:

> 'The South African government wishes to reiterate that the responsibility for the administration of Namibia during the transition period is the primary task of the Administrator General, which includes the responsibility for maintaining law and order in the territory.
>
> 'Particularly in light of the incursions which took place as from the night of 31st March 1989, and to avoid any misunderstanding which may arise in future, the South African government wishes to make it clear that the Administrator General has the right to use such measures and means as he would deem appropriate to counter activities of an aggressive, violent or intimidatory nature emanating from whatever quarter.
>
> 'The South African government trusts that you and the members of the Security Council will ensure that all political parties appreciate the importance of adhering scrupulously to the provisions of the relevant agreements.'

23rd May – UNTAG spokesman, Cedric Thornberry, advised that South Africa was reducing her troop levels ahead of schedule. The majority of the SWA Territory Force, which had been remobilised specifically to deal with the April incursion, would be demobilised again by the end of the week.

Units of the SADF would be withdrawn to South Africa.

24th May – The UN Secretary General, Dr Javier Perez de Cuellar, publicly rebuked South Africa for claiming it had the primary authority for governing Namibia until it was independent.

He warned that South Africa had no right to take unilateral action.

The British Ambassador to the UN, Sir Crispen Tickell, told the press the Council members supported the Secretary General in his efforts to implement the mandate he had been given for Namibia.

1st June – Brigadier Johan Louw, Chief of Staff (Operations and Planning) for South African forces in Namibia, announced there were less than 4 000 South African troops left in the territory.

He warned that Pretoria would not hesitate to step in and provide the police with the 'necessary support' on 'very short notice' should the security situation deteriorate.

9th June – The Secretary General, Dr Perez de Cuellar, announced he had appointed Botswana's Ambassador to the UN, Mr Legwaila Joseph Legwaila, as the deputy head of UNTAG.

1st July – Foreign Minister Pik Botha said in a statement that South Africa had supplied the MPLA government of Angola with full information and details regarding the presence of SWAPO elements south of the 16th parallel.

'In addition,' he said,' the South African government was informed that the

MPLA had decided to remove all SWAPO elements, including those north of the 16th parallel, to north of the 15th parallel, in order to further reduce any potential threat they may pose.'

Mr Botha said reports of continued violations of SWAPO's commitments would be raised as a matter of urgency at the next meeting of the JMMC in Luanda on the 7th July.

'These violations cast a shadow over the entire security situation in northern Namibia, creating a climate which is not conducive to the lessening of tension in the area.'

He had also requested South Africa's diplomatic representative to the UN to raise the matter with the Secretary General and convey concerns about the situation, urging him to take appropriate steps to ensure SWAPO complied with its commitments.

7th July – South Africa once again brought up the question of SWAPO elements being below the 16th parallel at the meeting of the JMMC in Angola.

Nothing positive regarding this question resulted.

15th July – According to police intelligence, further SWAPO elements had infiltrated Namibia, but this had not yet been confirmed.

17th July – Chief Inspector Derek Brune of the SWA Police, said at a news conference that there were, according to Intelligence reports, some 2 000 SWAPO insurgents deployed and active in Angola in the border areas close to Namibia.

18th July – SWAPO's former UN representative and Secretary for Foreign Affairs, Mr Theo-Ben Gurirab suggested that Mr Pienaar was creating a 'war situation' by alleging there was a massive build up of armed guerrillas in southern Angola and in Owambo.

Secretary General Dr Perez de Cuellar arrived in Namibia for a four day visit.

22nd July – At the end of the OAU summit, the African heads of state said the size of UNTAG was inadequate to 'guarantee even the minimum conditions for free and fair elections'.

They made no mention of the inadequacy of UNTAG forces in Angola.

19th August – Cuban President Fidel Castro threatened to delay the withdrawal of Cuban troops from Angola because his soldiers 'had been attacked by UNITA'.

24th August – Chief Inspector Kierie du Rand, SWA Police Public Relations Officer, announced in Windhoek that police had found two more SWAPO arms caches in northern Namibia.

One, 'freshly' buried in the veld near Grootfontein, held five 60mm mortar bombs and ten booster charges. The other, eighteen kilometres south west of Ruacana, consisted of thirteen M60 rifle grenades, eight 60mm mortar bombs, ten 82 mm mortar bombs, five 50mm mortar bombs, four anti personnel mines and an RPG-7.

29th August – The UN Security Council, at the instigation of the Non Aligned Movement, of which SWAPO is a full member, passed a resolution demanding strict compliance, especially by South Africa, with the UN independence plan for Namibia. It also demanded the disbandment of all para military forces in the territory, especially Koevoet.

There was also a call for more UN monitors for Namibia.

The resolution was a watered down version of a draft which would have focused more heavily on South Africa for allegedly 'failing to comply with the independence plan' and which called for UNTAG's military forces to be increased from 4 650 to 7 500.

In the debate, the permanent members of the Security Council opposed increases in the size of UNTAG's military component.

South Africa's UN representative, Mr Jeremy Shearer, said afterwards he was pleased 'the original draft, which was clearly an attempt to whitewash SWAPO, was not acceptable to important sensible members of the Council'.

1st September – Foreign Minister Pik Botha on behalf of the South African Government, made a strong protest to the UN on the contents of the Security Council resolution taken earlier in the week.

But, really, what was the use.

So by the end of August what had SWAPO achieved?

South African troops, which had been reduced to a mere 1 500 men, were confined to base. What remained of the old SWA Police Counterinsurgency Unit, Koevoet as it was once called, had been confined to bases far from the border.

The country was uncomfortably open for a major SWAPO incursion.

The original intention behind the peace plan had been pure and simple.

At the end of it all, after 'free and fair' elections had been held, the country would have been at peace, with only a police force.

The SWA Territory Force wouldn't exist and neither would its command structure.

PLAN wouldn't exist and neither would its command structure.

The SADF would have returned to South Africa.

This would have made it impossible for any party to resume the war, should they end up as the loser in the election.

Naturally, if SWAPO won the election, they would be at liberty to reform their forces, adding in any other elements they felt like, to create a new national army.

If another party, like the DTA won the election, they would likewise be at liberty to reform the SWA Territory Force, if they wished, or they could create a totally new army incorporating SWAPO elements.

This didn't happen in reality?

The SWA Territory Force was disbanded, as intended, and its command structure dismantled.

UNTAG made sure of that.

The most important part of the police force has been confined to base and could face disbandment before the November elections, which had never been intended.

The 1 500 members of the SADF still left in Namibia, have been confined to base.

What about SWAPO?

SWAPO never had any intention of disbanding PLAN, nor breaking down its command structure.

It hasn't.

Neither did SWAPO intend moving its forces north of the 16th parallel in Angola.

If they have, which seems doubtful, they were moved back struggling and screaming by the Angolans.

Unfortunately, the intention that PLAN should be disbanded was never translated into an agreement, so in the end no obligation was placed on SWAPO to do that or to dismantle its command structure.

SWAPO's 'responsibilities' were vicariously agreed to and then assumed by a number of policemen nations and the UN.

The question of seeing SWAPO's fighters redeployed north of the 16th parallel, was primarily an Angolan responsibility with the UN having a duty to monitor it.

For them to take part in the election, their weapons had to be placed in storage in Angola, Zambia or Botswana and they had to return to Namibia 'as civilians', meaning, it seems, they couldn't wear uniform.

The supervision of this was the duty of SWAPO's host countries and the UN.

The only agreement SWAPO entered into was a ceasefire, and that was through the UN and not directly with South Africa.

In retrospect, the dangers of SWAPO not being a directly involved party in at least a ceasefire agreement negotiated directly between Cuba, Angola and South Africa, and ratified by the Security Council, are self evident.

When the 1st April incursions of some sixteen hundred men occurred, at least some elements of the Angolan military must have been involved. It would have been impossible to mount an operation of that magnitude without someone being aware of it.

It would have required a massive logistical operation in Angola prior to the start, with a need for transport and so on. The feeding of 1 600 odd men alone, must have been a major operation.

Then there was the question of movement to north of the 16th parallel, after SWAPO's invasion of Namibia had failed.

By then, when it became impossible to deny it, the Cubans and Angolans agreed SWAPO had been south of the 16th parallel before the 1st April.

So who had known?

According to Fidel Castro's speech in Havana on the 9th July, the Cubans had been virtually in charge of the Angolan government in 1988, which means they would hardly have withdrawn completely in 1989. They would, at the least, have continued to service in councils, on committees and so on. It is undeniable they remained committed militarily.

So, if the top echelons of the Angolan Government knew, then it seems likely the Cubans did as well.

On the other hand a SWAPO prisoner questioned by the author, who had belonged to a mixed Cuban-SWAPO unit, told how it had been disbanded before the incursion.

This points towards the Cubans not being involved.

Maybe certain elements of the Angolan military, because of their long standing close links with SWAPO, rendered assistance on a freelance basis without the central government's knowledge.

If this happened, though, it would have needed to have been a powerful element indeed, because otherwise the Angolan government would have produced scapegoats afterwards to stop fingers being pointed at them.

They didn't.

There are two main difficulties in resolving the question.

Angola is an African third world totalitarian State.

It's actions cannot be measured or analysed with the same yardsticks applying to a democratic first world state.

But what happened after that?

Until South Africa pushed, Secretary General Perez de Cuellar did little to ensure that after the incursion SWAPO moved north of the 16th parallel.

He had done nothing about it before the 1st April either.

UNTAG spoke vaguely about 'sovereign states' and so on, saying they couldn't do the same things in Angola and Zambia as they could in Namibia.

But why couldn't they?

Both Angola and Zambia had agreed in writing with the UN they would allow UN personnel to monitor SWAPO bases in their countries.

This agreement had been one of the corner stones which had led South Africa to go ahead with the peace plan.

Surely Zambia and Angola, having agreed, were not in a position to dictate to the UN, and say they could only have this number or that number of UN monitors.

That was surely a UN decision.

If the Secretary General thought the number of UN monitors allowed was inadequate, why didn't he say so?

If those countries had become the subject of an unfavourable UN Security Council resolution, they would soon have come into line.

But the Secretary General didn't.

His only interest seemed to be the whitewashing of SWAPO's actions with an indecent haste to appease the Non Aligned Movement.

His attitude was that if Angola, Cuba and SWAPO said the PLAN fighters were north of the 16th parallel, then surely they must be.

Particularly, if the 100 odd UN men in Angola confirmed it. In spite of their Brazilian leader being on record as saying he trusted the Cubans to stick to the rules.

Well, they were not north of the 16th parallel – certainly not all of them anyway.

On the 15th May South African Intelligence estimated there were 600 PLAN fighters south of the 16th parallel.

The Angolans and Cubans denied it.

UNTAG said they were checking.

By August there were 2 000, according to South African Intelligence.

The UN gave assurances, saying they were not there, indicating that only a small minority of PLAN remained in Angola.

The rest had been disarmed, their weapons greased and placed in armouries by the Angolans and had returned to Namibia as 'civilians'.

In spite of those assurances, one is left with more than a lingering doubt as to what the truth really is.

Perhaps if the Secretary General had ordered UNTAG to display an equal diligence and zealousness towards monitoring SWAPO in Angola and Zambia from the very start, as they had done towards the Security Forces in Namibia, then that doubt wouldn't have been there.

According to SWA Police intelligence sources, at least a 1 000 PLAN fighters have returned to Namibia via the UN's refugee repatriation plan Namibia.

Nothing much wrong with that on the face of things. They had returned in civilian clothes, without weapons, and if they hadn't returned they wouldn't be able to vote in the election.

According to SWA Police intelligence, although they returned in dribs and drabs they had hardly been demobilised. In fact, their commanders had returned with them.

Each man had been given route instructions detailing where he should go on arriving back in Namibia.

Their destinations were the main and secondary refugee camps scattered the length and breadth of Namibia, particularly those the UN had allowed the SWAPO supporting Council of Churches for Namibia – CCN, to establish and run.

Once there, although without weapons and uniforms, they had been reformed into their original units – mostly SWAPO Special Forces.

In some camps they are believed to be in platoon strength, in others in company strength and in others even in detachment strength. But how could they have just stayed there?

The refugee policy had been that returnees would stay in the camps for a few days, perhaps a week, then once it was established where had to go, they would be moved on.

Unenvisaged problems had soon developed.

Time in Africa is rarely important and nor are deadlines imposed by organisations regarded as charitable. Many of the less sophisticated refugees wanted to remain in the shelter of the camps, unwilling to relinquish the guaranteed food and shelter.

There was a more sinister reason as well.

SWAPO had passed the word, it had even been monitored on *Radio Freedom* broadcasting from Angola, that refugees leaving the camps should be careful because Koevoet would kill them.

SWAPO had clearly decided it was in their interests to ensure the refugee camps remained as full of people as possible. Secondary refugee camps, without exception run by the Council of Churches for Namibia, had been started to house 'refugees' who couldn't immediately be resettled.

In them, as might be expected, were a sprinkling of old people whose families had moved away or died since they had originally left Namibia.

Obviously those are the sort of people one would anticipate being there.

Others in those secondary camps, though, are young hard men of military age.

The map shows where they are in Namibia.

What about armaments and weapons?

That is why SWAPO established arms caches in the northern border area, border patrols have been reduced to a minimum, because large numbers of police have been confined to their bases.

Consequently, no one can be certain how much in the way of arms and ammunition is being brought in from Angola, or how many cadres are being infiltrated. There are rumours of another possible source of arms for SWAPO.

The Kenyan contingent of UNTAG.

Kenya is a member of the OAU, which organisation is openly 100% partial so far as SWAPO is concerned.

In the April incursions SWAPO brought large quantities of brand new Kenyan uniforms, the same as worn by the Kenyan contingent, and that has never satisfactorily been explained.

It would obviously have been very convenient for SWAPO, if elements of their fighters had intended to masquerade as Kenyan soldiers.

If the Kenyans were cooperating it would not be difficult.

It would be similar to UNTAG counting SWAPO heads in Angola.

A man speaking English and wearing a Kenyan uniform, would be judged as Kenyan, particularly as few people in Namibia speak Kenyan dialects.

There have been rumours, but no hard evidence.

There was an affidavit from a man in Owamboland, saying he had seen Simon

Nipunya, an Owambo, in Kenyan uniform. Simon had left Namibia in 1974 to join SWAPO.

The local population in the country areas speak of alleged Kavango speaking 'Kenyans'. One was said to have used Kwangali, a Kavango dialect, and was identified as a man who had schooled at Nkurenkuru, and who was said to have left Namibia in 1984 to join SWAPO.

Some reports, too, were received from Otjiwarongo, about Kenyan UNTAG who spoke fluent Owambo.

At Okahanja, two Kenyans were identified as Namibian exiles, one of them Damara speaking.

On the 19th May, a NANSO member, accompanied by about twenty NANSO members and two UNTAG Kenyans, called at Police Otjiwarongo to lay a charge. One of the 'Kenyans' spoke to the complainant in Afrikaans.

All this, however, could be dismissed as rumours.

Another factor is more disturbing.

On the 21st April the Kenyan UNTAG contingent brought in what seemed a routine consignment of ammunition, via the South African port of Walvis Bay, under import permit number 7/89.

One item was 12 295 grenades.

The normal scale for an enlarged infantry battalion like the Kenyan contingent to UNTAG, would be about 4 000 grenades as a total for first and second line supply.

This is a maximum, in fact over generous figure, based on scales for an enlarged infantry battalion of the British Army, which the Kenyan Defence Force models itself on.

So what were the other 8 000 plus grenades needed for?

Then there were 709 X 81mm mortar bombs, approximately double the needs of an infantry battalion's first and second line supplies.

Next came the question of 7 62mm ball and tracer ammunition, for their basic infantry weapons.

In weight they had 50 245 kilograms – in quantity it was 1 049,016 rounds.

A battalion of soldiers can fight a lot of battles with that.

UNTAG and even the Administrator General stressed, when a newspaper published the figures, that it was standard practise for units to carry their 'normal' complements of infantry weapons, ammunition, explosives and so on.

But when does an 'abnormal' complement become a 'normal' complement?

Also, UNTAG is a 'monitoring' force, not a 'peacekeeping' force.

It did not go to Namibia to wage war.

16

Whatever Happened to the Refugees?

Refugees: Prisoners of SWAPO

Ever since the war's beginning, refugees from Namibia had spilled out into Angola and Zambia, many in the first instance at least, were political refugees in the true sense, SWAPO supporters or sympathisers. But others were non political refugees, people who wanted to escape the unenviable position of being caught in the middle between the Security Forces and SWAPO, or from SWAPO's murderous intimidation.

But the war grumbled on, mostly at a low key, for almost three decades, and in those years the perceptions of many of the black Namibian refugees, the times themselves and certainly SWAPO, changed.

SWAPO when formed thirty years ago, had broad democratic objectives when looked at through African eyes, but with Soviets and other Warsaw Pact and socialist/communist leaning countries to show them the way, it soon adopted a strictly Marxist-Leninist policy and direction.

Its leader, Sam Nujoma, ruthlessly strengthened the party's organisation and by this means his own position, quickly becoming a virtual dictator, whom few within SWAPO dared to oppose.

But it says much for the independent spirit of the black Namibian people, particularly the Owambos – the heart tribe of SWAPO, that many of them did. A surprisingly large number objected to the idea of Namibia becoming a communist totalitarian state, many others outside the Owambo tribal grouping hated the bias against them within SWAPO, and even more because for many different reasons SWAPO hadn't lived up to the promise expected.

Some weren't even opposing SWAPO, they were merely denounced in the classical communist fashion as 'South African' spies, revisionists, puppets of the Imperialists, sellouts to the cause and so on.

Others were unfortunate enough to fall victims to the jealousies of internal disputes, power struggles and so on.

A few who fell from grace, the more fortunate, escaped in time from SWAPO's clutches and fled Zambia or Angola and made their way back to Namibia.

Once back in the relative safety of Namibia, many joined opposing parties so they could fight SWAPO in the political arena. Others more bitter, swelled the ranks of the SWA Territory Force, particularly 101 Battalion, where they fought bitterly with machineguns and rifles, many giving their lives in the process, to ward off the possibility of a SWAPO take over of Namibia.

For the less fortunate dissenters of all types and persuasions, unable or not quick enough to make good their escape from SWAPO tyranny, a common fate awaited them. This was arrest, imprisonment without trial and the probability of being done to death after all that.

The largest single grouping of people detained at one time, were the supporters of the Caprivi African National Union – CANU, a party which had once amalgamated with SWAPO, but then splintered off again in the late 1970s, because of discrimination against non Owambo cadres.

President Kaunda of Zambia, at Sam Nujoma's request, ordered their mass arrest and incarceration in SWAPO detention camps. Probably more than a thousand people were arrested and detained during this Zambian/SWAPO purge.

Some were imprisoned in Zambian detention centres in Zambia, some were moved to Angola. Many eventually ended up in the infamous Mboroma detention camp in Zambia, when Joshua Nkomo's ZIPRA moved out at the end of the Rhodesian War.

The detention facilities at Mboroma were well documented by the Rhodesians, who mounted a Security Force raid on it to free prisoners. They consisted of raw and dank Vietcong style bunkers dug deep in the naked earth, without washing and only rudimentary toilet facilities, in which prisoners spent months on end without seeing the light of day.

They were hell holes in the truest sense.

Another detention centre of infamy is nearby, or maybe even within the Makena Transit Camp For Refugees, Zambia.

The most famous refugee from SWAPO is Andreas Shipanga, who was a top official in the organisation. After a disagreement on policy while in Zambia, President Kaunda, at SWAPO's request, ordered his arrest in 1976. A writ of *habeas corpos* was applied for in the Zambian High Court, but Kaunda had him flown out and detained in Tanzania before the hearing came up.

He, like SWAPO, prefers Kangaroo courts to judicial ones.

Fortunately for Shipanga, he possessed that which most of SWAPO's detainees didn't – international friends of influence, and much agitation commenced for his release.

There can be little doubt that if he hadn't been in that fortunate position, he would have disappeared like so many of the rest. Instead, after two years of horrific detention, he was released without explanation.

He is still in politics and back in Namibia, but he is one of the many who certainly doesn't want to see Sam Nujoma and SWAPO come into power.

In Angola, a communist totalitarian state, there have been rumours of many SWAPO detention centres. Some have remained unidentified, either because no one has escaped them and returned to Namibia, or because prisoners there are invariably liquidated. Every SWAPO base or camp has detention facilities of some kind or another.

Seven of SWAPO's special prisons or concentration camps in Angola have been positively identified. They are:

(1) SWAPO's Central Prison – This is 16 kilometres east of Lubango, just off a tar road. The detention facilities consist of pits in the ground, probably similar to those already described at Mboroma. Reports say prisoners are held there for 'crimes' like suspicious behaviour, activities against SWAPO's police, theft, murder and desertion.

Toilet and washing facilities are primitive to the extreme and no medical attention is provided.

(2) Camp Etale – This is found to the east of the Greenwell Matango 'Education' Centre. It is primarily for, as SWAPO describes them, spies, informants of the 'Boers', protesters against SWAPO policies and criticisers of the SWAPO leadership, all generally lumped together as counter revolutionaries.

Rumours that have filtered out of Angola, suggest that those still alive when SWAPO 'frees' Namibia, will be tried afterwards by People's Courts.

The prisoners at Camp Etale, estimated at about 250 in 1988, are said to be serving life sentences – although none have been judged in a court of law.

SWAPO's incarceration policy is strongly reminiscent of the Nazi death camps of World War-2. Anyone who dies there, no matter the cause, is marked down as having committed suicide. Guards doing duty there are never transferred to other work, in case the horrific goings on filter back to SWAPO's rank and file.

(3) Security Prison. This is near the old Tobias Hainyeko Training Centre and is predominantly used for political prisoners 'sentenced' to death. The prisoners are either liquidated by SWAPO firing squads or are thrown into some sort of deep pit or quarry known as the 'green hole'. This found in the area between Lubango and the Mulumba Logistics Base.

(4) Vienna Prison. This is ten kilometres to the east of Luanda and is used for the detention of prisoner serving short sentences for petty offences, like being absent without leave, drunkenness etc.

(5) Haidongo Prison. This is about ten kilometres to the west of Cuvango on the road to Dongo, some 500 meters off the road to the north. Prisoners there are mostly PLAN fighters imprisoned for disciplinary offences.

(6) Kamati Prison. This is a kilometre to the east of Haidongo Prison and apparently used for much the same purposes as that one.

(7) Nyango Prison. This is found within the Namibian 'Education' Centre at Camp Nyango. Prisoners are detained there for 'crimes' like lack of discipline, theft, insubordination, unacceptable behaviour, poor attitude towards educators, drunkenness and absence without leave.

The cells are made from wooden poles and cement and are windowless. Prisoners are chained to fastenings in the concrete floor and are fed once a day on a diet of beans and mealie meal porridge.

Prisoners accused of serious crimes, which by SWAPO definition can mean anything, are detained in solitary confinement and subjected to brutal interrogations. If someone decides they are guilty, they might be kept in Central Prison as a transit measure, until final incarceration in Etale Prison. If it has been decided to kill them, they are sent to the Security Prison for liquidation.

There is said to be a 'court' at Nyango, but few prisoners have appeared before it.

At one stage a few SWAPO cadres were sent to Mosi, Tanzania, for legal education, but this was soon discontinued.

SWAPO prisoners are not allowed the benefit of legal counsel.

The first people to agitate for international action to be taken to in action group comprising about 150 relatives and loved ones of missing SWAPO members.

In 1987 the Parents' Committee produced impressive and comprehensive documentation and evidence relating to SWAPO's violations of human rights.

One example dated 5th February 1985, of which the Parents' Committee can produce many similar examples, originated from a lady who gave her address as c/o UN High Commissioner for Refugees, PO Box 32542, Lusaka, Zambia, read as follows:

'I'm sure it will surprise you to receive a latter from an unexpected person. My dear, I am still doing fine, hope to hear the same from you.

'I am out of SWAPO, I haven't got any more time to sit and look how people disappear and are murdered by Owambos in SWAPO. Sululu and Sila are also out. People are going almost every day.

'In am with (name withheld). Accommodation and foodwise is okay. The only demoralising thing is that we don't get clothes. My sister, before I go anywhere, I first want to send my child home. You may have heard that Apies, Lukas, Boois, Eric, Aaron, Seibeb, Koesieb and almost everyone who is Nama/Damara speaking have disappeared in Angola.

'Just imagine, Pastor and Master Willem Kanjore were here in November of last year and had discussed the problem, but there is still no change, people are still disappearing. All the boys who played in the SWAPO band, were jailed and Agies shot himself. Andries Basson was also murdered. Tauno Hatukuilipi was also murdered in a very brutal way.

'Well, it is very sad that innocent people should be murdered like that. We are watched, they say they will make sure and get and beat and discipline us, which they will not succeed in doing. Tell Dickson, Alie also walked out. They wanted to send him to Angola.

'As your two brothers have also disappeared, you should stay away from here. Look for a big house for us, as I am looking for a sponsor to go to Britain.

'Answer as soon as possible, let me known where you stand. SWAPO told me, I have to stay in the camp with the child, until Namibia is free. For some time now I have not received anything from the magazine, not even food for my child. When will you be finished? I have written home and told Gows to tell sister Elis that both her brothers have disappeared in SWAPO.'

The phrase 'SWAPO told me I will have to stay in the camp with the child, until Namibia is free' is highly significant because it shows SWAPO has been 'recruiting' refugees, playing the numbers game as it were.

This could have been for the political reason of showing the world how many people had fled the South African regime in Namibia, or because they did everything to keep the numbers up due to the steady and lucrative rip off of refugee aid they had been engaged in.

It was probably for both reasons.

On the 13th August 1987 three representatives of the Parents' Committee, quite per chance, found themselves face to face with Mr Sam Nujoma at the European Parliament in Strasbourg. Not wishing to waste such an opportunity, Ms Talita Schmidt, confronted him and asked what had happened to her two missing cousins, adding that he should release the Namibians he was keeping in custody.

He responded by shoving her away. She returned and he dealt her a hard backhander to her face saying: 'You will die'.

244

At a press conference later, Nujoma was questioned on the assault by a journalist from *The Luxemburg Word*.

Nujoma answered that he wanted to 'categorically state that SWAPO excuses itself to no one'. He added: 'I would like to say to those who were sent by the South Africans, that they will be hit by one of their bullets, if they should appear in our area'.

When the inevitable storm broke, the really quite excellent SWAPO propaganda machine – honed to a fine edge by not only the Soviets but by many other left wing organisations including agencies of the UN, swung smoothly into action. They portrayed the incident as an 'invention by sympathisers of the South African apartheid regime'.

Some press reports about the assault appeared, but most newspapers ignored it, as did the electronic media in its entirety.

Yet it happened.

Impeccable witnesses, completely impartial, are still available, as is the tape recording of Nujoma's death threat at the press conference.

The truth, as always, is that outside of southern Africa, few people believe or wish to believe Sam Nujoma or SWAPO are capable of wrongdoing.

The stories of beatings, murders and disappearances of prisoners in SWAPO's hands are legend, but in the main the world ignores them because of the comfortable approach arising from the myth that SWAPO is an organisation engaged in a just fight for Namibian freedom and democracy . . . and 'apartheid' South Africa is 'the enemy', not them.

Western governments have refrained from demanding or taking part in active investigations of human rights violations by SWAPO, which they could easily have done.

It would be difficult for the Zambian and Angolan governments and SWAPO to resist major international demands for them to open their camps and prisons for immediate inspections by say the Red Cross, but no such demanded have been made.

Governments rest easily on the vague promise that as the United Nations Commission for Refugees is somewhere involved, reports of the illtreatment of prisoners at the least, or atrocities at the most, would have been brought to light.

This, however, is a promise unlikely to be fulfilled, because not only has UNHCR failed to make a complaint or raise a query about the treatment of SWAPO's prisoners, they have not even prepared documentation to show they exist.

Phil Christenson who prepared a report for the US Senate made some disturbing revelations. According to him the UNHCR offices in Frontline States denied help to black refugees fleeing the ranks of the African National Congress of South Africa, because it would be detrimental to the 'struggle for liberation' in South Africa.

This indicates the awful probability that refugees fleeing the clutches of SWAPO or the ANC, who ask for their help in the Frontline states, are denounced and handed back to them.

It seems the UNHCR have an unofficial policy of regarding the pressganging of recruits for the so called liberation movements as lawful, looking on it a kind of national service. It is evident that such abandonment of a refugee, at the best, would lead to his incarceration by SWAPO. At the worst it would signal his eventual execution before a firing squad.

Is that what a refugee agency is for?

If it is, the UNHCR should be disbanded and its work handed over to the Red Cross.

As evidence of such practises exist, it casts serious doubts on the vital neutrality and integrity of the UNHCR.

Because SWAPO's actions have remained internationally protected at almost every level and from almost every angle, it is rare for them to bother to even answer allegations made against them, but they have occasionally let slip highly prejudicial admissions illuminating their callous disregard for human rights and the sanctity of human life.

One telling example was the damaging admission made by SWAPO representative, Thelma Ashipala, at a public meeting held in Devon, England, on the 20th January 1987.

In answer to a question she said that SWAPO prisoners 'still alive' in the camps are being 'reeducated'.

The connotations of that statement need no amplification.

The next organisation to take up cudgels on behalf of prisoners held by SWAPO in Angola and Zambia, was the influential International Society of Human Rights, which has offices in Australia, Austria, Belgium, Ecuador, France, Great Britain, Israel, Italy, Mauritius, Spain, Switzerland, United States of America, West Germany, Soviet Russia. It also has contact groups in Argentina, Canada, Denmark, Finland, Mexico, Norway and Sweden.

SWAPO propagandists have at times slyly suggested, with success in some circles, that the ISHR is a front for one of 'apartheid' South Africa's intelligence organisations.

In the first place the ISHR has never had an office in Namibia, let alone in South Africa. In the second, it would be stretching credibility beyond reasonable limits, to believe that South Africa has successfully established two 'front' offices in Soviet Russia, one in Moscow and the other in Leningrad.

The International Society For Human Rights has fought a long and hard uphill battle to bring the atrocities committed by SWAPO against its dissenters into the international light of day . In 1985 they published their *Human Rights in South West Africa/Namibia,* in 1986 their *SWAPO And Human Rights* and in September 1988 their *Human Rights Violations In SWAPO Camps In Angola and Zambia,* which have received wide coverage.

They have done much in support of the Parents Committee, and between them they have created the beginnings of a lobby of church leaders, politicians and other public figures, particularly in Europe.

Meanwhile Amnesty International also began to show interest in the question and the following appeared in the Namibian chapter of their 1987 report:

'During 1986 Amnesty International was concerned about reports that the external wing of the South West Africa People's Organisation – SWAPO, was holding prisoners in its camps in Angola. Those held were alleged by SWAPO to have spied for South Africa, but other sources suggested that they had been detained as a result of political disputes within the organisation . . .

'Amnesty International was concerned also by reports that the external wing of SWAPO was holding prisoners at a camp or camps in southern Angola. Those detained were alleged by SWAPO to have infiltrated the organisation and spied for South Africa, but other sources suggested that they have been detained because of internal disputes within SWAPO. In February SWAPO officials admitted that more than 100 people had been detained but they did not disclose all their identities. The detainees were reported to include at least two men who had previously been of concern to Amnesty International when they were detained by the South African authorities in Namibia in the late 1970s.'

Organisations like the Parents' Committee and the International Society For Human Rights, are careful not to spoil their case by overstating it, and according to their records in September 1988, they had listed 184 dissidents believed to be prisoners or unaccounted for at the hands of SWAPO.

The problem is that refugees leaving Namibia over the years to swell the ranks of SWAPO in Angola or Namibia, have done so clandestinely and not through recognised immigration channels. Many did not tell their relatives they were going. In type they have ranged from the virtual primitive to the sophisticated, and regretably it is only those in the upper levels of that range who are likely to have been missed and reported as missing.

Dissenters who have escaped back to Namibia rarely talk of SWAPO's prisoners as being in the hundreds, but rather at levels ranging from 1 000 – 2 000, sometimes even more.

A petition signed by Namibian refugees on the 20th May 1988, which had been smuggled out of the Makena Refugee Camp, Zambia, reached its destination, the Canadian Embassy in Cape Town, on the 16th February 1989.

They complained that evidence existed to show that SWAPO intended to kill all Namibian refugees who did not support them.

25th May – Cedric Thornberry said at an UNTAG press briefing that 'confirmation had just been received from UNTAG military observers in Angola that they had seen a group who were apparently former detainees of SWAPO – 199 adults and a number of children – yesterday.

'The military observers had met them at SWAPO camps north of Lubango and had questioned them, ascertaining identification and other details. Details would come to the Special Representative's office tomorrow; meanwhile, it was reported those interviewed had been well dressed and seemingly well cared for. UNTAG military personnel had been told that all had been registered by the UNHCR, and arrangements would be made for their return in accordance with the settlement proposal.'

Asked by a journalist if the UN was satisfied that those interviewed were really at liberty, Thornberry replied that 'the military observers, who were so far the only UNTAG staff to have seen the individuals in question, seemed to have interviewed the persons whom they had seen. The situation would be examined in detail, and the UN would, of course, do all that was necessary to ensure their freedom to return to Namibia.'

When asked by another journalist to comment on Sam Nujoma allegedly saying the detainees had been isolated because they were 'misguided' and must not be allowed to influence the forthcoming elections, Thornberry declined to comment.

29th May – Cedric Thornberry, at an UNTAG press conference, revealed he had received a list giving names and details of the 201 former detainees released by SWAPO in Angola. This was being compared with consolidated UN documentation relating to the release of 280 political prisoners and detainees of SWAPO.

When answering questions, Thornberry said none of those released had been seen by the Red Cross and ways to return them to Namibia were being worked out.

30th May – Cedric Thornberry, in answer to a question at a press briefing, said the analysis of the list of freed detainees against the lists of SWAPO detainees held by UNTAG 'was still going on'.

A reporter asked him to comment on a report that some of them had appealed to UNHCR 'to get them out of the SWAPO camps'.

Thornberry denied this saying UNTAG military observers in Angola had reported that those interviewed had been registered by UNHCR and had 'indicated that they were content to remain in the camps pending their repatriation'.

1st June – Nicholas Bwakira, chief of UNHCR in Namibia, in answer to persistent questioning about the security of the 201 former SWAPO detainees at Lubango, said that 'Angola was responsible for their protection and UNHCR was providing material assistance as needed'.

He said they would be 'repatriated in the same manner and at the same time as the rest of the returning Namibians', making clear the point they would not be getting any 'special treatment'.

Why ever not, surely they merited some sort of special treatment?

9th June – The pro SWAPO, The Namibian, carried a report by John Lieben-berg, who with two other journalists, was flown to two SWAPO detention camps near Lubango in Angola, apparently at the behest of SWAPO, to interview some of SWAPO's former detainees.

Top officials, SWAPO's Secretary General, Mr Andimba Toivo ja Toivo, and Administrative Secretary, Mr Moses Garoeb, were present and listened impassively while the detainees related harrowing tales of torture and suffering.

A woman displayed her baby and said it was the fruit of rape by a camp guard.

At a camp for males one said: 'For more than ten years I have been forced to incriminate others, and told that we are agents of the South African regime.

'We have suffered harassment and torture in order to cow us into submission. Hundreds have been killed, maimed and lost. We were given two options: To agree to integration within SWAPO, or to be handed over to South Africa which would prove our collaboration with the regime.'

Moses Garoeb said later that SWAPO 'had made mistakes,'but pointed out it had been an organisation at war.

It seemed SWAPO, by arranging this visit, had decided to test the water themselves, before allowing the media as a whole to question their former prisoners once they were in a free country.

The reaction, which was highly unfavourable, obviously decided them on a course of not releasing too many.

28th June – The Angolan government, according to the Star's Africa News Service, has requested UNHCR to visit SWAPO detainees formerly held in camps.

4th July – 153 former detainees of SWAPO were flown into Windhoek Airport from Luanda. They were first reported by Cedric Thornberry of UNTAG on the 25th May as numbering 199 adults and a number of children. This was corrected to '201 persons' by Thornberry on the 29th May.

Neither UNTAG or the UNHCR explained the discrepancy between the original 201 in custody, and the 153 who arrived.

They were the people who UNHCR's Nicholas Bwakira had said on 1st June wouldn't be getting 'any special treatment'.

UNTAG's Cedric Thornberry described them on the 30th May as 'content to remain in the [SWAPO] camps until repatriation'.

This indicated UNTAG accepted the SWAPO detention camps as jolly holiday camp type places, in which all the objections of a prisoner, once he was out from behind bars, would quickly melt away.

Thornberry's suggestion, as it turned out, was as inappropriate as suggesting former Nazi death camp prisoners would want to return each year for their annual holidays.

They spoke of illegal detentions, executions and torture including tales of people being buried alive, being hung upside down and beaten with sticks and so on.

A woman who fell pregnant as a result of rape by a guard, explained how she had been beaten even while in that condition.

Mr Jephat Isaack, asked by a reporter if any of his friend had disappeared while he was in prison said: 'There are so many I can't count them'.

Mostly people had been detained as 'South African spies'.

It was revealed that in February 1989, SWAPO had attempted to reduce the number of detainees held by them, obviously so they wouldn't have to be sent back to Namibia, by offering prisoners the opportunity of reintegration into SWAPO, or 'being returned to the South African government,' implying they would then be arrested and imprisoned in South Africa.

The suggestions was made to the prisoners by SWAPO's Secretary General Toivo ya Toivo, and men with him were heavily armed, so as Mr Isaac, a former SWAPO officer bearer said, 'we decided to be reintegrated'.

SWAPO afterwards destroyed the detention camp.

Some of the former prisoners escaped into the bush and eventually managed to make contact with the International Red Cross, which ultimately arranged their repatriation to Namibia.

An uncounted number of others were less fortunate.

SWAPO's former prisoners have collectively confirmed, that in their opinions, at least 2 000 more were still be held in SWAPO's Angolan and Zambian detention camps.

6th July – Foreign Affairs Minister, Pik Botha, expressed concern over the safety of detainees still in the hands of SWAPO, saying he feared they could be murdered. He said he intended taking the matter up at the next meeting of the JMMC.

On the same day Mr Richard Boucher, a US State Department spokesman, said: 'We are deeply concerned about the mistreatment of Namibians by SWAPO. We've asked for a full accounting of the status of all detainees.

'We have raised the question of accounting for all SWAPO detainees with several countries in the region and have asked them to use their influence with SWAPO to ensure the safe repatriation of all SWAPO detainees to Namibia.'

Despite the international furore, the United Nations Commission for Refugees, blandly announced it had accepted SWAPO's contention that it had released all detainees, ignoring allegations by freed prisoners there were probably at least another 2 000 in SWAPO's hands, and a list of 300 named people still missing which had been provided by the Parents' Committee.

7th July – It was announced the freed dissidents had formed themselves into a pressure group, led by former SWAPO Politburo member, Mr Rinndja Ali Kaakunga, who said they were deeply anxious about the fate of hundreds of other detainees of SWAPO, who might have still be in detention, or who had died from illness or were executed in front of SWAPO's firing squads.

The pressure group named themselves the Political Consultative Council. It would not be associated with any political party, but they would work to unite 'all forces opposed to tyranny'.

At a meeting in Khomasdal Township, Windhoek, the former detainees stripped off clothes and displayed burns and marks of beatings inflicted while they were in SWAPO custody, to an angry and indignant crowd of more than a 1 000 people from widely differing political parties and ideologies.

Mr Kaakunga said that between 1980–1989, SWAPO's camps in Zambia and Angola had become 'hunting grounds' for suspected South African spies. Hundreds of people had been detained on false charges. SWAPO had built prison camps with 'torture chambers' and had sent dissidents to 'production units'.

He accused SWAPO of wanting to establish 'a fascist military dictatorship' in Namibia.

9th July – *Sapa-Reuter* reported from London that an unnamed SWAPO spokesman replied to the accusations of the freed SWAPO dissident, Ottniel Kaakunga, saying 'the claim by the South African spies that SWAPO had killed 100 detainees and is holding 1 000 others is a malicious fabrication.' He said SWAPO didn't condone torture, but 'if any such method was used, it was a case of excess dictated by the extreme conditions of a brutal war that South Africa has imposed on the Namibian people'.

On the same day, SWAPO leader, Mr Theo-Ben Gurirab, speaking at an election rally at Rehoboth about allegations made by returnees said: 'We don't condone torture under any circumstances. If that happened I apologise to them and to their parents. We considered them as spies, but not as enemies'.

He then went on to say that UN representatives as well as the international media had access to the detainees and their numbers were verified by UN personnel.

If anybody is prepared to believe this in the face of the overwhelming evidence to the contrary, they will believe anything.

18th July – The newly formed Political Consultative Council, after consultations amongst themselves, released a list of 94 people they knew had been in SWAPO's detention camps and who were missing feared dead or murdered, and another 439 described as missing, believed held by SWAPO in Angola or elsewhere.

2nd August – Speaking at an Institute of Strategic Studies conference on Namibia held in Pretoria, UN Special Representative, Mr Martti Ahtisaari, said the release of [SWAPO's] prisoners was a 'critical provision of the settlement plan . . . We have had some success in this regard [but] I am not satisfied that all political prisoners and detainees have been released and I am pursuing the question with all concerned governments and with SWAPO'.

At the same conference Mr Louis Pienaar said 'an unsettled matter is the return of all detainees held by SWAPO, which in terms of resolution 435, does not seem to be anybody's responsibility'.

8th August – It was confirmed the list of 94 presumed dead and 439 missing detainees held by SWAPO, compiled by the Political Consultative Council, had been handed to the Administrator General, Advocate Louis Pienaar, with the request he use his good offices to secure the release of those still detained before the November elections.

Spokesman Mr Kaakunga said it was a specific provision of resolution 435 that all political prisoners be released. The organisation was able to provide not only the names of those detained by SWAPO, but details of when and where they were last seen alive in SWAPO prisons.

11th August – Former SWAPO detainee, Mr Stephen Motinga, described after arriving in Windhoek, how he and 83 other prisoners had been 'released' from custody by SWAPO on 15th May.

'We were given the choice, 'he said,' as it was put, of being thrown away in the bush or to make a pledge that we would support and vote for SWAPO after our release.'

As 'thrown away in the bush' was a euphemism for being killed, they not surprisingly signed the declaration.

They were taken to the camp of SWAPO's First Mechanised Infantry Battalion and instructed not to move more than four kilometres from there, not to go to other SWAPO camps, or into the town of Lubango.

He said they spent two months there.

'We were never presented to UNHCR. We were simply hidden away.'

Eventually sixteen of them took the chance and fled the camp, registering for repatriation with the UNHCR, after which they were returned to Namibia without SWAPO's knowledge.

While in SWAPO detention Mr Motinga described how he was beaten for two weeks and hung naked and upside down from a tree. He said all detainees were tortured, with always the same result: 'Either death or a false confession. He said how prisoners had been held in holes in the ground, with no blankets and only a tin for toilet facilities except.

'It is time that SWAPO accounts for all these people,' he demanded. 'We call on the UNHCR, the International Committee of the Red Cross and UNTAG, to do all in their power to have these people released and repatriated.'

25th August – In an amazing revelation, Johannesburg's *Weekly Mail*, an authoritative newspaper so far as alternative politics are concerned, said it had been privately confirmed by a top level SWAPO official, although publicly denied by SWAPO headquarters, that at one stage the 'absurd paranoia and spy obsession' was so rampant that Sam Nujoma's wife, Mrs Kowambo Nujoma, was arrested as a South African spy and held at Minya Detention camp near Lubango.

It was believed she had since reconciled with the movement and was in East Germany. According to a SWAPO official in Windhoek she, 'will return to Namibia with her husband'.

In the same article the Green Party in West Germany, who described their organisation as long standing SWAPO supporters, took SWAPO to task in an open letter saying it had learned of the terrible conditions in 'your camps, torture and the arbitrary use of force, as well of killings.

'We ourselves have talked to a number of former prisoners . . . there is hardly any doubts in our minds that the reports are essentially true'.

In a report from New York, Abed Titus, founder president of the United Party of Namibia, formed after a split with SWAPO, complained that the UNHCR's office and UN officials in New York were still maintaining their pro SWAPO stance.

He had applied to UNHCR in March, but months later was still being given the 'run around'. Eventually he was promised a reservation on an aircraft carrying returning SWAPO members, but this was cancelled without reason at the last minute.

He said he was keeping close contact with South African Ambassador to the UN, Jeremy Shearer, who had already challenged the UN's proclaimed objectivity on the question of refugee repatriation.

Refugees – Pick a Number

5th September 1978 – According to newspaper reports, UN Special Representative Martti Ahtisaari, had carried out an investigation into the question of Namibian exiles and made a report to the then Secretary General and recently much discredited Kurt Waldheim.

He had estimated a total of 40 000 exiles, including SWAPO personnel, would have to be moved back to Namibia. 30 000 were said to be in Angola, 20 000 would be flown home and the rest sent by road. The remaining 10 000 were accounted for by an estimated 5 000 in Zambia, while the rest were spread out in various countries around the world.

As the years ticked by after the 1978 failure to implement UN resolution 435, the number of refugees said to be sustained by SWAPO in their Angolan and Zambian camps, had escalated sharply until by 1988 they claimed the number was in the region of 75–80,000.

SWAPO undoubtedly inflated these figures, but amazingly the numbers were never physically checked or even subjected to a query by the United Nations High Commission for Refugees. This indicates one of two things, either gross inefficiency or a widespread and blatant conspiracy to defraud the nations donating to the welfare of refugees.

Countries contributing towards the upkeep of refugees, like Sweden and others, and the UNHCR itself, made payments on a per capita basis, so playing the inflation of numbers game, was a highly profitable business for SWAPO.

The embarrassments for both SWAPO and the United Nations High Commission For Refugees, began when the truth came out after the 22nd December 1988, when resolution 435 once more came on line for implementation.

Naturally, all Namibian refugees had to be readied for repatriation. The UNHCR was obliged to send representatives to the SWAPO camps in Angola and Zambia to document the exiles. In terms of the peace agreement, they had to be questioned and afterwards properly documented to prove they were Namibian by birth, or had been born outside the country of Namibian parents.

The UNHCR delegations sent to check the camps were, according to a highly placed source, amazed and red faced to discover, in the first instance at least, that SWAPO could produce no more than 18 000 refugees to document.

Understandably, there were no quick answers available – the camps were deep in the often roadless African bush and easy to accept as difficult to audit. Fortunately, it seems, some embarrassment was saved, when SWAPO were able to bolster their numbers of refugees with more Kwanyama tribesmen, who pose a particular problem in southern Angola.

The tribal area of the Kwanyamas was bisected by the international border line when it was arbitrarily drawn in the old colonial days.

This left one third of the tribe in Namibia and two thirds, including the Chief and his royal kraal, in Angola.

In spite of this it is still the largest tribe in Namibia.

They have always regarded the border cutting through their tribal area as non existent and a blind eye has always been turned towards their toings and froings by both the Namibian and Angolan authorities.

The result for a long time, however, has been that some of the Kwanyamas have fluctuated between being sometimes Namibians and sometimes Angolans – depending on which nationality best suited them at a particular moment.

When things became hot within Namibia, because of the bush war, they hopped the border and became Angolans, but when the eastern part of Kwanyama territory inside Angola became UNITA's western operational area and a war zone to boot, then they moved south.

SWAPO had long ago claimed the Kwanyamas in Angola as 'their' refugees.

Obviously the more refugees they had, the more valid was their claim that Namibians were suffering and flocking to Angola to join them.

And the more refugee revenue they could convert to sustain their war effort.

UNHCR relief, channelled through SWAPO, soon became available for the Kwanyamas in Angola. Many came to rely on it and even gave up tilling for crops. They were unsophisticated peasant farmers in a harsh land. When the rains came their bellies were full, but in times of draught they starved. At the best of times, life allowed them little more than to eke out a precarious living.

Having got the taste for it, being a refugee became a definitely better way to live. A man, his wives and their many children, just sat around and waited for the trucks or the aircraft to come in. One week it would be food, the next clothing and a goodly supply of blankets for winter, and so.

For some, it became a way of life.

One former senior political commissar who deserted SWAPO and returned to Namibia, explained how he had originally crossed the Namibian border and joined SWAPO in Botswana. From there he was taken to Angola where he underwent military training and then to Liberia where he completed his high schooling. Being a man with political ambitions he was selected as a potential political commissar and sent to Soviet Russia for training.

On his return he was sent to southern Angola to assist with the administration of the Kwanyama 'refugees'.

'I got sick and tired of dealing with the Kwanyamas,' he explained. We used them as refugees, but they are not refugees. Most of them are not even Namibians, they are Angolans. Eventually, I couldn't take them any more, so I ran away from SWAPO'.

Which focuses on the most important points about the Kwanyama refugees.

Are they truly refugees?

If they are, are they truly Namibian refugees from the fighting in Namibia or are they Angolan refugees from the UNITA/MPLA fighting in Angola?

People who know the Kwanyamas, suggest that because of the tribal tradition of cross-border movement, it will be difficult, in most cases, to prove a particular person is or is not an Angolan or a Namibian.

This will be aggravated by the attitude of those who have come to rely on UN refugee relief. It seems certain many will have fabricated their family backgrounds, in their determination to follow the relief C-130s and the UNHCR cooking pots from Angola to Namibia.

3rd May – Cedric Thornberry said at an UNTAG press briefing that the registration of returnees hadn't been completed, but it looked as if 40 000 would be registering for return to Namibia. He stressed that this did not indicate the total number of refugees, since some were intending to complete schooling before returning and others would eventually make their own way back to Namibia without assistance.

A report by *The Star's Africa News Service* of the same day said the number of refugees expected to return was estimated at 50 000.

11th May – Nicholas Bwakira, in charge of the UNHCR program in Namibia, told a Windhoek press briefing that the UNHCR offices in Zambia and Angola had been strengthened to assist with the registration of returnees. He said registrations had not been completed, but 32 950 had been documented to date.

He said the majority would be returning by air, with the main points of entry being Windhoek, Grootfontein and Ondangwa. The operation would be ready to commence on the 15th May.

21st May – A report in the *Sunday Times* said Mr Olusey Bajulaije of Nigeria, deputy head of UNHCR in the Oshakati/Ondangwa region, had said the organisation was expecting '58 000 refugees, mainly from Angola and Zambia. Others will be flown in from Botswana, Cuba and various points in Europe'.

25th May – The Star reported that US Senator Mr Steve Symes had demanded the US Administration examine the funding of the Namibian refugee program in the light of suspected fraud by SWAPO.

He contrasted claims by SWAPO that it had been supporting between 70- 80 000 refugees in its camps, and securing funding for that number for many years, with current reports by UNHCR that there are actually less than 33 000.

'I believe,' said Mr Symes, 'the UNHCR has either acted in cooperation with SWAPO in submitting grossly inflated figures as a means of securing additional funding, or is completely unaware of the situation in Angola and Zambia.'

According to the same news report, UNHCR in New York, without apparently feeling the least bit abashed, told the *Washington Times*, that it 'had never taken a census of the Namibian refugees, so it had no explanation for the apparent discrepancy between SWAPO's figures and its own registration tally'.

Andreas Shipanga told the *Washington Times* that if 'Sam cannot produce these 80 000 refugees within the next few weeks, he will be exposed either as a con man or as a murderer'.

26th May – Anton Verwey, UNHCR representative in Zambia, told the press arrangements had been made to start flying more than 30 000 exiles home from Angola and another 4 400 from Zambia a week later.

28th May – *The Star's Africa News Service* spoke of an estimated 35 000 refugees in an article.

30th May – UNTAG spokesman, Fred Eckhard, told a Windhoek press conference that he believed 40 000 was the 'latest figure' of refugees who had so far registered with the UNHCR.

On the 1st June, Nicholas Bwakira, Director of UNHCR operations, confirmed at a press conference in Windhoek that 'some' 41 000 refugees had until then registered for repatriation, with more registering daily.

He was asked why the number of refugees receiving UNHCR assistance, was so much greater than those registered for repatriation. 'Had previous figure been dishonestly inflated?'

To quote the UNTAG press release Nicholas Bwakira said 'there were 69 000 refugees receiving UNHCR assistance in Angola, 6 000 to 7 000 in Angola, 200 in Botswana, and a number in other countries for whom he could not give exact figures'.

This totals 75 200 – 76 200, without including those in other countries.

Giving the numbers receiving UNHCR assistance, didn't mean they existed, particularly when the accusations of fraudulent falsification were as much against that organisation as they were against SWAPO.

Bwakira stressed the 'voluntary nature of the repatriation exercise' and that just because somebody had received aid did not 'mandate' his return. He added that 'refugees who did not return at the earliest opportunity would be entitled to continued assistance until Namibian independence. At that time a determination would be made as to whether they still qualified for refugee status. If the conditions that had given rise to their departure was seen to have disappeared, they would no longer be entitled to assistance'.

He then added 'the fact that not as many had registered to return as had been registered to receive assistance, indicated not only that some were electing not to return right away, but also that some were returning without availing themselves of further UNHCR assistance. In any repatriation exercise, there were always substantial numbers of refugees who returned spontaneously, without registering with UNHCR'.

9th June – *The Star* reported the International Society for Human Right had accused the UNHCR, SWAPO and Angola of signing an agreement in April 'that exiles not wishing to be repatriated to Namibia must remain in Angola'.

The Society said it was surprised that only 41 000 exiles had been registered, when 77 000 'had fled the country'.

It demanded an independent investigation be carried out in SWAPO camps in both Angola and Zambia, without SWAPO being present, to determine if those said to be unwilling to return were doing so of their own accord.

11th June – The *Sunday Times*, following the figure quoted by Nicholas Bwakira, spoke of '41 000 exiles'.

14th June – *The Citizen* in an article spoke of 'over 40 000' refugees. This also follows the Bwakira figure.

16th June – Nicholas Bwakira told an UNTAG press briefing that up until that date, 2 333 refugees had been repatriated from Angola and Zambia. The numbers were lower than had been anticipated because of technical problems with aircraft, which hopefully would be overcome after discussions with Zambia Airways.

A reporter asked what kind of technical problems were responsible for aircraft arriving only half full. He expressed a point which had become generally known in Windhoek, because the pilots flying the refugee aircraft in had said so.

UNHCR were scratching to fill the aircraft, which had been chartered to fly home a far greater number of refugees than were available.

Often aircraft were much less than half full.

Sometimes they didn't bother to fly, because there were insufficient refugees around to justify take off.

It was then the 'technical problems with the aircraft' excuse became hackneyed by Bwakira. 20th June – UNTAG spokesman Fred Eckhard said 5 381 refugees and exiles had moved into reception centres in the country.

21st June – *Die Republikein* in Windhoek claimed that SWAPO's *Radio Freedom* which broadcasts from Luanda nightly, had been warning refugees to be careful because they could be murdered by 'agents of the Boers'.

22nd June – According to *The Star's Africa News Service*, refugees who were supposed to stay in reception camps for no more than seven days were not budging from them. At DoBra reception centre outside Windhoek it was reported that 'very few' refugees had left so far and the camp was 100% full.

12th July – Jean-Pierre Hocke, a Swiss national and the UN High Commissioner for Refugees, said at Windhoek during a brief visit, that so far the UNHCR had repatriated 18 000 of the 41 000 refugees who had registered to go back. Nearly all refugees from neighbouring countries should be returned by early next month. After that, the UNHCR would arrange for the return of various other groups scattered about the world.

He added that the overcrowding problem in the refugee transit camps at Dobra, close to Windhoek, and at Okahanja, had been solved by allowing returnees to stay for no more than seven days.

This sounded as if the UNHCR had bumped its head against certain 'professional' refugees, perhaps some of those Kwanyamas from southern Angola. Clearly SWAPO had told them they could just stay in the camps, after returning to Namibia.

1st August – In a broadcast on *SWABC*, UNHCR's Nicholas Bwakira announced the UN was hoping to complete its repatriation of 41 000 refugees 'by the end of this week'.

1st August – According to a report in *The Citizen*, UN Special Representative Mr Martti Ahtisaari announced, intentionally or unintentionally softening the ground for the big let down, 'the repatriation of refugees is an entirely process process' and all those living abroad 'have a free choice to return.'

He added 'the target is now to see that those who have expressed their desire to come back, will come back.'

3rd August – UNTAG spokesman, Fred Eckhard, told a media briefing in Windhoek that the airlift of refugees and exiles from Angola and Zambia could be completed by the 7th August.

He said 32 464 of the 41 000 Namibians seeking repatriation had arrived in the country and 27 711 had been resettled since the operation began on 12th June.

And so, without a word of criticism by anybody in UN authority, the great refugee con trick was finally bulldozed through to finality.

It started with 80 000 refugees – the number the UN had been paying SWAPO to feed for ten years.

Then the great jump around began.

3rd May – UNTAG's Thornberry said it looked like 40 000.

11th May – UNHCR said 32 950 documented for return so far.

21st May – UNHCR representative, Bajulaije of Nigeria, said 58 000.

25th May – UNHCR in New York admitted there were only 33 000 refugees.

26th May – UNHCR representative Verwey said 34 000 expected.

1st August – UNTAG's Ahtisaari said every refugee had a free choice as to whether to return or not.

3rd August – UNTAG's Eckhard announced the end of the exercise with 32 464 having returned.

When the numbers were originally dropped from 80 000 to 40 000 it was explained that some were finishing their education etc and would be returning later.

40 000 refugees written off at a stroke.

After this the figure fluctuated wildly, but UNHCR's Bwakira steadfastly maintained the figure was 41 0000, although UNHCR in New York admitted there were only 33 000.

Finally, when the operation was completed on 3rd August, only 32 464 had returned, which is close to what a lot of people had conceded in the first place.

And so another 7 000 refugees were written off.

This meant 47 000 of the original 80 000 had elected to stay behind in Angola or Zambia.

Who was the UNHCR, particularly Nicholas Bwakira, trying to kid?

What he had implied was that almost half of the 'refugees' were either so comfortable they didn't want to return to Namibia, or they had sufficient funds of their own to enable them to transport themselves and their families by aircraft, bus or train – or perhaps by their owns cars – the thousands of kilometres back to their homes.

This would indicate a new breed of truly wealthy refugees.

But no one can suggest this is a likely or even a remotely reasonable explanation.

The reasonable and likely explanation is the more obvious one.

Multi millions dollars worth of refugee aid was fraudulently obtained and criminally converted by SWAPO. High officials in UNHCR were probably accessories before and after the fact to this fraudulent conversion.

If by a remote chance they were not, then the neglect revealed is so gross a lot of people should be sacked.

The main question uncomfortably lingers on. Why the cover ups by UNHCR and UNTAG?

Is it because they are far from impartial in the Namibian situation?

That everything is secondary to the main effort directed from New York, of which is seeing Nujoma and SWAPO installed as the government of Namibia, no matter the cost.

17

Whatever Happened to Koevoet?

By the end of the Mount Etjo conference on the 9th April, the world in general had been forced to reluctantly accept that the massive heavily armed incursion into Namibia by SWAPO's PLAN fighters had been made illegally and with aggressive intent.

Although Nujoma's reasons for mounting the invasion had remained unclear for some, others accepted his intentions had been to establish PLAN bases within Namibia from which he could launch a massive campaign of intimidation against the local populace, in much the same way as Robert Mugabe and his ZANU P/F had done in Zimbabwe in 1980.

Their defeat at the hands of the SWA Police during the April incursion did not, however, signify the end of the war, it was to them just another battle lost.

They were used to that and the human sacrifice mattered not a jot to SWAPO's leadership.

SWAPO, however, had lost none of its determination to win, whether by fair means or by foul, or whether before or after the November 1989 elections.

They were determined, and so were their various allies in the so called Non Aligned Movement, the OAU, the United Nations, Canada, the Scandinavian countries and elsewhere, that by the end of the year SWAPO would be the government of an independent Namibia, with Sam Nujoma as its Marxist president.

The next battle would be to destroy those who had destroyed them – the SWA Police.

The anti Security Force pro SWAPO propaganda, which had been dished out in such large dollops on a daily basis while the fighting was on, and which had been discredited by the world's acceptance that SWAPO had been the aggressor, was merely continued in the same vein and escalated.

Why not?

Yesterday's newspapers were yesterday's news.

It would soon be forgotten.

It would also soon be forgotten that SWAPO had done anything wrong in the first place.

The old discredited stories could be used again, and it would not be long before they were accepted as the truth.

It was important they be continued without a hiccup.

And this is what happened.

SWAPO's propagandists indeed knew that Hitler's Dr Goebbels was right. The campaign to discredit the counterinsurgency elements of the SWA Police, has become a propaganda classic of its kind, as much as was Hitler's campaign to show the Sudetenland Germans were oppressed by the Czechs, resulting in them being forced to hand the area over to Nazi Germany by reason of the Munich Agreement.

SWAPO's Propaganda War – Target Koevoet

9th April – The London *Sunday Telegraph* contained a report by its Defence correspondent, in Namibia for the peace process, saying he had looked at the corpses of SWAPO fighters laid out outside the Oshakati mortuary and 'none of the bodies showed the familiar signs of mutilation by heavy machinegun bullets of the type used by the South African led Security Forces.

'I asked the police tracker if the SWAPO guerrillas had been killed after surrendering. "What does it matter," he replied. "They are SWAPO, and they area dead. That is all that matters."'

This was no scoop for the reporter concerned. Every newsmen in Oshakati at the time was invited to view the bodies. Hundreds of photographs, which later appeared in newspapers all around the world, were taken.

Other newsmen, who had followed conflict around the world, saw nothing significant about the wounds on the SWAPO dead.

The story, however, would develop.

10th April – The *Times of Namibia* said more than 2 000 people attended a commemoration service and solidarity rally for PLAN fighters killed by the Security Forces.

The Council of Churches of Namibia, CCN provided a brass band.

Father Jackie said in his sermon 'the brothers who had been killed by the 'killers' of South Africa knew quite well that the success of the struggle lies in their actions and in the hands of God'.

A nice bit of 'liberation theology', if ever there was.

Mr Ben Ulenga, trade union and SWAPO official said: 'Our weapon is determination for our liberation. That is what broke the US in Vietnam and the Portuguese Empire in Africa'.

He said that when the PLAN fighters were 'fired upon while about to hand themselves over to UNTAG, the Boere decided to use the opportunity to wipe them out'.

Visiting speaker, Mr Dullah Omar, representing the South African UDF and COSATU, lashed out at the media saying: 'They think that the struggle for freedom has something to do with the writing of the law. Freedom is something for which you must fight'.

11th April – *The Namibian* said: '"Informed sources" have confirmed rumours that a Koevoet hit list has been drawn up containing names of prominent members of the community in the north sympathetic to SWAPO'.

Under a report headed: 'Apartheid for the Dead', it suggested Koevoet cared so little for their black policemen killed in the fighting, that they tossed them into mass graves together with the bodies of the SWAPO dead. It added: 'In nearby houses the families of known Koevoet members were in mourning. As one "eye witness" said: "The wives and children of the Makukunyas don't know where their husbands and fathers are. They have their suspicions that they are among those who are dead. They are all very, very, worried."'

As a matter of record, full military funerals were held for all black policemen killed in action.

12th April – A SWAPO official in Lusaka said UN Special Representative Martti Ahtisaari 'is dripping with blood of innocent Namibians killed using South African forces. We cannot work with such a person'.

A Mr Manning said 'eyewitness accounts confirmed SWAPO's accusations that the recent fighting started because South African forces hadn't been confined to their bases.

18th April – *The Namibian* reported that UNTAG had confirmed that allegations of violent intimidation had been received. It said the reports had originated from 'concerned individuals, church organisations and other 'progressive' groups.

Most of the reports, the newspaper alleged, concerned intimidation by the SWA Police.

20th April – The Administrator General announced the formation of a commission of enquiry under the chairmanship of Mr Bryan O'Linn, long standing pro-independence advocate of the Windhoek Bar and Chairman of the Namibia Peace Plan 435 study group.

The commission would sit continuously.

Its brief would be to thoroughly investigate any acts of intimidation or unlawful conduct by police, the defences forces, by political activists and even by UNTAG. Its findings would be reported to the Administrator General on an ongoing basis. Complaints could be laid with it by any source, including the general public.

20th April – *The Citizen* reported that South Africa is to register a strong protest in the United States over the screening of the documentary film accusing the Security Forces in Namibia of effectively executing SWAPO guerrillas who crossed the border on the 1st April.

The protest was being made, even though the documentary's impact in the United States is likely to be limited. Globalvision who produce the weekly television program, *South Africa Now*, is widely recognised as an agent of the radical left, and the main channels normally avoid screening their products. Consequently, it was likely to be screened on no more that thirteen cable stations, with off peak viewing.

South Africa Now was formed in Harare in 1986 as an anti South African propaganda organisation, with funds provided by the Non Aligned Nations through the Africa Fund. This is administered by Jennifer Davis, a long standing member of the South African Communist Party, with helpers from the African National Congress.

21st April – *The Citizen* reported UNTAG had set up separate investigations into allegations of harassment and intimidation, particularly in northern Namibia where 279 insurgents and 27 members of the Security Forces had been killed in the fighting.

21st April – *The Star* reported that 'residents of northern Namibia say Security Forces shot civilians and tore down villages during the recent fighting. The story followed recent allegations by a US television film that Security Forces 'effectively executed' SWAPO fighters after capture.

21st April – *The Weekly Mail* in a full page article on Namibia included the following: 'If anything, the Katutura resident's concern is voiced more bluntly by civilians in Owamboland. There it is firmly believed that when SWAPO guerrillas came across the Angolan border just before and on the first day of the transition process, they were ambushed by the SWA Police'.

23rd April – An article in the *Sunday Star*, generally derogatory of the Security Forces, said amongst other things: 'But where is the logic in demanding that SWAPO disarm when the SADF does not. And what about Koevoet, whose activities defy the imagination'.

23rd April – The *Sunday Times* carried an article by David Braun headed 'All out bid to smear SA over alleged Namibian atrocities.' In it he says ' a television documentary on the allegations was screened this week to a select group of congress people. It was claimed South African Security Forces executed between 18–24 members of SWAPO after they had been captured and confined early this month. Members of the UN Namibia Council have now seen the film.

'A spokesman for Globalvision, which produces the weekly television magazine program *South Africa Now*, which is broadcast on an 'alternative channel and which featured the atrocity documentary in its most recent show, said in an interview today the 31 nation Namibia Council had been perturbed by the documentary.

'Several ambassadors said it was apparent from the report, based on allegations by two British newsmen working for the London *Sunday Telegraph*, that South African Security Forces had acted brutally against captured SWAPO fighters'.

It went on to say that Mr Peter Zuze, Chairman of the Namibia Council and Zambia's Ambassador had 'deemed the evidence of atrocities to be clear' and he wondered whether other SWAPO fighters besides those photographed had not also been 'eliminated' after their capture.

5th May – A report in the *New Nation* continued the story. By this time the bodies had been 'concealed in a courtyard at the Oshakati police mortuary.' It also alleged 'experts' had confirmed the fighters had been shot through the backs of their heads, after 'examining the photographs' with a magnifying glass.

8th May – Secretary General Perez de Cuellar was reported as saying a senior police officer in northern Namibia had been 'discharged' following complaints by UNTAG.

The SWA Police's PRO, Chief Inspector Kierie du Rand described the report as 'rubbish' and 'wishful thinking of UNTAG'.

10th May – UNTAG spokesman Mr Cedric Thornberry said the UN was investigating allegations of fifty incidents of intimidation, assault and misconduct in northern Namibia. 'Some of the allegations are dismaying. I don't know if they are justified, but we are investigating them'.

The allegations involved military personnel, political parties and officials.

This figure did not, it is believed, include the case where UNTAG members allegedly brutally raped a 49 years old coloured woman.

18th May – The Administrator General, Mr Louis Pienaar, told *The Times* of London, he was 'very perturbed' about allegations made against former members of Koevoet. He pointed out, however, that no reports of these allegations had been made to the police.

18th May – Zimbabwean President and Chairman of the Non Alligned Movement of the UN, Robert Mugabe, accused the Security Council of 'outright mismanagement'. He went on to say: 'UNTAG and its leadership cannot escape criticism for the slowness with which they began their work, as well as the "outrageous" decision to unleash the South African forces against the Namibian people'.

He made no criticism of SWAPO which, coincidentally, is a full member of the Non Aligned Movement.

19th May – At an UNTAG press conference, when asked UNTAG's specific role regarding 'the atrocities' alleged to have been committed by the Security Forces, Mr Thornberry said 'UNTAG military monitors and observers were responsible for monitoring the SADF And SWA Territory Force'.

23rd May – At an UNTAG press conference Mr Thornberry said in answer to a question that 'UNTAG was monitoring all SWAPOL's activities to the best of its ability. It was, of course, looking forward to the arrival of more police monitors, mine resistant vehicles and radios'.

24th May – At an UNTAG press briefing held by Cedric Thornberry, a correspondent pointed out that although Koevoet had been disbanded, but it was well known its members had been integrated into SWAPOL and its founder was now the SWAPOL commissioner for the northern region. Was that not a problem for UNTAG's perspective, and would it not undermine the confidence of returnees?

The answer, by a person not stated in UNTAG's press release, was that he was 'not certain that the organisation had been disbanded. Once the SWA Territory Force and other citizen forces had been demobilised and confined the base, attention would have to be given to this urgent and important question, which had also been dealt with by the Secretary General in his 23rd January report to the Security Council'.

30th May – At an UNTAG press briefing, Mr Fred Eckhard, said it had been agreed after discussions between the Administrator General and the Special Representative, that an 'enhanced investigative process' had been agreed on to handle complaints of harassment and intimidation.

Six SWA Police investigating teams had been sent from Windhoek to Oshakati, 'where UNTAG had so far reported to SWAPOL about 120 such complaints, most of them involving allegations of official misconduct on the part of one or other element of the Security Forces. (*The Star* reported this as 'most of them against the police force.'

Cedric Thornberry explained the decision had derived in part from the discussions within the joint working group (AG and Special Representative) on all aspects of impartiality. A consensus had emerged that the number and gravity of complaints from Oshakati and the need for an effective investigative procedure, demanded that SWAPOL strengthen its internal review mechanism.

A reporter questioned the wisdom of SWA Police investigating complaints against its own members and Thornberry pointed out every police force looked after its own housekeeping saying: 'In most democratic societies, the police had found ways to reassure the public that their internal review procedure were independent and objective'.

This appeared to imply the society was not democratic, and neither were the police review procedures objective.

31st May – The Namibian National Students Union – NANSU, a SWAPO front organisation, instituted a class boycott in northern Owambo. They were demanding all members of Koevoet be returned to bases and dismissed from the police force during the territory's transition to independence.

31st May – A news report in *The Star* said teachers had joined the boycott. Also that the National Union of Namibian Workers – another SWAPO front so say representing 60 000 workers, was threatening to join the strike if the students demands were not met.

2nd June – At an UNTAG press briefing a pressman recalled a visiting British

MP and human rights lawyer, had said UNTAG should insist that 'Koevoet should be completely withdrawn; that UNTAG police monitors accompany all police patrols; and that all Casspirs be confined to base'.

Mr Eckhard noted that Security Council resolution 632 called for Koevoet to be disbanded. The functioning of police monitors was a matter for Commissioner Fanning. As for Casspirs, their mine resistant capabilities were still 'essential' in the north. The settlement plan, however, called for the SWA Police to be lightly armed, so heavy armaments should be removed from those still in use.

Another reporter said Koevoet members had been seen 'roving' around the north at night, without monitoring. Mr Eckhard confirmed such reports had been received from UNTAG police monitors and said the matter would 'continue' to be raised with the Administrator General.

The term 'roving' obviously referred to patrolling, which is a routine and essential duty for any police force. Maintaining law and order was a duty given to the SWA Police in terms of the peace plan. It stretches one's imagination as to why the matter 'would continue to be raised with the Administrator General'.

Asked if the issue of reintegration of Koevoet members into SWAPOL was being raised with the police commissioner, he said Koevoet as such was supposed to have been disbanded in accordance with the peace plan. He declined to comment when asked if UNTAG was demanding that every single former Koevoet member be withdrawn from service.

He was asked how many complaints against Koevoet were being investigated by UNTAG. He said 'he recalled 120 complaints – not all of them involving Koevoet, however – had been reported to UNTAG monitors in the Oshakati region alone. They had been referred to SWAPOL for investigation, which would, of course, take place under UNTAG police monitor supervision'.

6th June – According Mr Gerhard Roux, spokesman for the Administrator General, there was an almost complete stayaway from schools in Owamboland. About 1 000 teachers were also on strike. All strikers demanded that former Koevoet members be discharged from the SWA Police. Many of the children 'on strike' were nine years of age and some were younger, which clearly indicated that SWAPO intimidation was involved.

9th June – The *New Nation* claimed that South Africa had formed an assassination squad to murder some 200 SWAPO and UNTAG personnel, who have been put on a secret death list.

13th June – Dr Nickey Iyambo, a senior SWAPO official, arrived back in Windhoek as a returnee. In a statement to the press he said former members of Koevoet should be withdrawn from the normal police force.

'The Koevoet are people trained to kill and that is what they are still continuing doing and they should stop that.'

Seeing he had just arrived back in Namibia after many years of absence, he could hardly have been the most knowledgeable person around.

14th June – At an UNTAG press briefing a reporter asked whether UNTAG had access to all police bases in the north as there had been reports of UNTAG monitors being refused access to SWA Police premises. In the words of the press release 'Mr Eckhard replied that UNTAG must have free access to SWAPOL premises in order to properly carry out its monitoring function, and the matter was being discussed'.

This was clearly an allegation that UNTAG monitors were being refused entrance to police stations, which was untrue.

17th June – It was revealed in New York that Mr Ahtisaari had sent a strongly worded letter a week before to Mr Louis Pienaar. He complained that police units equipped with heavy weapons and armoured vehicles were intimidating people in the north of the territory and had been involved 'in a number of incidents'.

He said the SWA Police 'appear to have created an atmosphere of fear and intimidation . . . the activities in which they have been engaged render its members, in my opinion, unfit for continued service in the police during the transition period, in view of the need to ensure the necessary conditions for free and fair elections'.

He was asked to rectify the situation.

22nd June – The Administrator General issued a statement denying press reports that he had refused to replace ex-Koevoet members serving with SWA Police in the northern regions.

'In my letter of 21st June to Mr Ahtisaari, I said I was prepared to consider the progressive removal of former members of the counterinsurgency unit from Owambo as the threat posed by PLAN recedes.

'Clearly this must be undertaken with the minimum of disruption of normal police duties and with due regard to the security situation in the north.

'. . . I have together with the SWA Police a responsibility to ensure that we do not undermine our ability to maintain law and order in all areas of this country. This is a responsibility which the settlement plan has imposed on me and I must bear this requirement in mind in my efforts to resolve this problem.

'. . . It will be understood, however, that I cannot consider a blanket removal of former counterinsurgency members on the basis simply of general and unsubstantiated complaints or accusations.'

27th June – At a meeting of the UN Security Council, Secretary General Dr de Cuellar described the continued deployment of Koevoet as a 'grave' problem. He said Mr Louis Pienaar's proposal for a phased withdrawal did not go far enough.

28th June – The Catholic Church's Justice and Peace Commission said it believed all Koevoet bush fighters should be withdrawn from the regular police force, as a step in restoring the 'credibility of the force' in the eyes of the public'.

28th June – The Administrator General released the following statement: 'According to press reports, the Secretary General, Mr Perez de Cuellar has again referred to the continuing presence in the SWA Police force of former members of the counterinsurgency unit. This unit was reactivated by necessity after the SWAPO incursions of 1st April. They have since been disbanded and reintegrated in the conventional police force.

'The situation in the northern regions is complicated. Conditions remain abnormal and I have a duty to ensure that the police force remains capable of dealing with any eventuality which may arise.

'. . . There is no easy solution. I cannot, for instance, contemplate a blanket withdrawal of all former members of the counterinsurgency unit while replacements are not immediately available.'

29th June – *The Star* reported that Mr Sam Nujoma, speaking in London, said South Africa was in breach of resolution 435 by allowing Koevoet 'to terrorise the population . . . They are killing people and the South African government must accept UN resolution 435 . . . That means dismantling Koevoet and the SWA Territorial Force.

Nujoma said he had raised the issue with British Foreign Secretary, Sir Geoffrey Howe and a spokesman afterwards said the British were concerned about Koevoet and they had repeatedly raised the issue with South Africa.

4th July – Mr Martti Ahtisaari said after a three day visit to Owambo, that the population there continued to feel insecure and was 'frequently intimidated' by elements of the SWA Police.

Mr Martti Ahtisaari, was told by (SWAPO fronting) organised labour, that unless Koevoet members were immediately removed from the police, a mass strike by workers and students 'would start tomorrow'.

6th July – Administrator General Louis Pienaar launched an action through the Supreme Court in Windhoek seeking an urgent order that the strike by Owambo pupils and teachers, and which had recently been extended to civil servants, was illegal.

The application was expected to be heard in chambers.

The strike was over demands that members of Koevoet be removed from the police force.

11th July – US Assistant Secretary for State, Herman Cohen, said in Windhoek that: 'We took very seriously the complaint of the UN Secretary General about the excessive use of force in northern Namibia and the abuses by the police forces'.

He revealed the United States had made diplomatic efforts to ensure the situation of excessive force and abuses by police was eliminated.

'I believe the profile of the police is being lowered and the number of "intimidating" vehicles and weapons is being diminished.'

13th July – A spokesman for UNTAG announced that Secretary General de Cuellar would be paying a visit to Namibia for the period 18th-21st July.

18th July – Secretary General de Cuellar spoke on his arrival in Windhoek of the necessity for free and fair elections 'in which all people of Namibia will determine their future in an atmosphere untainted by fear or intimidation.'

19th July – SWAPO officials in Windhoek suggested to the press that convoys of military material were being sent to the far northern border for use by Koevoet. They said they intended crossing into Angola and then returning to Namibia 'disguised as SWAPO', so South Africa could get an excuse 'to let loose its soldiers'.

21st July – Dr Javier Perez de Cuellar speaking in Oshakati said the issue of Koevoet 'against which many allegations of intimidation had been made' was 'a matter of concern.'

The road between Oshakati and Ondangwa was lined by ululating and dancing SWAPO supporters, waving placards welcoming the UN and demanding the removal of Koevoet members from the SWA Police.

Dr de Cuellar lunched with prominent members of the SWAPO supporting Council of Churches for Namibia – CCN. One can have little doubt what the main subject of conversation centred around.

21st July – The *New Nation* announced that both the Organisation of African Unity – OAU, and the Non Aligned Movement – NAM, have 'called for the expulsion of members of the "dreaded" Koevoet unit that have been "infiltrated" into the SWA Police'.

They said that 'in terms of resolution 435 the responsibility of ascertaining the suitability of personnel for service in SWAPOL was the responsibility of the Secretary General and the UN Special Representative'.

'We therefore demand and insist that the Special Representative should ask the Administrator General that Koevoet be disbanded immediately.

'General Hans Dreyer, the founder and leader of Koevoet, should be removed from his present post as commander of police in northern Namibia.'

They asked why UNTAG had decided to use the 'dreaded' Casspirs and said: 'The Use of Casspirs by UNTAG or SWAPOL must be banned.'

'The recent ... campaign by elements of SWA Police and the Koevoet Paramilitary Forces in northern Namibia has underscored the urgent need to further increase the police and military components of UNTAG.'

They also said enough UNTAG police had to be found to accompany and monitor each SWAPOL patrol.

22nd July – *The Citizen* under the banner headline 'UN CHIEF- GET RID OF KOEVOET MEN', reported that Dr Javier Perez de Cuellar told a news conference before leaving for Pretoria that he had asked South Africa to consider 'dismissing' more than 2 000 members of the SWA Police who had served in Koevoet.

He said the main threat to 'free and fair elections' concerned charges of intimidation against former members of Koevoet. He said they had created an atmosphere of mistrust' in northern Namibia.

He told the news conference that Mr Louis Pienaar had rejected his request to dismiss all Koevoet members from the police force. He said he would move them from the northern regions into less tense regions, but would dismiss policemen only if misconduct was proved against them individually.

'I am sorry to say I am not totally satisfied with Mr Pienaar's decision,' the Secretary General said. 'Elimination [of Koevoet] would create a better situation.'

Foreign Minister Pik Botha told reporters after meeting the Secretary General that the dispute over Koevoet ' was not an insurmountable problem'.

24th July – *The Citizen* reported that Zimbabwe's President, Robert Mugabe, together with twenty other heads of state had arrived to attend the OAU summit in Addis Ababa.

A resolution adopted by the OAU Council of Ministers strongly criticised the UN decision to release South African Forces against SWAPO 'on the eve' of the implementation of resolution 435. It attacked South Africa's 'massacring' of members of SWAPO and their present failure to completely demobilise the notorious' Koevoet.

25th July – Secretary General Dr Javier Perez de Cuellar, who had stopped off on the way at Lusaka to meet with President Kaunda and Sam Nujoma, addressed the OAU summit in Addis Ababa. He said members of Koevoet, which had earned an 'evil reputation' in northern Namibia, had been reabsorbed into the SWA Police.

'They are not suitable for continued employment in the police force under the terms of the UN plan,' he declared.

27th July – Mrs Glenys Kinnock, wife of Britain's leader of the opposition, Neil Kinnock, had a fright when a bomb was exploded at a police base nearby the Eenhana Voter's registration centre she was visiting.

She later said she had been told by 'elderly residents' that intimidation of villagers by Koevoet was continuing.

28th July – The Etale police base in Owamboland was subjected to a stand off bombardment during the night by SWAPO elements using a Soviet supplied 60mm mortar.

A Russian ATM landmine was found in the vicinity the next morning after police, press and UNTAG vehicles had passed over it. It was fortunately not detonated. The culprits made good their escape.

30th July – Mrs Glenys Kinnock called for an end to the use of police Casspirs on the roads because of their 'intimidatory effect'. It was noticeable that she baulked at calling for the discharge of all former Koevoet members from the police force. Instead she more responsibly said 'the Koevoet command structure should be disbanded'.

1st August – *The Star* reported that Police Commissioner, Lieutenant General Dolf Gouws of the SWA Police, ruled out disbanding Koevoet at a briefing for military correspondents in Pretoria, saying it was the only thing preventing anarchy from overrunning the orderly peace process in the territory.

He said that if 'Koevoet were removed, the way would be open to 'lawless government.'

General Gouws said police were being used as a 'target' because there was no legal way of getting rid of them.

He stressed there was no legal way Koevoet members could be dismissed.

The use of Casspirs 'which featured in most intimidation claims against the SWA Police' had been scaled down in certain areas, but not on the border.

Since the scaling down, four landmines boosted with dynamite, had been found on roads near Oshakati, Ongidiva and Ruacana. 'The aim of the allegations,' he said, 'has been to get us off the Casspirs. This has placed us in a difficult position because we cannot ride soft skinned vehicles under these conditions.'

Advocate Louis Pienaar said at the same briefing he was not 'prepared to have the police force's numbers reduced.

4th August – Addressing a seminar organised by the Institute for Strategic Studies in Pretoria, Mr Ahtisaari said that Secretary General Perez de Cuellar had stated during his recent visit to Namibia there was no place for the continuation of counterinsurgency operations under 435. He said it was essential the police fulfilled the normal law and order functions only, 'under UNTAG monitoring'.

9th August – Mr Vezera, Director of the Windhoek based pro SWAPO Churches Information and Monitoring Service – CIMS, told a press conference that one of the biggest threats to the Namibian independence process lay in the continued use of Koevoet. He expressed the hope that the 'situation created behind Koevoet' would not make a 'bumpy peace an explosive one'. He suggested the security threat was there 'partly by [not a SWAPO] design' and could play a 'make or break role'.

He accused Pretoria, despite denials, of still maintaining Koevoet bases in the north of Namibia

He said 'more than "400" complaints surrounding the activities of Koevoet had been filed'.

10th August – Mr Ahtisaari, speaking at Stellenbosch, said problems still needing to be addressed in Namibia included the 'policing situation in the north . . .'. He said there was an increasing victimisation of political parties. 'Harassment is taking forms that are really unacceptable'.

Later, in response to questions, he said former members of Koevoet had been going through kraals trying to identify SWAPO's PLAN fighters.

10th August – A delegation of the Council of Churches in the Netherlands, said in Windhoek, that former members of Koevoet should be withdrawn from the SWA Police.

Professor Bob Goudzward urged the Administrator General 'to find ways of "reeducating them" in order to assist their "reintegration into society"'.

What a staggering piece of patronisation.

16th August – Chief Inspector Kierie du Rand, PRO of the SWA Police, announced that police had made safe another SWAPO laid Russian TM57 landmine, which had been buried on a secondary dirt road in Ovambo.

16th August – Administrator General, Mr Louis Pienaar, gave way to world pressure brought about by SWAPO's propaganda war and announced that former members of Koevoet would be removed from northern Namibia and confined to bases elsewhere.

He said he had previously promised he would review the situation, and the reduction of SWA Police forces in northern Namibia, if the potential threat posed by PLAN had receded.

Mr Ahtisaari had told him the majority of PLAN elements had returned to Namibia as civilians and that PLAN's command structure had been dismantled in the sense that a number of PLAN commanders had returned to the country as civilians and that PLAN's weapons were stored and greased and were under lock and key in Angola.

He said Dr de Cuellar had 'reaffirmed the assurances given to me by Mr Ahtisaari'.

'He added that in his and Mr Ahtisaari's view PLAN no longer had the capability of posing a threat,' Mr Pienaar said.

He said he had accepted these assurances.

'Acting on these assurances and in accordance with earlier undertakings given by me, I am prepared to remove from duty in the northern regions a total of 1 200 members of the SWA Police force.

'This number represents the remnant of the counterinsurgency component.'

He said they would be confined to bases 'where they will undergo reorientation and retraining to equip them for roles which are to be redefined in the light of the changed circumstances.

'This decision, which affects a substantial percentage of police deployed in the north, will enable me to restructure the command system in that area in the coming weeks.' He conceded the development would reduce SWAPOL's capability to respond to an untowards eventuality, but the decision had been taken on the basis of the solemn assurances given to him by the Secretary General and the Special Representative.

He added that UNTAG was welcome to monitor their confinement to bases.

Koevoet – The Truth

In the first place Koevoet was a misnomer, it didn't exist, because its successor the SWA Police Counter-Insurgency Unit, SWAPOL COIN, had been disbanded in December 1988, before the commencement of the peace process.

Its personnel were duty branch policemen serving with the unit.

Instead of with that unit they could have been serving with the CID, the Dog Section, Riot Squad, the Crime Prevention Unit and so on. In fact, after a spell with SWAPOL COIN they would likely be posted to any of the other police sections available within the broad spectrum of the police force.

True a lot of the white constables, some sergeants and a few warrant officers were on attachment from the South African Police, but this is because the SWA Police is a relatively small police force, and due to the war, an inordinate number of personnel were engaged in paramilitary border control duties.

This, in normal circumstances, would have resulted in an unduly high proportion of their men spending time on border duty away from normal police work, with the

Force as a whole suffering because of an unavoidable lowering of general police standards.

Fortunately for the SWA Police, because Namibia was South African administered, they had a big brother – the South African Police – SAP, with its personnel pool of plus 60 000 men and it created no problem for them to allow their men to volunteer and spend periods on attachment in Namibia. In fact, it added to the experience of their own Force.

The majority of black policemen serving in the unit had little general duty branch experience it is true, but this was because their situation was different to the white policemen, as drawing black volunteers from the SAP personnel pool wasn't practical because of language and tribal barriers. A Zulu would be lost in Owamboland.

But why, the uninitiated might ask, should policemen from anywhere do a paramilitary job anyway?

The answer is that it has always been traditional in Africa, and certainly in those territories which once forming part of the old British Empire, as was the case with South Africa.

The SAP had been formed from an amalgam of famous old para military police forces. In the Western Desert campaigns of World War-2, the SAP supplied the men for an elite fighting division.

Even UNTAG Commissioner Fanning of Ireland, had came from a para military police force.

What was the evidence against Koevoet, to keep to the nomenclature of the propagandists, anyway?

If one is to believe the adjectives used in describing them, even since the 9th April, then they had to be pretty bad on a 'where there's smoke there's fire' basis – probably worse than the Waffen SS of World War-2 infamy.

Men who could be variously described in the earlier pages of this chapter, as killers of South Africa, the dreaded Koevoet, violent dismaying intimidators (according to UNTAG, individuals, church organisations and other progressive groups), who shot civilians, tore down villages, compiled hit lists, who wiped out innocent SWAPOs about to hand themselves over to UNTAG, who executed prisoners, who disposed of their comrade's bodies by callously tossing them into mass graves, who engaged in activities defying the imagination, who created an atmosphere of mistrust, who terrorised the population, who used excessive force and who were in need of reeducation to assist their reintegration into society.

Men who someone as elevated as the Secretary General of the United Nations Security Council, could describe as a grave problem, a matter of grave concern, men with an evil reputation and who should be dismissed from the police force out of hand.

It just goes to show how effective SWAPO's propaganda campaign was. SWAPO, in the interests of UN impartiality, should be regarded as just another political party, but there seems no hope of that.

The Non Aligned Movement (which has SWAPO as a full member) should be dealt with at arms length, because its Africa Group is completely aligned to SWAPO's cause. So far as Dr Javier Perez de Cuellar is concerned, it seems clear he is a man with the strength of character needed to drift along with the current.

If the Non Aligned Nations could muster sufficient nations to vote with them, it is possible he could be voted out of a job – as nearly happened in the first week of April – except the five permanent members of the Security Council beat them to it by passing a vote of confidence in De Cuellar.

That didn't mean, of course, that he hadn't had a lucky escape, or that he would get away with it next time. So since then he has obediently toed the line and gone along with the Non Aligned Movement.

So what about those obviously terrible cases of intimidation the SWA Police has been involved in?

Well, most don't exist. They were products of SWAPO's lively imagination and accepted as fact by the Special Representative, Martti Ahtisaari, the Secretary General and others down the line.

None of those terrible cases, which spokesmen at UNTAG press conferences had experienced difficulty in finding words to describe – so they never did – had been reported to the police.

Now surely if those awful allegations against the police were that bad, and the complainants had the reassurance of knowing the UNTAG police were there to look over the shoulders at the SWA Police while they made their report, then reasonable people would have reported them.

If they didn't, one must assume they didn't happen.

Many accusations about which UNTAG made a lot of noise, just faded away once the publicity had died down.

Like the insinuations that the police had executed prisoners after capture, the evidence being certain bodies displayed to the press at Oshakati.

It was said they had been shot in the backs of their heads at close range with small calibre weapons. International experts even examined photographs with microscopes, pronouncing it was true.

The correspondent from London's *Sunday Telegraph* who started it all, was surprised the bodies hadn't been cut to pieces. He had heard the police were equipped with 50 calibre Brownings and 20mm cannons which create those wicked sort of injuries.

Obviously what he didn't know was that men can also be killed by R-5 bullets, although most are killed by shrapnel – and a tiny piece can be fatal.

As a result bodies were exhumed at the request of UNTAG and post mortems were carried out. The pathologists found no evidence to suggest that insurgents had died from any other way except in battle.

This, of course, was a non story, so it never found its way into the London *Sunday Telegraph*, or got a mention on the radical *South Africa Today* program in the United States.

Then the burial of the insurgents in mass graves became an atrocity story in itself. First there was the most disgracefully untrue story of them all from the SWAPO supporting, *The Namibian*, that because of apartheid, the white policemen just tossed the bodies of their black comrades killed in action into the mass graves with the dead SWAPO.

It obviously took a ghoul of incredible ingenuity to think that one up.

But it was obviously one of those inventive days, because it was in the same issue they said Koevoet had a hit list.

The bigger the lie again.

After this came the sob story of how could the police just throw their dead enemies into mass graves. Why didn't they compile a police docket on each one, get an undertaker to lay out the corpse, provide a coffin, get in mourners and conduct a proper burial.

The 'callousness' was supported by photographs of bodies being tossed into mass graves from the backs of lorries – enough to conjure up the Auschwitz syndrome for the world press.

Well, in short and to put it bluntly, it was war.

There were none of the niceties one would have expected in Croydon or Boston.

The battles happened in the raw and remote bush of Africa – in the bushveld of Owambo and in the mountains and deserts of Kaokoland.

Where they could, the police buried their dead foes where they fell, which has been the custom in war since time eternal.

The British still do it, which is why soldiers killed in the Falklands are buried in the ground they fought to conquer.

Surely there can be no disgrace in that?

Often, though, the police didn't have time, because of the exigencies of war, to properly sweep for bodies. So many have remained undiscovered to this day.

Those picture of insurgents being buried in mass graves, were pictures of them being reburied in mass graves, because they had already been exhumed for post mortems to be carried out at the request of UNTAG.

This explains the use of face masks – to cover up the stench of death.

Yet, in spite of this, the SWA Police, short of manpower as they have been, have still done their bit at UNTAG's insistence, by having investigation teams engage in the supreme waste of time of searching for so far undiscovered bodies – so they can prove beyond all reasonable doubt they were not 'murdered' by police during the first nine days of April.

This has kept another set of policemen out of SWAPO's hair, allowing them to continue their intimidation program undisturbed.

What intimidation cases against police have been reported?

Mostly they are the proverbial bags of beans.

Anything will do and SWAPO have had a heyday.

It is from this that 'intimidation cases' originated from police driving their Casspirs while on routine patrols past SWAPO supporter's kraals.

This is intimidation?

Yes, in the opinion of the UNTAG Police Commissioner Stephen Fanning of Ireland.

It reminds one of the time just prior to Malawi's independence, when the British government ordered a Royal Commission to look into who had stood on a particular black lady's foot.

Each intimidation complaint has had to be investigated by the SWA Police, with UNTAG police looking over their shoulders to see they do their jobs properly.

It is from this that UNTAG and the Secretary General came to talk of threatening vehicles.

UNTAG have conceded publicly that Casspirs are needed, they have even hired some themselves, because SWAPO are still planting landmines and the Casspir is the finest mine protected vehicle in the world.

But the question remains.

How can there be such a thing as a threatening vehicle?

And this encouraged to be regarded as a crime by a man who described himself in his CV as formerly being the most senior policeman in Ireland – the country whose nationals were responsible for the *Oxford English Dictionary* adding the word 'kneecapping' to its lists.

Now kneecapping is intimidation, real intimidation.

So is threatening someone with death, if they don't vote for SWAPO.

But a policeman on duty driving past a SWAPO kraal in a 'threatening vehicle'!

It makes one wonder what sort of police work Commissioner Fanning was doing in his climb to the rank of major general?

Certainly his men couldn't have done much patrolling in vehicles, unless, of course, having a 'threatening vehicle' isn't a criminal offence in Ireland.

It seems strange that a senior police officer could have a completely rationale approach to police work in his own country, but once with UNTAG, he behaves like he is Alice and Namibia is Wonderland?

The statistics of 'intimidation' complaints against police in what has become a Mad Hatter's tea party, can hardly be said to justify the international furore. They are:

Found 'False':	29
'Unfounded' – Prosecutor declines to prosecute:	12
'Undetected':	6
'Under Investigation':	25
With Attorney General for instructions:	2
'Pending trial':	1
With O'Linn Commission for investigation:	1
Total complaints April – August 1989:	76

Further, of the two 'positive' cases – the one pending trial and the other with the O'Linn Commission at the end of August, one cannot say if convictions will eventually result.

One concerns an incident where a policeman drew a gun on a SWAPO supporter. The policeman alleges it was in self defence, while the complainant says it wasn't.

The other case concerns an illegal meeting held by SWAPO which was broken up by DTA supporters. The police were called and they asked all parties to go to the police station so the matter could be sorted out. On the way a free for all developed and the police arrested twelve of the brawlers. Later, when the political affiliations of the fighters had been sorted out, it was discovered they were all SWAPO members.

No DTA members were arrested, so SWAPO complained of intimidation.

Would that have been intimidation in Ireland, or Britain or anywhere else?

Surely someone somewhere must have lost his sense of perspective.

The UNTAG police expressed dissatisfaction with the standard of police investigation in only one of those complaints against police, and that matter is still under investigation.

Obviously a SWA Policeman could be convicted of intimidation. That is why all complaints are investigated. Policemen everywhere face prosecution for illegal activities. None, however, have been convicted since the 1st April.

The UNTAG police have a duty laid down by resolution 435 'to accompany the police forces in the discharge of their duties'.

Resolution 435 lays down that 'the primary responsibility for maintaining law and order in Namibia during the transition period shall rest with the existing police forces', which is the SWA Police.

The intention of the resolution was clearly that UNTAG policemen should be attached to police stations and accompany the SWA Police in their day to day duties to see to fair play.

They have not done this.

Instead, even in remote areas, they have been ordered by Commissioner Fanning not to base themselves at police stations, ride in SWA Police vehicles, mix with SWA Police members, go into police canteens and so on.

Their 'non fraternisation' rule is reminiscent of the orders given to Allied troops when Germany was occupied at the end of World War-2.

Yet Namibia is not an occupied country and the SWA Police are not the enemy.

Both police forces have their duties.

South Africa is cooperating fully in this unique UN exercise to bring Namibia to independence.

UNTAG police have accompanied SWA Police personnel, always in separate vehicles, only during the investigation of intimidation cases. Until the middle of August they had not accompanied police on any other routine patrols or investigation.

With the campaign mounted by SWAPO to discredit them, it was obviously important to the SWA Police that they should.

One would also have thought it important to UNTAG.

Even SWAPO thought it was important and demanded it publicly on many occasions.

The Administrator General asked for it many times and said so publicly. So did the SWA Police, at first politely and at a low key. Then, when desperation at UNTAG police inactivity set in and all else had failed, SWA Police Commissioner, General Dolf Gouws, arranged to appear on SWA Television and asked UNTAG publicly, in front of a million witnesses.

Still nothing happened.

The excuse at first was that the UNTAG police didn't have mine protected vehicles. There were too many SWAPO landmines around for their men to risk their lives.

They wanted to lease some Casspirs – those 'threatening and intimidating' vehicles the UN were demanding the SWA Police stop using.

So they got Casspirs on lease.

The first ten were signed for on the 16th June by Dermot Hussey, UNTAG's chief procurement officer.

Paragraph 4 of the lease agreement between the Commissioner SWA Police and UNTAG reads: 'The Lessee hereby acknowledges that the vehicles have been delivered to him by the Lessor and that it is (sic) in good condition and proper working order'.

It is clear this was more than just a routine clause in an agreement.

The vehicles hired were valuable, with a stipulated value of R1 3 million. The rental for the duration of the agreement totalled R496 000.

They would hardly have been accepted, unless they really were in good condition and proper working order.

Yet, suddenly, as soon as the UNTAG police had taken delivery of them, they were invariably 'broken down' or 'out of order'.

The result – UNTAG still didn't accompany SWA Police on routine patrols and investigations.

Eventually, there was an unexpected response by UN Special Representative Martti Ahtisaari.

He recommended to the Secretary General that in terms of resolution 435, he had decided all policemen who had previously served in Koevoet were 'unfit for continued service in the police during the transition period'.

He demanded they be arbitrarily dismissed.

A drastic demand indeed, and one that could, by the stroke of a pen, end some 1 200 careers.

The careers of men who had done well for their country and who deserved better treatment than even the suggestion of dishonourable discharges.

Resolution 435 lays down '... Special Representative shall ensure the good conduct of the police forces and shall take the necessary action to ensure their suitability for continued employment during the transition period'.

So he was quite within his rights.

But what on earth did he base his decision on?

The Secretary General took up the demand.

The stridency of demands by the Non Aligned Movement increased to a crescendo.

Finally, the Administrator General bowed to pressure and confined men who had served in SWA Police COIN to bases away from the border area.

SWAPO had got its way – the Angolan-Namibian border in the north had been stripped of its defences.

Suddenly, the UNTAG police were available to accompany the SWA Police on routine patrols and investigations.

Not every patrol and investigation, mind you, about 20% at the most.

In certain instances, however, they refused point blank.

They wouldn't accompany border patrols, go out at night or accompany foot patrols.

So they still weren't adequately monitoring the SWA Police.

One is left wondering who gave the orders that UNTAG police monitors shouldn't accompany the SWA Police in the first place.

Could it have been Major General Fanning, the UNTAG Police Commissioner?

The author questioned Commissioner Fanning at the opening of the UNTAG Police post at Katutura Township in April, and recorded his replies.

Stiff: 'Commissioner, will your forces accompany patrols in the northern part, along the border?'

Fanning: 'They will indeed, that is one of their chief functions.'

Stiff: 'They will be going out in the bush with the patrols?'

Fanning: 'They will be going out on patrols when they deem it appropriate. When the Special Representative of the Secretary General deems it appropriate for our monitors to travel with SWA Police patrols, they will do so.'

Stiff: 'So that is not immediate?'

Fanning: 'It is immediate as from tomorrow morning – they will be travelling with patrols both here and in the north.'

When this conversation took place, contacts between the SWA Police and SWAPO insurgents were still a regular occurrence. The author, curious as to how the UNTAG police would protect themselves in the event of a contact asked:

Stiff: 'Mister Commissioner, one last question. Will your men be carrying firearms?'

Fanning: 'My men are unarmed, except on special occasions. The only time they will carry a firearm is when they are going on a patrol where their life may be in danger from wild animals or bandits. Where they may be out on patrol for days in the desert, and where a bandit armed with a normal bow and arrow could take the vehicle from them, and leave them buried in the desert.'

Stiff: 'What about a bandit with an RPG-7?'

Fanning: 'We have no right to allow . . . thank you. But they will only be armed for very special occasions, for certainly . . . protective purposes.'

UNTAG Police, as has already been shown, didn't 'immediately' and 'as from tomorrow' accompany SWA Police patrols.

Perhaps it was because they discovered the main danger out in the bush didn't lie with bandits armed with bows and arrows.

The most likely explanation, however, is that Special Representative Martti Ahtisaari gave the order, perhaps on the instructions of Secretary General Javier Perez de Cuellar himself.

There could be only one reason.

UNTAG, even then in April, was plotting and planning to set up the situation where they could neutralise the main strength of the SWA Police on the northern border.

If they had allowed SWA Police activities to be monitored, they would have had no option but to admit they were far from being unsuitable for police duties, and that the very reverse was the case.

Without the reports of monitors to call them liers, they could do what they liked.

Well, there certainly has been intimidation – but it looks like the SWA Police is the main victim.

18

Swapo's Intimidation Campaign

Roland Gaucher in his book, *The Terrorists*, explained succinctly that the goal of terrorism is not to kill or to destroy property, but to break the spirit of the opposition. It is a politically inspired act to subject the people to a power that is challenging the established one.

SWAPO's terror campaign, commenced nearly three decades ago, had not succeeded in mobilising the masses of Namibia behind it. In spite of the death of more than 2 000 innocent civilians at the hands of SWAPO during the bush war years, the spirit of the population had not been broken. Instead, as the years passed by, the will of resistance against the organisation had grown, manifesting itself in things like the formation and quick expansion of the SWA Territory Force, the SWA Police and the founding and growth of many democratic political parties in opposition to SWAPO.

Contrary to SWAPO's claims in public that they will attain up to 90% of the vote in the November elections, it became clear the SWAPO leadership was really worried about the election outcome.

While SWAPO's April invasion as a military operation might have failed, it didn't signal an end to their ongoing campaign of political intimidation, with its objective of cowing the population so the people would vote them into power. Their theme has been clear – if they lose the election they will return to the bush and the war with all its consequent suffering for the people of Namibia will continue.

This campaign has been supplemented by a major propaganda effort, using OAU, Canadian and Scandinavian money, to create an acceptable 'democratic' face of SWAPO. Their major targets have been the media and white owned big business, using the tactic of soothing noises and tut-tutting at the very suggestion of there being nationalisation, a lack of democracy and Marxist oppression 'when' SWAPO comes to power.

The marketing of this image is not seminared by the hard face of the bush fighting revolutionary, and certainly not by Nujoma who invariably puts his foot in it and says the wrong thing anyway, but by smooth talking, well educated black men who exude sound common sense and pragmatism. As one can expect the media, in the main, have played into SWAPO's hand by representing the SWAPO point of view as the truth to millions of readers, viewers and listeners around the world.

Newspapers like *The Times* of London, to their everlasting shame, did much the same thing for Adolf Hitler before World War-2.

The prophet urge in newspapermen is strong, which perhaps explains why they throw all their bags on what seems to be the fastest train, even if all evidence indicates it as the quickest transportation to a country's hell.

To fully illustrate SWAPO's recent intimidation story, would take a complete book in itself, but the random samples quoted here paint a horrifying picture.

31st March – Ten black Namibian inhabitants of Kavango, including a policeman and soldiers, applied to the Supreme Court of Namibia for relief against intimidation by SWAPO and NANSO and their members:

In a sworn affidavit, Petrus Muti, said that during October 1988 he and a friend attended a SWAPO meeting at Rundu. They were told that soldiers are puppets and were ordered to leave the meeting.

His brother Festus Sipopa, a member of SWAPO and NANSO threatened that he would be thrown into the river when he leaves the army.

'He will force my head under the water and my body will only be recovered after six days.'

In his affidavit he asked the court to protect him for he feared that after 1st April, when the army disbanded, members of SWAPO and/or NANSO would cause him serious harm or even kill him.

In another sworn affidavit, Markus Kwandu Lenguria, said he had been threatened with death by members of SWAPO and NANSO on several occasions.

He said a shopowner, Bastius Vitumbo, had refused to serve him because he was a soldier. He also showed him a firearm which he would use to kill him.

A soldier from 202 Battalion said in his affidavit that his house had been burnt down by SWAPO members and he had been assaulted by a scholar and teachers from the Rupana High Primary School.

Costa Makasa said in his affidavit that he had been threatened by members of NANSO, who had said all members of the army would be killed after 1st April.

In another affidavit placed before the Supreme Court, Manfred Haikera stated that on several occasions he had been threatened and intimidated by members of SWAPO.

He said a certain Willem Mudiki had threatened 'he will make me his slave and even when he goes for a shit I will have to clean him'. He also said that 'all soldiers are Botha's dogs and were bought by money. After 1st April, we won't receive any more money and SWAPO will see to it that we are killed.'

On 7th March, Paulus Mangundu, threatened him that all soldiers of the Territory Force would be castrated and turned into 'oxen'. 'The "tools" of the fat ones will be removed so that they can be yoked to work. Those who are too thin, will be roped round the neck and left in the bush to die'.

In other affidavits before the Supreme Court, Rudolf Matheus and Simon Sinyundu said they had been assaulted and threatened by SWAPO members.

Pius Sikango and Lyamu Peruka Paulus Semete said that on several occasions they had been threatened by SWAPO members. As a consequence they feared for the lives of themselves and their families.

Judge Mouton, acting president of the Supreme Court of South West Africa/ Namibia, issued a *rule nisi* in favour of the ten applicants and SWAPO, NANSO and 26 members of the two organisations. He ordered that the *rule nisi* serve as an interim interdict by which the respondents were:

(i) Prohibited from intimidating, or threatening to assault or trying to kill the applicants and/or their families;

(ii) Prohibited from contacting the applicants and/or their families by any means;

(iii) Prohibited from entering, damaging or destroying the residences of the applicants and/or their families;

(iv) Prohibited from damaging, removing or destroying the movable property of the applicants and/or their families;

(v) Prohibited from interfering with the freedom of movement, freedom of speech and freedom to hold or attend meetings, of the applicants and/or their families; and

(vi) Prohibited from proclaiming that the applicants, because they are soldiers, are bad and must be assaulted or killed.

16th April – Jefta Eiseb laid a charge of intimidation against SWAPO member Junius Andreas at Police Okahanja. Andreas, who had torn off his shirt and cut it into pieces, was convicted and sentenced.

23rd April – A 13 year old schoolboy of the Nausanabis Primary School near Leonardville, absconded from the school hostel after being threatened by hostel personnel for not taking part in SWAPO activities. He said they were forced to practice SWAPO songs in the afternoons and had once been taken into town with others to shout 'power' and give SWAPO clenched fists. Children wearing DTA t-shirts were beaten or given less food.

27th April – Likeus Hailkela reported to Police Oshakati that SWAPO members in a vehicle abused, threatened and swore at him.

27th April – Jeremia Ekoly complained to police that SWAPO members had sworn at, abused and threatened him.

27th April – Leopard Bhuuya complained at Police Ondangwa that he had been sworn at and threatened by SWAPO members.

27th April – Ms Fernardus Burger complained to Police Karasburg that a SWAPO member had told her he possessed a firearm and he would shoot her and all other whites.

27th April – Four residents of Ovamboland made an urgent application to the Supreme Court of South West Africa/Namibia for relief against SWAPO and four of its members.

In an affidavit Djolonimo Kandowa said he was a member of 101 Battalion and that Joseph Gosea had threatened him on several occasions, saying he would kill him with a panga after the implementation of resolution 435.

He stated that members of the local population had also told him they were being intimidated and threatened with death by SWAPO if they didn't support the organisation.

Daniel Simon, also a member of 101 Battalion, said in his affidavit that he feared for his own safety and that of his wife and two children.

He stated that SWAPO member Sila Kambonde had threatened him that SWAPO would use him as an ox in front of a plough when they came to power.

Also, that SWAPO member Stefanus Silvanus had threatened that he would have problems if he didn't join SWAPO.

In another affidavit before the Supreme Court, Moses Akanambo, told how the same threats had been made to him as well by Kambonde and Silvanus. David Haileka, another member of 101 Battalion and once a member of the Security

Branch of the SWA Police, said he dared not visit his parents home and hadn't done so since 1981, because SWAPO supporters in that region had ordered he be 'captured' and punished.

In 1984 armed SWAPO terrorists attacked his father's residence. They said they had been looking for him. He also said Immanuel had assaulted him, saying that SWAPO was going to take over the government of the country. When they did, all members of 101 Battalion would be killed.

In his affidavit, he also testified overhearing Josef Matheus addressing a group of scholars, saying that after the implementation of resolution 435, the members of 101 Battalion would become SWAPO's slaves.

He said that members of the local population had told him on several occasions that SWAPO fighters had concealed their weapons and uniforms and were hiding out in plain clothes amongst the tribespeople.

Edward Natonwe said in his sworn affidavit that he had been told by Rebecca and David, both SWAPO supporters, that all soldiers and policemen will be killed by SWAPO.

A *rule nisi* was duly issued against SWAPO and four of its members in favour of the applicants.

The Supreme Court ordered that the *rule nisi* would serve as a interim interdict by which SWAPO members, Josef Gosea, Josef Matheus, Silas Kambonde, Stefanus Silvanus and S Bondo were:

(i) Prohibited from intimidating, threatening, assaulting and/or killing the applicants and/or their families;
(ii) Prohibited from contacting the applicants and/or their families by any means;
(iii) Prohibited from entering, damaging or destroying the residences of the applicants and/or their families;
(iv) Prohibited from damaging, removing or destroying the moveable property of the applicants and/or their families;
(v) Prohibited from interfering with the freedom of movement, freedom of speech and freedom to hold or attend meetings of the applicants and/or their families;
(vi) Prohibited from proclaiming at meetings or by any other means, that the applicants, because they are soldiers, are bad and must be assaulted or killed.

The Supreme Court ordered SWAPO, as an organisation, to take all reasonable measures to ensure that its members didn't commit any of the above mentioned deeds.

And to take all reasonable steps to ensure the contents of the court order was communicated to all its members.

28th April – An urgent application was made to the Supreme Court in Windhoek by four adult males from the Kavango, acting on behalf of five minor school children, Kasinga Sesita, Kapika Sesita, Injala Sesita, Bernard Kasanga and Paula Luciano from the Sauyemwa High Primary School and Andreas Lipayi, a former scholar from the Ndonga High Primary School.

Mr Johannes Makondo, acting on behalf of his three brothers, Kasinga Sesita, Kapika Sesita and Injala Sesita, swore in an affidavit that his brothers had been expelled from school because of their refusal to become members of NANSO.

His statement was confirmed by affidavits from the scholars themselves.

Kasinga Sesita, ten years of age and a standard 1 pupil at the Sauyemwa High

Primary School, told how the headmaster had said that if they refused to become members of NANSO, they would have to leave the school.

He said his class teacher, Mr B Kansowa, told them to pay a R1 membership fee, after which they would get NANSO membership cards.

In his affidavit he told how another teacher, Mr Josef Siningwe, had ordered all DTA members to leave the school.

Kapika Sesita, 12 year old standard 3 pupil, stated that his class teacher, Mr Hausiku told him to leave school, because he wasn't a member of NANSO.

He stated that 25 pupils, in addition to himself and his two brothers, had been expelled because of their refusal to become members of NANSO. Intja Sesita, a 13 years old Standard 3 pupil at the Sauyemwa High Primary School, said in an affidavit that his class teacher, Mr J Shiningwe, had said he would only educate NANSO members.

He told the pupils he was going to work at the hospital, where he would kill DTA members going there for treatment.

He also lectured them on SWAPO doctrine and taught them how to sing SWAPO songs.

Josef Fenando, acting on behalf of his 15 year old sister, Paula Luciano, and his 13 year old brother, Bernard Kasanga, stated in an affidavit that both children had been expelled from school because of their refusal to become NANSO members.

Bernard Kasanga said in an affidavit put before the court, that teacher Moses had ordered all pupils who were not SWAPO or NANSO members to leave the Sauyemwa High Primary School.

Paula Luciano, a standard 4 pupil from the same school, testified that the teachers, including the headmaster, wore clothes which were either in SWAPO's colours, or displayed SWAPO's insignia.

She said she was expelled from school because of her refusal to sing SWAPO songs and become a member of NANSO.

Andreas Lipayi, a former scholar at the Ndonga High Primary School, said in an affidavit he had left the school because he could not endure the circumstances there and had since taken employment as a shop assistant.

He stated that two of his teachers, Manfred Haipopo and Bernhard Sikango, were both SWAPO members. He said they used to force pupils to sing SWAPO 'freedom' songs, and greeted each other with SWAPO salutes.

Mr Marbod Mupangwa Thikundeko, a teacher at the Lower Primary School Duyogha, said in an affidavit that the headmaster and hostel father of the Divandu High Primary School, Mr Karl Mukupi and Mr Johannes Thimbangu respectively, had threatened him because of his refusal to become a member of NANSO.

Mr Justice Levy granted a *rule nisi* in favour of the applicants against SWAPO, NANSO and the eight teachers, ordering that the *rule nisi* serve as a interim interdict which:

  (i) Prohibited the respondents from intimidating, threatening or assaulting the above mentioned children as well as applicant, Mr Mandod Mupangwa Thikundeko, for the purpose of persuading them to become members of SWAPO or NANSO;

  (ii) Prohibited the eight teachers from the Sauyemwa High Primary School, the Ndonga High Primary School and the Divandu High Primary School from forcing, allowing or persuading pupils to sing SWAPO songs;

  (iii) Prohibited them from expounding and propagating SWAPO's or its affiliated

organisations such as NANSO's, doctrines, principles, aims and achievements;

(iv) Prohibited the respondents from intimidating, threatening, assaulting or
attempting to kill the applicants or their families;

(v) Prohibited the teachers, other than in a school context, from contacting the
applicants or their families, or setting foot on the premises of the applicants
and their families;

(vi) Prohibited them from interfering with the freedom of movement, freedom
of speech, freedom to belong to the political party of their choice and the
freedom to hold or attend meetings, of both the applicants or their families.

The teachers were also ordered to allow all the expelled scholars back in their
schools and to allow them to continue their school education without hindrance.

1st-5th May – SWAPO supporting school children were involved in several
intimidation incidents in the Hoha region of Kavango. Their actions were instigated
by their headmaster who told them to harass DTA members and demobilised
former soldiers of 202 Battalion. They sung SWAPO 'freedom songs' near their
houses at night, challenging them to come out and fight SWAPO. They shouted
slogans like: 'Down with the army'; 'Down with DTA' and 'Down with Botha'.

4th May – A SWAPO supporting teacher, lectured his pupils saying SWAPO was
good and the DTA was bad.

4th May – During a SWAPO meeting at Musu in the Kavango, the speaker said
all black people working for Koevoet, or who had been soldiers, or who had
worked for white people, would suffer.

5th May – The headmaster of a school in the Sambyo tribal area, a prominent
SWAPO member, reprimanded a man for not greeting his mother with a SWAPO
clenched fist salute. He told him he would beat him up and that in future he would
be regarded as his enemy.

5th May – In an urgent application to the Supreme Court of SWA/Namibia, Mr
Abner Erasmus Nuule, a senior headman of Ovamboland, alleged that his two
minor daughters, Selina Nuule (14) and Miriam Nuule (16), were missing and he
feared they had been convinced by SWAPO, NANSO and four SWAPO supporting
teachers to go and join SWAPO in Angola.

Mr Nuule stated in his affidavit that on the 17th April, on returning from
Windhoek, he was told his two daughters had run away from school. He couldn't
believe it, because his children weren't like that.

The next morning he went to the Oshakati Secondary School to investigate.

He couldn't get any satisfactory answers from the staff, so he reported the matter
to the police, who undertook to investigate.

Not satisfied he had done all he could, he decided to go and talk to the army,
thinking it possible they had seen his daughters, because they always had patrols
out in the area.

A Colonel Dreyer at Oshakati, suggested the girls might have been abducted,
and offered to assist in the search as well.

The suggestion upsets Mr Nuule a lot, because it was common knowledge that a
lot of school children had disappeared over the years never to be seen again.

He knew about the Parent's Committee, whose aims were to find children who
had been abducted to Angola by SWAPO, where they were trained as terrorists and

where, in some case, the girls were put into so called baby farms or breeding camps, to produce future recruits for SWAPO.

He realised he had to act quickly, because once his daughters had crossed the border, he wouldn't see them again.

He sent his son, Ijamba Erasmus Nuule, to search towards Ruacana, while he concentrated on the area around Oshakati.

He approached Senior Headman Kautuima to ask for his assistance as well.

Late that afternoon his son 'phoned from Ruacana, saying he had found the missing girls at the home of a Mr Kaharero.

Kaharero had locked them in a room and refused to release them.

His son asked for help to effect the release of the imprisoned girls.

He saw Colonel Dreyer who organised a military helicopter to fly Senior Headman Nuule and two of his councillors to Ruacana.

When they arrived it was to learn that police had already freed his daughters and other four schoolgirls found there with them.

His son was already on his way back to Oshakati, with all six children.

When questioned by their parents and Colonel Dreyer, all the girls insisted to they had gone to Ruacana of their own free will.

It was obvious to the adults, though, that they were frightened and not telling the truth.

Their Pastor, Mr Hikumaha, was asked to assist. He spoke to them privately, gaining their confidence. They fearfully explained how they had been exposed to almost continuous indoctrination of SWAPO doctrine, dogma and propaganda over a long period at Oshakati Secondary School.

At the school they had been ridiculed, disparaged and intimidated by being continually referred to as the children of a 'puppet'.

Pressure to force them to join NANSO had been relentless, especially from teachers Mr Nabut and Mr Iiloha.

The children had been too frightened to discuss things with their parents or report it to the authorities, particularly as they had been warned they would be 'dealt with' if they mentioned anything. Eventually, being completely intimidated by then and not knowing which way to turn, they had given way and agreed to become members of NANSO.

Afterwards, they were told they must prove their loyalty by joining SWAPO in Angola, where they would be trained as 'freedom fighters', for the purpose of freeing Namibia from the racist Pretoria regime.

After hearing this, Mr Nuule seriously considered removing his daughters from school, but the pastor convinced him it would be all right to send them back, promising he to visit them regularly.

On 3rd May Mr Nuule sent the Pastor to the school to collect his daughters and bring them home, because the following day was a public holiday.

When he got to the school, he was very disturbed to see Mr Nuule's daughters participating in a mass rally, celebrating SWAPO's Cassinga day.

He asked but the school authorities refused to allow him to take the girls with him.

The Pastor returned to Mr Nuule and told him what was going on.

Mr Nuule immediately realised they were being intimidated and brainwashed with SWAPO propaganda, probably making them likely to accept the idea of going to Angola to join SWAPO.

He asked Pastor Hikumaha to return to the school and fetch his daughters.

The Pastor returned empty handed, saying the girls were missing and no one knew where they were.

After considering the affidavits and listening to the advocate's plea, the Judge President of the Supreme Court of SWA/Namibia, Hans Berker, issued a court order whereby SWAPO, NANSO, the headmaster of Oshakati Secondary School, Mr Kasupi, two teachers at the school, Mr Nabut and Mr Selm Iilaka, as well as a Mr Kaharero from Ruacana, under whose control or possession the two children might have been, were ordered to immediately hand over the children to the police at either Ruacana or Oshakati.

The respondents were further ordered to immediately provide the police with any information regarding the whereabouts of the two children.

The Supreme Court granted the police force in Ovambo the right to search any place or premises where the children might be held.

The court also issued a *rule nisi* serving as an interim interdict whereby the respondents were:

(i) Prohibited by any means, from intimidating, threatening or trying to persuade the daughters of the applicant and/or any school children from the Oshakati Secondary School, to go to Angola;

(ii) Prohibited by any means, from trying to abduct the applicant's two daughters and/or any other scholars of the Oshakati Secondary School to Ruacana or any other place, for the purpose of taking them abroad and/or to be of any assistance to allow and/or to take part in any such abduction;

(iii) Prohibited by any means, from interfering with the freedom of movement, freedom of speech and freedom of association of the applicant's two daughters;

(iv) Prohibited from intimidating the two daughters of the applicant and/or any other scholar of the Oshakati Secondary School, giving them lectures on SWAPO doctrine and propaganda, forcing them to sing SWAPO songs and/or participate in political rallies and/or political meetings during school time or after hours;

(v) Prohibited from intimidating the applicant's two minor daughters or any other scholar of the Oshakati Secondary School, or by any other means attempting to convince them to become members of SWAPO or NANSO;

(vi) Prohibited by any means, from intimidating, threatening, assaulting or harming the applicant, his family as well as the deponents of the application;

(vii) Prohibited by any means, from breaking down, ridiculing, disparaging, or questioning the authority of the applicant as a senior headman in Ovambo.

9th May – Workers at Rossing Mine near Swakopmund were told by the Mineworkers Union of Namibia – MUN, that all workers must become members of the MUN and vote for SWAPO.

9th May – SWAPO members at Mupapama in Kavango, tore a youngster's DTA t-shirt from his body and hit him on the head with a bottle.

A demobilised soldier of 202 Battalion was also assaulted.

11th May – Two prominent SWAPO members, one a primary school headmaster, gathered together school children living in the school hostel and forced them to practise SWAPO songs from 20:00–22:30, in readiness for a SWAPO meeting on the 20th May.

Many children not wishing to take part, ran away and hid in the bush.

12th May – A SWAPO member refused to allow a Mr Mokoya to enter his cuca shop, because he wasn't a member of SWAPO.

12th May – A group of six SWAPO members from Windhoek, driving a blue Toyota 4x4, arrived at Okandi in Ovambo. They told the locals to vote for SWAPO in the coming election. If they didn't, they would be arrested and sentenced to death by a People's Court.

13th May – A DTA political meeting scheduled to take place at Okahau in Owambo, was stopped by SWAPO orchestrated school children throwing stones at and adopting aggressive attitudes towards the DTA members. They also shouted slogans like 'down with DTA.'

14th May – People attending a SWAPO public meeting at Siya, 40 kilometres west of Rundu, were told that armed PLAN fighters were reentering the region the next day. From then on, they said, PLAN fighters would be available at any mission station in the Kavango.

15th May – Another urgent application for relief was brought before the Supreme Court of SWA/Namibia.

In an affidavit, Timoteus Gabriel said that Johannes Shikindo, the headmaster of the Sarukwe Primary School, and Mr Andreas Hainguru, a teacher and assistant headmaster at the Mawanze Primary School were well known to him as SWAPO members. He said both openly practiced politics in school, persuading people to join or support SWAPO.

He was present when both teachers told the headman's wife the children shouldn't go to school, but should attend a SWAPO meeting instead.

They said to Mr Gabriel that when Sam Nujoma returned to Namibia, all soldiers would become SWAPO's slaves.

He stated that he had personally seen both teachers allowing school children to sing SWAPO songs.

Children had told him they had been forced to sing SWAPO songs and attend lectures on the organisation.

They had also been threatened that if pupils didn't support SWAPO, they would have to leave the school.

Josef Hamupembe stated in an affidavit that on 24th April, he and seven other members of 202 Battalion had attended a SWAPO meeting wearing civilian clothes. Present were a few adults and about forty children between 8 and 21.

Stanislaus Kazana – headmaster of the Bunya High Primary School and supervisor of the SWAPO branch of Bunya, Alex Shimero – a teacher at the Bunya Lower Primary School and Chairman of the SWAPO branch at Nubya, Fidelius Neromba – Headmaster of the Bunya Lower Primary School and supervisor of the local SWAPO branch, Thereses Tenga – teacher at Bunya Lower Primary School and Magnus Nanyemba – teacher at Bunya High Primary School and Secretary of Information for the SWAPO branch at Bunya, were all speakers at the meeting.

Magnus Nanyemba tried to persuade the audience to join and support SWAPO. He said that anybody who was not a member of SWAPO would have problems when Sam Nujoma returned to Namibia in June 1989.

He criticised the South African Government and the DTA, saying they were bad.

He directed his words to the children, saying that after 1st April the country would be independent, so if they didn't join NANSO, they would be kicked out of school.

The other teachers addressed the meeting on much the same theme. They

284

praised Sam Nujoma, SWAPO and NANSO and condemned South Africa, the DTA and all other political parties and non supporters of SWAPO.

Fidelius Likuwa said in an affidavit that he attended the same meeting. He said his four children attended the school where the speakers were employed as teachers. His children had told him on several occasions that they had been forced to sing SWAPO songs and participate in school boycotts.

Two more affidavits by Alois Likuwa and Dionisious Hamutenya confirmed the other statements and said their children had also told them they had been forced to sing SWAPO songs and participate in school boycotts.

The presiding judge granted a *rule nisi* in favour of the applicants, which was also made an interim interdict whereby SWAPO, Mr Johannes Shikanda and Mr Andreas Hainguru were:

  (i) Prohibited from intimidating Mr Timoteus Gabriel or his family to become members of SWAPO;
 (ii) Prohibited from threatening, assaulting or killing Mr Gabriel or his family;
(iii) Prohibited by any means, from interferimg with Mr Gabriel's and his family's freedom of movement, freedom of speech, freedom of association and freedom to participate in politics;
 (iv) SWAPO and Magnus Nanyemba were prohibited from intimidating Josef Hamupembe, Fidelius Likuwa, Alois Likuwa and Dionisious Hamutenya or their families, to become members of SWAPO;
  (v) SWAPO and Mr Nanyemba were prohibited from threatening, assaulting or killing the above mentioned four applicants or their families;
 (vi) They were prohibited by any means, from interfering with the applicants' and their families', freedom of movement, freedom of speech, freedom of association and freedom to participate in politics;
(vii) SWAPO, NANSO, Stanislaus Kaganga, Alex Shiremo, Fidelius Neromba, Teresea Tenga and Magnus Nanyemba were prohibited by any means from intimidating, threatening or assaulting the children of Fidelius Likuwa, Alois Likuwa and Kionisius Hamutenya, for the purpose of persuading them to become members of SWAPO or NANSO;
(viii) The above mentioned correspondents were prohibited by any means from forcing, allowing or persuading the scholars at the Bunya High Primary School to sing SWAPO songs;
 (ix) The above mentioned respondents were prohibited by any means, at these schools, from propagating or proclaiming the doctrine, principles, aims and achievements of SWAPO, NANSO or its affiliated organisations;
  (x) SWAPO and NANSO were instructed to take all reasonable steps to assure themselves that their members didn't commit any of the abovementioned acts;
 (xi) SWAPO and NANSO were instructed to take all reasonable steps to assure themselves that the contents of the Supreme Court order was communicated to their members.

15th May – Scholars attending the Leevi Secondary School, complained they had been forced to attend regular SWAPO meetings in the school hall and also to participate in a class boycott on 13th May.

16th May – A PLAN member told scholars at Ongwediva that everybody must to vote for SWAPO, otherwise the war would continue. If SWAPO lost the election, all scholars would be forced to go to Angola to help with the 'struggle'. They were instructed to take away food, which had been provided the Security Forces, from the old people.

18th May – A teacher speaking at a SWAPO meeting at Suiriungu in the Kavango, said he would kill anyone wearing a DTA shirt. He added that Sam Nujoma will punish everyone who has worked for the whites.

18th May – A pistol carrying SWAPO official from Windhoek, told a SWAPO meeting at Kaisosi, near Rundu, that those who didn't buy SWAPO membership card would be killed by SWAPO/PLAN.

20th May – A Mr Shitunda was assaulted by three scholars in the Ndonga- Linena area. They threatened that he would be killed if he continued wearing a DTA t-shirt after 1st July.

20th May – A SWAPO official, addressing a public meeting at Kongola in the eastern Caprivi, invited SWAPO supporters to collect pistols from him and use them to kill soldiers of 701 Battalion, once they had been demobilised. He said they should kill them during the night, so the police would think it was the work of PLAN fighters.

20th May – Gabriel Kautuima – Senior Headman of the Kwanyama people in Owambo, Manasse Weyulu – elected Headman of the Kwanyamas in the Ondwi area, Johannes Kalangula – elected headman of the Kwanyamas in the Ometwe-wondjama area, Abner Erasmus Nuule – Senior Headman and leader of the Kwambi people and as such elected in terms of traditional law and custom, Andreas Shaliu – elected Senior Headman in the Oipunbu area, Okandjera, Owambo, Joseph Andreas – Chief of the Onabango area of Ndonga, Annanias Kamanya – elected Headman in the Kwalundhi area, Owambo, Sebastian Kam-wanga – elected Chief in the Gciruku area in Kavango, Angelina Matumbo Nakule – elected Chief in the Sambyo area, Kavango, Boniface Bebi Mamili Headman of the Mafwe tribe in Caprivi, and Matias Walaula, Senior Headman in the Okalongo area, Kwanyama, Owambo, brought an urgent application before the Supreme Court of SWA/Namibia, against eight respondents:

1. South West Africa Peoples Organisation – SWAPO;
2. Council of Churches of Namibia – CCN;
3. Namibia National Students Organisation – NANSO;
4. Namibia National Teachers Organisation – NANTO;
5. The Administrator General of SWA/Namibia;
6. Minister of Defence;
7. The UN High Commissioner for Refugees; and
8. The UN Special Representative for Namibia.

The applicants asked the full bench of the Supreme Court, the Judge President Hans Berker, Judge Harold Levy and Judge Johan Strydom, to issue a *rule nisi* upon which the respondents were called, to give reasons why an order of court with the following stipulations should not be issued against them:

A An order that the Administrator General and the Minister of Defence and the corporate bodies immediately take proper and sufficient precautions to protect the lives and property of the applicants and their families, the authorities of their tribes and the members of their tribes against illegal actions from the side of

SWAPO, the Council of Churches for Namibia – CCN, NANSO, NANTO or any other person or organisation which is directly or indirectly involved with the respondents;

B   An order that refugees returning to the area be prohibited to enter the area, unless proper and efficient precautions are taken by the Administrator General and the Minister of Defence to insure that such refugees will not take or endanger the lives or property of the applicants, their families or the members of their tribes or commit illegal acts against the applicants, their families or members of their tribes;

C   An order that the Council of Churches of Namibia – CCN, be forbidden to control or get involved with the repatriation of such refugees;

D   An order that no such refugees or any other person may enter, stay, reside or establish themselves in the areas of which the applicants are the captains, senior headmen or headmen, without the consent of the official headmen or senior headmen, and subject to the conditions set by them;

E   An order that if such a refugee or any other person who is permitted by the applicants to enter, stay, reside or establish himself in the area, the applicants will be entitled according to their tribal custom or customary law, to end such permission in case the captain, headman or senior headman involved, is of opinion that it is to the benefit of the tribe to take such action;

F   An order which forbids the construction, establishment or operation of a refugee camp, which is directly or indirectly under control of SWAPO, the Council of Churches for Namibia – CCN, or the UN High Commissioner for Refugees – UNHCR, without the consent of the applicants;

G   An order which forbids SWAPO, the Council of Churches for Namibia – CCN, NANSO and NANTO to take away or threaten the lives or possessions of the applicants, or members of their families or tribes or to act or allow any illegal actions against them.

In an affidavit, senior headman Gabriel Kautuima stated that he was the elected senior headman of the Kwanyama tribe and according to Ovambo tradition Law and custom, the counsellor spokesman and leader of the Kwanyama people.

The Kwanyama tribe is the largest in Ovambo and according to the 1986 census approximately 245 000 people belong to it. It is therefore the largest single tribe in Namibia and counting for about a fifth of the total population.

He stated that for several years SWAPO had been busy with a terror and intimidation campaign against the local population in Ovambo, which had intensified since 1978.

It was clear that SWAPO with its armed violence was trying to intimidate the local population for the purpose of subjecting them to its will. SWAPO was also busy with an inland intimidation campaign through its front organisations, like the CCN, NANSO and NANTO. This inland intimidation campaign, conducted by means of threats and false propaganda, had escalated over the past few years. This intimidation through armed violence had been manifested by the following acts of SWAPO, the CCN, NANSO and NANTO:

1 The traditional authorities are the basis of authority in Ovambo. There have been continuous attempts by SWAPO and its front organisations to, by the means of armed violence and other forms of intimidation, to break down these authorities. Several traditional leaders in Ovambo were murdered because they refused to submit to the views and doctrine of SWAPO. Most of the applicants have had to

ward off attempts on their lives by SWAPO. Mr Kautuima himself survived fourteen such attempts. He listed the names of nine headmen and senior headmen who had been murdered by SWAPO.

2 Some of the leaders in Ovambo had been intimidated through armed violence by SWAPO to such an extent that they had been forced to leave their homes and live under degrading and perilous conditions at tribal offices or elsewhere, where they had the protection of the security forces. Under such circumstances it was difficult for tribal leaders to control their people and much damage had been done to their authority.

3 The homes of the traditional leaders had been attacked regularly and burned down and their personal property damaged or destroyed by SWAPO. Their cattle had been stolen, impoverishing them to such an extent that they were no longer self supporting.

4 (a) School children are misused and taught to despise and ridicule the authority of the traditional leaders.

(b) Through continuous propaganda by NANSO and NANTO children are intimidated at school to ridicule, despise and reject traditional authority and customs.

(c) The intimidation of youth and school children is manifested by the following acts:

(i) Groups of school children in the streets shout insulting and despising remarks like 'Down with the headmen', and 'Viva SWAPO'.
(ii) Groups of school children sing SWAPO songs which propagate the breaking down of traditional and governmental authority.

(d) In the past the traditional leaders were always members of school committees and other social institutions, but in the present day they didn't even dare enter the school grounds.

5 (a) They were experiencing on a daily basis an intimidation and propaganda campaign by SWAPO, the CCN, NANSO and NANTO, in which they were accused of being 'puppets' of the South African government and that they are imitators who only execute the orders of that government.

(b) The truth was the traditional authority had for many years been the only authority, and it was the South African government who had reduced their powers and authority. Nevertheless, they still fulfilled an important role in maintaining law and order in their tribal areas.

(c) They find this false propaganda affects the youth, especially the children.

(d) The false propaganda has mainly been spread in schools, from SWAPO's own political stage and from the pulpit of member churches of the Council of Churches of Namibia – CCN, mainly the Evangelical Lutheran Ovambo Church – ELOC, and the Evangelical Lutheran Church in Kavango.

6 The traditional authority of the headman was always recognised and nobody established himself in an area without the permission of the headman.

According to traditional law and custom the territory of the tribe is the joint property of the members of the tribe and the captain, headman or senior headman controls the people who live there.

The permission for a person to live in an area can be suspended by the traditional authority of the area, if it is in the interest of the tribe.

Ovambo, as it is, has a weak infrastructure and is already over populated. If people are allowed to establish themselves without control, the problem can escalate.

The churches, who are members of the CCN, were allowed land long before the existence of the CCN, by the captains, headman and senior headman or their predecessors, for the exclusive purpose of building schools and churches to preach the Gospel and academically educate the children. In some cases permission was also given for the establishment of hospitals on such land.

They are now finding that ELOC and its sister church in Kavango are using their premises as if they are their private properties, allowing SWAPO to use them for political meetings and for the preaching of SWAPO propaganda from the pulpits. Intimidation of school children by teaching them SWAPO propaganda and doctrine is practiced in schools under the control of the Council of Churches of Namibia.

At ELOC church at Engela, UNTAG was allowed to establish a military base without either party consulting the headman of the area, which is Mr Kautuima.

He also found foundations had already been dug for a refugee camp, where refugees will be kept under the control of UNTAG and the CCN. Mr Kautuima said that in spite of SWAPO's intimidation campaign, some traditional leaders had managed to survive, mainly because of the support of their people and the protection given by the Security Forces.

He said the Security Forces protected the population, while SWAPO used a violent and escalating campaign against the people. They had planted explosives and bombs at shopping centres and butcheries, which had caused the death of many people, mainly innocent women and children.

Against this background of suffering and hardship over the last twenty three years, especially the last ten, his people had welcomed the peace initiatives which led to SWAPO's agreement to a ceasefire in August 1988 and the implementation of resolution 435 on 1st April 1989.

Headman Manasse Weyulu said in his affidavit that in 1978 he had fled for his life from his home in the Ondwi region, and had been living ever since in poor conditions at the Eenhana tribal offices.

In 1978 his sister, her baby and two other women were murdered by SWAPO.

His kraal had been burned down and 80 head of cattle and 250 goats stolen.

He dared not return to his homestead, which is 32 kilometres from the tribal offices.

He said he had been unable to work his land or maintain authority over his people. This had impoverished and humiliated him.

Headman James Kalangula said in his affidavit that SWAPO terrorists had attacked and burned down his homestead in 1983.

He was wounded in the attack, while his wife and children were abducted and taken back to Angola together with his cattle.

On the same day SWAPO had also attacked the homes of three of his deputy headmen.

Headman Andreas Shaliu said how SWAPO terrorists had already made two attempts on his life, forcing him to live in humiliating circumstances at the Okahau tribal office.

He said SWAPO politics were regularly preached from the pulpit by Pastor Annanias Iita, who once said in reference to him that he 'does not know what is going to happen to the "puppets" when the Security Forces withdraw.'

In his affidavit Headman Annanias Kamanya said he had been forced to settle at

Oshakati after SWAPO terrorists had attacked his home in the Oshandi region in 1981.

Resulting from this action he lost everything he possessed, including 6 000 head of cattle, stolen by SWAPO. He had since lost control of the people who fell under his tribal authority.

Headman Matias Walaula, in his affidavit, said his homestead which is two kilometres south of the Angolan border, had been attacked six times by SWAPO terrorists.

He was fully aware that PLAN still has two major bases near the Namibian border in the vicinity of Beacon 14 5 [in contravention of the peace plan] and that PLAN members in civilian clothing were still moving around his area of authority.

On the 29th May the Court granted the application and ordered the Administrator General to direct the Commissioner of the SWA Police to make the necessary arrangements in order to protect the lives and property of the applicants, their relatives and tribal office bearers against wrongful actions by the respondents SWAPO, Council of Churches For Namibia – CCN, NANSO and NANTO, or any other person or organisation which are directly or indirectly connected with the respondents, and which actions may threaten or affect the lives or property of the applicants.

The directions given were subject to the Commissioner of Police having sufficient personnel at his disposal to afford the required protection, but it stipulated he could avail himself of auxiliary support which was either at his disposal or could be employed for this purpose.

Other matters in this application were to be dealt with by the court at a later date.

UNTAG spokesman, Fred Eckhard, at a Windhoek press briefing on the 31st May, said when asked Mr Ahtisaari's response at being named as a respondent, that 'we are not aware of this action' adding that, in any case, the Special Representative was immune from local jurisdiction.

Purely another case of tunnel vision by UNTAG, where they kept their eyes and ears closed to anything they didn't want to see or hear.

Particularly, in this instance, where the full bench of the Supreme Court had found as fact their good friends, the Council of Churches for Namibia – CCN, had been aiding and assisting a Marxist terrorist organisation in its campaign to intimidate and murder people. In the meantime the CCN had been appointed as an agent for the UNHCR, to receive, accommodate and identify the refugees in Namibia.

21st May – The headmaster of the Eluva School for the Blind in Ovambo, reported getting a letter from SWAPO, which asked why his scholars had not taken part in the class boycott organised by the SWAPO fronting Namibia National Students Organisation – NANSO.

22nd May – A SWAPO official told a NANSO meeting held at Bukala in eastern Caprivi, that SWAPO members would soon be issued with pistols with which to 'defend' themselves. He cautioned people to be careful of the soldiers of 701 Battalion, but said they would soon get their chance to hit them.

22nd May – The parents of scholars at the Damara School in Mariental, complained their children were being indoctrinated with SWAPO propaganda by certain teachers.

24th May – A Portuguese speaking resident of Kaisosi, east of Rundu, laid a charge of intimidation against SWAPO members, saying they had been harassing former Angolan refugees.

25th May – Phillemon Moonza complained to Police Oshakati that SWAPO members had caused him to be discharged from the Namibian Taxi Association, because of his DTA membership.

25th May – Six PLAN fighters attended a braaivleis at the home of a teacher from Onagena School in Ovambo. They said they were still around, and had their firearms and uniforms which they used at night.

26th May – A former PLAN fighter threatened members of the Security Forces, saying he would report their names to SWAPO if they didn't resign from their jobs and start supporting SWAPO. He stressed that all those whose names were reported to SWAPO would be executed when they won the election.

27th May – SWAPO members tried to intimidate people in the Katimba area near Rundu, saying they were not to attend a DTA meeting. They said the DTA told lies and it belonged to the Boere, who give poisoned food to the people.

27th May – Salmon Haraib complained to Police Gobabis that the headmaster of a primary School at Witvlei had taught SWAPO slogans to school children. He had also instructed them on how to sing SWAPO 'freedom' songs.

29th May – Senior Headman Gabriel Kautuima applied to the Supreme Court in Windhoek for relief saying in his affidavit he had read in The Namibian newspaper, that the Namibian Teachers Union was established to promote the objectives and doctrine of SWAPO.

He told the court that one SWAPO song being taught to pupils in schools had the following substance and effect:

'SWAPO will win the struggle against the racist Pretoria regime;

'SWAPO's soldiers would drink the blood of Botha's grandmother and the blood of the headmen'.

He said school children were being used by SWAPO and its front organisations to ridicule traditional leaders by the following acts:

(i) Traditional leaders were insulted in public with derogatory remarks, like 'Down with the headmen' and 'Viva SWAPO'.

(ii) Groups of school children sung SWAPO songs propagating the breaking down of traditional and governmental authority.

Senior Headman Kautuima stated that SWAPO and its front organisations were busy daily with a full time intimidation and propaganda campaign, in which the headmen were being called 'puppets of the South African government.'

He said this false propaganda was being spread from SWAPO's political stage as well as in schools and in churches of the Evangelic Lutheran Church in Namibia – ELCIN.

The population of the country, especially the inhabitants of the northern region, were suffering severely from intimidation by members of SWAPO and its front organisations.

The intimidation was specifically aimed at school children and members of the demilitarised South West Africa Territory Force, who refused to become members of SWAPO and its front organisations.

The cases of intimidation were so extensive that the people were forced to turn to the Supreme Court for their rights to be protected.

A *rule nisi* was granted to the applicant by the Supreme Court.

29th May-3rd June – Two members of PLAN, wearing civilian clothes but armed with assault rifles and pistols, were seen in the Oshindobe area talking to civilians.

30th May – Willem Josef Haikera complained to Police Rundu that while visiting the local clinic, SWAPO supporters had told him that if he attended a DTA meeting, he would be assaulted and his home would be burned to the ground.

30th May – The student body of the A Shipena School in Katutura Township, had stood up to the Namibia National Students Organisation – NANSO, and refused to join the school boycott before the June examinations. NANSO officials had warned Shipena scholars to take care when leaving the school grounds, as they would be facing reprisals.

31st May – Scholars at the High Primary School, at Eenhana in Ovambo, who had declined to join the class boycott, had been forced to leave the school premises by SWAPO supporter.

A similar incident occurred the same day at the Ongwediva Lower Primary School.

31st May – Alexander Katemba complained to Police Rundu, that he had been threatened with assault at a cuca shop, because he was a soldier and not a SWAPO member.

1st June – A former PLAN fighter threatened black members of the Security Forces in Ovambo, saying he would give their names to SWAPO so they would be killed.

2nd-3rd June – A group of school children picketed the shop of a DTA organiser, preventing people from buying there.

A demobilised soldier was assaulted and told to inform his friends that they would have to pay for the deaths of their 'brothers' killed by the army.

3rd June – DTA supporters shopping at cuca shops in Okatope, were told by SWAPO members they would be killed if they went to them again.

3rd June – A well known SWAPO supporter tore a DTA flag from a vehicle at Bethanien. He publicly burnt it.

People wearing DTA t-shirts were forbidden to enter the Evangelic Lutheran Church at Bethanien.

5th June – A demobilised soldier of 202 Battalion complained to Police Bagani that SWAPO members had prevented him from entering a shop, then had insulted and threatened to assault him.

6th June – Police Rundu laid a charge of intimidation against a prominent SWAPO youth leader in the Kavango.

They also charged an employee at the Kavango Administration for intimidating workers refusing to take part in a strike organised by the pro SWAPO Namibia Public Workers Union.

6th June – A demobilised former soldier of 202 Battalion and a policeman laid charges against SWAPO members at Police Nkurenkuru, after they had been assaulted.

8th June – SWAPO members at Olune announced they didn't believe in peace negotiations, saying Sam Nujoma wanted to see more blood flowing.

8th June – All classes at the Lower Primary School at Ongwediva were hurriedly stopped by the headmistress because she feared for her life after a 'phone call from the SWAPO fronting Namibian National Student's Organisation – NANSO, in Windhoek. They demanded to know why her school wasn't taking part in the NANSO organised school boycott and said if she was a freedom fighter, and not a 'puppet', she would close the school.

9th June – A former PLAN fighter campaigning for SWAPO in Kaokoland, told people that if they didn't vote for SWAPO in the coming elections they would be killed.

13th June – Mr A Saikote complained to Police Rundu that he had been refused treatment at a clinic because he wasn't a member of SWAPO.

14th June – Mr Fernando Petrus laid a charge at Police Oshakati after he and a friend, Ndemuloko Mulike, had gone shopping at a cuca shop. The owner locked them up for an hour because they didn't support SWAPO.

14th June – SWAPO officials told repatriated refugees at Ongwediva that they shouldn't leave the camps, because Koevoet would kill them.

16th June – Stones were thrown by SWAPO supporters at a bus carrying DTA supporters in the Kapako area.

16th June – A SWAPO member at Okahanja stabbed a DTA member with a knife and said the DTA was a 'puppet' party.

17th June – Children attending a SWAPO meeting at Kangango were told to burn their parents' DTA membership cards and force them to join SWAPO.

17th June – A DTA youth meeting was disrupted by two SWAPO supporting teachers, one was armed with a pistol. They threatened everyone present and told the organiser he was a marked man.

17th June – Andries Makumba complained to Police Katutura that three SWAPO supporters had called at his house and threatened him with death because of his DTA membership.

19th June – A group of SWAPO supporters, drinking liquor in a cuca shop, attacked a policeman when he walked in. Two other policemen patrolling nearby came to his assistance, but were themselves attacked and an attempt made to disarm them. After fruitlessly firing warning shots, one of the assailants was fatally wounded in the stomach. He died the next morning in hospital. One of the policemen was also medically treated for injuries sustained.

20th June – Mr Peter Katijova, a DTA Party worker, was assaulted by four SWAPO supporters while on his way home.

20th June – A DTA organiser wearing a party t-shirt entered a shabeen at Mondisa, Swakopmund, for a drink. A well known SWAPO supporter ripped the shirt from his back and cut it into pieces. The party worker has stated that he is now too frightened to continue with his political work.

20th June – Mr Sipunga Kaduma complained to Police Rundu that a teacher allowed the school children to sing SWAPO 'freedom' songs and shout SWAPO slogans.

20th June – At a SWAPO meeting at Rundu it was announced that a member of the SWA Police would be killed.

21st June – A threat by SWAPO to the life of headman Dawid Frederik of Nama's was received.

22th June – SWAPO Youth League members had intimidated the inhabitants of the Okatope and Onankale areas. The people there had become frightened for their lives and afraid even to talk to a policeman, let alone mention the possibility of laying charges.

23th June – A member of 202 Battalion complained that a minister of the Dutch Reformed Mission Church had refused to baptise his child. He said the father must change his political views. According to him members of the DTA were not christians – he would only baptise children of SWAPO members.

24th June – DTA party worker, Joram Kandjeo, was forced to stop his car by SWAPO supporters on the road between Ohangwena and Oshakati. They argued that DTA members weren't allowed to use the public road. The SWAPO supporters began tearing DTA election posters from his vehicle. He tried to stop them, but they assaulted him, threatened to kill him and said they would burn his vehicle. Eventually he broke free, started his car and drive off.

24th June – Two DTA cars were stoned by SWAPO supporters near Onga, injuring a DTA supporter.

24th June – Mr Johannes Nodore and Miss Helmi Mpasi complained to Police Rundu that a SWAPO member had sworn at them and threatened them with death because they were wearing DTA t-shirts.

24th June – Mr Reinhard Somseb complained to Police Rundu that SWAPO members were forcing him to support SWAPO. If he didn't they said he would be assaulted and shot.

25th June – A Mr Anuius reported to Police Oshakati that a SWAPO member had threatened him with death.

25th June – Three DTA members, Messrs Lansaria Nikolaye, Johannes Alfeas and Mrs Marta Ipundula complained to Police Oshakati that members of SWAPO had thrown bottles at them.

26th June – Constable P Nakule reported to Police Oshakati that a member of SWAPO at Ondangwa had threatened him with death.

26th June – A former PLAN member told people at the FNDC Hardware Shops, Oshakati, that PLAN was ready to assist SWAPO, should something go wrong with the election.

28th June – Two members of SWAPO had spread the word that SWAPO members would be getting rifles with which to kill all DTA supporters. They said men working with the Security Forces would be executed after SWAPO took over.

June – In a petition directed to the UN Special Representative and to the Administrator General, twenty two traditional leaders [paramount chiefs, chiefs, senior headman and headmen] said it was evident a persistent intimidation and propaganda campaign had been commenced by SWAPO and its front organisations, to undermine the prevailing structures of authority, especially the traditional structures of authority of chiefs and headmen.

In particular they complained about school children being indoctrinated by SWAPO supporting teachers with SWAPO propaganda, in order that they should disregard and ridicule traditional structures of authority – not only those of the chiefs and headmen, but of parental authority as well.

They alleged that school children were being intimidated by SWAPO and its front organisations, in particular NANSO, to accept revolutionary ideologies and to reject and ridicule all forms of authority, to attend SWAPO and NANSO meetings, to take part in political processions, and to sing SWAPO songs in public.

1st July – The SWAPO supporting headmaster of a primary school near Omege, Owambo, told a SWAPO meeting that everyone must vote for SWAPO, because it is the largest party, while the DTA is the party of the Boere.

He said the names and vehicle registration numbers of all 'puppets' in Ovambo were known and they would be 'captured' after the election.

11th July – A black domestic worker reported that SWAPO men had called at her neighbours' hut at Ondangwa and given them voter's registration forms. When they explained they had no intention of voting for SWAPO, they were physically assaulted. After that they were told the intimidators had registered them as SWAPO voters, which compelled them to vote for SWAPO at the election.

This was not the end of SWAPO's intimidation campaign.

It was just the beginning.

19

The Future?

By the end of August 1989 the situation in Namibia was uncertain.

UNTAG, takings its lead from Secretary General Dr Javier Perez de Cuellar, seemed to have developed an almost open partiality to SWAPO.

Some 2 000 of SWAPO's political prisoners in Angola and Zambia have disappeared, most since January 1989.

Evidence that they existed is incontrovertible.

From stories coming out of Angola and Zambia, it seems they had either been intimidated into rejoining SWAPO or 'thrown away in the bush' – as a SWAPO officer euphemistically called being done to death when offering the choice to a prisoner.

The prisoner later escaped to tell his story in Namibia.

The last thing SWAPO wants is to have their own dissidents back in Namibia.

They released an experimental 200 and allowed them to return to Namibia, but the resultant storm of adverse publicity – relating to torture, deprivation and murder of prisoners – caused so much damage to SWAPO's image, both nationally and internationally, that they obviously decided they couldn't take the risk of releasing another 2 000.

The United Nations High Commission for Refugees apparently agreed, accepting SWAPO's word there were no more returnees left in Angola and Zambia.

Well, they would, wouldn't they? to quote the immortal words of Mandy Rice-Davies.

UNTAG, it seems, except for an occasional bout of muttering that something should be done, has done nothing.

One wonders if Mr Ahtisaari has forgotten what he said on arrival at Windhoek Airport on the 31st March.

'Those who are in exile, must have the chance to come here.'

Is it that SWAPO's prisoners don't count in this equation?

Latterly one has been hearing expressions like: 'There is no real evidence,' and suchlike, from all sorts of quarters.

The same sort of stories, similarly dismissed, filtered out of Nazi occupied Europe during World War-2, yet Auschwitz, Bergen-Belsen, Buchenwald, Riga and many other Nazi death camps were no figments of imagination.

Then there are South African Intelligence allegations of there being an estimated 2 000 SWAPO fighters south of the 16th parallel in Angola.

Angola, Cuba, SWAPO and UNTAG deny they exist.

What an encouragement for SWAPO if they do.

Next comes the allegation that a 1 000 or more PLAN fighters, who returned as refugees, are waiting, reformed in their military formations, but without uniforms, in the various secondary refugee camps run by the SWAPO supporting Council of Churches for Namibia-CCN, scattered around Namibia.

Their weapons are either in caches already, or are probably being brought in across the Angolan border at night, now that police patrols have been severely curtailed as a result of action by the Security Council brought about by agitation of the African members of the so called Non Aligned Movement.

The African states in the Non Aligned Movement, are determined SWAPO will be installed as the government of Namibia by the end of the year.

Robert Mugabe, the man with all the experience in these matters and the outgoing chairman of NAM, wanted Nujoma to do a repeat of what he did himself in Zimbabwe with his ZANU P/F in 1980, during the run up to independence.

He assisted with the supply of many additional uniforms for PLAN before the April incursion.

Each infiltrating insurgent took with him at least three sets, which were for kitting out SWAPO sympathising tribesmen.

The intention was to demand base camps within Namibia from UNTAG, and flood both fighters and freshly uniformed and equipped civilians into them, and use them as centres from which to 'politicise' the people into supporting SWAPO at the November elections.

Because of the valour of the SWA Police, however, this plan was foiled.

In spite of this SWAPO could still win the elections by means of the intimidation factor, which is truly horrifying.

On the other hand this has worked against them to a large extent, so one cannot be emphatic about the likely results at the polls because the DTA might win. Certainly SWAPO is not that confident, by all reports, and judging by their actions.

Since April, though, much has changed and so have SWAPO's plans, with the active support and assistance of the Non Aligned Movement.

With South African forces having been drastically reduced, the SWA Territory Force demobilised and the old SWA Police COIN confined to base, the country's defences are much weakened. Various scenarios are possible, because one thing which seems certain is that Nujoma and SWAPO, if they lose the election, will try to take over the country by force.

They are already passing the word that if they lose they will go back to the bush and the war will continue.

The only road to peace is a vote for SWAPO.

Mugabe's ZANU P/F terrorists gave the same message to the black populace of Zimbabwe and it worked for him.

One worrying matter, particularly considering the international nature of the agreements between Angola, Cuba and South Africa, is that Cuba has recently threatened to halt its withdrawal of troops from Angola.

Another is that peace talks between the MPLA government and UNITA seem to have broken down.

Perhaps the reality of this is that the Angolan-Cubans intend to destroy UNITA, rather than talk to them, particularly now that the South Africans have vacated their Caprivi military bases, so no direct supply lines for providing them with military aid remain.

An apocalyptical projection, which cannot be dismissed out of hand because it

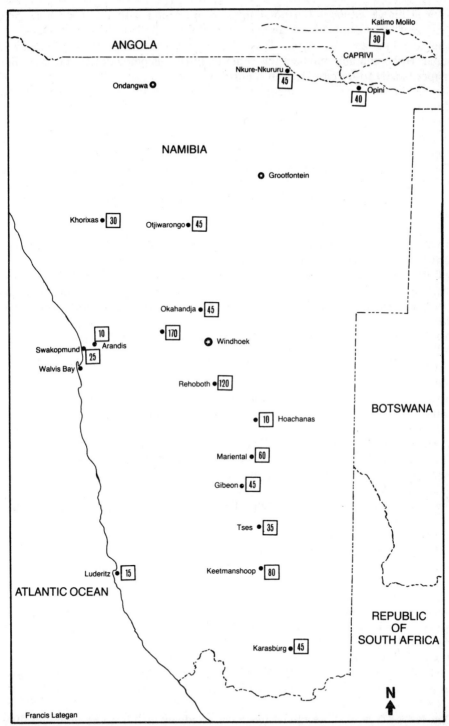

Map showing distribution of PLAN in Angola and Namibia, according to South African Intelligence, as at the 15th May 1989.

rates well above being just a possibility, is concerned with intelligence reports filtering out from Zimbabwe, Zambia and the Non Aligned Movement.

This suggests an 'All Africa Force', consisting of troops from Zimbabwe, Zambia, Botswana and maybe a few other countries, is being quietly put together on paper, ready to be mobilised in a hurry.

Support in the way of air elements, C-130 and other transports, has been offered by Libya.

The PLAN hatched up by SWAPO and the African members of the Non Aligned Movement, is that if the election goes against SWAPO in November, there will be a 'popular' uprising against the newly elected regime.

This will involve PLAN fighters storming over the border from Angola, while the 1 000 PLAN fighters scattered around the country in the Secondary Refugee camps, will start military operations designed to topple the government.

400 PLAN fighters based at Sesheke in Zambia, will immediately move south and invade the Caprivi Strip, with the active support of the Zambians.

It will be remembered these units made hostile moves southwards towards the Caprivi during the April incursions, but withdrew.

400 PLAN fighters have been reported as moving to a base at Dowe, in north western Botswana, and they will cross the border into north eastern Namibia.

The prognosis is that UNTAG will do nothing, because it is a monitoring force and not a peacekeeping one.

Also, it will not have the will and will bow in confusion and accept the disinformation of SWAPO and the Non Aligned Movement.

The Security Forces, it is expected, will by then have their hands effectively tied by the UN and be incapable of intervening.

A call will be made to 'Africa' by the CCN and the unions to restore order in the country, and the Libyan C-130s, and other aircraft standing by to be loaded with troops, will take off from various airports in Zambia, Botswana and Zimbabwe and the 'All Africa Force' will head for prearranged destinations in Namibia.

The address of the outgoing Chairman, Robert Mugabe of Zimbabwe, when presenting his report to the ninth summit of the Non Aligned Movement on the 5th September was significant.

'There is a grave possibility,' he said, 'that the Namibian people may be cheated out of genuine self determination.'

Now what on earth did he mean by that?

Cutting through the double talk, it meant SWAPO might fail at the polls, so the NAM will lead the hue and cry to have the election declared invalid.

'It is clear,' he went on,' this summit will need to consider what further "action" the movement needs to take on Namibia.'

One can guess what sort of 'action' he meant. He said the report of a group of eighteen representatives of the Non Aligned Movement who had visited Namibia made disturbing reading.

It would be interesting to see that report.

Meanwhile, moderates of the NAM apparently wanted to talk about debt, environment, human rights and so on, but Namibia was the Africa Group's obsession.

One can be certain those moderates have no idea which is going on behind the scenes.

This might well be an option being planned, but there are many reasons why it could fail.

298

In the first place the certificate that the election was 'free and fair' is not going to be certified by Robert Mugabe of Zimbabwe or by the Secretary General of the UN, but by UN Special Representative Martti Ahtisaari, and although he has performed some amazing tightrope acts in the past months since the 1st April, he appears, in the main, to be playing the game straight down the middle.

It seems, at the moment, he is happy with the way things are going in the lead up to the election. Those things that are wrong, the intimidation and so forth, are unlikely to effect his final judgement on the 'free and fair' issue so long as there is not open conflict.

In fact, there is no reason to suppose he has changed his view which he expressed clearly on the day he arrived in Namibia.

'When the Namibian people have chosen, the outcome must be accepted and respected by all.'

If, for instance the DTA and allied parties win, and SWAPO and the NAM decide to attempt the apocalypse solution, things could go sadly wrong for them, no matter how grand their ideas.

In the first place a non SWAPO election winner, if there was a 'popular uprising', would probably ask South Africa to help them restore order.

Although South Africa has made the diplomatic decision to withdraw from Namibia, this does not mean she will merely stand by and watch a revolutionary grab for power take place.

As the former governing power, and the only regional power, such a request could hardly be denied.

UNTAG, whether it was liked it or not, would have no moral or legal say in the matter.

The 'All Africa Force' notion, however, has long been a pipe dream of men like Robert Mugabe and Kenneth Kaunda, but they have never been able to get their act together, except perhaps in Mozambique, which has hardly been a marked success.

But an 'All Africa Force' or even a part Africa force, would certainly be in for a rude awakening if it found itself matched against the SADF.

Quantity is no substitute for quality.

They should ask the Angolans and have a confidential chat with Fidel Castro. He will no doubt repeat what he said in public on the 9th July, when he said that a relatively small number of SADF personnel nearly 'defeated his whole revolution'.

It must have made him thankful he'd never faced up to the SADF in the good old Sierra Madres days.

If SWAPO fails at the polls, they will try to make the country ungovernable and more, but whether they succeed or not is another question.

If, however, SWAPO wins at the polls, things will be different.

South Africa is committed to accepting the result, no matter what, and if SWAPO comes in, she will quietly complete her final withdrawal from the country, and that will be the end of it.

There are sinister divisions coming to light within SWAPO itself, however, and it would not be surprising if a few heads amongst the leadership, perhaps even Nujoma's himself, rolled before the election in last minute struggles for power.

It seems probable that white SWAPO leader, Anton Lubowski, who was assassinated outside his Windhoek home on the 12th September, was murdered by SWAPO as a sacrificial lamb.

There is much to suggest he had been killed by an IRA hit man brought in expecially for the job, on orders of SWAPO's top leadership, as an example to those agitating against Nujoma's presidency of SWAPO.

It is doubtful Lubowski was involved in such plotting, but he was generally resented within SWAPO and undoubtedly regarded as expendable.

The warning was probably directed at the highly placed Hamutenya Hidipo, who it is said, is being backed for the SWAPO presidency by PLAN's top military commanders.

Windhoek, a sleepy hollow until now, seems to have a violent future lying ahead.

It will be ironic, however, if SWAPO, with its hackneyed slogans and Marxist policies as outdated as Joseph Stalin himself, which have failed and brought so many African states to ruin, wins the election.

The failures have not just been African either.

It has happened with oppressed peoples the world over. But formerly suppressed hopes of democracy are now spreading like wildfire, jumping from one socialist republic to another in the USSR, in China, in Poland, in Hungary, and in many other countries as well.

All of them, gradually but scornfully, edging communistic socialism into the dustbin of history where it belongs.

One can only hope the democratic states of the UN, at least, will suddenly wake up and realise the Namibian people, by not voting for SWAPO, are really not opting for the retention of apartheid and South African rule.

Both will be Namibian history by November anyway.

Their choice is between Marxist totalitarianism and democracy.

A people elects the government it deserves, they say.

One must hope the Namibians realise they deserve freedom and democracy.

And, that the world will not stop them from having it.

APPENDIX 1

Western Proposal for Settlement/Security Council Document S/12636

Letter dated 10th April 1978 from the Representatives of Canada, France, West Germany, United Kingdom and the United States of America addressed to the President of the Security Council.

On instructions from our governments we have the honour to transmit to you a proposal for the settlement of the Namibian situation and to request that it be circulated as a document of the Security Council.

The objective of our proposal is the independence of Namibia in accordance with resolution 435/1976, adopted unamimou sly by the Security Council on 30th January 1976. We are continuing to work towards the implementation of the proposal.

(Signed by Permanent Representatives to the UN of the above States)

Proposal for a settlement of the Namibian situation

(i) Introduction

1 Bearing in mind their responsibilities as members of the Security Council of the UN, the Governments of Canada, France, the Federal Republic of Germany, the United Kingdom and the United States have consulted with the various parties involved with the Namibian situation with a view to encouraging agreement on the transfer of authority in Namibia to an independent government in accordance with resolution 385/1976, adopted unaminousl[by the Security Council on 30th January 1976.

2 To this end, our Governments have drawn up a proposal for the settlement of the Namibian question designed to bring about a transition to independence during 1978 within a framework acceptable to the people of Namibia and thus to the international community. While the proposal addresses itself to all elements of resolution 385/1976, the key to an internationally acceptable transition to independence is free elections for the whole of Namibia as one political entity with an appropriate UN role in accordance with resolution 385/1976. A resolution will be required in the Security Council requesting the Secretary General to appoint a UN Special Representative whose central task will be to make sure that conditions are established which will allow free and fair elections and an impartial electoral process. The Special Representative will be assisted by a United Nations Transition Assistance Group – UNTAG.

3 The purpose of the electoral process is to elect representatives to a Namibian Constituent Assembly which will draw up and adopt the constitution for an independent and sovereign Namibia. Authority would then be assumed during 1978 by the Government of Namibia.

4 A More detailed description of the proposal is contained below. Our governments believe that this proposal provides an effective basis for implementing resolution 385/1976 while taking adequate account of the interests of all parties involved. In carrying out his

responsibilities the Special Representative will work together with the official appointed by South Africa (the Administrator General) to ensure the orderly transition to independence. This working arrangement shall in no way constitute recognition of the legality of the South African presence in and administration of Namibia.

(ii) The electoral process

5 In accordance with Security Council resolution 385/1976, free elections will be held, for the whole of Namibia as one political entity, to enable the people of Namibia to freely and fairly determine their own future. The elections will be under the supervision and control of the UN in that, as a condition to the conduct of the electoral process, the elections themselves, and the certification of their results, the UN Special Representative will have to satisfy himself at each stage as to the fairness and appropriateness of all measures affecting the political process at all levels of administration before such measures take effect. Moreover the Special Representative may himself make proposals in regard to any aspect of the political process. He will have at his disposal a substantial civilian section of UNTAG, sufficient to carry out his duties satisfactorily. He will report to the Secretary General of the UN, keeping him informed and making such recommendations as he considers necessary with respect to the discharge of his responsibilities. The Secretary General, in accordance with the mandate entrusted to him by the Security Council, will keep the Council informed.

6 Elections will be held to select a Constituent Assembly which will adopt a Constitution for an independent Namibia. The Constitution will determine the organization and powers of all levels of government. Every adult Namibian will be eligible, without discrimination or fear of intimidation from any source, to vote, campaign and stand for election to the Constituent Assembly. Voting will be by secret ballot, with provisions made for those who cannot read or write. The date for the beginning of the electoral campaign, the date of elections, the electoral system, the preparation of voters rolls, and other aspects of electoral procedures will be promptly decided upon so as to give all political parties and interested persons, without regard to their political views, a full and fair opportunity to organize and participate in the electoral process. Full freedom of speech, assembly, movement and press shall be guaranteed. The official electoral campaign shall commence only after the UN's Special Representative has satisfied himself as to the fairness and appropriateness of the electoral procedures. The implementation of the electoral process, including the proper registration of voters and the proper and timely tabulation and publication of voting results will also have to be conducted to the satisfaction of the Special Representative.

7 The following requirements will be fulfilled to the satisfaction of the UN's Special Representative in order to meet the objective of free and fair elections:

    A Prior to the beginning of the electoral campaign, the Administrator General will repeal all remaining discriminatory or restrictive laws, regulations, or administrative measures which might abridge or inhibit that objective.

    B The Administrator General shall make arrangements for the release, prior to the beginning of the electoral campaign, of all Namibian political prisoners or political detainees held by the South African authorities so that they can participate fully and freely in that process, without risk of arrest, detention, intimidation or imprisonment. Any disputes concerning the release of political prisoners or political detainees shall be resolved to the satisfaction of the Special Representative acting on the independent advice of a jurist of international standing who shall be designated by the Secretary General to be legal adviser to the Special Representative.

    C All Namibian refugees or Namibians detained or otherwise outside the territory of Namibia will be permitted to return peacefully and participate fully and freely in the electoral process without risk of arrest, detention, intimidation or imprisonment. Suitable entry points will be designated for these purposes.

    D The Special Representative with the assistance of the UN High Commissioner for Refugees and other appropriate international bodies will ensure that Namibians remaining outside of Namibia are given a free and voluntary choice whether to return. Provision will be made to attest to the voluntary nature of decisions made by Namibians who elect not to return to Namibia.

8 A comprehensive cessation of all hostile acts shall be observed by all parties in order to ensure that the electoral process will be free from interference and intimidation. The annexure describes provisions for the implementation of the cessation of all hostile acts, military arrangements concerning UNTAG, the withdrawal of South African forces, and arrangements with respect to other organized forces in Namibia, and with respect to the forces of SWAPO. These provisions call for:

(a) A cessation of all hostile acts by all parties and the restriction of South African and SWAPO armed forces to base.

(b) Thereafter a phased withdrawal from Namibia of all but 1 500 South African troops within twelve weeks and prior to the official start of the political campaign. The remaining South African force would be restricted to Grootfontein or Otjivelo or both and would be withdrawn after the certification of the election.

(c) The demobilisation of the Citizen Forces, Commandos, and ethnic forces, and the dismantling of their command structures.

(d) Provision will be made for SWAPO personnel outside of the territory to return peacefully to Namibia through designated entry points to participate freely in the political process.

(e) A military section of UNTAG is to make sure that the provisions of the agreed solution will be observed by all parties. In establishing the military section of UNTAG, the Secretary General will keep in mind functional and logistical requirements. The Five Governments, as members of the Security Council, will support the Secretary General's judgement in his discharge of this responsibility. The Secretary General will, in the normal manner, include in his consultations all those concerned with the implementation of the agreement. The Special Representative will be required to satisfy himself as to the implementation of all these arrangements and will keep the Secretary General informed of developments in this regard.

9 Primary responsibility for maintaining law and order in Namibia during the transition period shall rest with the existing police forces. The Administrator General to the satisfaction of the UN Special Representative shall ensure the good conduct of the police forces and shall take the necessary action to ensure their suitability for continued employment during the transition period. The Special Representative shall make arrangements when appropriate for United Nations personnel to accompany the police forces in the discharge of their duties. The police forces would be limited to the carrying of small arms in the normal performance of their duties.

10 The UN Special Representative will take steps to guarantee against the possibility of intimidation or interference with the electoral process from whatever quarter.

11 Immediately after the certification of election results, the Constituent Assembly will meet to draw up and adopt a Constitution for an independent Namibia. It will conclude its work as soon as possible so as to permit whatever additional steps may be necessary prior to the installation of an independent Government of Namibia during 1978.

12 Neighbouring countries shall be requested to ensure to the best of their abilities that the provisions of the transitional arrangements, and the outcome of the election, are respected. They shall also be requested to afford the necessary facilities to the UN Special Representative and all UN personnel to carry out their assigned functions and to facilitate such measures as may be desirable for ensuring tranquillity in the border areas.

Annexure – Schedule of the Peace Process (Updated by the 1988 agreements)

1st APRIL 1989

Namibia

1 Commencement of implementation of UN Security Council resolution 435/78, the reduction of South African forces and confinement to their bases in Namibia.
2 Release of prisoners/detainees.

Angola

Completion of the withdrawal of 3 000 of the estimated 50 000 Cuban troops from Angola. Commencement of the step by step withdrawal of the remaining 47 000 troops and their simultaneous and gradual redeployment to the north. Commencement of the confinement of SWAPO combatants to their bases in Angola and Zambia.

14th MAY 1989

Namibia

1 South African forces reduced to 12 000 men and commencement of return of exiles and publication of election rules.
2 Completion of the repeal of discriminatory legislation.
3 Dismantling of command structures of Citizen Forces, Commandos and ethnic forces and confinement of their military equipment under UN supervision.

11th JUNE 1989

Namibia

South African forces reduced to 8 000 men and repatriation of refugees completed.

1st JULY 1989

Namibia

South African forces reduced to 1 500 men confined to base and election campaign begins.

1st AUGUST 1989

Angola

All the remaining Cuban troops in Angola will have been withdrawn to the north of the 15th parallel.

31st OCTOBER 1989

Angola

All the remaining Cuban troops in Angola will have been withdrawn to the north of the 13th parallel.

1 NOVEMBER 1989

Namibia

Election for Constituent Assembly

Angola

25 000 of the 50 000 Cuban troops (50%) will have been withdrawn from Angola.

1 WEEK AFTER THE CERTIFICATION OF THE ELECTION

Namibia

All the South African forces will have been withdrawn.

1 APRIL 1990

Angola

33 000 Cuban troops (66%) will have been withdrawn from Angola with the remainder deployed north of the 13th parallel.

1 OCTOBER 1990

Angola

38 000 Cuban troops (76%) will have been withdrawn from Angola.

1 JULY 1991

Angola

All Cuban troops will have been withdrawn from Angola.

APPENDIX 2

Secretary General's Report – Security Council Document S/12827 of 29th August 1978.

Report of the Secretary General submitted pursuant to paragraph 2 of Security Council Resolution 431/1978 concerning the situation in Namibia

Introduction

1 At its 2082nd meeting on 27th July 1978, the Security Council adopted resolution 431/1978. By that resolution, the Council, recalling its resolution 385/1976 and taking note of the proposal for a settlement of the Namibian situation contained in document S/12636 of 10th April 1978, requested me to appoint a Special Representative for Namibia in order to ensure the early independence of Namibia through free elections under the supervision and control of the United Nations. The full text of Resolution 431/1978 reads as follows:

> The Security Council, Recalling its resolution 385/1976 of 30th January 1976, taking note of the proposal for a settlement of the Namibian situation contained in document S/12636 of 10th April 1978,
>
> (i) Requests the Secretary General to appoint a Special Representative for Namibia in order to ensure the early independence of Namibia through free elections under the supervision and control of the United Nations;
>
> (ii) Further requests the Secretary General to submit at the earliest possible date a report containing his recommendations for the implementation of the proposal in accordance with Security Council resolution 385/1976;
>
> (iii) Urges all concerned to exert their best efforts towards the achievement of independence by Namibia at the earliest possible date.

2 Immediately following the decision of the Security Council, I appointed Mr Martti Ahtisaari, the United Nations Commissioner for Namibia, as my Special Representative for the purposes of the resolution.

3 Mindful of the Council's further request contained in paragraph 2, I requested my Special Representative to undertake, at the earliest possible date, a survey mission to Namibia for the purpose of gathering for me all the information necessary for the preparation of the present report. To assist him in this task, I placed at his disposal a team of UN officials and military advisers.

4 This report, which is based on the survey of my Special Representative, is submitted to the Security Council in accordance with paragraph 2 of resolution 431/1978, in which the Council requested the Secretary General 'to submit at the earliest possible date a report containing recommendations for the implementation of the proposal in accordance with Security Council resolution 385/1976'.

(i) The survey mission

5 As stated above, my Special Representative, accompanied by a staff of UN officials and military advisers, visited Namibia from 6th-22nd August for the purpose of carrying out a survey of all matters relative to the implementation of resolution 431/1978.

6 In addition to relative to the implementation of resolution 431/1978.

6 In addition to meetings with the Administrator General of the Territory and his staff, as well as with the South African military and police commanders and local authorities, the Special Representative had the opportunity to consult extensively with representatives of political parties, churches, the business community and individuals. His consultations in this regard covered a wide spectrum of public opinion within the Territory. In this connection, the Special Representative and his staff, by travelling extensively within the Territory, were able to familiarize themselves with local conditions which would have relevance to the effective organisation and operation of UNTAG entrusted with the tasks set out in the proposal for a settlement of the Namibian situation contained in document S/12636.

7 In the course of his meetings and consultations, the Special Representative was able to obtain the views of not only the Administrator General and his staff but the representatives of the Namibian people on a broad range of important topics relating to the necessary conditions for the holding of free and fair elections and to the role of the UN. Among the principal subjects discussed were the repeal of all the remaining discriminatory or restrictive laws, regulations or administrative measures which might abridge or inhibit the objective of free and fair elections; arrangements for ensuring the release of political prisoners and detainees, as well as the voluntary return of Namibians; the arrangements and dispositions required to ensure the cessation of all hostile acts; the electoral process; the composition and work of the Constituent Assembly; and the timetable for the accomplishment of the above stages. The military aspects of the operation, with special reference to the introduction and functioning of the military component of the UNTAG, were also fully discussed. In addition, the Special Representative also discussed with the Administrator General the manner of ensuring the good conduct of the police and the arrangements necessary to assure the free and unrestricted discharge by the UN staff of the tasks assigned to them.

(ii) General guidelines

8 The implementation of the proposal in paragraph 2 of resolution 431/1978 will require the establishment of a United Nations Transition Assistance Group – UNTAG, in the Territory, consisting of a civilian component and a military component. Because of the unique character of the operation and the need for close cooperation between them, both components will be under the overall direction of the Special Representative of the Secretary General.

9 The Special Representative will report to me, keeping me informed and making such recommendations as he considers necessary with respect to the discharge of his responsibilities. The Secretary General, in accordance with the mandate entrusted to him by the Security Council, will keep the Council fully informed of developments relating to the implementation of the proposal and to the functioning of UNTAG. All matters which might affect the nature or the continued effective functioning of UNTAG will be referred to the Council for its decision.

10 The deployment of both components of UNTAG must take into account the specific geographic, demographic, economic and social conditions prevailing in Namibia. These include, in particular, the vast distances and varied nature of topography and vegetation; the broad ranges of climatic conditions; the scarcity of water; the population distribution and existing communication network; the distribution and concentration of ethnic groups; and

the lack of an adequate infrastructure in the north, such as roads and other communications and facilities. All these factors, when analysed, make it evident that sizable resources, both military and civilian, will be required to provide the close monitoring called for in document S/12636.

11 In performing its functions, UNTAG will act with complete impartiality. In order that the proposal may be effectively implemented, it is expected that the Administrator General and all other officials from within the Territory will exhibit the same impartiality.

12 For UNTAG to carry out all its tasks effectively, three essential conditions must be met. First, it must at all times, have the full support and backing of the Security Council. Second, it must operate with the full cooperation of all the parties concerned, particularly with regard to the comprehensive cessation of all hostile acts. Third, it must be able to operate as a combined United Nations operation, of which the military component will constitute an integrated, efficient formation within the wider framework of UNTAG.

13 To monitor the cessation of hostilities effectively, to maintain surveillance of the Territory's vast borders and to monitor the restriction to base of the armed forces of the parties concerned, the cooperation and support of the neighbouring countries will be necessary. Such cooperation will be most important particularly during the early stages.

14. Implementation of the proposal, and thus the work of UNTAG, will have to proceed in successive stages. These stages, which are detailed in the annexure to document S12636, can be grouped as follows:

(a) Cessation of all hostile acts by all parties and the withdrawal, restriction or demobilisation of the various armed forces;

(b) Conduct of free and fair elections to the Constituent Assembly, for which the preconditions include the repeal of discriminatory or restrictive laws, regulations or administrative measures, the release of political prisoners and detainees and voluntary return of exiles, the establishment of effective monitoring by the United Nations and an adequate period for electoral campaigning;

(c) The formulation and adoption of a constitution for Namibia by the Constituent Assembly;

(d) The entry into force of the constitution and the consequent achievement of independence of Namibia.

15 The length of time required for these stages is directly related to the complexity of the tasks to be performed and to the overriding consideration that certain steps are necessary before it can be said that elections have been held under free and fair conditions. It will be recalled that the proposal envisaged a series of successive stages, spaced so as to provide a sufficient lapse of time before the holding of the elections. This should permit, among other things, the release of political prisoners and detainees, the return and registration of all Namibians outside the Territory who may wish to participate in the electoral process, the deployment of United Nations military and civilian personnel and electoral campaigning by all parties in an atmosphere of tranquility. The timetable set out in the proposal called for the lapse of approximately seven months from the date of the approval of the present report by the Security Council to the holding of the elections.

16 In his discussions with the Special Representative, the Administrator General said that the South African authorities, having previously established 31st December 1978 as the date of independence, felt that they were committed thereto and that, consequently, the elections should take place as scheduled, regardless of the fact that it would necessitate substantially reducing the timetable necessary for completion of the preparatory plans. A majority of the political parties was of the opinion, however, that it was essential to maintain the orderly phasing of the preparatory stages and to allow sufficient time for electoral campaigning in order to ensure free and fair elections. Further, it was pointed out that the actual date of independence would fall within the competence of the Constituent Assembly.

17 It will be recalled, however, that at the time the proposal was first formulated, the date of 31st December, 1978 was consistent with completion of these steps. The delay in reaching agreement among the parties now makes completion by this date impossible. It is therefore recommended that the transitional period begin on the date of approval of the present report by the Security Council and proceed in accordance with the steps outlined in document S/126366. Using the same timetable that earlier provided the 31st December 1978 date, an appropriate date for elections would be approximately seven months from the date of the approval of the present report.

18 Estimates the periods of time required for completion of stages (a) and (b) of paragraph 14 above are included in the annexure to document S/12636. In view of the fact that the periods required for stages (c) and (d) of paragraph 14 would be determined by the Constituent Assembly, it is expected that the duration of UNTAG would be one year, depending on the date of independence to be decided by the Constituent Assembly.

19 UNTAG will have to enjoy the freedom of movement and communication and other facilities that are necessary for the performance of its tasks. For this purpose UNTAG and its personnel must necessarily have all the relevant privileges and immunities provided for by the Convention of the Privileges and Immunities of the United Nations, as well as those especially required for the proposed operation.

20 The military component of UNTAG will not use force except in self defence. Self defence will include resistance to attempts to prevent it from discharging its duties under the mandate of the Security Council. UNTAG will proceed on the assumption that all the parties concerned will cooperate with it and take all the necessary steps for compliance with the decisions of the Security Council.

(iii) Establishment of UNTAG

A. Military Component

21 The functions which will be performed by the military component of UNTAG are set out in paragraph 8 of document S/12636 and in the annexure thereto. These include, in particular:

    (a) Monitoring the cessation of hostile acts by all parties, the restriction of South African and SWAPO armed forces to base, the phased withdrawal of all except the specified number of South African forces and the restriction of the remainder to specified locations;

    (b) Prevention of infiltration as well as surveillance of the borders of the Territory;

    (c) Monitoring the demobilisation of Citizen Forces, Commandos and ethnic forces, and the dismantling of their command structure.

22 The military component will assist and support the civilian component of UNTAG in the discharge of its tasks.

23 The military component of UNTAG will be under the command of the UN, vested in the Secretary General, under the authority of the Security Council. The command in the field will be exercised by a Commander appointed by the Secretary General with the consent of the Security Council. The commander will report through the Special Representative to the Secretary General on all matters concerning the functioning of the military component of UNTAG.

24 The military component will be comprised of a number of contingents to be provided by member countries upon the request of the Secretary General. The contingents will be selected in consultation with the Security Council and with the parties concerned, bearing in mind the accepted principle of equitable geographical representation. In addition, a body of selected officers to act as monitors will form an integral part of the military component of UNTAG.

25 The military component, including the monitors, will be provided with weapons of a defensive character, consistent with the guidelines set out in paragraph 20 above.

26 In order that the military component might fulfill its responsibilities, it is considered that it should have a strength of the order of seven infantry battalions, totalling approximately 5 000, plus 200 monitors, and in addition, command communications, engineer, logistic and air support elements totalling approximately 2 300. The infantry battalions should be fully self sufficient.

27 It will be essential to establish an adequate logistic and command system at the very outset of the operation. It will therefore be necessary to obtain urgently from governments the elements of such a system. In this connection it may well be necessary to use also the services of civilian contractors for some logistic functions, as appropriate. In the nature of the physical circumstances pertaining to this operation, UNTAG may have[to rely to a considerable extent on existing facilities and installations in Namibia.

B Civilian component

28 The civilian component will consist of two elements. One of these elements will be the civil police, whose function will be to assist the Special Representative in implementing the tasks set out in paragraphs 9 and 10 of document S/12636.

29 The duties of the civil police element of UNTAG will include taking measures against any intimidation or interference with the electoral process from whatever quarter, accompanying the existing police forces, when appropriate, in the discharge of their duties and assisting in the realization of the function to be discharged by the Administrator General to the satisfaction of the Special Representative of ensuring the good conduct of the existing police forces.

30 In order that the UNTAG police may fulfil their responsibilities, as described above, it is considered, as a preliminary estimate, that approximately 360 experienced police officers will be required. It is hoped that police officers will be made available by governments on a secondment basis, bearing in mind the accepted principle of equitable geographical representation, as well as the language and other requirements of the assignment.

31 The non police element of the civilian component of UNTAG will have the function of assisting the Special Representative in implementing paragraphs 5 to 7 of document S/123636 and the relevant sections of the annexure thereto. These tasks will consist, in particular, of the following:

(a) Supervising and controlling all aspects of the electoral process, considering the fairness and appropriateness of the electoral procedures, monitoring the balloting and the counting of votes, in order to ensure that all procedures are strictly complied with, and receiving and investigating complaints of fraud or challenges relating to the electoral process;

(b) Advising the Special Representative as to the repeal of discriminatory or restrictive laws, regulations or administrative measures which may abridge or inhibit the objective of free and fair elections;

(c) Ensuring the absence of, or investigating complaints of, intimidation, coercion or restrictions on freedom of speech, movement or peaceful political assembly which may impede the objective of free and fair elections;

(d) Assisting in the arrangements for the release of all Namibian political prisoners or detainees and for the peaceful, voluntary return of Namibian refugees or Namibians detained or otherwise outside the Territory;

(e) Assisting in any arrangements which may be proposed by the Special Representative to the Administrator General and implemented by the Administrator General to the Special Representative's satisfaction intended to inform and instruct the electorate as to the significance of the election and the procedures for voting;

31 Bearing in mind the vast size of the Territory, the dispersal of the population and the lack of adequate communications, it is considered, as a preliminary estimate, that approximately 300 professional officers, as well as the necessary supporting staff, will be required initially until the cessation of hostile acts has been achieved. Thereafter about 1 000 professional and 200 field service and general service staff will be required during the electoral campaign and the period of balloting in order to cover all the polling stations. The staff will, among other duties, be required for 24 regional centres and more than 400 polling stations.

33 It is anticipated that some of these officials will be provided from among existing UN staff and that some will be persons appointed especially for this operation. In addition, it is my hope that a significant number of officials can be seconded or loaned by governments. All such seconded or loaned personnel will be required to assume the responsibilities incumbent on UN officials.

34 It is also my intention to conduct consultations concerning the designation of a jurist of international standing whose appointment as legal adviser to the Special Representative is provided for in paragraph 7 B of document S/12636.

(iv) Proposed plan of action

35 Subject to the approval of the present report by the Security Council, it is my intention to initiate the operation as quickly as possible.

36 It is my intention to appoint as Commander of the military component of UNTAG Major General Hannes Philipp, who has extensive experience of UN peace keeping operations and is already familiar with the situation in Namibia.

37 Immediately following such a decision by the Security Council, the Special Representative, accompanied by the commander of the military component, the key elements of their staffs, together with essential command and logistic elements, will proceed to Namibia in order to establish the headquarters of UNTAG and begin operations as quickly as possible.

38 A number of Governments have already expressed their interest in providing military contingents for UNTAG. Immediately upon the approval of the present report by the Security, it is my intention to consult the Council and the parties concerned on the composition of the military component, bearing in mind the principle of equitable geographical representation, on the one hand, and the necessity of obtaining self sufficient units, on the other. Every effort will be made to begin the deployment of the military component within three weeks and to bring it to its full strength within twelve weeks. For this to be achieved, it will be necessary to determine the composition of the military component at the earliest possible time.

39 It is also my intention to approach governments to provide military personnel to serve as monitors. In the initial stages, given the urgency of deploying at least some of the monitors, it may be possible to draw upon officers already serving with other existing UN operations. This may also apply to key staff positions.

40 As regards civilian personnel, it is likewise my intention, as stated in paragraphs 30 and 33 above, to approach governments to make available on secondment or loan experienced police officers to serve as police monitors and other experienced officials to serve in the civilian component of UNTAG. In recruiting civilian staff for UNTAG, I shall bear in mind both the accepted principle of equitable geographical representation and the urgent need to deploy a large number of experienced staff within the shortest possible time.

(v) Financial implications

41 At present there are too many unknown factors to permit an accurate assessment of the cost of UNTAG. Based on the numbers of personnel specified in this report and the envisaged duration of twelve months, and taking into account the magnitudes and elements of the financial requirements experienced in other peacekeeping operations, the indications are that the financial requirements for UNTAG could be as high as $300 million. Of this,

approximately $33 million will be required to finance the return of refugees and exiles. In view of the nature of the operation, due regard should be given to the fact that some elements of the operation might be phased out before the end of the mandate and that alternative arrangements might be possible which could result in lower costs.

42 The costs of UNTAG shall be considered expenses of the organisation to be borne by the member states in accordance with Article 17 (2) of the Charter.

Index

314